A TRAILS BOOKS GUIDE

Paddling NORTHERN Wisconsin

85 Great Trips by Canoe and Kayak

TEXT AND PHOTOS BY

Mike Svob

trails books
AN IMPRINT OF BOWER HOUSE
DENVER

Photography by Mike Svob
Maps by Mapping Specialists, Ltd.

Library of Congress Catalog Card Number: 2006934273

ISBN 978-1-931599-86-3

10 9 8 7 6 5 4

Contents

Paddling through rice beds on the upper Wolf.

Acknowledgments

Since I was asked in March 1996 to write this book, many a day has been spent talking on the phone or in person with innumerable resource people, poring over maps, driving to and from rivers, paddling in good weather and bad, filling up note pads, hunkering down over my computer, and checking and rechecking the million and one details associated with the 82 recommended day trips. Fortunately, I've had a lot of help throughout the process. I can't begin to thank everyone who has assisted me along the way, but I would be remiss if I did not mention some of my key helpers.

Most of all, I'm grateful to my wife, Donna, for putting up with my frequent absences and my constant agonizing over this or that; to my friend and enthusiastic paddling companion M.J. Kewley; to my neighbors and good friends Bill and Donna Kallner (Bill taught me most of what I know about paddling); and to my editor, Liz McBride, for judiciously mingling her roles as facilitator, constructive critic, counselor and advocate.

Thanks also to the following "locals" for spending time with me and providing especially useful information about specific rivers: Lawrence Stelzel and Irvin Trout of Rib Falls (Big Rib). Randy Gustafson of Northwoods Wilderness Outfitters in Iron Mountain (Brule). Mike Schuck of North Central Power Company, Ed Zahn at Murry Rock, and Harold Flater of Flater's Lodge (Chippewa). Pete Segerson of the Antigo DNR office (Eau Claire). DeWayne Zuck of the Flambeau Lodge (Flambeau). Bob Arnold and Erica Pucci of Hawk's Nest Outfitters (Manitowish). Mike Mehne of Argosy Adventures in Niagara, and Randy Gustafson (Menominee). Rick Swartz of Northern States Power Company at Saxon Falls (Montreal). Mike Krieger of Namekagon Outfitters in Trego and Terrence O'Halloran and Branda Long of the Trego Visitor Center (Namekagon). Bill Spanbauer of the Bagley Rapids area and Gary Zimmer of the Lakewood USFS ranger station (Oconto). Dan Kosir of Kosir's Rapid Rafts, Gail Coss of the Rock Dodgers Canoe Club, and Laurie Fike of the Peshtigo DNR office (Peshtigo). Jim LaChapelle and George Pakos of the Florence Wild Rivers Interpretive Center, and Randy Gustafson (Pine and Popple). Pete Segerson (Prairie). Gary Bedient of Barron and Rick Cornelius of the Barron DNR office (Red Cedar). Jerry Dorff of Wild River Outfitters in Grantsburg, Rick Gulden of Gulden's Campground in Danbury, Lindsay Paquay and Jesse Lovelace of the USFS headquarters in St. Croix Falls, and John Burrill of Marine Landing (St. Croix). Dave Kelly of Flambeau Sports & General Store in Lugerville, and Mike Denny of the Winter DNR office (South Fork). Sonny Tresness of the Tomahawk area and Mark Brandt of the Woodruff DNR office (Tomahawk). George Phillips of Drummond and Paul Paulson of Bear Country Sporting Goods in Drummond (White). Phil Valitchka and Sam Morgan of the Wisconsin Valley Improvement Company in Wausau (Wisconsin). Bill and Donna Kallner and Jamee Peters of Langlade (Wolf). John Burzynski of Gilman (Yellow).

A big thank you also to the many public agencies, companies and businesses that agreed to act as sources of water-level information; the Wisconsin DNR and U.S. Forest Service were particularly gracious in this regard.

Introduction

Northern Wisconsin is very rich in remote, unspoiled rivers. This guidebook presents the best of them. Every type of canoeing and kayaking opportunity is represented: quietwater, whitewater, intimate streams, and wide, powerful rivers. The book is intended for novice, intermediate and advanced paddlers alike, and is especially for those who love nature and scenic beauty. It's my hope that if more people become aware of how blessed this part of the state is to have such rivers, the effort to preserve them will grow.

Which Rivers Are Included

"Northern Wisconsin" can be defined in many ways, of course. For the purposes of this guidebook, it refers to the area north of Highway 29—north, that is, of an arcing line from Green Bay in the east to Prescott in the west. There is a multitude of rivers in this part of the state, and it's a shame that all of them can't be included. The fact is, however, that some are more canoeable than others.

In deciding which river sections to include in this book, I looked for trips on which paddlers could reasonably expect to have a safe, enjoyable time, free (wherever possible) of long, windy lakes, polluted water, annoying and sometimes dangerous obstructions (dams, limbs, brush, etc.), laborious portages and heavy motorboat traffic. Preference has been given to stretches that have scenic value, good accesses, generally adequate water levels, convenient canoe-camping possibilities or challenging whitewater. Rivers that have sufficient water to paddle for only a few days a year (such as the Totogatic) have not been included. Also generally excluded are the upper reaches of most rivers. While they have a certain charm for hardy, venturesome explorer-types, most people tire quickly of beaver dams, alder jungles, mosquito swarms and the other "niceties" of headwater paddling.

Obviously, an element of subjectivity came into play in the selection process. I personally have paddled every foot of the 961 miles of river included here, together with another 160 miles that turned out not to meet the above criteria.

What's in the Book

In addition to a map that shows roads, put-ins and takeouts, significant rapids, mileage and other information, each trip is described in a detailed narrative. After a general summary, each description covers camping opportunities, water levels, gradients, shuttle routes, canoe rentals and/or shuttle service (when available) and accesses. Then the paddler is led systematically down the river. There is nothing obligatory about the length of each trip: Alternate accesses, which are identified, can be used to shorten or otherwise vary a trip. I do not estimate the time it might take to paddle a section because that depends upon so many factors—speed of current, individual paddling skill, type of boat, wind conditions, etc. Two to three miles per hour is a good rule of thumb for making a rough estimate.

Maps

The maps in this guidebook are designed to provide all of the essential information that boaters need to get to the designated stretch of river and paddle enjoyably and safely down it. I have resisted the temptation to include superfluous pieces of information in the maps, in order to keep them as simple and uncluttered as possible. Six essential components and their symbols are indicated in the key to each map: accesses, mile markers, railroads, rapids, cities or villages, and campsites. Mile markers begin at the designated put-in for a trip and continue to the end of each map. Calculating mileage for a river, however, is not an exact science. We have done our best to be as accurate as possible.

Most rapids and riffles are mentioned in the trip narratives, but only significant rapids (Class II, III and IV) are marked on the maps with hash marks; some rivers have so many Class I rapids that a map that noted them would be almost totally covered with marks. If a riffle or Class I rapids has been named by locals and paddlers (e.g., Suzie's Rapids near Oconto), its name and location are shown on the map with an arrow, not hash marks. For the criteria used to classify the difficulty of rapids, see the section below on "Special Safety Factors."

Rapids are most common on rivers with relatively high gradient (i.e., the rate of descent, usually expressed in feet per mile), so the gradient for each section is noted in the description. As a rule of thumb, a gradient of 10 feet or more per mile is a good predictor of significant whitewater; thus, when you see that a stretch has a gradient of 15, say, or 25, you should be forewarned. Gradient by itself, however, is not always an accurate indicator of difficult rapids. For example, some "pool/drop" stretches like the Menominee Reservation portion of the Wolf have not only several big drops but also a great deal of flatwater, averaging out to a deceptively low gradient number.

You can determine where you are on the river at any given time by observing such features as creek mouths, bends, rapids, bridges, prominent islands, etc., and comparing these with the map. A compass is helpful if you are inclined to use one.

If additional maps are desired, three kinds are recommended. For detailed information on elevation contours, wetlands, woods, etc., consult the topographical maps available from the U.S. Geological Survey in various scales. To obtain free indexes and catalogs and to order maps, contact USGS Information Services, Box 25286, Denver, CO 80225. Another very useful resource is the *Wisconsin Atlas & Gazetteer* (published by the DeLorme Mapping Company and available in bookstores), which provides 104 grid maps of the state. These are especially helpful in locating back roads. In addition, many counties publish excellent recreation maps that provide all kinds of information; these are available from chambers of commerce and visitor centers.

Camping

Only public campgrounds and campsites are mentioned, except in situations where private campgrounds are located on the river. Many of the rivers in northern Wisconsin lend themselves to multiday canoe-camping trips because of conveniently located riverside campsites.

Rafting the Wolf.

Water Levels

For each river section, a source of water-level information has been provided. Water level is one of the most important pieces of information that you need to have before going paddling. Ideally, the water will be flowing at a safe, pleasant level. But if it's too low, you can be in for a miserable time, dragging your boat through shallows. If it's too high, your life can be in peril. **Every river in this book is dangerous when high, especially in the spring.** Stay home or do something else when the water is high; risking your life isn't worth it. Bear in mind, too, that when springtime rivers in the southern part of the state are flowing nicely, northern rivers are often still frozen.

You will find that some sources of water-level information are more reliable than others, for a variety of reasons. The methods of judging water conditions as a criterion for canoeability are somewhat inconsistent, varying from place to place and person to person. Gauge readings are arbitrary and localized, and terms such as "low" and "high" tend to have different meanings for intermediate and expert paddlers. Nevertheless, when you have been informed by a local source that a river is low, medium or high, you are wise to take heed, especially if told that it's high. Ultimately, you yourself are responsible for deciding whether to paddle or not. For some indicators of high water, see the section below on "Special Safety Factors."

The best source of current and historical water level information is the United States Geological Survey website that presents "real-time streamflow data." At this Internet location you can obtain recent readings (i.e., within the last 24 hours) from over 200 active gauges located on rivers, creeks, lakes, and other waterways throughout Wisconsin. This data may be accessed at **http://waterdata.usgs.gov/wi/nwis/current/?type=flow.** For more information about USGS water data, see **http://waterdata.usgs.gov/nwis.**

Whenever an active gauge is located on or near a given section, this book indicates the station number of the gauge in the trip description. The current reading for each station is presented in terms of (1) a water level number (e.g., "Stage feet above datum") that is based on an arbitrary gauge, and (2) streamflow expressed in cubic feet per second (cfs). By themselves, these figures do not tell you whether the stream is low, medium, or high, unless you have paddled it many times before and can make a correlation. Fortunately, you can obtain graphed historical data from USGS for the previous week, month, or other period of time, thus giving you a good idea of how high or low a given stream gets and what the current gauge reading means.

Shuttle Routes

The easiest shuttle route from the put-in to the take-out is indicated for each trip. Occasionally, there is a slightly shorter route, but it usually involves rough or undependable roads. Please bear in mind that the shuttle route described may need to be altered if you choose to modify the trip by using a different access to take out or put in.

Canoe Rental and Shuttle Service

Whenever there is a known provider of canoe rentals and shuttle service, that information is included. Some outfitters provide shuttles only for customers who rent canoes, but others will shuttle canoeists' boats and vehicles for a fee. Incidentally, these service providers are often an excellent source of water-level information.

Accesses

Put-ins and take-outs range from attractive and convenient park landings, to easily missed clearings on the riverbank, to extremely difficult accesses requiring great caution. When you're in doubt about spotting an inconspicuous take-out (especially when something ominous lies downstream), it's a good idea to hang a bright bandanna or piece of surveyor's tape from a branch at the landing. Only public landings, or private ones that are commonly used by the public with permission, are included in this book.

Trip Descriptions

After these preliminaries, the trip description itself provides a verbal road map of the river section, conveying a lot of information that is not on the map. Except for a few rivers that are normally paddled in the springtime, such as the Popple, the descriptions are based on normal summer flows, that is, neither low nor high. Places where it is appropriate to scout and, perhaps, portage are pointed out, together with still-visible historical sites (like the remnants of old logging dams), pleasant lunch spots, alternate accesses, scenic highlights, etc. With only a few exceptions, the descriptions do not tell you how to run a given rapids. Often there is more than one way to negotiate a rapids, and the routes sometimes vary with the water level. Occasionally, familiar "lines" through rapids change unexpectedly when ice or flood moves trees and rocks into previously unobstructed places.

Usually, when the river upstream or downstream from the described section is not included in the book, an addendum briefly summarizes that part of the river.

Fishing Opportunities

Drawing upon a variety of sources—mainly direct observations of what fishermen are catching, conversations with anglers and DNR fisheries personnel, and material gleaned from published works—I have mentioned the fish that are commonly found in various sections of river. Not all of the stretches included here are great producers of fish, of course, but some are outstanding. Portions of the Brule, Bois Brule, Wolf, Oconto, Prairie, Eau Claire and White, for example, are deservedly well known as trout streams.

Several written sources are especially informative:

Steve Born, Jeff Mayers, Andy Morton and Bill Sonzogni, *Exploring Wisconsin Trout Streams: The Angler's Guide* (Madison, Wis.: University of Wisconsin Press, 2007). Features many detailed analyses of Wisconsin rivers and streams, including the Bois Brule, Namekagon, White, Prairie, Peshtigo, Oconto, Wolf, Pike and Eau Claire rivers.

Jim Humphrey and Bill Shogren, *Wisconsin & Minnesota Trout Streams* (Backcountry Publications, 1995). Two veteran fishermen profile 120 trout streams, with practical advice on tactics. Included are discussions of the Bois Brule, Brule, Eau Claire, Menominee, Namekagon, Oconto, Peshtigo, Pike, Pine, Prairie, Red Cedar, Red, St. Croix, White, Wisconsin and Wolf.

John Motoviloff, *Flyfisher's Guide to Wisconsin* (Wilderness Adventures Press, 2003). Covers 250 of the best flyfishing waters in Wisconsin, with good maps, directions, and practical information about fly shops, etc.

Wisconsin Department of Natural Resources, *Wisconsin Muskellunge Waters*. This 40-page booklet, updated in 1995, provides information on where muskies may be found in 42 counties.

Wisconsin Department of Natural Resources, *Wisconsin Trout Waters*. This 60-page booklet provides access maps for the best trout streams in the state.

Private Property

Much of the shoreline along the rivers in this book is owned by the state, a county or the federal government, but the majority is privately owned. Please respect the rights of property owners whenever you're looking for an access, a lunch stop, a campsite or a scout/portage trail. If in doubt about a given location, don't step foot on it, or else ask permission to do so. Once in a while, you will be presented with ambiguous situations and must use your common sense and good judgment.

Unlike many more-restrictve states—such as neighboring Illinois—Wisconsin has clearly established the right of canoeists and kayakers to paddle most streams in the state. According to the DNR, "Navigability determines whether a waterway is public or private. Navigable lakes and streams are public waterways. A waterway is navigable if it has a bed and banks, and it is possible to float a canoe or other small craft at some time of the year—even if only during spring floods. Because they are public, you may use navigable waters for fishing, boating, swimming, or other recreational activities, provided public access is available, or you have permission of the landowner to cross their property to reach the waterway. Once on a navigable waterway, as long as you keep your feet wet, you may walk along the bed of the stream, fish, swim, or boat in any navigable lake or stream."

A 2001 revision of the state statutes reinforced the "keep your feet wet" rule of thumb, asserting that boaters and fishermen may access the exposed shoreline "only if it is necessary to exit a body of water to bypass an obstruction."

River Reading and Maneuvers

Some of the river sections described in this guidebook are normally placid and suitable for beginners. But most sections involve situations that require at least a modicum of ability to "read" the river and to maneuver a boat. Moreover, even the peaceful stretches occasionally present obstructions and other hazards for the unwary paddler. Thus, for both enjoyment and safety, all paddlers should master the basic principles of river dynamics and boat handling. Moving-water technique is much more complex than lake paddling.

In addition to knowing about equipment (boats, paddles, life jackets, boat flotation, throw-ropes, etc.), canoeists and kayakers should learn the fundamentals of river current: for example, current differentials, downstream and upstream Vs and waves, and the effects of obstacles, such as eddies, trees and limbs, "holes," horizon lines, ledges and falls, and "rock gardens."

In order to maneuver a boat in moving water, boaters need to become familiar with six basic paddling strokes: forward and back, draw and pry, sweep and brace. These allow paddlers to move forward efficiently, to stop movement downstream or even go backward, to turn, to move the boat sideways, and to prevent it from capsizing. By combining these strokes with the ability to read the river, paddlers can execute the essential river moves: sideslips, eddy turns, peel-outs and ferries.

Confidence and skill in river reading and maneuvering are essential for safe paddling on the rivers of northern Wisconsin, especially those with whitewater. An added bonus, however, is the spirit of playfulness that such skill makes possible. It is fun to "run" a river, certainly, but it is pure joy to be able to slow things down and play in it leisurely.

A canoe wrapped around a rock on the South Fork of the Flambeau.

Since this is a guidebook, not a manual on canoeing and kayaking, detailed information on river-reading and maneuvering must be found elsewhere. Of course, the best source of such information is a class at a paddling school. Other excellent sources are books and videotapes that introduce the basics of paddlesport. Still another way for novice paddlers to learn about the basics is to accompany safety-oriented, experienced boaters on nonthreatening trips; watch, ask questions, follow the example of accomplished boaters, and don't be reluctant to walk your boat around situations that don't feel right.

Special Safety Factors

Canoeists and kayakers paddle for many reasons, including relaxation, communion with nature, excitement, fellowship and self development. But whatever their intent, all paddlers should have one overriding consideration at all times: safety for themselves and their companions. Knowledge, skill and good judgment are essential to having a good, safe time on the river, unmarred by damaged equipment, injuries or perhaps worse. To that end, the following 10 potential hazards warrant special emphasis. All are encountered somewhere on the river sections described in this book, and all demand extra care.

1. Broaching

In general, you must keep your boat parallel to the current, particularly in rapids. Otherwise, you are at risk of

Springtime paddling can be fun, but hypothermia is a potential hazard.

pinning the boat sideways on an obstruction (a "broach"). The force of moving water is awesome, and can quickly "wrap" your craft, with you in it! Potentially catastrophic though a broach is, however, you can usually avert disaster by staying calm and aggressively leaning the boat toward the obstruction so that the onrushing water won't flip the boat and fill it. Maintaining the downstream lean, you can often work your boat off the obstruction by "scrunching" it forward or backward a few inches at a time, then continuing on downstream. Sometimes if the situation allows, you can step out onto an obstructive rock, free the boat, and climb back in. Fellow paddlers can be of assistance, too. Broaching is especially problematic in the boulder gardens that are plentiful in northern Wisconsin rivers.

2. Cold

Usually the ice begins going out in mid-April on the rivers described in this book. From then until early June, rivers flow forcefully, and boaters enthusiastically take their equipment out of winter storage. Unfortunately, these months are prime times for hypothermia, a potential killer. Water temperature below 60 degrees is dangerous; immersion can quickly take away your strength and even your will. A useful rule of thumb is to wear a wet suit or dry suit whenever the air and water temperatures don't add up to 100. Unless you are skilled, properly equipped and clothed, and accompanied by other skilled paddlers, you should not venture out under such conditions.

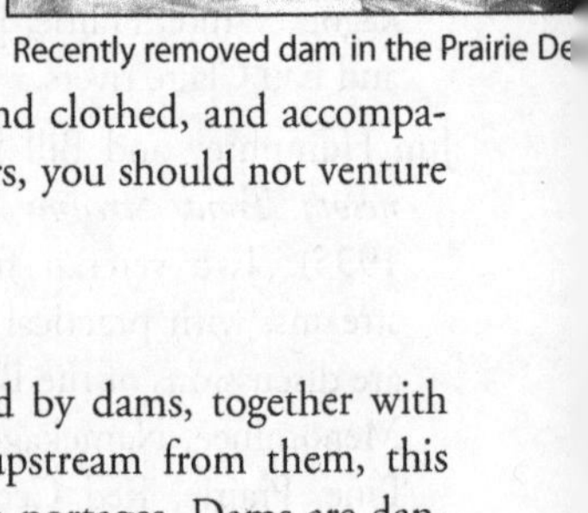

Recently removed dam in the Prairie De

3. Dams

Because of the danger posed by dams, together with the monotonous flowages upstream from them, this book includes only two dam portages. Dams are dangerous in many ways and should be given a wide berth, particularly so-called low-head dams (low, uniform structures that may appear innocuous but are often fatal because of the recirculating current downstream, which can pull you into danger and keep you there). If you put in below a dam, be sure to launch your boat as far downstream as possible to assure that you don't get

A classic hole at Little Bull Falls on the Popple.

pulled into the turbulence. If you choose to paddle on an impoundment, take out as far upstream from the dam as possible. Most dams in Wisconsin have designated portage trails.

4. High Water

During the spring and after downpours, all of the rivers in this book can become dangerously high, a situation that causes fast current, huge waves and big holes; requires quick decision time; takes away slow, shallow recovery areas; and increases the odds that you will encounter fallen trees and floating debris. Add the likelihood of cold water, and you have a high-hazard situation. No one has any business being on a river when it is in flood.

Tell-tale signs that a river is dangerously high are water flowing through the trees or shrubs; fast, turbulent, muddy, sometimes "boiling" current; water close to the bottom of bridges; and floating debris.

5. Holes

When swift water flows over a rock or ledge, it sometimes creates a downstream depression into which the surrounding water rushes turbulently, creating a "hole" (also known as a "hydraulic" or "reversal"). The recirculating current in particularly strong holes, which are called "keepers" or "stoppers," holds onto a boat and traps swimmers. Small, weak holes can easily be run (and even played in by skilled boaters), but large "sticky" ones should be avoided, by portaging, if necessary. Some river sections in this book develop significant holes even when the water is at moderate levels (e.g., the "Roaring Rapids" of the Peshtigo, the Reservation portion of the Wolf, and Piers Gorge on the Menominee).

Sulllivan Falls on the Wolf: a 7-foot waterfall.

6. Ledges & Falls

River-wide ledges are fairly common on the rivers in this book: Beaver Dam Rapids on the Flambeau, Bagley Rapids on the Oconto, and the May Ledges on the Bois Brule, for example. Falls are comparable but more dramatic, involving a sudden vertical drop of several feet or more (for example, Big Smoky Falls on the Wolf and Missicot Falls on the Menominee). Both ledges and falls usually are indicated by a horizon line—a uniform line across the river where it suddenly drops off, sometimes accompanied by mist and noise. When approaching a falls or a significant ledge, take out upstream and scout to determine whether it is safely runnable. Portage if in doubt. Some ledges and falls develop significant holes in moderate to high water.

7. Strainers

Fallen trees and limbs can be potentially lethal on all of the rivers of northern Wisconsin, and should always be avoided. Small rivers like the upper Peshtigo and upper Oconto are especially prone to such "strainers"—so-called because water rushes through them, trapping boats and boaters. Be especially watchful for strainers on the outside of bends, at the bottom of drops and under bridges.

Downed trees and limbs don't look like much, but they're potentially deadly: Give them a wide berth.

Try to stay upstream from your boat when you dump (Monastery Falls on the Red).

8. Swimming After a Capsize

All boaters "dump" sooner or later. For properly equipped paddlers on a warm day in calm, unobstructed water, it's no big deal. But coming out of your boat in whitewater is a different matter. Try to stay upstream from your boat, lie flat on your back with your feet pointed downstream, and back-paddle to slow yourself down. Do not try to stand up until you're in very shallow, slow water; otherwise, you're in danger of trapping your foot in a crevice, a not-uncommon cause of drowning. In the hands of someone who knows how to use it, a throw-rope can be used to advantage in rescuing capsized boaters.

9. Waves

In a rapids, standing waves (or "haystacks") are often formed when water rushes through a chute or runs into slower water below. Waves can mark the deepest, most unobstructed channel for paddlers to follow, but in high-water conditions they can be large enough to "stall out" a canoe and swamp it. Often, big waves can be skirted along one side or the other to avoid the biggest ones.

10. Rapids

For seasoned whitewater paddlers, rapids are what canoeing and kayaking are all about. There is nothing quite like the heady sense of exhilaration that comes from working your way through a complex rock garden or negotiating a difficult drop. Indeed, rapids are beautiful and exciting—a wonderful complement to the much more plentiful quietwater stretches. Remember, however, that rapids pose dangers, especially for the inexperienced and unskilled; even veteran paddlers sometimes run into trouble when they attempt rapids that exceed their skill level, paddle when the water is too high, fail to scout, or simply "have a bad day."

Rapids can be a playground for experienced whitewater paddlers, but they always demand respect and caution.

Rapids are infinitely varied, ranging in difficulty from easy, relatively unobstructed riffles and waves to extremely violent water that threatens the lives of all boaters, including experts. In order to provide a consistent method of comparing rapids worldwide, the International Scale of River Difficulty was devised, a system that categorizes rapids in six classes, from "easy" to "extreme." The following adaptation of this scale reflects the criteria used by experienced Wisconsin whitewater paddlers and is the rating system used in this book. Please note that whenever the water is high and/or cold, rapids are usually considered at least one class higher.

Class I: Fast water with some waves and obstructions but easily negotiated; requiring little maneuvering and involving slight risk; suitable for paddlers with some moving-water experience. Class I rapids are one step up from "riffles": fast, wavy, unobstructed water that is usually quite easy and safe to run. The St. Croix and Namekagon rivers have innumerable riffles and Class I rapids.

Class II: Fast water with awkwardly located rocks, ledges, sizeable waves and other river features requiring considerable river-reading ability and maneuvering skills; broaching a possibility; suitable for trained and experienced (intermediate) whitewater paddlers. At medium levels, Boy Scout Rapids on the Wolf, Little Falls on the Jump, and Cedar Rapids on the Flambeau are good examples of Class IIs. The term "Class II" encompasses a significant range. Some rapids, for instance, are fairly short and have no great consequences downstream, while others seem to go on forever, making rescue difficult and the potential consequences more serious.

Class III: Very difficult rapids with large, often irregular waves and curlers, "pushy" current, big drops of 3 feet or more, difficult-to-determine routes, holes and other features requiring complex maneuvers and precise boat control; often involving negative consequences in case of a dump, including difficult rescue; suitable only for advanced whitewater paddlers. Horserace Rapids on the Peshtigo, Washburn Falls on the Popple, and Big Falls on the Jump, at low to medium levels, are IIIs.

Class IV: Intense, powerful, turbulent, sometimes unpredictable and dangerous rapids involving large, often unavoidable holes and big waves; necessitating fast "must-do" maneuvers under pressure; consequences of capsize often nasty; rescue quite difficult; suitable only for highly skilled paddlers with a great deal of demanding whitewater experience. Missicot Falls on the Menominee is a IV.

Class V: Long, obstructed, violent and extremely dangerous rapids, with such features as big drops, constricted routes, undercut shorelines and rocks, broaching and pinning situations, and "keeper" holes; grave danger to life and limb; little chance of rescue; suitable only for teams of experts under optimal conditions of weather, water level, etc. Despite its short length, the left channel of Big Smoky Falls on the Wolf—under

The outwash from dams and powerhouses can be dangerous. Pictured is the powerhouse at Grandfather Dam on the Wisconsin River.

the footbridge—is a V because of the high, steep drop, circuitous route and numerous obstructions on the way down (sometimes including logs).

Class VI: Super difficult, unpredictable and dangerous; all of the above criteria carried to an extreme; injury or death a strong possibility; suitable only for suicidal fools. Superior Falls on the Montreal River is a Class VI.

REMEMBER: Whenever in doubt about what lies ahead, especially when you suspect a hazard of some kind, do not hesitate to get out and scout. (Incidentally, be careful when scouting. Slippery rocks and other shoreline hazards can be just as injurious as the rapids themselves.) If scouting reveals something that you're not sure you can handle, portage. Never let false pride, peer pressure or daredeviltry push you into situations that exceed your skill and experience level. Always wear a suitable PFD (life jacket) and—in whitewater—a helmet. And never paddle alone.

River Etiquette

Along with the delight of paddling the magnificent rivers of northern Wisconsin come certain responsibilities for all of us:

1. You will be pleased to see that littering and other abuse of the river environment are seldom problems on the rivers described here. Please do your part to help preserve the wilderness experience.

2. All of the rivers of northern Wisconsin have at least some private property on their shoreline. Always put yourself in the place of the property owner and respect his or her rights. Whenever possible, ask permission before stepping foot on private land, and express your gratitude.

3. Be considerate of other paddlers when you're on the river. Keep other members of your group in sight at all times, for instance, and designate lead and "sweep" (rear) paddlers. Inexperienced boaters need particular attention.

4. Observe the boating etiquette that governs the use of popular play spots on the river. One such convention calls for boaters not to hog surfing waves; enjoy yourself, but give the next person a turn. Another "rule" establishes the right-of-way of paddlers running a rapids or drop; if other paddlers are playing at the bottom, they must yield.

Big Rib River 1

Highway 64 to County F (7 Miles)

The little-known Big Rib River is delightful for both whitewater and flatwater enthusiasts, and is especially enjoyed by paddlers who prefer intimate little streams. Much of its length is canoeable—from Rib Lake in northeast Taylor County to Lake Wausau in Marathon County—but the most pleasant and reliable portion begins at Highway 64 near Goodrich. Two rapids are definitely for highly skilled paddlers only, but the rest of the river is suitable for novices.

The 18 miles described in this book are generally rather narrow (40 to 80 feet wide), with many pleasant riffles, beautiful stone formations, clear water, a winding stream bed and unspoiled seclusion (almost no houses!). Only super-low water or a grouchy temperament stands between paddlers and a wonderful time on the Big Rib. It certainly deserves to be better known by canoeists.

Camping is not available on the river, but there are campsites at the Rib Lake village park a few miles north, and at the Medford city park to the west.

Water levels are best in the spring, and after sustained rainfall other times of the year. Like all of the rivers in this book, however, the Rib can be quite dangerous when the water is high—especially in the first couple of miles after Highway 64. The tightness of the river also makes fallen trees and limbs a definite hazard in high water. At droughty times of the summer, previously enjoyable riffles and rapids are annoyingly scratchy and even impassable. There is no USGS gauge on the river. In order to determine whether there's enough water for a good trip, check the Class I rapids alongside the park at the County F bridge: There should be enough water flowing over the rocks to float a boat comfortably without getting hung up.

> **The Streams of Taylor County**
>
> When the subject of great northern Wisconsin canoeing counties arises, several obviouscandidates come readily to mind, including Rusk, Forest and Mari-nette counties. Lesser known as a paddling destination, Taylor County certainly deserves more attention.
>
> In addition to the delightfully intimate Big Rib River, which starts in the northeastern corner of the county and ends up in the Wisconsin River in Marathon County, Taylor offers three other pleasant paddling streams. The Black, famous for its tumultuous whitewater in the Neillsville area, is small, winding and remote before exiting Taylor County to the south. The Yellow River, originating in an even more remote area in the Chequamegon National Forest, greets paddlers with rapids near Gilman before heading west toward the Chippewa. North-ward, the Jump River serves up some tough whitewater at Little Falls and Big Falls, then flows more calmly through a couple of popular sections in the northwest corner of the county. Try these, and you're sure to have as good a time as on Wisconsin's better-known rivers. For details see the trip descriptions in this book.

The average **GRADIENT** is a steep 12.8 feet per mile.

Canoe and kayak rentals are available at Silent Glide Canoe & Kayak Shop in Medford (715-748-0148 or www.silentglidecanoeandkayakshop.com). The **shuttle route** for the first stretch is via Highway 64, Rinehart Drive, Bungaloo Road and County F. Boaters who wish to paddle only the whitewater portion can take out earlier at the County Line Road landing (shuttle route via Highway 64 and Greiner Road). Trips of other lengths can be arranged by using County A as a take-out or put-in.

PUT IN at the **Highway 64 bridge** 13 miles east of Medford, upstream- or downstream-left. There is little room alongside the highway for parking.

The river begins quite narrow and swift, flowing between grassy banks heavily wooded with maple, pine, elm, cedar and popple. A house appears on the left soon after the put-in, but evidence of human habitation is rare for the next 18 miles.

After only a mile of fast, sometimes-riffly water, the **Rib Dells** suddenly appear after a short left bend. There's an eddy on river-left, opposite a cabin on the right shore. Be sure to get out on the left and scout the entrance to the dells, taking care not to fall on the slippery rocks. A mile of unbroken Class II+ rapids begins immediately downstream, so a swim is definitely not desirable. The surrounding terrain is rugged, and a portage difficult. On the other hand, high water can turn the first few hundred yards of the dells into a mean succession of Class III+ holes and exploding waves that make portaging prudent.

Take the time to admire the beauty of the rocky mini-canyon of the dells. The river constricts here, plunging over several drops and big boulders, then "settles down" into a very long Class II boulder garden. In low water conditions, the rocks and steady gradient result in scraping, bumping and perhaps walking. Only advanced paddlers should venture onto this part of the river, and everyone should stay away when the river is in flood. Dell Avenue runs down to the river here, but the riverside area is private and gated.

After the dells and the following rapids, the river flattens out and flows southeast, then south, paralleling Greiner Road for about a mile. At the point where Greiner Road meets County Line Road, a short dirt road leads to a **landing** on river-left: This is a good take-out for paddlers who wish to run only the whitewater stretch, or an alternative put-in for less experienced boaters who wish to avoid the dells. Baldwin Creek enters on the right a short distance upstream from this access.

The river continues to be narrow, riffly and winding, occasionally widening to 80 feet, but always with good current. Small or medium-sized islands occasionally appear. Deadfall is seldom a problem, but some of the narrower channels around islands demand caution.

You'll encounter pleasant gravel bars throughout the trip—great places to stop for lunch, relaxation and swimming. Fishermen often wade the river for trout, especially in swift, bouldery areas and in pools. The surroundings are rugged and isolated all the way to County F, which is preceded by a hundred-yard-long Class I boulder garden.

TAKE OUT at **Amco County Park,** downstream-left from the bridge. An excellent **access,** this lovely park provides good parking, picnic facilities, playground, toilets and water, and is a popular swimming, fishing and picnicking spot on weekends.

Big Rib River 1

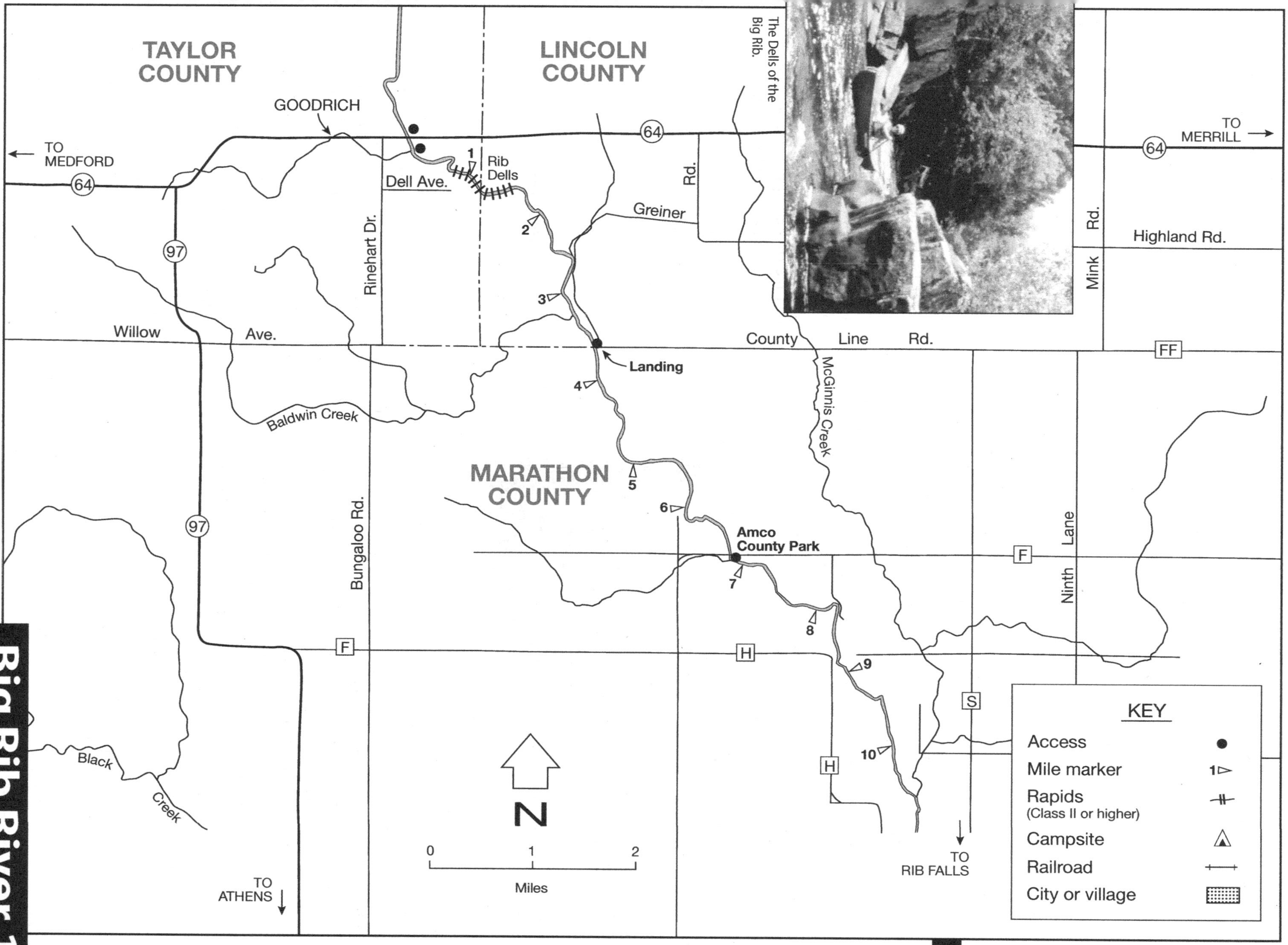

The Dells of the Big Rib.

Big Rib River 2

County F to Rib Falls (11.3 Miles)

Even more isolated than the upstream stretch, this section of the Rib River provides an enjoyable day trip for both novices and experienced paddlers. Tight, clean, curving and totally undeveloped, it flows through a variety of settings, with attractive stone outcroppings, swift riffles and inviting gravel bars along the way. The Rib River Valley is flanked by beautiful, heavily wooded hills, and the scenery is always a delight. Eagles, heron, ducks and deer are common, and local fishermen catch smallmouth and walleye.

Camping is available within a few miles' drive at the Rib Lake village park, the Medford city park and Rib Mountain State Park.

Water levels are usually best in the spring, through June and after periods of rainfall. The river's many riffles become very scrapy in low-water conditions, necessitating a lot of walking. Check the small rapids downstream from the County F bridge to make sure there's enough water to float comfortably.

The **GRADIENT** of this section is 5.3 feet per mile.

A ledge on the Big Rib.

The **shuttle route** is via County F and County S. The trip can be shortened to 4.2 miles by taking out at County A, or to 7 miles by putting in at County A.

PUT IN at the **County F bridge,** downstream left. Marathon County maintains an attractive park here, with parking, picnic facilities, playground, drinking water and toilets. A short Class I rapids immediately follows the put-in, on both sides of a small island.

Except in a few wider and deeper spots, good current continues all the way to the take-out at Rib Falls. Riffles are somewhat less frequent than upstream, but still plentiful. You'll see no houses between County F and Rib Falls.

McGinnis Creek enters on the left a half mile before the County A bridge. A short dirt road leads to the **access** 150 feet downstream-right, near a small side channel.

River width varies between 50 and 80 feet, and small islands occasionally appear. You'll spot beautiful stone outcroppings along the shoreline. Gravel bars and large boulders in the stream bed (easy to avoid) become more common.

After the mouth of Einert Creek on the left, the river goes into a long southwest straightaway, followed by a long stretch of lovely stone formations on the right in a left-hand bend. The river is fairly deep and slow here. Immediately after the stone formations, the river narrows and is crossed by a ford (dirt tracks can be seen on both sides); this location is just south of Ninth Avenue. Huge boulders line the left shoreline downstream. From the crossing to the take-out, the river tends to be deeper, with more boulders along the shore and in the stream bed.

Finally, after a big grassy island and some old wooden pilings, the river curves sharply to the left toward the village of Rib Falls. A creek enters on the right in the curve, followed by many large boulders and stone formations on the right shore. Some traffic noise can be heard from nearby County S and County U.

In the half-mile straightaway approaching the take-out, the river is deep and slow, backed up by the falls. When the river turns right, Class III **Rib Falls** can be heard and seen ahead. The County S bridge is several hundred feet downstream from the falls.

TAKE OUT upstream from the falls at the bank on the left. A trail leads from the bank to **Rib Falls County Park,** which provides parking, picnic facilities, playground, toilets and drinking water. The village of Rib Falls is nearby.

Take the time to get a close-up view of the falls from the shoreline. A dam was once located here to provide power for a sawmill and a grist mill. The old dam was washed out in the 1960s, but remnants can still be seen along the shore.

Other trips: South of Rib Falls, the Big Rib River crosses Highway 29 and thus is outside the scope of this book. A fairly popular trip takes paddlers from County S to Marathon City (a slow float, with many sandbars). Marathon City to Lake Wausau is a somewhat longer float trip. The river is considerably wider below Rib Falls, with diminished current.

Big Rib River 2

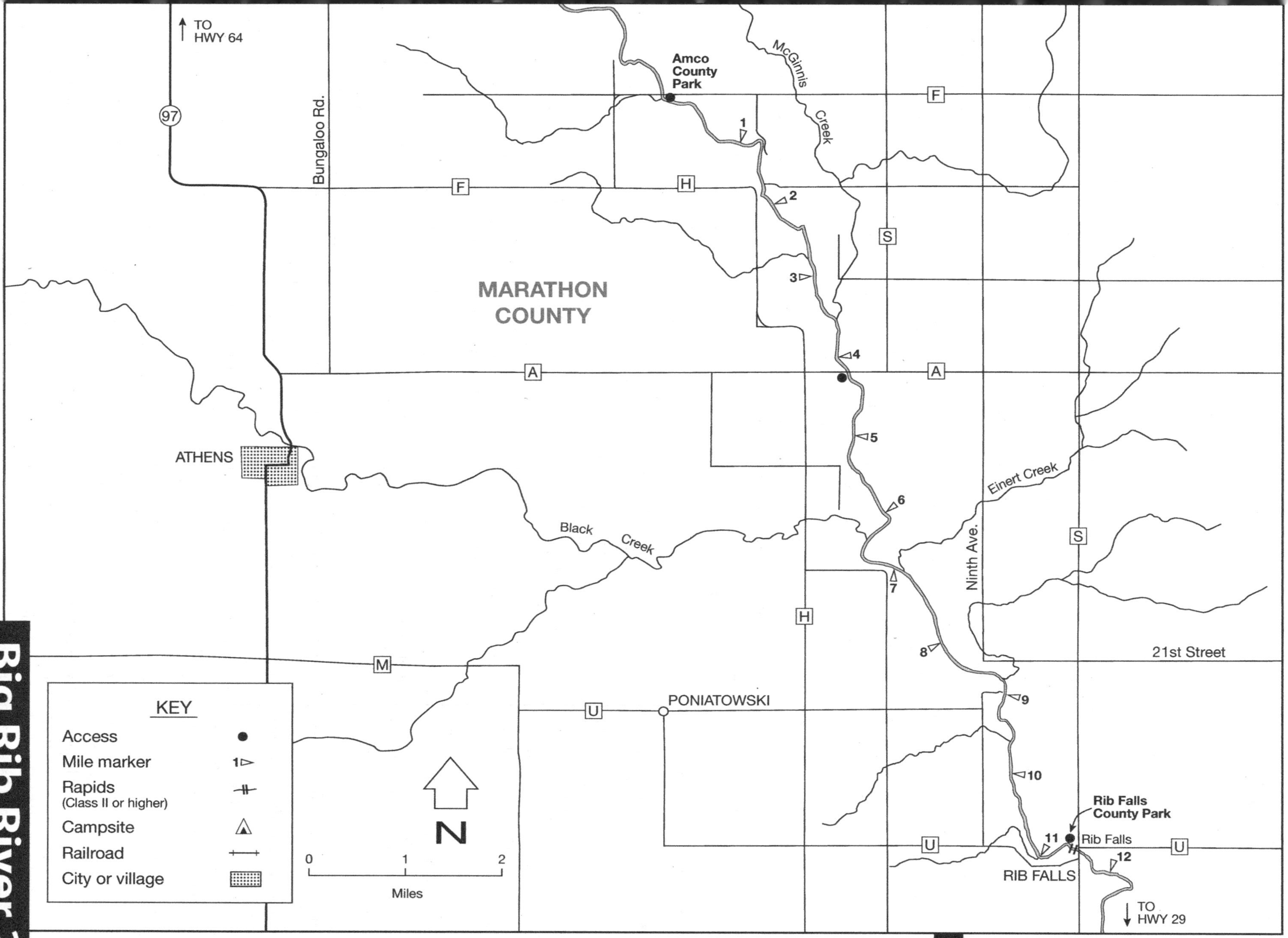

Black River

Highway 64 to Bridge Road (12.4 Miles)

Originating near the tiny community of Chelsea in Taylor County, the Black River changes character many times as it flows southwestward to the Mississippi near Trempealeau. The 40 miles of river that lie north of Highway 29 are pleasantly winding and undeveloped, and run through a varied setting of marsh, farmland and forest. Nowhere on this part of the river does one encounter the boulder-strewn whitewater stretches that are common downstream.

The most canoeable portion of the upper Black lies west of Medford, where Highway 64 provides a convenient access point. This day trip winds through a peacefully remote area that is mostly wooded lowland, with many riffles and islands. Numerous gravel bars make wonderful places to stop for relaxation or lunch. Deadfall is often a possibility but seldom a real problem. Although suitable for beginners, the stretch does require an ability to maneuver through an occasional tight spot. Adjoining farmland is never intrusive, and only a few buildings are seen. Eagles are common.

Camping is not available on the river, but there are a number of public campgrounds nearby: Medford city park to the east and several campgrounds in the Chequamegon National Forest to the north (Chippewa, Eastwood, Kathryn Lake, North Twin Lake, Spearhead Point and West Point).

Water levels are best in the spring and after sustained rainfall in the summer and fall. In medium-to-high water conditions, be watchful for strainers; consider another form of recreation when the water is high. On the other hand, very low water means walking your boat through the seemingly endless succession of riffles and Class I rapids. As a rough guide to canoeability, check the channels alongside the small island just downstream from the Highway 64 bridge, or the rapids 150 yards upstream from the bridge. Although much farther downstream, the USGS gauge at Neilsville (#05381000) may give some idea of the water level; see "Water Levels" in the introduction.

The average **GRADIENT** is 6.4 feet per mile.

The **shuttle route** is via Highway 64, County DD, County A, County T and Bridge Road. **Canoe and kayak rentals** are available at Silent Glide Canoe & Kayak Shop in Medford (715-748-0148 or www.silentglidecanoeandkayakshop.com).

PUT IN upstream-right at the **Highway 64 bridge** near County DD. There is room for a few cars alongside the road.

The river begins about 70 feet wide, flowing between grassy, wooded banks. The water is clean but usually a little dark from organic material—thus the name "Black River." Not far downstream, you'll see a gravel pit on the right, followed by the first of many riffles. There is a house on the right where a creek enters, then two islands.

Inviting gravel bars appear. After a place where vehicular tracks lead down to the river on both sides, a wooded lowland area begins. A big island precedes another dirt road leading down to the river on both sides. Riffles and Class I rapids become more frequent after a long, sweeping left-bend with 10-foot cutbanks on the right shore.

A pasture and gravel road appear on the left, then a pile of concrete rip-rap. From this point there's a long stretch of winding, often narrow and fast water with a circuitous channel, islands and occasional downed trees. Maneuvering through is usually no problem, but be careful.

The first house in a long time appears on the left just downstream from the mouth of Trappers Creek (7.2 miles). The river widens here, heads into a northwest straightaway and emerges temporarily from the lowland setting. As the river bends back to the southwest toward the County A bridge, there are sandy pine-topped cutbanks on the right. The river is mostly narrow, deep and slow down to the bridge (8.5 miles), except for a spot a half mile upstream where the channel narrows to 20 feet and becomes swift; beware of deadfall here.

After a farm on the left, there is another winding area with riffles, gravel bars and islands; choose the channels with the most water and look out for limbs. Power lines pass overhead at the beginning of a large island. After an abrupt right turn, then another to the left, the railroad bridge appears 1.2 miles upstream from Bridge Road.

TAKE OUT downstream-left at **Bridge Road,** where there's room for a few cars alongside the road. An alternative take-out, upstream-right at the County X bridge west of Withee, adds about 5 miles to the trip.

Other trips: Just upstream from the above section, the Black meanders through approximately 10 miles of lowland. Putting in at Highway 64 near County E is not recommended because there is so much deadfall in the tight, winding bends. For maps and descriptions of the much-better-known southern sections of the river, see *Paddling Southern Wisconsin.*

The View from Wisconsin's Highest Place

Mount Everest it's not, but it is the highest place in Wisconsin. And when you're paddling the Black, Big Rib, Jump, Yellow, Tomahawk or South Fork of the Flambeau, it's in the neighborhood.

Timm's Hill, located in a 220-acre Price County park, is 1,951 feet above sea level, and rewards hikers with a lovely view—especially from the observation tower at the top. The setting is particularly pretty in the fall.

An added bonus is the 10-mile trail that connects the park with the Ice Age Trail to the south. The Timm's Hill National Scenic Trail passes through some densely wooded glacial hills and skirts a couple of lakes. The southern end features interpretive signs conveying information about the glaciers and logging operations once found in the area. Both hikers and mountain bikers may use the trail.

To get to the park, take Highway 102 east from Rib Lake, then County C north, and finally County CC east.

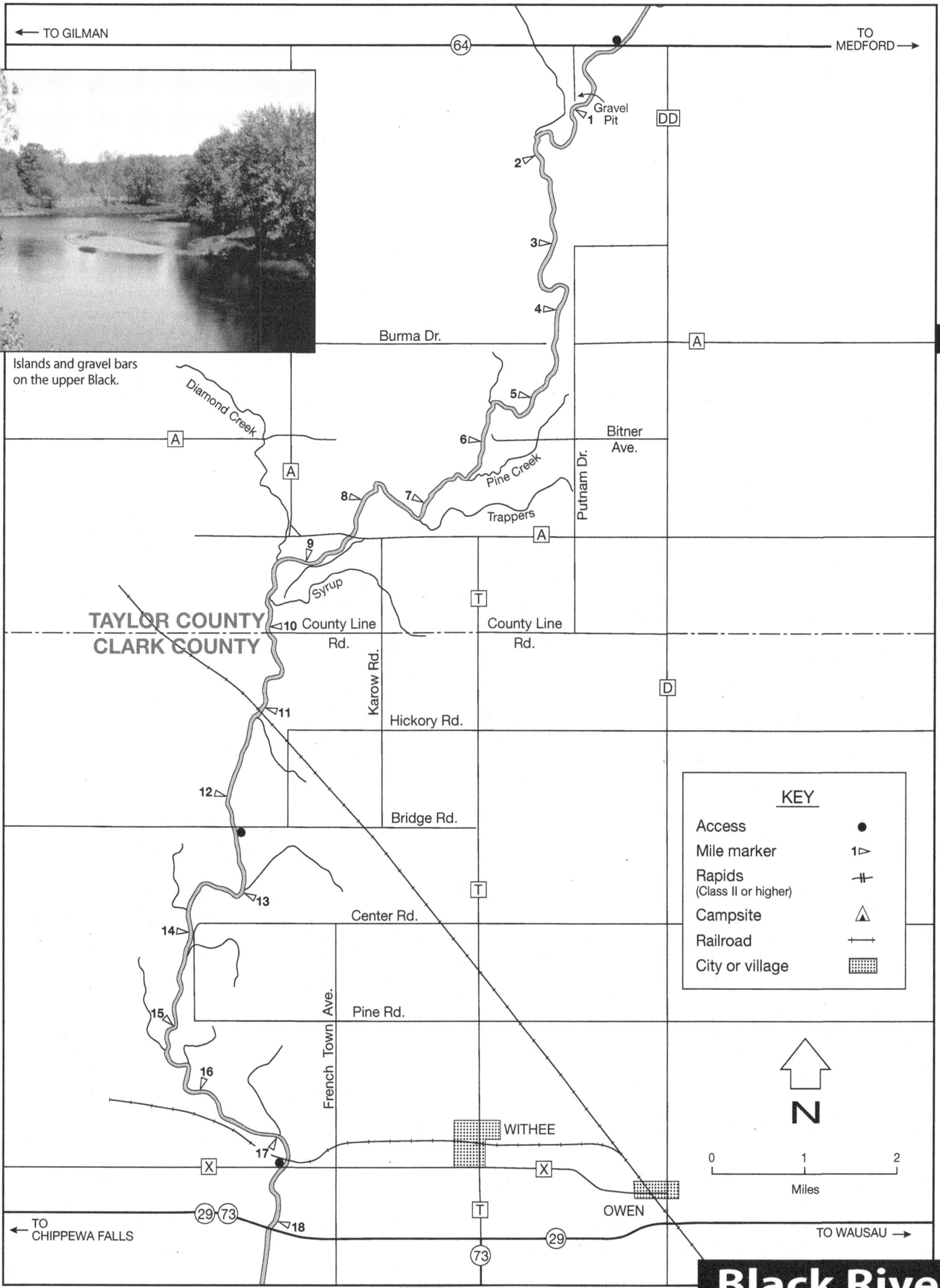

Islands and gravel bars on the upper Black.

Bois Brule River 1

County S to Highway 2 (12 Miles)

One of the most famous rivers in the Midwest, the Bois Brule is also one of the most popular canoeing streams in Wisconsin. Part of the reason for its popularity is its unspoiled character: The entire river lies within the 52,000-acre Brule River State Forest, 12,000 acres of which are owned by private landowners who take pride in helping preserve the wild character of the shoreline.

Another factor that keeps canoeists coming is the river's diversity. Beginning as a tiny meandering stream in a cedar and spruce bog, the river straightens through several lakelike wide spots. It then runs a series of gentle rapids, passes lovely rustic homes, and winds quietly between wooded banks before dropping for several miles over turbulent ledges and rocks. In short, the Bois Brule appeals to paddlers of every preference—with renowned trout fishing as well. Incidentally, the name of the river is a French translation of the original Ojibwe name meaning "burned woods."

The 12-mile stretch from County S (Stone's Bridge) to Highway 2 is the most popular day trip on the river. Its mostly quiet water and relatively easy riffles and rapids make it an excellent paddle for less-experienced canoeists.

Even a River Can Change Its Mind

The bogs, ledges, banks and even the direction of flow of the Bois Brule are all a result of the river's unique geological history.

As the last glacial period neared an end, a huge mass of melting ice occupied the general area of what is now known as Lake Superior. The meltwater poured southward, carving the valley through which the Bois Brule and part of the upper St. Croix rivers now flow. The water carried rocks along with it and deposited them in places that were later covered by many feet of decayed vegetation to form bogs. The glacial torrent also cut through the volcanic rock and sandstone of the Copper Range, where today you'll find the Bois Brule's most challenging rapids.

As the waters receded, deep deposits of clay were left behind. Then, because of a ridge between the Brule and St. Croix watersheds, the river changed direction and began flowing north into Lake Superior. It penetrated the clay and created the Bois Brule's characteristic high banks.

Almost the entire section is privately owned. Please respect the rights of property owners and obey the occasional no-trespassing signs.

The State Forest office asks that canoeists use only designated landings (as described in this book) and not bring cans or bottles onto the water

Camping is available at the Bois Brule Campground, which is accessed by canoe at 10.6 miles or by car from Highway 2. Another State Forest campground, Copper Range, is located farther north along the river.

Water levels are very dependable, thanks to the gradual discharge of water from the extensive bogs and swamp wetlands of the Upper Bois Brule. For general information on water levels (high, medium or low), call the office of the Brule River State Forest (715-372-5678) or Brule River Canoe Rental (715-372-4983), which provides shuttles and **canoe/kayak rental.** There is a USGS gauge (#04025500) on the river downstream from the village of Brule; see "Water Levels" in the introduction.

The **GRADIENT** is 4.1 feet per mile.

The **shuttle route** is via County S, Highway 27 and Highway 2. The trip can be shortened to 8.6 miles by taking out at County B.

PUT IN at the developed **landing** downstream-left from the County S bridge (Stone's Bridge).

The river is quite intimate at the beginning, only 30 feet wide and passing through an attractive lowland covered with cedar, spruce, balsam, tamarack and alder. Occasional rock wing-dams have been placed in the stream bed to enhance the otherwise shallow flow. The water is clear, with a sandy bottom and many rocks.

About 2 miles from the put-in, McDougal Springs enters on the right. No houses are encountered until the private Cedar Island estate, where a boathouse appears on the left, followed by a couple of charming footbridges that cross to the island itself, then more buildings. The estate is the biggest and best known of the fishing lodges that were built on the river by well-to-do sportsmen as early as the late 1800s.

For about a mile after Cedar Island, the river channel narrows and there is a series of riffles and Class I rapids. At times, trees canopy the river, heightening the sense of intimacy. This is a particularly beautiful part of the river. At one point, the river widens into a short pool, with a picnic shelter to the left. Just downstream are more Class I rapids, called **The Falls** and **Twin Rapids.**

At 5 miles, the river widens to about a quarter mile (Big Lake), then narrows to pass through easy **Wildcat Rapids** and widens again to form Lucius Lake. If the wind is out of the north, paddling up the lakes isn't easy.

You'll see many attractive homes from this point on. Frequent stands of white pine appear on the bluffs, together with occasional high sand banks and picturesque wooden bridges.

At 8.6 miles, the **Winneboujou canoe landing** is located upstream-left at the County B bridge. This excellent access can be used as an alternate take-out if a shorter trip is desired. Winneboujou is the name of an Ojibwe god: the Great Hare.

After Winneboujou, there is a series of exciting Class I rapids almost all the way to the campground. You'll hear the only rapids of consequence, **Little Joe,** upstream; it comes at 10.4 miles after a right-hand turn. Get out and walk the river-right path to scout this Class II rapids, which has a couple of big rocks in the center that you will want to avoid. A log-driving dam was located here a century ago.

After Little Joe, the **Bois Brule Campground** follows not far downstream, on the right. **Doodlebug Rapids** (easy Class I) follows the campground.

TAKE-OUT: The river winds quietly for a mile to the **landing** upstream-left from Highway 2.

Bois Brule River 1

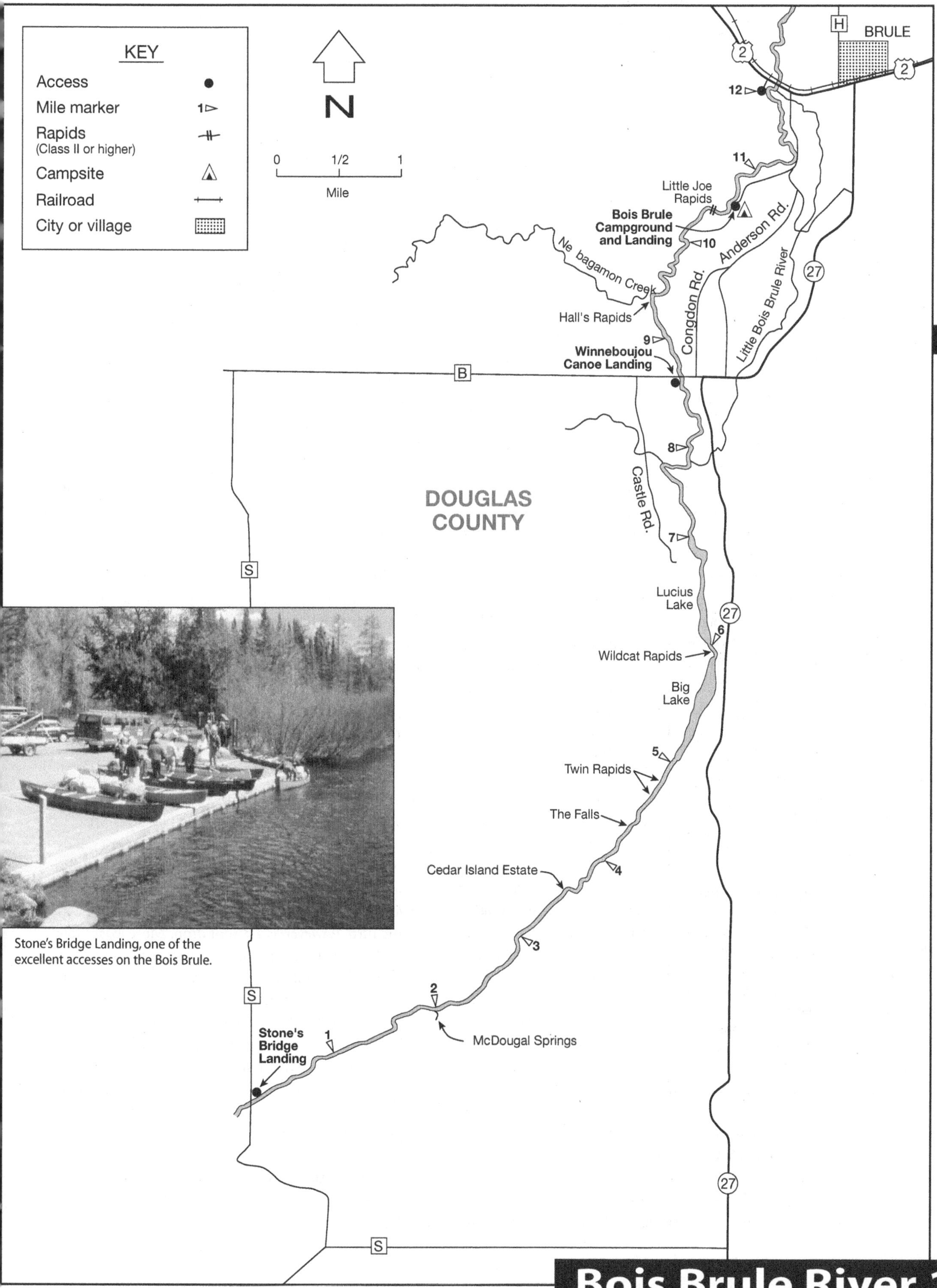

Stone's Bridge Landing, one of the excellent accesses on the Bois Brule.

Bois Brule River 2

Highway 2 to Highway 13 (15.5 Miles)

Don't generalize about this stretch of the Bois Brule based on what you'll encounter in the first half. While the beginning 7 miles contain the quietest water offered by the river, the next 8 are almost continuous whitewater and include two series of very challenging Class II ledges. Thus, this section is usually paddled in shorter portions: Highway 2 to Pine Tree Landing (or Copper Range Campground) by those who want a placid flatwater float, and Pine Tree Landing to Highway 13 by whitewater seekers. Beginning canoeists should not venture beyond Pine Tree, especially in medium to high water.

The course of the river, while generally straighter upstream from Highway 2, twists and turns in this stretch as the river cuts through a narrow valley. Near the Copper Range Campground, the river gradient increases conspicuously, resulting in many miles of riffles and rapids. The wild scenery, curving river bed and almost continuous whitewater (mostly Class I) make the section from Pine Tree Landing a joyous run for experienced boaters. Once you've paddled it, you're sure to return.

The River of Presidents

How many rivers have drawn five presidential fishermen? Only the Bois Brule can claim that distinction. Grant, Cleveland, Coolidge, Hoover and Eisenhower have all visited this river in pursuit of trout.

During their fishing trips, the three most recent presidents were guests at nearby Cedar Island, a 4,000-acre private estate that includes many charming cedar log buildings and spring lakes.

Some observers maintain that the quality of the Bois Brule fishery isn't what it used to be, but the river is still quite popular with anglers. Brookies, rainbows and browns reside here (especially upstream from County B near Winneboujou Landing), and coho, Chinook, pink salmon and steelheads annually migrate up the river from Lake Superior to spawn.

For recommendations on where and how to fish the river, see *Wisconsin & Minnesota Trout Streams* by Jim Humphrey and Bill Shogren (Woodstock, Vt.: Backcountry Publishers, 1995).

Camping is available at the two state forest campgrounds on the river, one on this section at Copper Range and another upstream from Highway 2.

Water levels are almost always adequate for pleasant paddling. For information, call the DNR's Brule River State Forest office (715-372-5678) or Brule River Canoe Rental (715-372-4983), where you also can **rent a boat** or arrange a shuttle.

The average **GRADIENT** for the whole section is 12.9 feet per mile, but the final 8 miles are much steeper.

The **shuttle route** is via Highway 2, County H and Highway 13, with Pine Tree Landing as an alternate take-out or put-in. The Copper Range Campground can be accessed only by campers.

PUT IN at the developed **landing** upstream-left from the Highway 2 bridge.

The 7.5 miles from Highway 2 to Copper Range Campground wind slowly back and forth through a peaceful, heavily forested area. Pine, ash, popple, maple, birch, spruce and balsam are plentiful along the shoreline, and steep clay banks are prevalent. This area of the river is generally known as The Meadows.

The Meadows is a good stretch for a lazy fishing trip. Many varieties of trout inhabit the river, and this section features a number of deep holes where lunkers are found. One of the better known fishing spots is the Boxcar Hole, located downstream from Casey Creek at 3.6 miles.

The river north of Highway 2 all the way to Lake Superior has numerous parking lots and access points for fishermen, so you will often encounter anglers along the banks and wading in the river.

After more deep holes and occasional steep banks, the river begins to change character. As you approach Copper Range Campground, slow, deep water gives way to Class I rapids. Paddlers who have registered for a campsite may take out at the campground on river-right. Use of the Copper Range bridge, just downstream from the campground, is discouraged as an access. An excellent public access soon follows at 7.8 miles: **Pine Tree Landing.**

After Pine Tree, the river is very winding and narrow, with almost constant Class I rapids. Two miles downstream from the landing—shortly after a gas-line clearing, a wooden footbridge and a sharp left turn—the **Lenroot Ledges** (solid Class II) begin. Get out on the right and walk along the fisherman's path (accessed from County FF) to scout the four drops. The chutes over the ledges are usually fairly easy to read, but scouting is a good idea. Look for an unexpected boulder in the middle of the final drop. Portage the ledges if necessary.

Rapids continue to be numerous after Lenroot, increasing a little in difficulty. There are usually big waves before and after the County FF bridge.

About half a mile below FF come the biggest rapids on the river—the **May Ledges** (Class II+). Like Lenroot, this series of four drops begins with a left turn. The first ledge, just before the turn, is an easy one; located in the turn, however, is a 3-foot drop. More ledges follow. Because the chutes are not apparent from river level, paddlers should take out on the right and scout the whole series. Before you start your canoe trip, you can pre-scout the May Ledges from Koski Road.

After a couple of small ledges downstream from the May series, rapids are still frequent but become easier. A few cabins are seen along the shore. Many high bluffs of clay and sand appear, and the red clay increasingly clouds the water. Several big bends precede Highway 13.

TAKE OUT at the excellent **landing** upstream-right from the Highway 13 bridge.

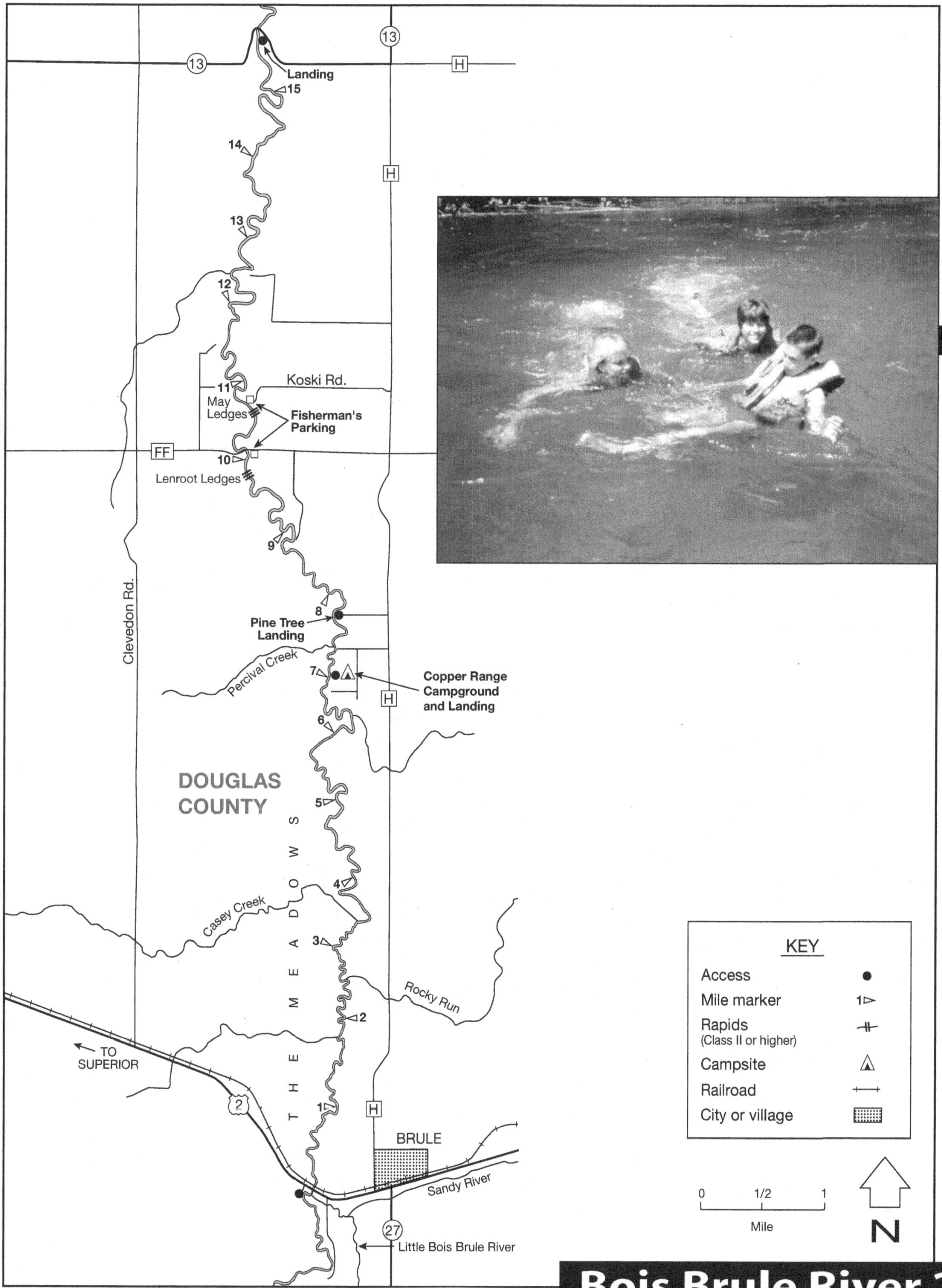

Bois Brule River 2

Bois Brule River 3

Highway 13 to Lake Superior (8 Miles)

Few canoe trips end as spectacularly as this one: One moment you're paddling down the calm final stretch of the Bois Brule, still enthusiastic about the gorgeous scenery and periodic riffle/rapids, and the next moment Lake Superior looms before you. It's always an exciting experience, whether the lake is mirror-smooth or windswept.

Canoeists spending a two- or three-day weekend on the river will find this a perfect run for Sunday morning before heading home. Easily paddled in three hours or less, this stretch of river provides considerable variety: easy rapids, attractive banks, some quiet water, an interesting lamprey barrier and, of course, the dramatic finish. Paddlers who don't mind a longer day (almost 16 miles) can put in farther upstream at the Pine Tree Landing, and thus include the river's best whitewater stretch. The current is always good, so you can move right along if you choose to do so—or dawdle, if you like.

Camping is not available on this section, but Brule River State Forest campgrounds are located along the river in each of the two upstream sections.

A Tough Way to Get There

The ancient water route from Lake Michigan to the Mississippi via the Fox and Wisconsin Rivers is well known. Less commonly known, however, is the much more difficult route that was used for centuries by Native Americans, explorers, traders and missionaries to travel from Lake Superior to the Mississippi. The journey from Green Bay to Prairie du Chien was a piece of cake compared to the arduous canoe trip up the Bois Brule, followed by a two-mile portage to Upper St. Croix Lake and a long voyage down the St. Croix River to the Mississippi.

The explorer Duluth is thought to have been the first white man to make the trip, in 1680. Not until the mid-1800s was the route superseded by roads. Today it is still possible to hike the portage trail: It begins near the boat landing at the north end of St. Croix Lake.

Water levels are very dependable year-round. For general information on water levels (high, medium or low), call the Brule River State Forest office (715-372-5678) or Brule River Canoe Rental (715-372-4983), which provides shuttle service and **rents boats.** Inexperienced paddlers should not paddle this section when the water is high.

The average **GRADIENT** for this section is a lively 12.5 feet per mile.

The **shuttle route** is via Highway 13 and Brule River Road.

PUT IN at the excellent **landing** upstream-right from the Highway 13 bridge. After Highway 13, the river continues to be very winding, with many riffles and Class I rapids. Because of the clay banks, the water becomes progressively cloudier.

Two miles into the trip, warning signs indicate the approach of a **dam.** Just upstream from a row of orange buoys, a portage trail appears on river-left. Take out carefully and carry your equipment around this impressive concrete structure, which prevents lamprey eels from swimming upriver and decimating the trout population. The dam replaces a less effective electric weir that once was located downstream.

Clay darkens the water of the Bois Brule.

A tributary stream enters on the left shortly after the dam. Half a mile later, the river goes under a small iron bridge at McNeil Road. From here to Lake Superior, the DNR has provided numerous fishermen's parking lots near the river (none of which can be seen from the water).

Gentle rapids continue, with many high banks. Creeks enter on the left at 3.5 miles and on the right at 4 miles, followed by an old bridge abutment on the left. As you continue downstream, the banks grow higher. All of a sudden, within approximately a mile of the lake, the current slackens and cool lake air can be felt. Half a mile upstream from the mouth, another logging-era dam was located a century ago: Here logs were sorted before they were rafted across the lake to mills in Duluth.

The river widens in its final reaches, and then the great expanse of Lake Superior comes into view.

TAKE OUT on the **sandy beach** to the right just before the mouth of the river. A long sand-spit extends to the left, thus protecting the river from waves coming in from the lake. Up the hill to the right is a DNR scenic overlook, with parking, picnic tables and toilets. The view from the top of the hill is glorious: You'll want to spend some time there before hitting the road. A detailed historical marker near the overlook conveys many interesting facts about the river.

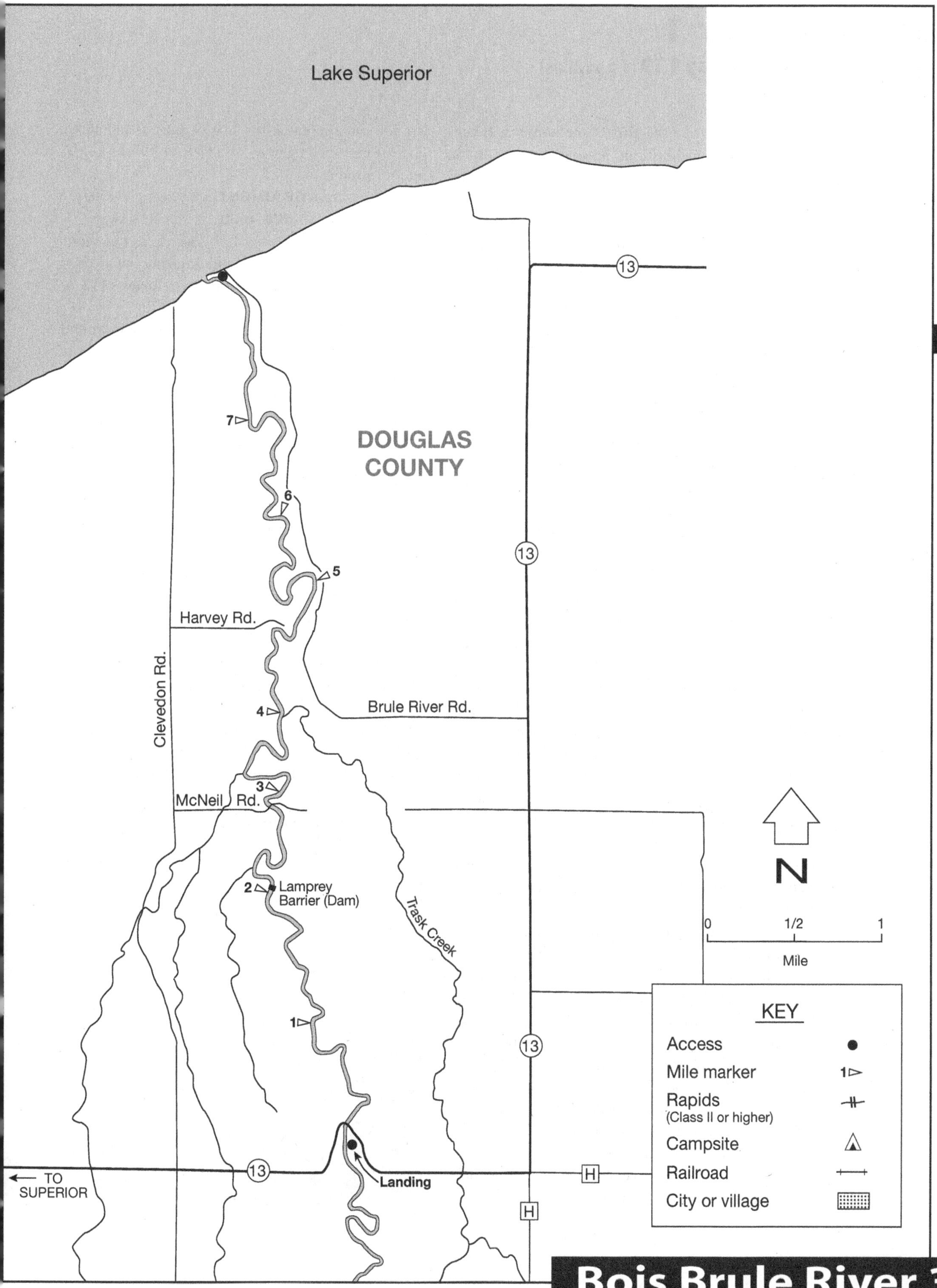
Lake Superior
DOUGLAS COUNTY
13
7
6
5
Harvey Rd.
Clevedon Rd.
4
Brule River Rd.
3
McNeil Rd.
2
Lamprey Barrier (Dam)
Trask Creek
1
N
0
1/2
1
Mile
KEY
Access
Mile marker
Rapids
(Class II or higher)
Campsite
Railroad
City or village
TO SUPERIOR
Landing
H

Brule River 1

Highway 55 to Highway 139 (13.5 Miles)

The Brule River forms part of the border between Wisconsin and Michigan, flowing southeast to its confluence with the Michigamme River (where the Menominee River begins). A lovely little river with steady current, it runs quietly through an environment that is, for the most part, wild. Here you'll encounter deer, eagles and beaver, along with numerous riffles and Class I rapids. Once you have paddled the Brule, you'll wonder why there aren't more canoeists on it.

The river is suitable for novices (taking proper precautions), except when the water is high. The first section, from Highway 55 to Highway 139, has no rapids but does have numerous pleasant riffles. Thanks to its cleanness, remote setting and riffly sections, the Brule has a good reputation as a fishery for brown and brook trout. Stands of pine, maple, elm, cedar and birch, together with a profusion of alder bushes, line the banks, and marsh grass grows in the lowland sections.

Most of the land on the Wisconsin side of the river is in the Nicolet National Forest, while much of the Michigan side is owned by the Michigan DNR. However, there are patches of private land here and there. In this first section, you'll encounter private land in the big bend at the 3.5-mile point and in the stretch between 10 and 11 miles on the Wisconsin side.

Camping is allowed anywhere on national forest land, but prior permission must be obtained to camp on Michigan DNR land. Good, undesignated campsite locations can be seen occasionally on the Wisconsin shoreline, for example, near the mouth of Allen Creek at 8.5 miles. The USFS Brule River Campground at the put-in provides 11 sites in a beautiful grove of pine and balsam fir. Other public campgrounds are located within a few miles' drive: at Perch Lake, Chipmunk Rapids, Lauterman Lake, Lost Lake, Stevens Lake and Windsor Dam.

Water levels are relatively constant, but are occasionally too low for comfortable paddling. Like any river, the Brule develops a number of danger spots in high-water conditions. Information on water levels can be obtained from the Florence Wild Rivers Interpretive Center (715-528-5377 or 888-889-0049) or by calling Northwoods Wilderness Outfitters in Iron Mountain (800-530-8859 or 906-774-9009), which also provides shuttle service and **canoe/kayak rental**. Rentals are also available at Wild Rivers Adventure Company in Florence (715-952-8027). There is a gauge under the Highway 141 bridge; as a rule of thumb, there's enough water to paddle the Brule if the gauge reads 3.5 or higher. You can also check the USGS gauge (#04060993, located near the Highway 2 bridge); see "Water Levels" in the introduction.

The average **GRADIENT** is 5.9 feet per mile.

The best **shuttle route** is via Highway 55, Highway 70 and Highway 139. The trip can be shortened considerably by putting in or taking out at alternate access points reached via Forest Roads 2172 or 2454, which run north from Highway 70.

PUT IN at the USFS **Brule River Campground** near Nelma, Wisconsin, on Highway 55 just south of the Michigan border.

The river begins narrow and marshy, then widens after the Highway 55 bridge. Occasionally, you will see houses on the Michigan side.

The current picks up and the river narrows a little after Forest Road 2172 (an alternate **put-in** or **take-out**) comes in from the right, at the 4.3-mile point. There are many alder-covered islands and pleasant riffles.

A nice primitive campsite appears on the right at 8.5 miles, near the outlet of Allen Creek. Forest Road 2454 (another **access**) comes in from the right a half mile downstream from Allen Creek.

At approximately 10.5 miles, a house appears on the right, with a clearing on both sides of the river and old pilings.

The river continues narrow and riffly with good current past the mouths of Huff Creek and Chuks Creek on the right and all the way down to Highway 139.

TAKE OUT on the upstream- or downstream-right side of the **Highway 139 bridge.** There is parking space for a few cars.

A misty morning on the Brule.

Brule River 1

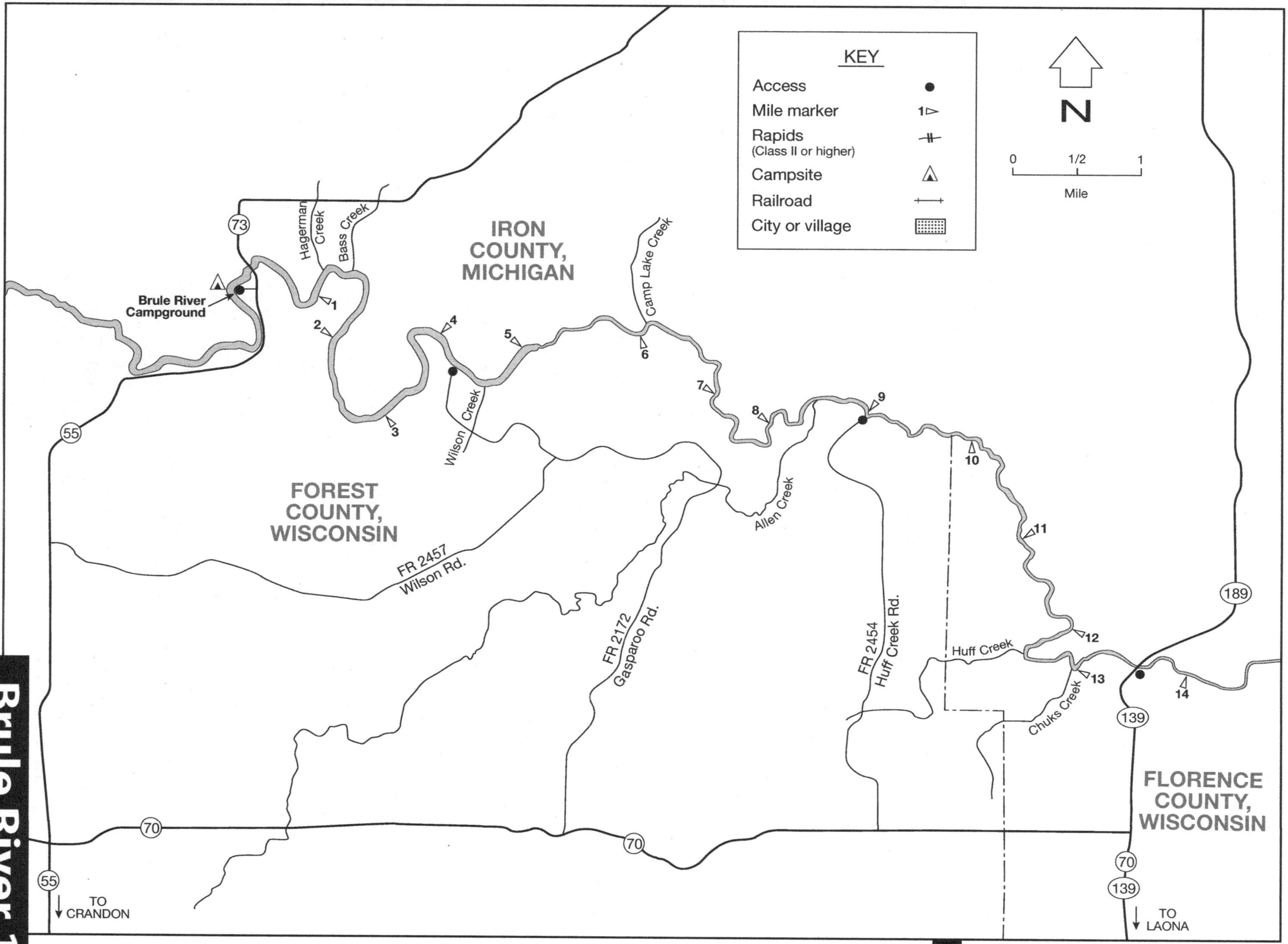

Brule River 2

Highway 139 to FR 2150 (16.2 Miles)

This section of the Brule, like the previous stretch, is winding and remote but throws in a few Class I–II rapids for good measure. Novice paddlers should be prepared to scout (and perhaps portage) some of the rapids. The setting is quite varied and includes swift narrows, wide shallow areas, rock gardens, ledges and heavily wooded shoreline. Wildlife is often spotted. Trout fishing is good, and smallmouth are occasionally caught.

Most of the shoreline is publicly owned, but there are several short stretches of private land on the Wisconsin side: shortly after the Highway 139 put-in, on both sides of Forest Road 2152, in the big right bend along the railroad tracks 1.5 miles north of Pentoga, and in part of the last mile before Forest Road 2150.

Camping is allowed anywhere on national forest land on the Wisconsin side, but you must obtain prior permission to camp on Michigan DNR land. Occasionally, you will see undesignated primitive campsites along the river, near Twin Rapids and Two-Foot Falls, for example. For other public campgrounds see Brule 1.

Water levels are fairly constant throughout the canoeing season, but be careful when the water is medium or high, especially in the area above and below Pentoga where there are several Class I–II rapids in bends. Always be on the lookout for strainers, and scout whenever in doubt. This stretch tends to be a little deeper than the upstream portion, especially after the mouth of the Iron River. For sources of water-level information, and for **canoe rentals** and shuttle service, see the description of Brule 1.

The average **GRADIENT** is 4.3 feet per mile.

The best **shuttle route** is via Highway 139, Highway 70 and Forest Road 2150. (The trip can be shortened by using one or both of the forest roads—2152 and 2446—that run north from Highway 70.)

PUT IN on the upstream- or downstream-right side of the **Highway 139 bridge.** Some parking is nearby.

For the first 6 miles, there are a number of wide, shallow spots and a few riffles. Current persists, however.

Wisconsin Slough enters from the right at 2.1 miles, and Wisconsin Creek enters, also from the right, at 6.1 miles.

The Iron River enters from Michigan at 6.5 miles, often cloudy in color because of mining residue. A railroad bridge crosses the Brule below the mouth of the Iron River.

At 7.3 miles, Forest Road 2152 (an alternate **access**) touches the river on the right. There is a constriction here, with a tongue and wave. After FR 2152, the river gets narrower and swifter, with more riffles and small rapids.

Olsen's Creek enters from the left at 7.8 miles, followed a quarter-mile later by **Fisherman's Eddy Rapids** (an easy Class I rock garden).

A mile later (9.3 miles) comes the longest rapids on this stretch, **Twin Rapids.** The first part consists of a series of easy Class I rapids, followed by several hundred yards of flatwater, then another set of rock gardens; the second set (Class I–II) is more difficult than the first and requires more maneuvering. There is a primitive campsite along the right shore.

At 10.8 miles, **Railroad Rapids** (Class I) occurs at a point where railroad tracks run along the river on the left and the river begins bending to the right.

Downstream (12.1 miles), the main river channel emerges from behind a couple of islands at the Forest Road 2446 bridge near Pentoga, Michigan (another alternate **access** point). If you wish to get out here, take out upstream from the bridge on the right, where there is a big eddy. If you continue, be careful: The bridge is rather low, making clearance a problem in high water, and the current is swift.

The river narrows after the Pentoga bridge, and the current quickens.

Two miles downstream from the bridge (14.1 miles) comes **Two-Foot Falls** (Class I–II). As you approach, you can hear the roar and see a horizon line. Take out on the right shore just upstream from this river-wide 2-foot bedrock ledge; there is a well-established scout/portage trail that leads up to a very nice campsite on a wooded bank. Most canoeists run the drop on the right side, where there's a tongue; immediately after the drop, the river veers to the left. Make sure that there are no strainers below the drop. Negotiating the drop requires boat control; portage if you are unsure of your skills.

TAKE-OUT: After two more quick miles, Forest Road 2150 (Rainbow Road) appears on the right. The **landing** is easy to miss because there isn't much of a clearing. A house comes into view on a hill before the landing, and you will see the concrete remains of old bridge pilings on the left side of the river opposite the landing. The current is brisk here. If the weather has been wet, the last couple miles of FR 2150 can be messy: Be careful not to get stuck as you drive out.

Angling for trout on the Brule.

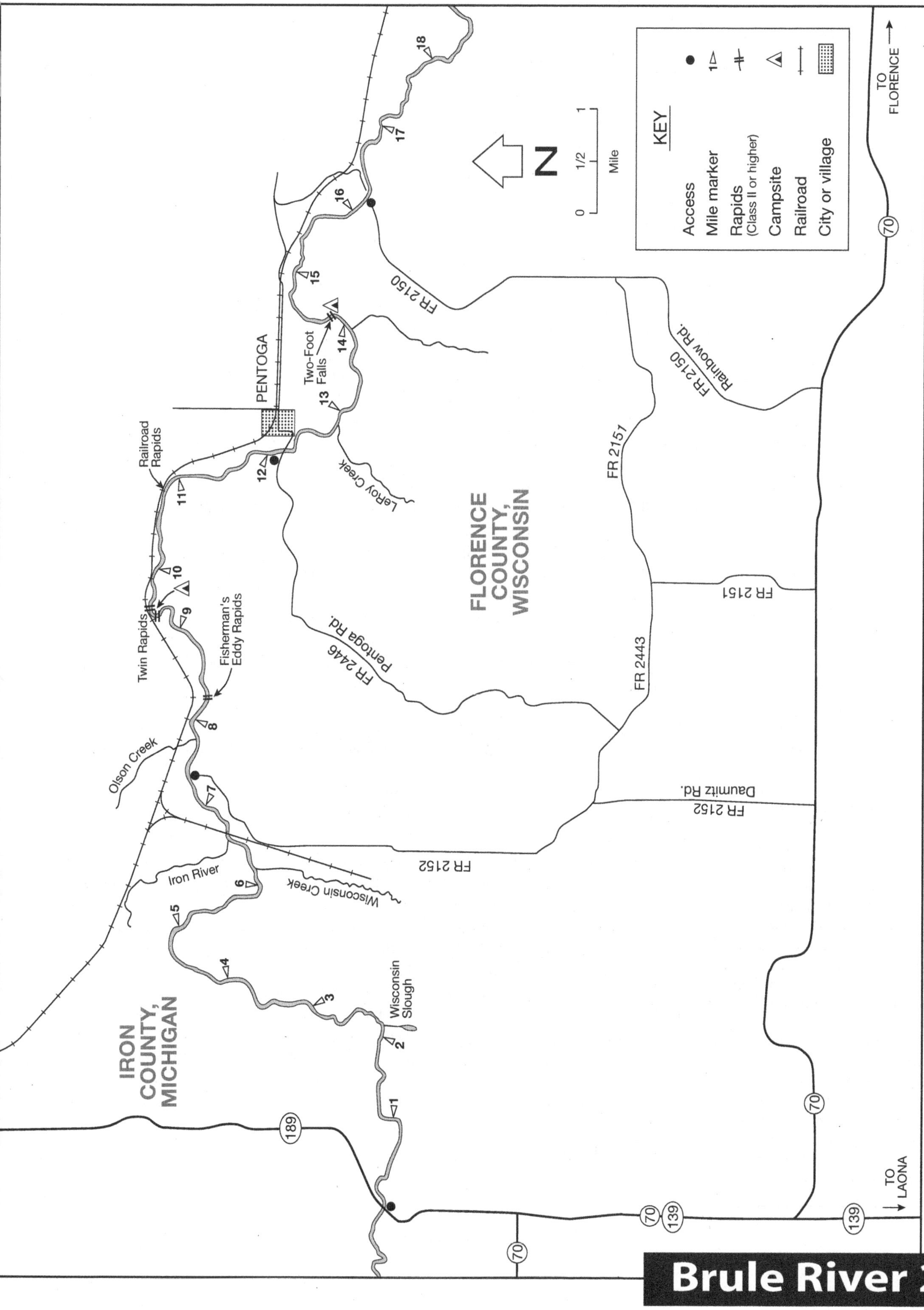

Brule River 2

Brule River 3

Forest Road 2150 to Brule Flowage (14 Miles)

You'll see few signs of human habitation on this wild stretch of the Brule. Majestic cedars frequently hang over the river from grassy, wooded banks. Mostly flatwater, the stretch includes many delightful riffles and the last Class I–II rapids on the Brule before it becomes the Menominee. Eagles, deer, muskrats and mergansers are common as the river winds its way toward the dam of the attractive and relatively narrow Brule River Flowage; below the dam, the Brule and Michigamme come together to create the high-volume Menominee River.

Camping on the river is sparse. Unlike the shoreline along the two upstream sections, most of the land here is privately owned. (Because individual property owners have large tracts of land, however, there are only a few dwellings along the entire stretch.) On the Wisconsin side of the river, the Nicolet National Forest ends near the mouth of Riley Creek. You will find several public campgrounds within a few miles' driving distance: Perch Lake (on the access road to the put-in), Lauterman Lake, Chipmunk Rapids and Lost Lake.

For **water levels** and **canoe/kayak rental,** see Brule 1.

The average **GRADIENT** is 6.4 feet per mile.

The **shuttle route** is via Forest Road 2150, Highway 70, Chapin Road and River Landing Road. Shorter trips can be arranged by utilizing alternate accesses at Carney Road (Michigan) or the Highway 2/141 bridge.

PUT IN at the river-right **landing** at the end of FR 2150 (Rainbow Trail); there is also an access here on the Michigan side of the river. Rainbow Trail runs 5 miles north from Highway 70 to the river; in wet weather, the last couple miles can be rather mushy.

After the put-in, the river is narrow, with riffles and the first of many islands. Riffles continue in curves for 2 miles, and the predominant setting is low wooded banks. Clear water flows over a gravel bottom.

But Which Brule?

No small amount of confusion is caused by the fact that different rivers in Wisconsin have the same name. In the northern portion of the state, for example, there are two Eau Claire rivers and two Pines—each of which is canoeable in certain sections.

Most confusing of all, however, is the "two-Brules" situation. Even though residents of northwest Wisconsin call their river "the Brule," as if there were no other, it officially is designated the Bois Brule by the U.S. Geological Survey and the state of Wisconsin highway map. It is deservedly one of the most popular canoeing and fishing streams in the Midwest.

The "other Brule," which partially divides northeast Wisconsin and the Upper Peninsula of Michigan, is often informally called the "Border Brule" to distinguish it from its better-known counterpart. Less dramatic than the Bois Brule, it nevertheless has considerable charms of its own.

Armstrong Creek enters from the left in a right-hand bend, followed by Riley Creek on the right (the eastern boundary of the national forest). After a southeast straightaway, the outlet of Pickerel Creek enters on the right in a left turn.

Half a mile downstream from a very high, grassy, wooded bank on the left, you'll encounter the **Michigan DNR landing** at the end of Carney Road on the left (3.5 miles). This is a pleasant grassy site with picnic facilities and toilets.

An orange post downstream warns of a buried gas pipeline, immediately preceded by an enjoyable ledge/riffle. Downstream, you'll see a cabin surrounded by thick cedar groves on the right.

Then, for several miles, the river straightens somewhat, widens and gets a little shallower as it heads southeast toward Highway 2/141. At one point, many islands appear in the river, and there are a couple of miles of delightful riffles. Occasionally, you'll find boulders in the stream bed and along the shoreline.

Not far downstream from an old railroad bridge (in a big left-hand bend), a large island precedes the Highway 2/141 bridge. Be careful of deadfall in the narrower right channel. If you're using the bridge as a **take-out** or **put-in,** the best access is downstream-left (10.2 miles).

A string of islands follows the bridge, together with a pretty stone outcropping on the right. Occasional riffles follow, and the river is generally a little wider.

After a river-right cabin, Class I–II **La Chapelle Rapids** runs for about a hundred yards in an S-curve. A series of riffles and Class I rapids follows.

In a right-hand bend, Florence Town Road E approaches the river on the right, opposite a farm. The Washburn Bridge was once located here; the old abutments remain.

Good current continues for a while, then slackens as the river widens at the west end of the flowage. There are high wooded banks on both sides for about half a mile before the landing.

TAKE OUT on the right at Wisconsin Electric Power Company Brule Recreation Area #28. WEPCO provides an excellent concrete **landing,** toilets and parking. To get to the access area, take Chapin Road north out of Florence, and turn left at the Y intersection onto River Landing Road.

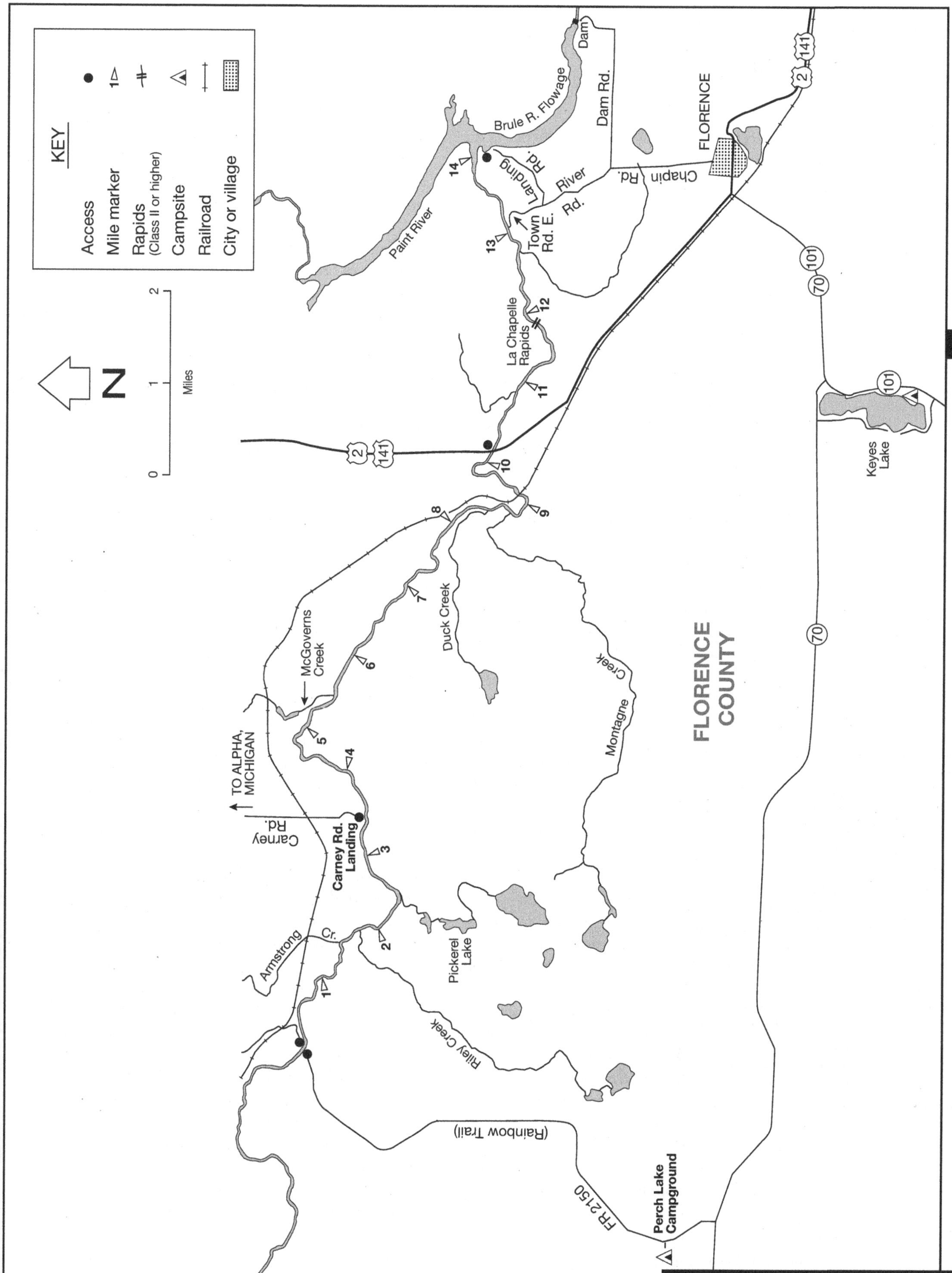

Brule River 3

Chippewa River 1

Winter Dam to Ojibwa (7.8 Miles)

Few rivers in Wisconsin are as historically rich as the Chippewa. Together with such tributaries as the Flambeau, Jump, Yellow, Red Cedar, Eau Claire and Couderay (Court Oreilles), the Chippewa drains 9,500 square miles—one-sixth of the total area of the state. In the 19th century, its watershed accounted for more than a third of Wisconsin's white pine forest, making it a "logger's paradise," in the words of famous lumberman Frederick Weyerhaeuser.

Dropping almost a thousand feet from its source to the Mississippi, the Chippewa had a dependable current for floating logs downstream to the sawmills of Chippewa Falls and Eau Claire. It was also relatively free of the major boulder gardens and drops that plagued loggers on such rivers as the Wisconsin and the Wolf. In 1892, at the peak of the Chippewa logging era, an estimated 632 million logs floated down the river.

The heyday of logging lasted 80 years, until 1918. Today, few signs of the camps, "rollways," driving dams and tote roads remain. Nevertheless, the Chippewa is basically the same wide and—for the most part—gentle river that the lumbermen knew.

Originating in Bayfield and Ashland counties, the west and east forks of the river meet in the Chippewa Flowage, a 17,000-acre wilderness lake created in 1923 by the construction of the Winter Dam. Below the dam, 50-plus miles of dependably canoeable river carry paddlers to the Flambeau River confluence. Except for some Class II rapids in the Radisson area, the Chippewa is generally suitable for novices. For beginning and experienced paddlers alike, however, care and good judgment are always required. The Chippewa is a big river that can be especially powerful and dangerous under medium and high water conditions. High volume can turn mild riffles into big, boat-swamping waves, and boaters must always be on the look-out for downed trees.

The first recommended trip is fairly typical of what you'll encounter all the way to the mouth of the Flambeau: good current; low, grassy, wooded banks; occasional riffles and Class I rapids; and few houses. Fishermen are a common sight, angling for northerns, walleye, muskie, smallmouth, catfish and panfish. A wide variety of wildlife inhabits or frequents the valley.

Try a Paddle/Pedal Weekend

For those who enjoy both canoeing and bicycling, Ojibwa Park is a wonderful place to set up camp. Take a day to paddle the Winter Dam to Ojibwa stretch of the Chippewa, spend the night at the Ojibwa Park campground, then pedal a nearby bike trail on day two.

The 366-acre park is bordered on the north by the river. At the southern edge is the Tuscobia State Trail, an abandoned railroad right-of-way used by mountain bikers, hikers, horseback riders and, in winter, snowmobilers. Running 75 miles from Tuscobia (north of Rice Lake) to Park Falls, the trail traverses beautiful countryside and passes through such communities as Radisson, Winter, Couderay and Loretta. Ojibwa is the halfway point, so you can jump on your bike and head either way on the second day of your paddle/pedal weekend. Be prepared for some soft or rough areas on the trail and a couple of short detours onto adjoining roads.

Camping is available near the river at Ojibwa Park (see below) and at several private campgrounds in the Chippewa Flowage area.

Water levels are almost always sufficient for enjoyable paddling, but boaters should stay off the river when it is high. Check the gauge at County G (#05356000) on the USGS website; see "Water Levels" in the introduction.

The average **GRADIENT** is 5.1 feet per mile.

The **shuttle route** is via Dam Road and County G.

Canoe/kayak rental is available at the Wannigan Resort, located on the river at County G (715-266-5141); at MI ZI ZAK Kayaks near New Auburn (715-651-0284 or www.mizizakkayak.weebly.com); and at Flambeau Adventures near Ladysmith (715-532-7733 or www.flambeauadventures.com).

PUT IN at the designated river-right canoe **landing** off Dam Road, several hundred yards downstream from Winter Dam. A long trail descends to the landing.

At the beginning, the river is only about 125 feet wide, bordered by pines and a variety of deciduous trees. Much of the shoreline is lined with boulders. Soon, the river bends to the right: Look for eagles on the left, a common nesting area. Despite the proximity of Dam Road on the right, the setting is very peaceful.

After the mouth of Chapple Creek and a cabin on the right, the river is considerably wider for a while. Small islands appear. Downstream from the mouth of Knapp Stout Creek on the left, pleasant riffles precede the County G bridge (3 miles). There is an **access** upstream-right at the bridge, near the Wannigan Resort.

After the bridge, County G is never far from the river, but paddlers are seldom aware of it. There are occasional riffles in shallow or narrow spots. Upstream from the mouth of Phalan Creek, the river deepens as it swings right to the southwest—this is purportedly a good fishing area.

Houses begin appearing on the right as the river heads south, then southwest toward Highway 70. The sound of traffic can be heard. After the highway becomes visible on the left, several piles of evenly spaced rock appear in the river—the remnants of an old pedestrian bridge. Just downstream, where power lines cross the river, there's a good roadside **access** (with parking and picnic tables); directly across the highway is **Ojibwa Park,** popular with campers and picnickers.

A long Class I rapids follows the roadside access. From here to the small community of Ojibwa, the river is wide and straight.

TAKE OUT at the **village park,** downstream-right from the County G bridge; parking, picnic facilities and toilets are provided.

Other trips. A few miles downstream from Ojibwa, the river slows for the Radisson Flowage, formed by the Arpin Dam. The next day trip (C-2) begins below the dam.

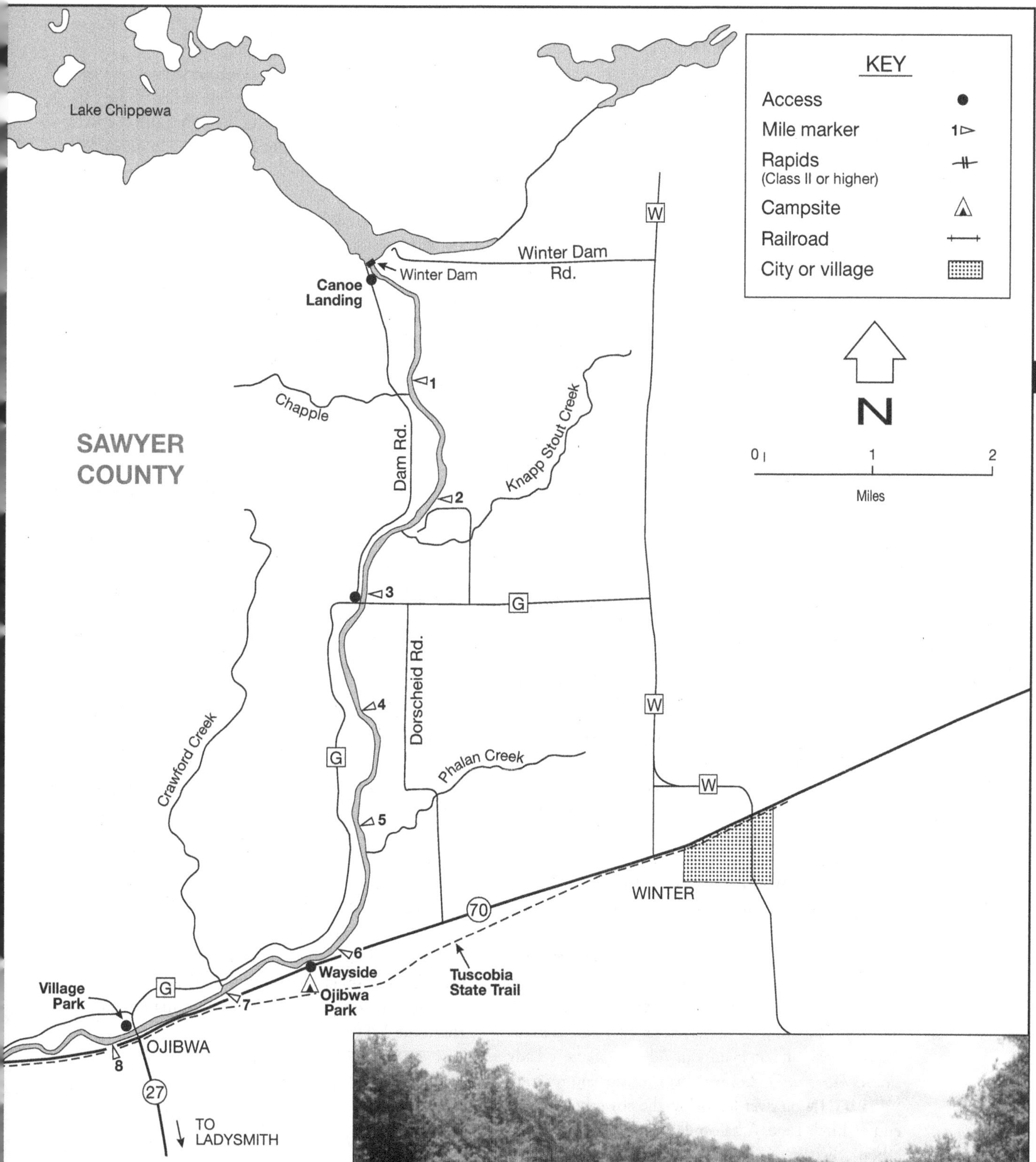

Within sight of Winter Dam.

Chippewa River 2

Arpin Dam to County D (8.5 Miles)

The Chippewa is held back by a second dam near the village of Radisson in Sawyer County. An unusual structure linking several islands, Arpin Dam was built by a lumber company in 1914 at the head of a long rapids called Belille Falls. Half a century later, a powerhouse was built at the end of a canal on the left. The best rapids on the Chippewa—more than half a mile of solid Class II boulder gardens and ledges—are here at Belille Falls, directly downstream from the dam. Most of the other significant logging-era rapids have disappeared from the river as a result of downstream dams at Chippewa Falls, Jim Falls, Cornell, Wissota and Holcombe.

Except for Belille Falls, the 8 miles below the dam are like most of the Chippewa: wide and occasionally riffly, with many islands and good current. The current can be deceptive: The river is so big that you tend to forget that you're being swept along. The whole stretch consists of a series of big, gradual bends. Fishing is popular here, as elsewhere on the Chippewa.

Camping is available a few miles northeast of Radisson at Ojibwa Park, to the south at the Bruce city park, and to the southwest at the Audie Lake and Perch Lake county parks.

Water levels are almost always adequate for good paddling. High water is dangerous, however, especially in the rapids below the dam. There are USGS gauges upstream at County G (see Chippewa 1) and downstream near Bruce (#05356500); see "Water Levels" in the introduction.

The **GRADIENT** averages 5.8 feet per mile.

The **shuttle route** from the powerhouse access is via Birch Lane, Swede Road, Old Highway 70, Highway 40 and County D. **Canoe/kayak rental** is available at the Wannigan Resort, located on the river at County G (715-266-5141); at MI ZI ZAK Kayaks near New Auburn (715-651-0284 or www.mizizakkayak.weebly.com); and at Flambeau Adventures near Ladysmith (715-532-7733 or www.flambeauadventures.com).

PUT IN on river-left below the powerhouse at the end of Birch Lane. A half-mile canal leads to the powerhouse, where good parking and a convenient access are available. There is also a commonly used private landing on river-right across from the powerhouse, alongside River Drive 1.3 miles south of Old Highway 70.

Only advanced boaters should consider paddling the **rapids** below the dam (put in on the right off River Drive just below the dam). The Class II rapids below the dam curve to the left, almost to the point where the canal rejoins the main channel. The rapids are not runnable when low but wild and woolly when medium or high. In the spring and late fall, they can be partially seen through the trees from River Drive. Scout at least part of the rapids before running them.

Below the powerhouse, the river is relatively narrow, but it soon widens for the remainder of the trip. There are numerous cabins on the right until the river swings to the left, away from River Drive. In the middle of the big left bend, the Couderay River enters on the right, followed by some riffles. For a while, Highway 40 can be heard and occasionally seen on the right.

After a house atop a left bluff, then a right turn, the Litke Drive bridge appears (**access** downstream-right). A historic marker on the left indicates that in 1840 this was the site of the Hotel Belille, a logging-era stopping place. The first white settler in Sawyer County was Charles Belille, from Quebec. Belille is also reputed to have run a portage service around the rapids named after him.

After the bridge, stay right (main channel) of the big island. You'll encounter a pleasant series of riffles in a big left bend, with houses on the right. The river briefly becomes quite wide where the river bends left again, alongside several cabins; riffles follow. You will pass several small grassy islands as the river begins a big right bend; tall forested banks line the river on the left throughout the curve.

As the river turns to the left again, you'll see Highway 40 on the right, riffles, then a couple of attractive wooded islands, followed by several white cottages. A long right bend leads to the next bridge, at Blomberg Road (**access** upstream-left).

The river is quite wide as it curves southeast toward the take-out but narrows before the approach to County D. During the last couple of miles, there are no houses or road noise. A huge boulder in midriver is followed by the mouth of the Brunet River on the left, then a riffle.

TAKE OUT at the County D bridge, downstream-left. This is a convenient access, with room for several cars along the road. A short distance west of the bridge is the small community of Exeland, so-called because two railroads crossed there during the logging era in the 1800s.

Beginning of Belille Falls below Arpin Dam.

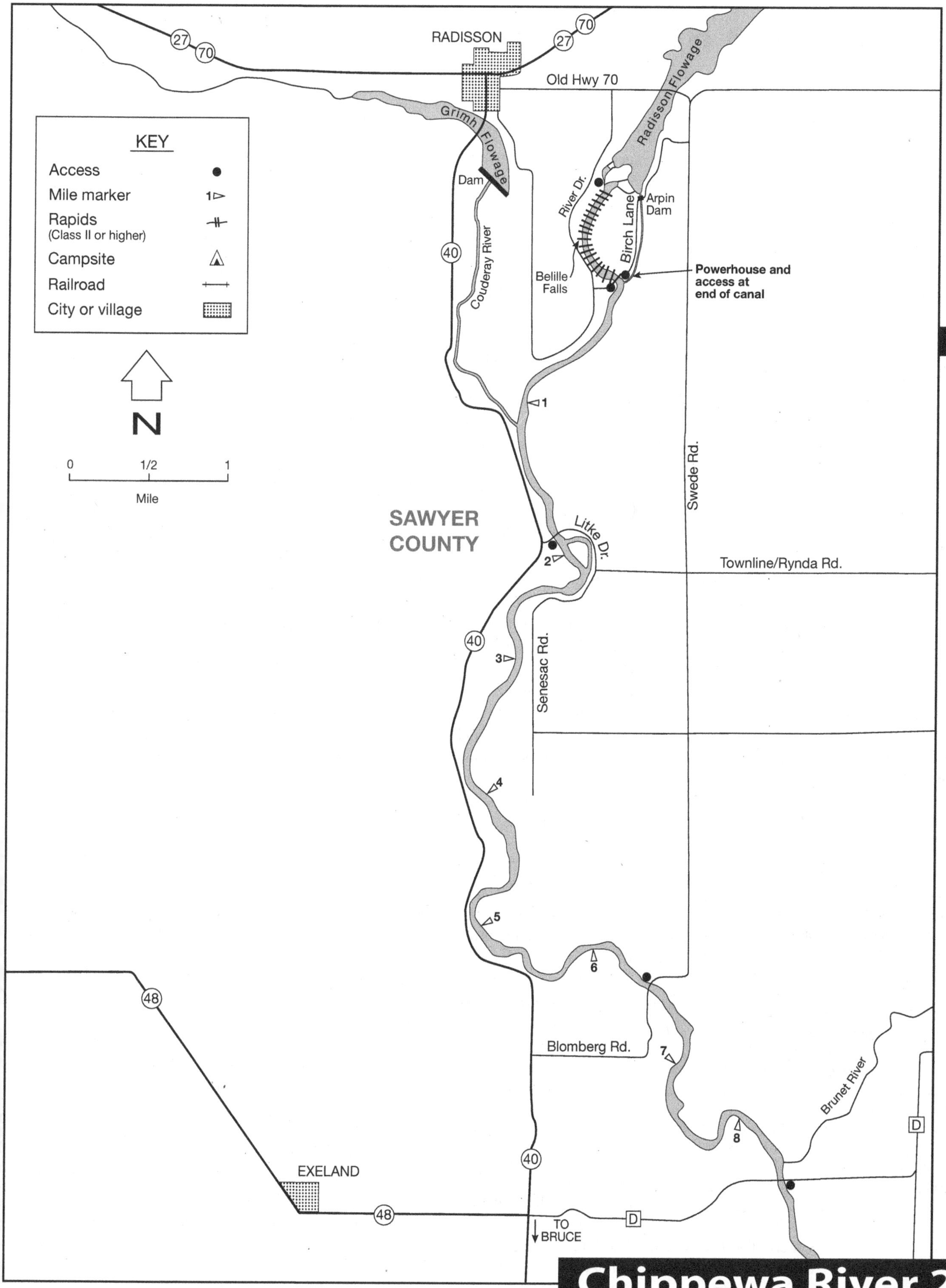

Chippewa River 2

Chippewa River 3

County D to County A (10.2 Miles)

Wildflowers along the Chippewa.

A very pleasant and varied stretch of river, this part of the Chippewa offers pretty scenery, steady current, and many riffles and rapids. A good section for "advanced-beginners," it nevertheless must command respect—especially when the water is at medium to high levels. The current is always present and the water volume is considerable, so paddlers must always be aware of the short closing speed when approaching obstructions. Most of the stretch is at least a hundred feet wide. Eagles, ducks and other birds are common. Fish caught in the river include muskie, northern, walleye, smallmouth, catfish and panfish.

Camping is available to the north at Ojibwa Park, to the south at Bruce city park and to the southwest at Audie Flowage and Perch Lake county parks.

Water levels are usually adequate for good paddling. Do not venture onto the river when it is high, however. Check the gauge at Bruce (#053565000), on the USGS website; see "Water Levels" in the introduction.

The average **GRADIENT** is 6.8 feet per mile.

The **shuttle route** is via County D, Highway 40 and County A. For **canoe/kayak rentals,** see Chippewa 2.

PUT IN downstream-left at the **County D bridge** near the small community of Exeland. There is room for a few cars alongside the road.

Riffles occur just downstream from the bridge, and there are grassy banks on both sides. The woods are mainly deciduous (oak, maple, aspen, birch, etc.), but pines and other coniferous trees become more plentiful downstream.

There are several riffles before a pine-covered rock ledge appears on the right (1.5 miles) —a popular stopping place. A big island follows the ledge.

A few hundred yards below the big island, in a left-hand bend, is a Class I rapids: A ledge runs partly across the river from the right, and a chute angles down the center toward the left. Like many of the riffles/rapids on this section, this constriction can develop big waves in high water. More riffles follow.

Two cabins and two pitches of Class I rapids are located where Nail Creek comes in on the left (3.4 miles). There will be no more dwellings until Murry Rock (named after an early settler). The river widens after Nail Creek, but good current and periodic choppy riffles continue.

The Nation's Greatest Pinery?

It's difficult to overestimate the volume of pine that came out of the Chippewa watershed between 1838 and 1918. Logging historians contend that the Chippewa Valley contained more white pine than any other comparably sized area in the country—as much as one-sixth of all the pine in the United States.

When the ice went out in the spring, huge quantities of logs floated down the Chippewa and its many tributaries, aided by several dozen dams. The river formed an excellent conduit for transporting hundreds of millions of logs to mills in Chippewa Falls and Eau Claire every year.

As in other areas of Wisconsin, the Chippewa pinery seemed inexhaustible at the time, but in the end it was cut down in merely 80 years.

Don't get complacent and drift without watching where you're going. The current can easily dump your canoe if you strike one of the many boulders just under the surface.

Class I rapids precede Murry Rock (5.2 miles), identified by big boulders and several buildings on the right shore, together with a small, rocky island.

Downstream, after a big island, an old railroad bridge crosses the river. Class I rapids begin under the bridge. Just below the short rapids at the bridge is a small rocky island.

Go to the left of the big island downstream from the railroad bridge. In this left channel is an enjoyable Class I rapids with a "whoop-dee-doo!" wave-train.

The river widens and slows. From here to County A there are numerous islands, all heavily wooded and some quite large. At one point, the river winds through a large group of islands. Some of the channels are narrow, and paddlers must be on the alert for fallen trees.

The Weirgor River—an important feeder stream in log-driving days—enters on the right (7.4 miles). You'll hear traffic noise as the river approaches Highway 40 on the right. There is a big red barn on the right as the river starts to bend to the left.

Clear Creek enters on the right, followed half a mile later by a very large island. Farther downstream another creek comes in from the right at an abrupt left-hand turn in the river. The pool here is a popular fishing spot.

The last mile before the bridge is wide and flat, but with good current. There is an attractive stand of red pine on the left.

TAKE OUT upstream-left at the **County A bridge** near the tiny community of Imalone. There is room alongside the road for a few cars.

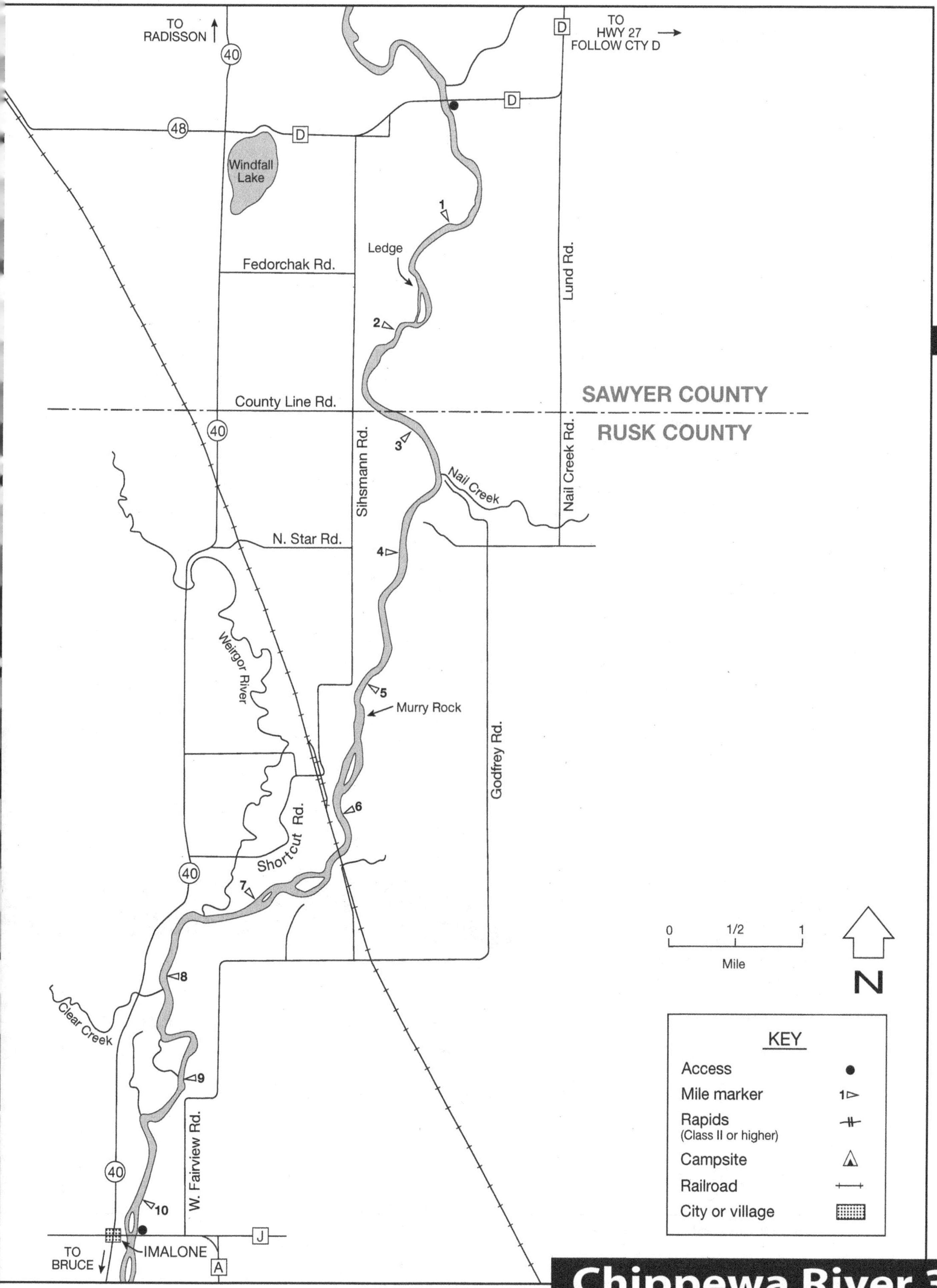

Chippewa River 3

Chippewa River 4

County A to Highway 8 (9 Miles)

Downstream from Imalone, the Chippewa widens and becomes progressively quieter. A good current flows between high grassy banks, and you'll come upon many attractive wooded islands. There are houses all along this stretch, but they are scattered and unobtrusive. A few spots on the river are popular with anglers.

Camping is available near the take-out at the Bruce city park and to the west at Audie Flowage and Perch Lake county parks.

Water levels are almost always adequate for good paddling, but paddlers should stay off the river when it is high. See Chippewa 3.

The **GRADIENT** averages only 1.6 feet per mile.

The **shuttle route** is via County A, Highway 40 and Highway 8. For **canoe/kayak rentals,** see Chippewa 2.

PUT IN at the **County A bridge,** upstream-left. There is roadside parking for a few cars.

The river widens after the bridge, but current persists.

After a long straightaway, there's a big bend, first to the left and then back to the right. Where the river bends back to the right, there is a house high up on the bluff and a series of enjoyable riffles. The river narrows a little in the bend.

Just downstream, the river widens again and there are several big islands. The next few miles are considered a good fishing area. Occasionally, traffic noise can be heard from Highway 40 on the right.

At 4 miles there is a **landing** on the left, opposite two small islands and immediately after a house on the left.

A big bend to the right begins soon after the landing. After the river starts bending back to the left, the wide mouth of Devil's Creek appears on the right. Note the footbridge over the creek.

Riffles occur occasionally all the way down to the old railroad bridge.

At 7.2 miles, there are three sets of power lines overhead. A nice riffle is located under the second.

The wide mouth of the Thornapple River—a major tributary during the logging era—appears on the left (8.4 miles). In the spring, incidentally, the lower Thornapple is a good canoeing stream.

Immediately thereafter, there is a railroad bridge. By now, you will be able to hear traffic noise from Highway 8 downstream.

TAKE-OUT: Go to the left around the big island just upstream from the Highway 8 bridge to take out at the public landing. Look out for strainers in the left channel. The upstream-left **landing** is accessed by a short paved road alongside Highway 8 east of the bridge. A short distance west of the bridge is the community of Bruce.

Many attractive islands highlight the Chippewa.

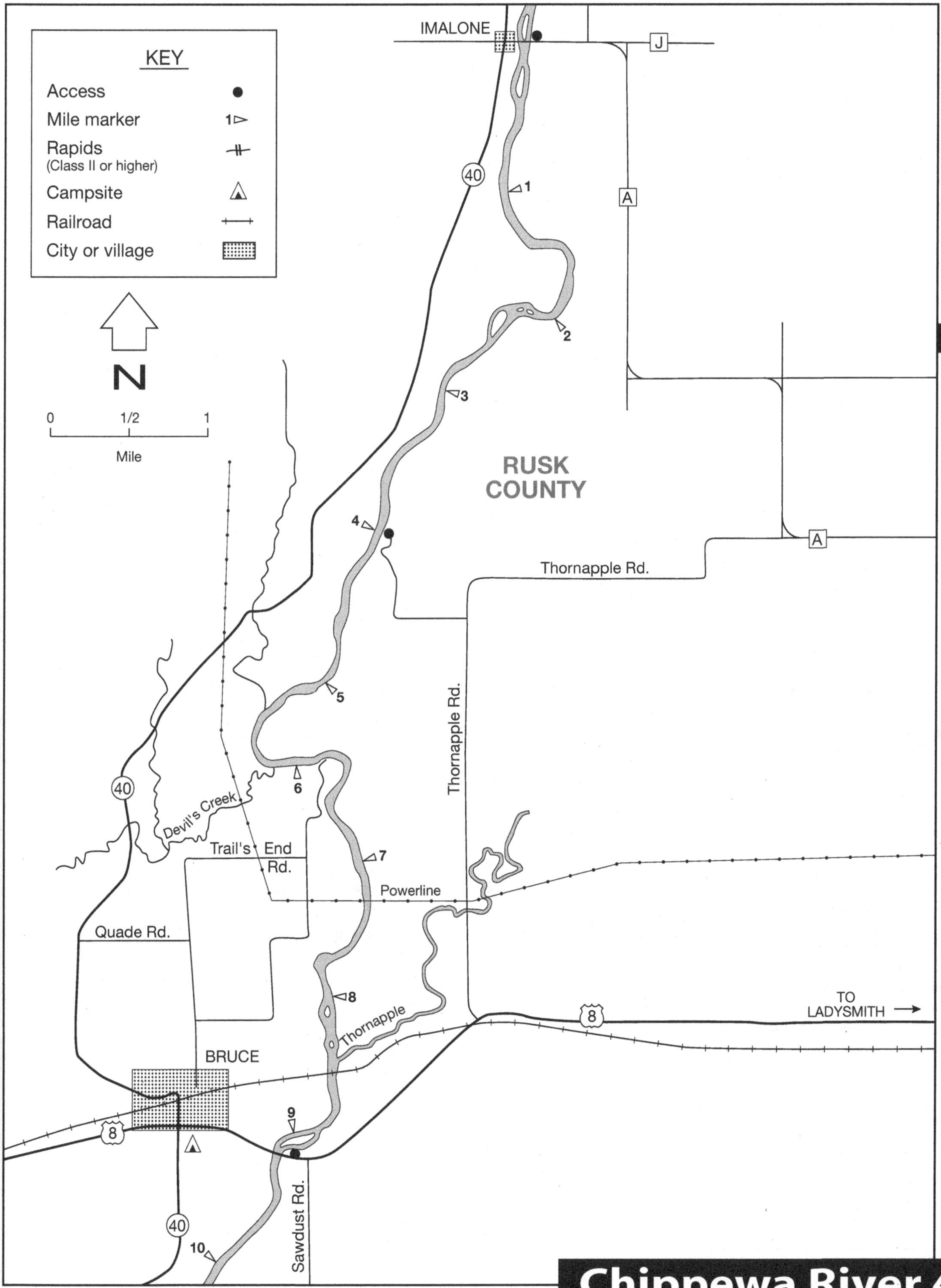
KEY
Access
Mile marker
Rapids
(Class II or higher)
Campsite
Railroad
City or village
N
0
1/2
1
Mile
IMALONE
J
40
A
RUSK
COUNTY
Thornapple Rd.
Thornapple Rd.
Devil's Creek
Trail's End
Rd.
Powerline
Quade Rd.
Thornapple
BRUCE
8
TO
LADYSMITH
Sawdust Rd.
1
2
3
4
5
6
7
8
9
10

Chippewa River 5

Highway 8 to the Flambeau (18 Miles)

In this long section before the confluence with its main tributary, the Chippewa becomes even wider. Riffles are not as common as upstream, but steady current persists. If there was any doubt in your mind about the Chippewa being a big river, this stretch will convince you. Woods, including some beautiful oak groves, continue to line the banks. Roads parallel the river at the beginning and end, but most of the stretch is undeveloped and scenic. Houses along the river are relatively scarce until the last few miles. Anglers are a common sight, fishing for northern, muskie, smallmouth, walleye, catfish and panfish.

Paddling the entire stretch at one time is more than most boaters want to undertake. Trip length can easily be shortened by using one or both of the intermediate landings as alternate accesses.

Camping is available near the put-in at the Bruce city park and 12 miles northwest of Bruce at the Audie Flowage and Perch Lake county parks. Flater's Resort, at the Chippewa/Flambeau confluence, contains campsites.

Water levels are always adequate for good canoeing, but paddlers should stay home or go elsewhere when the river is high. See Chippewa 3.

The **GRADIENT** is only 1.1 feet per mile.

The **shuttle route** for the entire section is via Highway 8 and County E. Shorter stretches using Hagerty's Landing and/or Hatch's Landing involve Sawdust Road and Hatch Road. **Canoe/kayak rental** and shuttle service are available at Flater's Resort at the Chippewa/Flambeau confluence (715-595-4771); MI ZI ZAK Kayaks near New Auburn (715-651-0284 or www.mizizakkayak.weebly.com); and Flambeau Adventures near Ladysmith (715-532-7733 or www.flambeauadventures.com).

PUT IN east of Bruce at the public **landing** near the Highway 8 bridge, upstream-left. A short access road leads to the landing.

Below the bridge, the river is obviously wider than upstream. The farther you go, the less current there is, but it's always present to assist paddling. In comparison with previous sections, there are relatively few islands and no riffles for the first few miles. Highway 40 gets quite close on the right at times. After a long, gradual bend to the left, there is an attractive high grassy bank as the river heads back to the right. Houses appear occasionally.

Downstream from the mouths of a couple of creeks, **Hagerty's Public Landing** appears on the left (6 miles). The landing is located at the end of a short gravel access road off Fletcher and McLean roads, with room to park a couple of cars.

After Hagerty's Landing, the river heads south for a couple of miles, then proceeds circuitously through several huge bends in every direction possible. Along the way are some deep fishing holes and big islands. Eventually, the river heads back toward the east after the Big Bend downstream from Potato Creek.

You'll find **Hatch's Public Landing** (12.5 miles) after the Big Bend, on the left, with a concrete ramp and room for parking. More islands, bends and fishing holes follow. Skrupky Rapids, a riffle, is found in the big right-hand bend downstream from Rice Creek.

The number of cabins increases as the river flows southeast between Chippewa Avenue and County D.

About a mile upstream from the mouth of the Flambeau, the Chippewa bends left. Here there is a small, undeveloped dirt **landing** alongside County D on river-right, immediately after the outlet of Mud Creek. The landing is behind a small island. Downstream, a number of trailers precede the confluence on the left.

TAKE OUT on river-left at **Flater's Resort,** located on the tip of land at the confluence.

Other trips. Downstream, the Chippewa slows and widens as it enters the Holcombe Flowage. Thereafter, one dam after another tames the river all the way to Eau Claire. From there it flows unfettered to the Mississippi at the southern end of Lake Pepin.

From Indian Trail to Modern Highway

When early explorers, traders, loggers and settlers moved into an undeveloped area, they typically took advantage of existing Indian trails. In the early decades of this region's logging era, which began in the late 1830s, such a trail was tremendously helpful in getting men and material up and down the Chippewa River from Chippewa Falls to what is now the Winter Dam area.

Known as the Chippewa Trail, the pathway headed north out of the Chippewa Falls area to Long Lake, then angled over to the Chippewa River at Big Bend, paralleling the river all the way to a stopping place called the "Trading Post" (where the southern end of the modern-day Chippewa Flowage lies). Along the way were numerous "hotels" where travelers could stay.

The trail was gradually enlarged and improved to form a roadway. Much of it is now Highway 40, Highway 70, County G and Dam Road.

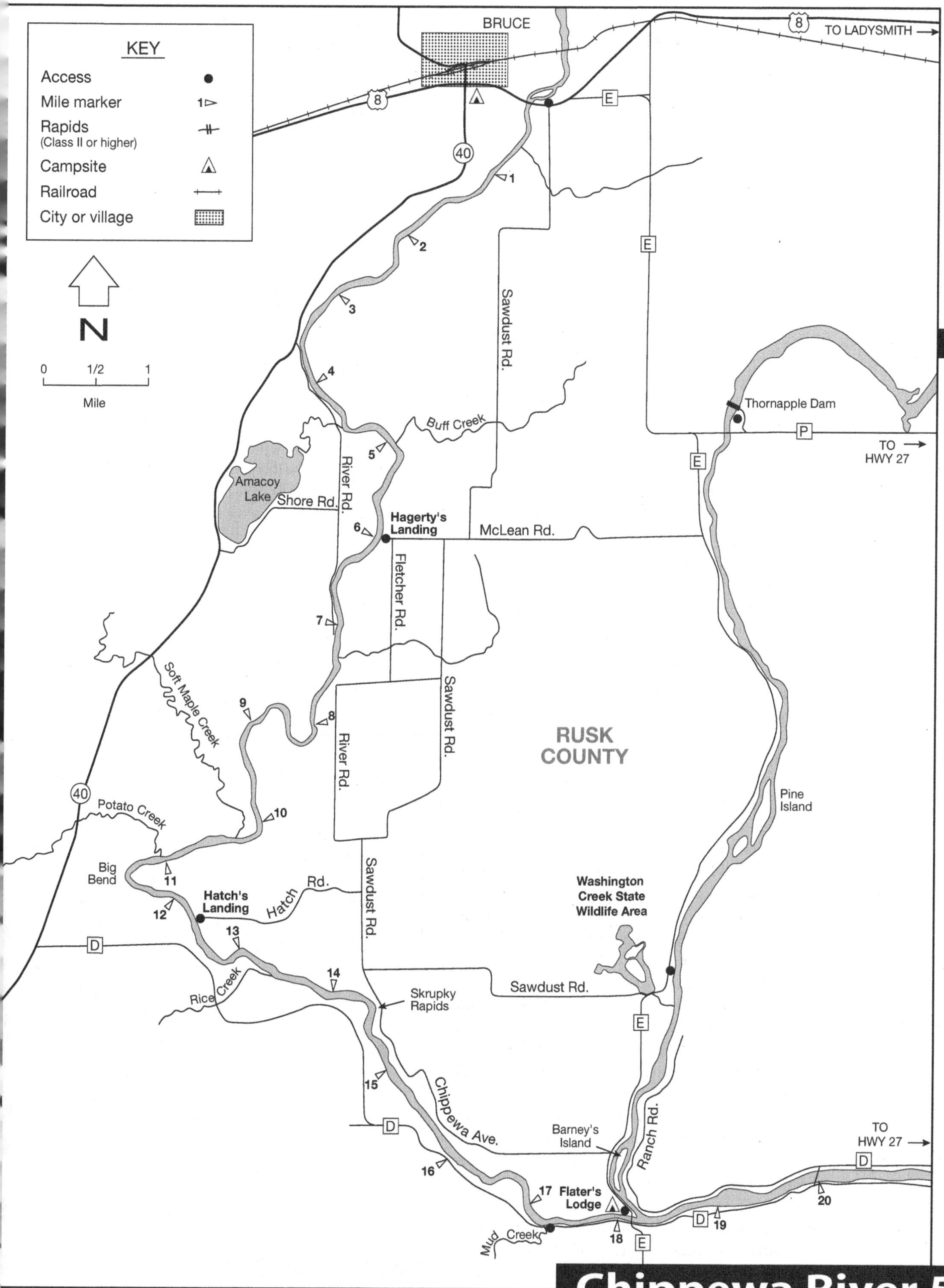

Chippewa River 5

Eau Claire River 1

Highway 64 to the Dells (17 Miles)

The west and east forks of the Eau Claire converge 3 miles west of Antigo. After that, the river has sufficient volume to enable canoeists to paddle all the way out to the Wisconsin River at Wausau, encountering three dams along the way. A small, pleasant river, the Eau Claire is best in the spring.

Most of the upper part of the river flows through farmland, but the banks are wooded and few homes are seen until Wausau draws near.

The portion from Bear Lake Road to County Z is especially scenic, with many beautiful formations of granite and other igneous rock. The Eau Claire is a good trout stream, though most of the choice trout habitat lies upstream from the put-in. Smallmouth bass are common in all stretches of the river. Most of the two sections described here are flatwater, but there is also some excellent whitewater, including a solid Class III–IV rapids that should be attempted only by expert boaters.

Camping is available at the take-out at Eau Claire Dells County Park and a few miles to the west at Marathon County Park in Wausau.

Water levels are usually adequate in April, May and early June, and after periods of sustained rainfall. For the first section, you are advised not to proceed if the put-in is scrapy. High water makes the river dangerous—especially downstream from Bear Lake Road. Although it is located a way downstream, the gauge at Kelly (#05397500) may be helpful in determining water level; see "Water Levels" in the introduction.

The **GRADIENT** averages 5.2 feet per mile.

The **shuttle route** is via Highway 64, County HH and County Y. The trip can be shortened considerably by using other accesses as put-ins or take-outs: County Y, Hansen Road, County G, Bear Lake Road or Highway 52. For a good whitewater run, put in at Bear Lake Road and take out at Highway 52 or at the Dells campground. Several accesses are on private land, so please be considerate of the owners.

PUT IN at the Willard Ackley historical marker alongside Highway 64, 3 miles west of Antigo. A dirt access road lies along the river at this point, with room for several cars.

All of the first section is narrow and winding, with many small islands, wooded shoreline, and fairly low banks. Occasionally, farmland approaches the river. Houses are infrequent except in the vicinity of bridges. Not until the trip is more than half completed does the first whitewater appear.

The first few miles of the river flow southward. A short paddle leads to the County Y bridge, which has a good **access** upstream-right (1.8 miles). Downstream, after the mouth of Owen Creek on the left, the Hansen Road bridge is **accessed** upstream-left. Shortly thereafter, you'll see the remnants of an old bridge abutment. The river loops to the west before County G (**access** upstream-right), at 7 miles.

The first rapids—a brief, easy Class I—occurs in a bend half a mile upstream from the Bear Lake Road bridge (**access** upstream- or downstream-left, at 9.7 miles).

The next portion of the trip is recommended only for experienced paddlers because a series of boulder gardens, constrictions, and small ledges. A boulder garden with two sloping ledges (Class I–II) is the first of these.

The next set of **ledges** is more difficult—a solid Class II—and is easily scouted or portaged on the right atop a rocky wall. Huge boulders are scattered for about a hundred yards, especially at the beginning and end of the rapids. The first ledge (about 4 feet) is run near the left bank after a left turn in the river, followed by fast water and finally another 4-foot ledge with a slot and tongue on the right side. This rapids is called **Three Rows Falls** by some locals and **Bader ledges** by others because of the three rows of rocks that appear in low water. In moderate to high water, be careful of the grabby curlers and hole below the first drop. The Highway 52 bridge at Hogarty follows (**access** downstream-right) at 13 miles.

The last few miles are quite attractive: The river gets increasingly rocky, with high wooded bluffs and several enjoyable Class I rapids. As the dam upstream from County Y draws nearer, the current slackens and several houses appear.

TAKE OUT on the right upstream from the dam, near the parking area and restrooms alongside the **Dells County Park campground** road. It's well worth the time to walk the trail along the river from the dam, across County Y, and into the park. The beautiful rock formations make this a very popular area for locals and tourists.

Running the final drop of Three Rows Falls.

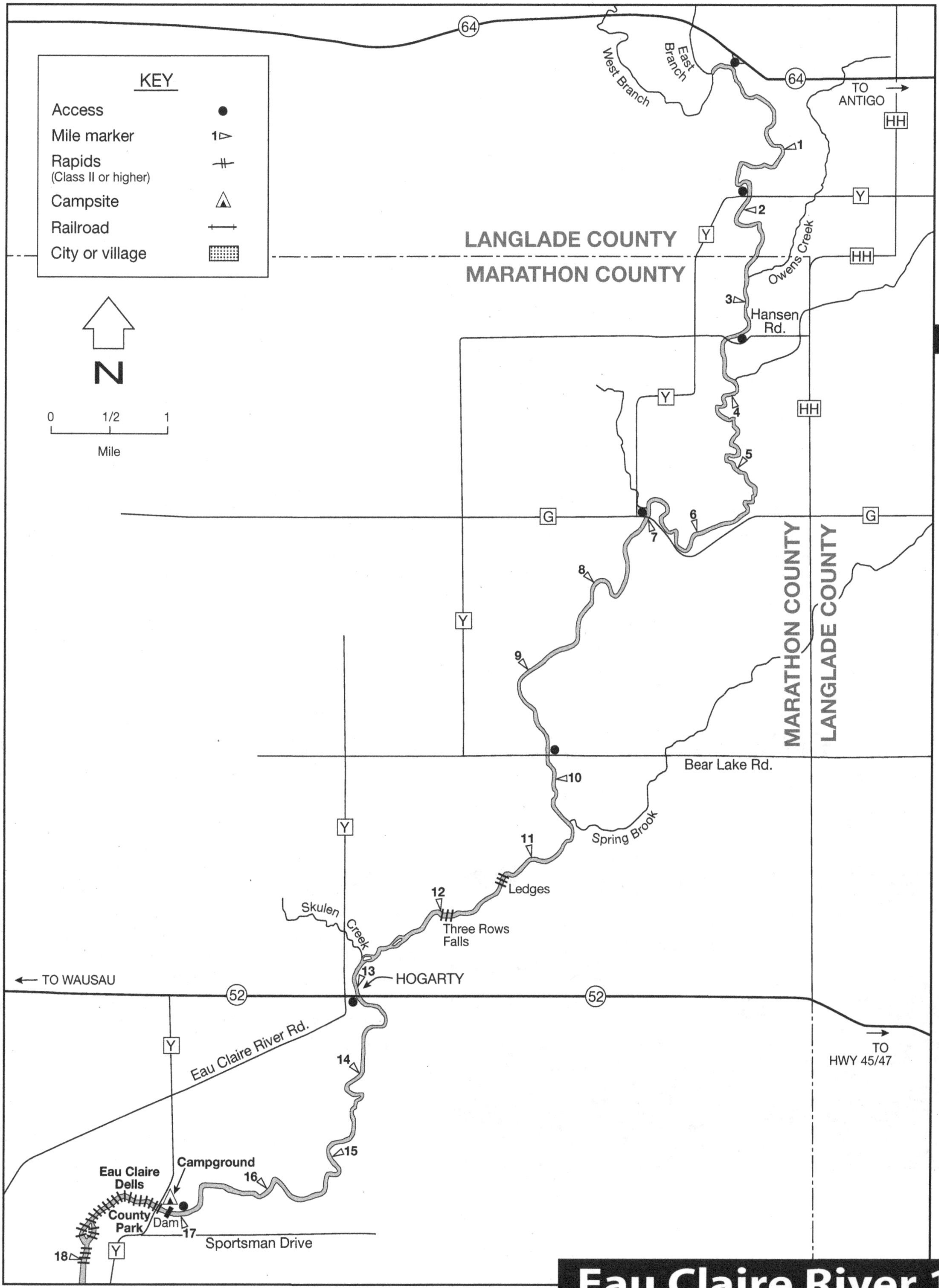

Eau Claire River 1

Eau Claire River 2

The Dells to Club House Road (10 Miles)

If you're looking for a section of river that begins with a bang and ends with a whimper, this is it. Below the dam upstream from County J, Class II rapids lead to the Dells, a complex and difficult (Class III–IV) maze of rock formations. Then, after 3 more miles of intermittent rapids, the river suddenly widens and slows for the rest of the stretch before emptying into a small flowage downstream from Club House Road. Beginning with a high wooded shoreline, rocky outcroppings and whitewater, the trip ends lazily with a wide, shallow stream bed and low, grassy banks. Novices should not attempt to paddle the portion upstream from County Z; even the Z-to-N stretch has a rapids that should be portaged by beginners.

Camping is available near the put-in at the Eau Claire Dells County Park, and a few miles to the west at Marathon County Park in Wausau.

Water levels are best in the spring and after sustained rainfall. High water, however, makes parts of this section hazardous. The Dells are always dangerous, but in high-water conditions they can be downright outrageous. During periods of lower water, the volume of water flowing from the dam to the County Y bridge can give you an idea of whether the stretch is paddleable. The long rock gardens downstream from the Dells can be quite miserable when there isn't enough water. For gauge information, see Eau Claire 1.

Stone formations below the Eau Claire Dells.

The **GRADIENT** is a lively 9 feet per mile.

The **shuttle route** is via County Y, County Z, Eau Claire River Road, County N, Eau Claire River Road and Club House Road. Good accesses at County Z and County N make it easy to vary trip length.

PUT IN at the **county park** below the Dells by carrying your boat past the picnic shelter and down the fairly steep bank.

When water levels aren't too high, expert kayakers and canoeists have run the Dells, putting in from the path below the dam (river-right), accessed by the campground road on the east side of County Y. It is recommended, however, that everyone portage.

Class II **boulder gardens** continue downstream for a couple of miles, with an exciting S-curve about a mile below County Y. A scenic trail winds along the shore from the county park, crossing the river on an attractive footbridge. Class I–II **rapids** follow a large island until some power lines pass overhead; from here to County Z, the river flows quietly, except for a Class II constriction a quarter mile upstream from the bridge. All the way from County Y to County Z, there are numerous picturesque stone formations along the shoreline.

The County Z bridge (2.2 miles) can be accessed downstream-left. Half a mile below the bridge, there is a large wooded island with Class II **rapids** on both sides. The left channel is narrower and more difficult, with several small drops. Take out at the head of the island and walk along either side to scout. After a few hundred yards of rapids below the island, the remainder of the trip is flatwater.

Downstream from the bridge at Badger Road (4.6 miles), the river widens and becomes more shallow. Houses appear for a while until the County N bridge at 6.5 miles (**access** upstream-right). More meadows and farms are seen along the shoreline. Houses again appear frequently as River Road parallels the river on the right in the last couple of miles before Club House Road.

TAKE OUT upstream-right or left at the **Club House Road bridge,** where there is room to park a few cars.

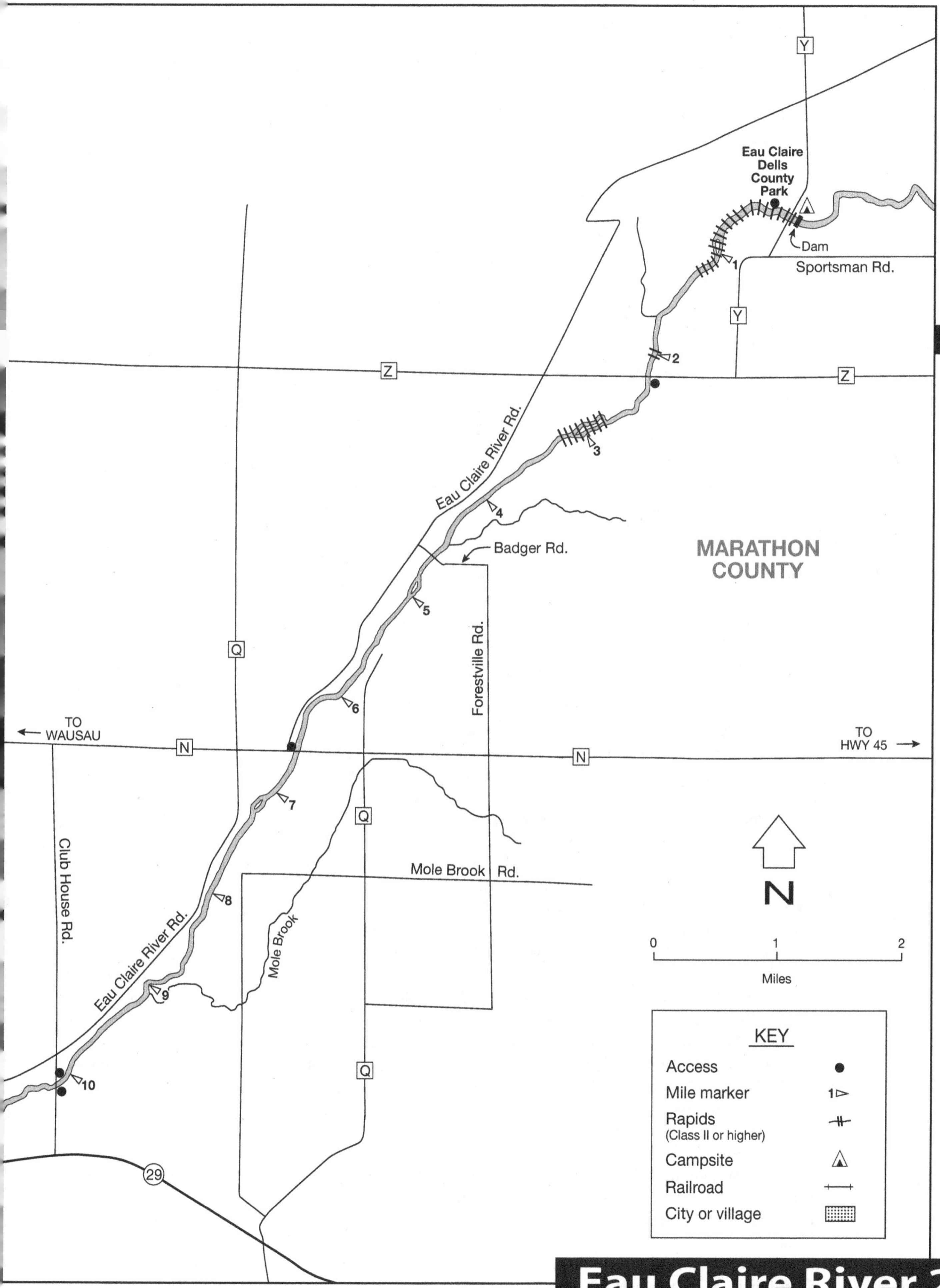

Eau Claire River 2

Flambeau River (North Fork) 1

Turtle-Flambeau Dam to Agenda Landing (14.2 Miles)

Originating in Iron County where the Manitowish and Bear rivers come together, the newly formed Flambeau flows only a few miles before entering the vast Turtle-Flambeau Flowage from the east. When it emerges from the dam on the west side of the flowage, it is already a fairly large river. For 19 miles it flows southward before encountering four dams.

The most popular canoeing section of the river is the 40 miles below these dams, from Nine-Mile Creek to Beaver Dam Landing. But the less paddled stretch northeast of Park Falls is at least as enjoyable. It has exciting rapids, pleasant flatwater, visible remnants of the logging era and gorgeous scenery.

You'll see almost no houses, thanks to the inclusion of a 300-foot strip of land on both sides in the Flambeau River State Forest. Fishing is said to be good for muskie, smallmouth, northern and walleye. Beautiful high banks, profusely forested with birch, pine, hemlock, balsam, cedar and maple, are common all along the stretch. Commonly observed wildlife includes eagles, osprey, ducks, herons, deer and muskrat. Numerous rock outcroppings add to the picturesque scenery.

Camping: No improved campsites are provided along this section of the river, but Hines City Park in Park Falls, which has a river-left **access** 4 miles downstream from Agenda Landing, has campsites, picnic facilities, toilets and good parking; the park is just upstream from the Upper Dam. There are also numerous private campgrounds in the flowage and Park Falls areas.

Water levels are very dependable for good canoeing as a result of constant releases from the dam. Stay off the river when the water is high, however. The rapids increase greatly in difficulty and danger. For general information on water levels, call the DNR's Flambeau River State Forest Headquarters (715-332-5271).

The average **GRADIENT** is a deceptive 3.5 feet per mile.

The **shuttle route** is via Dam Road, County FF, Creamery Road, River Road and Flambeau Lane. Shuttle service and/or **canoe rentals** in the immediate area are available from the Flambeau River Lodge (715-532-5392), Nine-Mile Tavern (715-762-3174), Big Bear Lodge (715-332-5510), Oxbo Resort (715-762-4786), Flambeau Sports Outfitters (715-339-2012), and Flambeau Adventures (715-532-7733).

PUT IN at the Turtle-Flambeau Dam canoe **landing** at the end of Dam Road, river-right. The landing is located well below the dam, just downstream from a rapids.

The river begins narrow and winding, with several Class I rapids all the way to **Notch Rock Rapids,** a fast Class II that rushes in a wave-train for about a hundred yards past a rocky wall on the right. Look for the notched boulder on the right near the end. Flatwater with good current follows.

A big, beautiful island with a picnic bench appears downstream; go left in the deeper main channel. Island Rapids (Class I–II) S-curves along the island for several hundred yards. Riffles follow, then a long quiet stretch.

Spring Creek enters on the right, followed by riffles. Wider, slower water succeeds the riffles all the way to the mouth of Swamp Creek on the right (3.5 miles), followed immediately by lovely pine banks on both sides. Drift-wood is abundant. After a home appears on the right, there's a short riffle, followed by more flatwater.

Bear Skull Rock (6.4 miles) appears in the middle of the river—a huge boulder that looks like a bear's head from river-right; a cedar grows from the top. A short, easy Class I rapids follows, with a pretty little island in the middle. Just downstream, there is a long, slender island alongside the mouth of Deer Creek.

Quinn's Rapids, a noisy and steep Class II boulder garden about 50 yards long, comes after a right turn at 8 miles. There is a nice campsite on the left shore. After Quinn's, the river widens, turns left past a creek, then constricts and turns right through a Class I rapids.

Flatwater follows to **Holt's Public Landing** on the right, near a house (10 miles). In the bend below Holt's can be seen old logging-bridge footings, river-right.

The next couple of miles feature a series of enjoyable rapids, starting with **Pine Tree Rapids,** a sequence of easy Class I pitches ending with a Class I–II wavy ledge with an overhanging pine tree; avoid the big boulders in the middle.

The Ledge, a 200-yard Class I–II boulder garden, winds around a rocky island, beginning in a right bend within sight of Pine Tree.

The Ledge is followed by a big island with the remnants of an old logging dam on the right side; go left. Calm water leads to another big island, the left channel of which is obstructed by a logjam. Paddle the right channel, which drops over a Class I–II boulder garden for about 75 yards, then becomes flat again. Another rapids occurs just before the end of the island, followed by a few more brief Class I–II rapids in close succession. The current then slacks off as the river enters a big left bend.

TAKE OUT on the right at **Agenda Landing,** near several houses.

Other trips: Four more miles of slow paddling on the Upper Park Falls Flowage leads to Hines City Park, then the first of four dams. Two more miles of flowage lead to the Lower Park Falls Dam, followed by approximately 5 miles of water before Pixley Dam and, finally, another 6 miles to the Crowley Dam. Below Crowley, the Flambeau again flows freely for almost 50 miles before another dam blocks its path.

Flambeau River (North Fork) 1

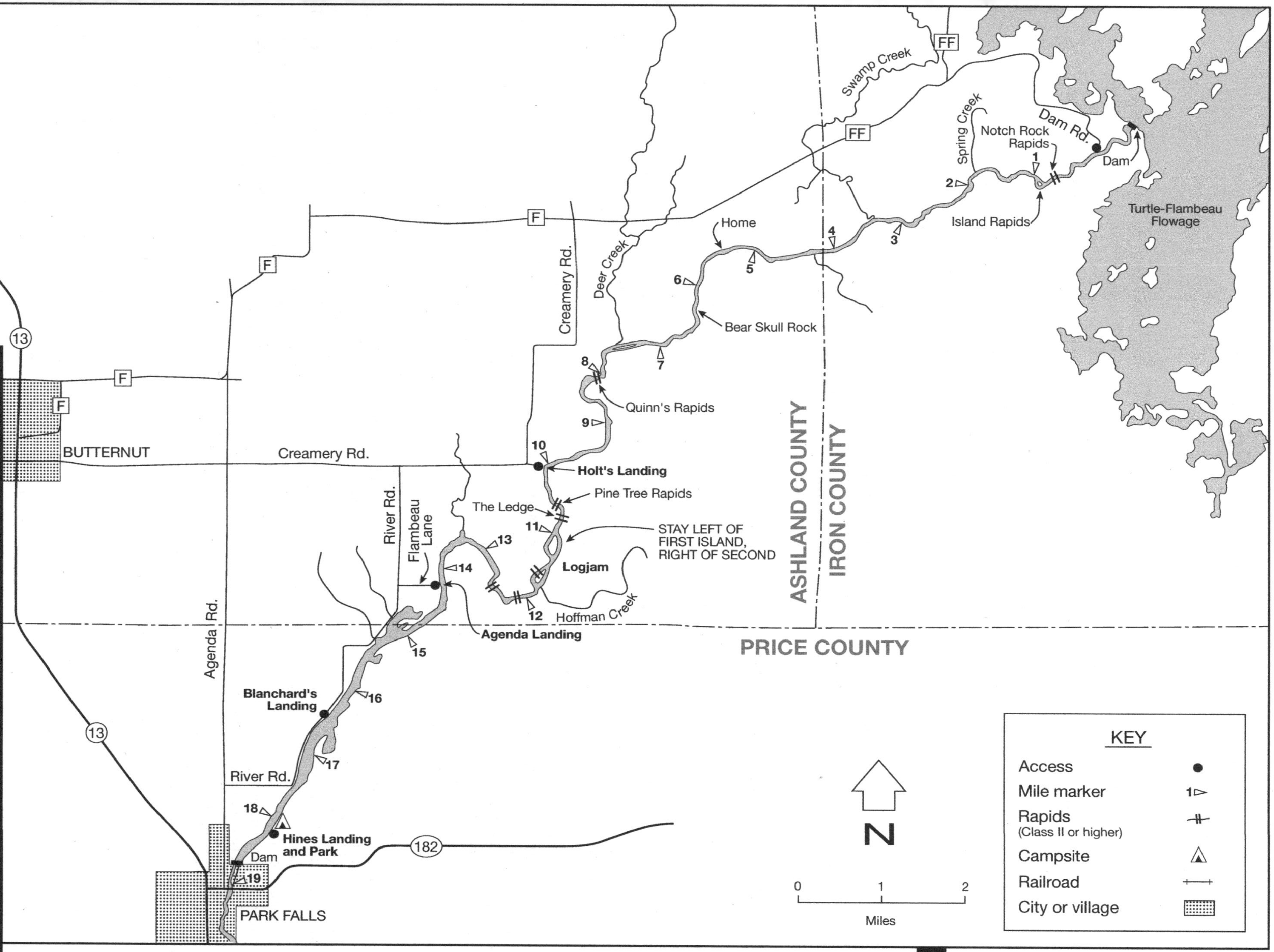

Flambeau River (North Fork) 2

Nine-Mile Creek to Oxbo (11.7 Miles)

This stretch, an ideal trip for beginning canoeists, is also very popular with fishermen and quietwater enthusiasts in general. Most anglers are in pursuit of muskie, northerns, walleye, smallmouth bass and panfish. Wildlife is varied. You're sure to see eagles and other birds, and there is much evidence of beaver activity. A mixed forest lines both shores of this big, wide section of river, which lends itself to a leisurely float.

Camping: Almost the entire section lies within the Flambeau River State Forest, which maintains canoe-campsites along the way. Camping is allowed only at designated sites, marked by signs showing a brown teepee. These excellent sites invite multiday canoe-camping trips; two-to-three-day trips are common. Public camping is also available nearby at the Connors Lake and Lake of the Pines campgrounds. Moreover, there are several private campgrounds in the area.

Water levels are almost always sufficient for good paddling, but all sections of the Flambeau are dangerous when high. For general river conditions, call the headquarters of the Flambeau River State Forest (715-332-5271). Maps and information on canoeing, camping and fishing the Flambeau can be obtained by calling this number or by checking the website at www.dnr.state.wi.us/forestry/StateForest/SF-Flambeau.

The average **GRADIENT** is 3.4 feet per mile.

The **shuttle route** is via Highway 70. For shuttle service and **canoe rental,** see North Fork 1.

PUT IN at the **Nine-Mile Landing** on river-left alongside Highway 70, near the bridge over Nine-Mile Creek. Toilets, water and plenty of parking are available.

The river is 200 feet wide here, with fast current, and begins with a big sweeping bend to the left that puts you back alongside Highway 70 for a while.

LeTourneau Creek comes in from the left as the river bends to the right. The first pitch of **Barnaby Rapids** (usually somewhere between a riffle and Class I) appears as the river bends back to the left. Rapids continue downstream, but you should have no trouble riding the waves and dodging rocks.

The river gets wider and the current a little slower after the next bend to the left. Several houses appear on the left on the stretch down to Deadman's Slough (also on the left); Butternut Creek comes in from the right in the middle of this stretch.

After a bend back to the right by an island, the river once again flows alongside Highway 70 for a while. Another right bend follows, and the Flambeau begins a 6-mile loop that will take it to Oxbow (the local spelling is "Oxbo").

Downstream on the left, just before an island, is the County Line Campsite (a typical Flambeau campsite, with toilets, picnic tables and room for two tents).

A mile downstream from the mouth of Rock Creek, on the right, the river abruptly swings left for a long southwest stretch. Pine Creek enters from the right in the midst of this turn.

Farther down, alongside a big island and within sight of the old Highway 70 bridge, is the Oxbo campsite on the left.

TAKE OUT at the **Dix-Dox Landing** on the left, upstream from the old bridge. An access road leads to the landing from Highway 70. Several houses are located here, including a resort on the left after the old bridge.

A typical campsite on the Flambeau.

Folk Art, Anyone?

Paddling on the Flambeau will take you close to the city of Phillips, where an unusual display of American folk art sits alongside Highway 13. You'll never see anything else quite like it.

Beginning in 1950, a local tavern owner and retired farmer named Fred Smith created more than 200 life-size concrete figures of lumberjacks, historical characters and animals, and decorated them with bits of colored glass and other materials. Located in the rock garden next to the tavern where he tended bar, the figures attracted a lot of attention from tourists over the years.

When Fred died in 1976, the Kohler Foundation bought the "Wisconsin Concrete Park," restored it, and gave it to Price County. Now maintained and preserved by the county, this one-of-a-kind park is well-worth a visit.

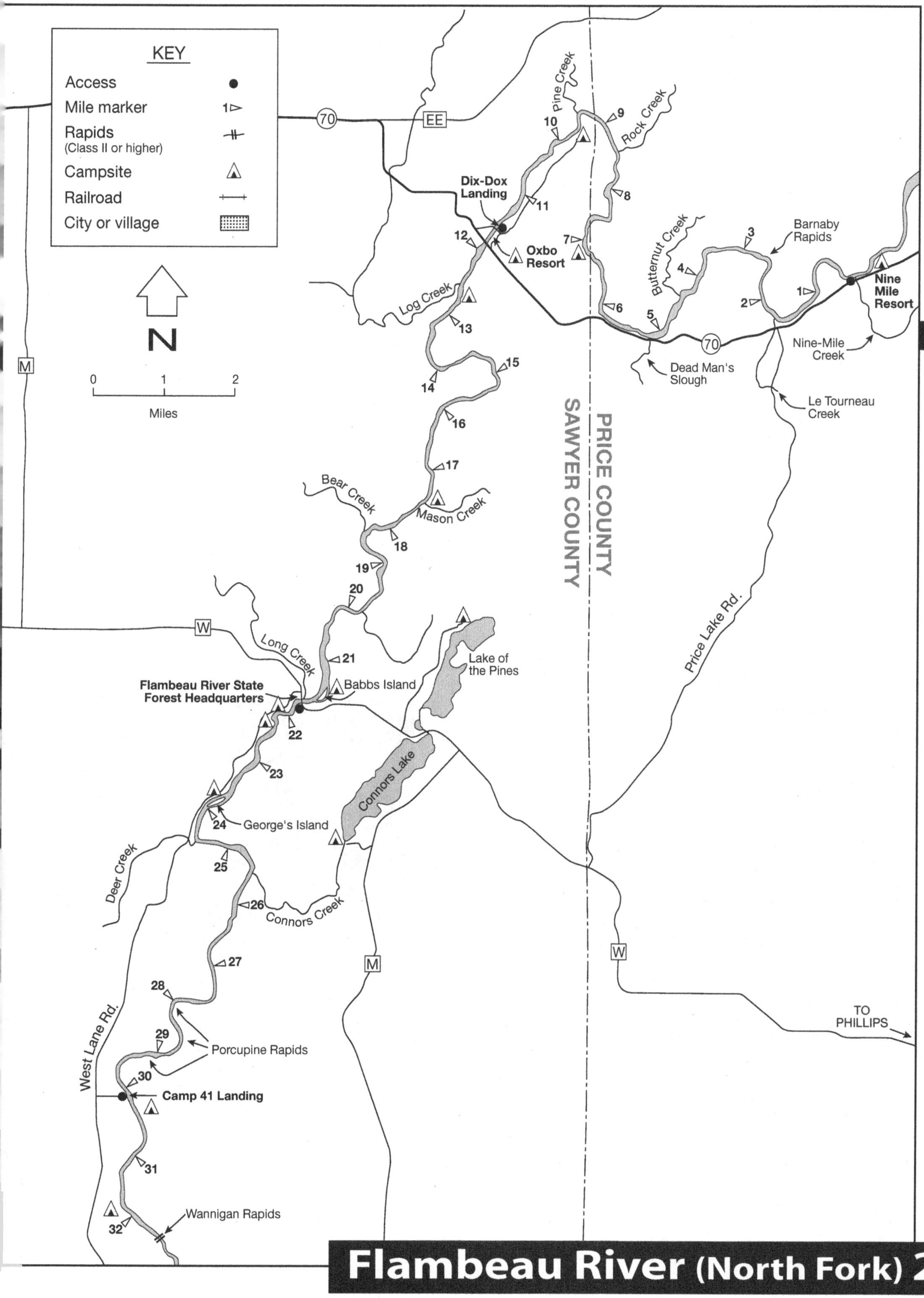

Flambeau River (North Fork) 2

Flambeau River (North Fork) 3

Oxbo to Camp 41 Landing (18.3 Miles)

Most of this section is like the previous 12 miles: wide, fast, heavily wooded and quiet. Not until the take-out approaches do you get a taste of whitewater. Thus, this section is a good one for novice paddlers. Always bear in mind, however, that the Flambeau is a big river; mishaps can and do happen to canoeists who are inattentive or paddle when the river is high. This trip can be shortened by using the access at County W (described below).

Campsite selection is excellent: Half a dozen sites lie between the put-in and take-out, making it clear why the Flambeau is so popular as a canoe-camping river. Public campgrounds are also located nearby at Connors Lake and Lake of the Pines.

Water levels are almost always adequate for good paddling. For information, call the headquarters of the Flambeau River State Forest (715-332-5271).

Average **GRADIENT** is 3.2 feet per mile.

The **shuttle route** is via Highway 70, County M, County W and West Lane Road. For shuttle service and **canoe rental** see North Fork 1.

PUT IN at the **Dix-Dox Landing,** upstream-left from the old bridge at the Oxbo (accessed from Highway 70). Houses and a resort follow the old bridge, and there are riffles between the two bridges.

About a mile downstream, a campsite is located on the left shortly after Log Creek enters on the right.

After a couple of big bends and a straightaway, the Mason Creek Campsite appears on the left, upstream from the mouth of Mason Creek.

Wood pilings from an old lumber company bridge can be seen on the left side of the river near the mouth of Bear Creek, which comes in on the right.

A series of smaller islands announces the approach of Babbs Island. A very attractive campsite is located on the left just before Babbs Island, which is followed by the County W bridge.

There is a public **landing** downstream-left from the bridge, directly across the river from the headquarters of the Flambeau River State Forest. More campsites are available on the right just downstream from the headquarters building.

In the long stretch south from County W down to the mouth of Deer Creek, more campsites appear on the right: Boy Scout and George's Island.

There are a couple of houses just upstream from the mouth of Deer Creek where the river swings to the left. At a large island, it turns back to the right; Connors Creek enters at the end of the right-hand bend.

Now begins a 5.5-mile stretch to the south that ends at Camp 41. Here you will encounter the only whitewater on this section.

In the mile and a half before Camp 41, there is a long, curving series of riffles and Class I rapids, known as **Porcupine Rapids.**

TAKE OUT at the **Camp 41 Landing** on the right. The Camp 41 campsite is located on the other (left) side of the river. Camp 41 Landing is accessed from West Lane Road.

Wisconsin's Answer to Quetico

Near the source of the Flambeau River lies the massive Turtle-Flambeau Flowage. Formed in 1926 when a dam was built on the Flambeau just downstream from its confluence with the Turtle River, the flowage is a complex impoundment of 14,000 acres with 230 miles of shoreline and 195 islands. In 1990 the state of Wisconsin acquired the flowage, including 95 percent of the shoreline, thus assuring that it would remain natural and undeveloped.

The flowage teems with wildlife and is a great place to fish. Sixty campsites are scattered on islands, accessible only by boaters. Multiday canoeing trips are popular, and in recent years the area has attracted sea kayakers. Venture out onto the waters here, and you'll swear you're in Canada.

Good campsites make the Flambeau popular for overnight trips.

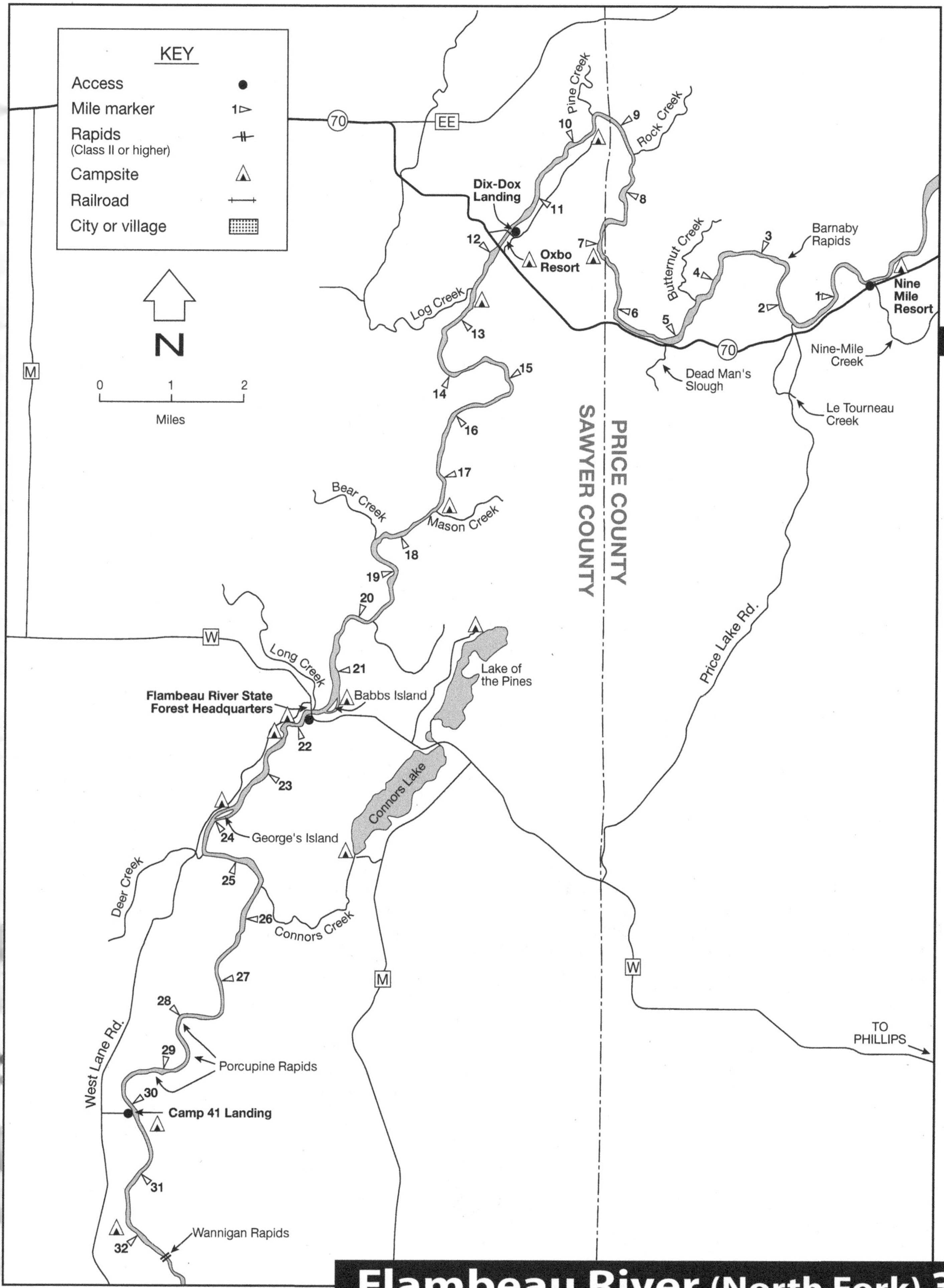

Flambeau River (North Fork) 3

Flambeau River (North Fork) 4

Camp 41 Landing to Beaver Dam Landing (11.4 Miles)

When canoeists tell stories about whitewater paddling on the Flambeau, this is probably the section they're talking about. Like those upriver, this stretch offers beautiful scenery, comfortable campsites and good fishing, but the resemblance ends there. Rapids begin within a couple miles of the put-in and alternate with quietwater all the way to the end. Two of the rapids are particularly memorable. You should have experience and good boat control before you venture onto this section, and should avoid it when the water is high.

Riverside **camping** is available at several designated sites, and at the privately owned Flambeau Lodge.

Water levels are almost always adequate for good paddling. For general information on river conditions, call the headquarters of the Flambeau River State Forest (715-332-5271).

The **GRADIENT** averages 5.2 feet per mile.

The **shuttle route** is via West Lane Road. For shuttle service and **canoe rental,** see North Fork 1.

PUT IN at the **Camp 41 landing,** river-right, accessed from West Lane Road.

The river is fast, wide and quiet for a mile. Riffles begin as the river turns left, leading into **Wannigan Rapids** (Class I–II). Wavy and rocky, Wannigan is not difficult for most experienced canoeists. Wannigan campsite is located on the right before the rapids.

Flambeau Falls (Class II) comes a half-mile downstream, at a wide point in the river. Dode's Island lies between the two pitches of this rapids, which is a little more challenging than Wannigan. There are some big rocks to avoid, but routes aren't difficult to find.

Beaver Dam Falls: the biggest drop on the Flambeau.

Half a mile farther is the confluence with the South Fork of the Flambeau, which enters from the left. A beautiful campsite (the "Forks") is found on the left just after the confluence. Bear Run campsite appears on the left farther downstream, and Hervas Landing and campsite (5.8 miles) not long thereafter.

A cabin on the right, a left-hand bend and a campsite on the right announce the beginning of **Cedar Rapids** (7.2 miles). The river is quite wide here. An island separates the river, and the rapids is usually run between the island and the left bank, over a ledge that has several chutes. Don't let down your guard after the drop; a brief rock garden follows. A solid Class II, Cedar Rapids should be scouted from the well-established trail on the left. Once you're on the trail, you'll see why this is a favorite vantage point for taking photographs.

The second, third and fourth pitches of Cedar Rapids follow in the next couple of miles (Class I–II). These widely scattered rapids are found in places where the river drops gradually through boulder beds for several hundred yards. Routes are not difficult to find.

Beaver Dam Rapids (10.8 miles), the biggest drop on the North Fork, is within sight of the last pitch of Cedar Rapids. This solid Class II+ rapids has a sheer drop of 4 feet, and its roar can be heard far upstream. Take out on the left to scout the main drop, which consists of a river-wide ledge strewn with huge boulders. There is usually a good slot near the middle, but backrollers can develop in high water. Inexperienced canoeists should portage; boaters have drowned in this area. If you decide to run the rapids, go slow and keep your boat lined up with the current. A short boulder garden follows the drop.

TAKE-OUT: Shortly after the rapids, **Beaver Dam Landing** appears on the right, accessed from West Lane Road.

Other trips: Some canoeists who aren't averse to lake paddling continue for another 4.5 miles to the Flambeau Lodge on the right. Class I rapids occur a mile downstream from Beaver Dam, but then the head of the Big Falls Flowage begins a mile later. The Big Falls Dam is 13 miles downstream from Camp 41. Three more dams (Dairyland, Ladysmith and Thornapple) hold back the next 22 miles of the Flambeau. After that, only 8.5 miles of the river remain before it flows into the Chippewa.

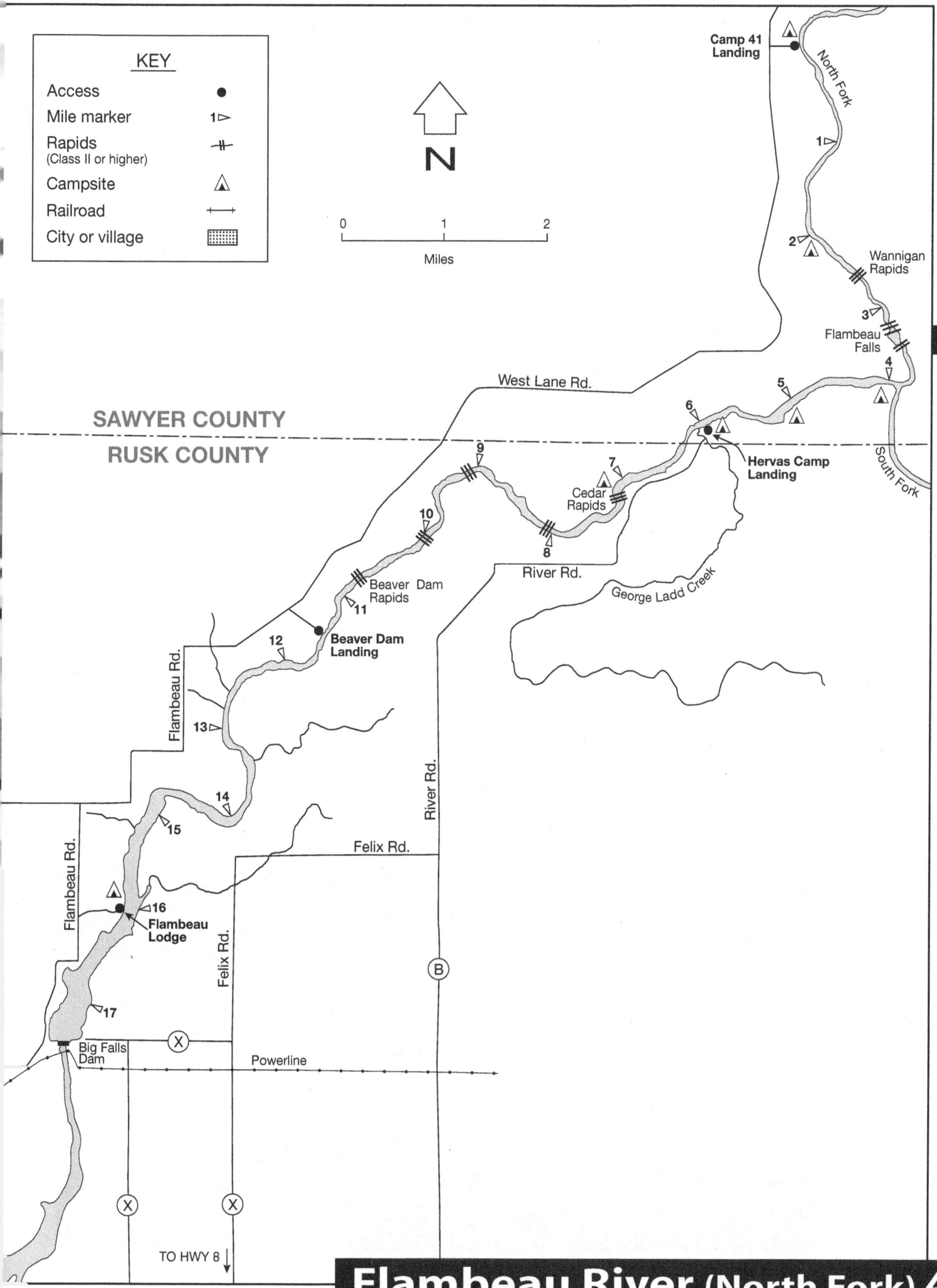

Flambeau River (North Fork) 4

Flambeau River (North Fork) 5

Thornapple Dam to the Chippewa River (8.1 Miles)

In its last hurrah before flowing into the Chippewa, the Flambeau is almost urban in character compared with the wilderness setting of the upstream sections. Almost from the put-in, County E runs close to the right bank, and development has taken place on both sides of the river. Thus, you'll see many homes and cabins on this stretch. Nevertheless, the river and its environs are attractive, and the current continues to move right along. Two huge islands add variety. Because of its accessibility, scenic value, quietwater and brevity, this final section of the Flambeau is a popular day trip.

Since most of the shoreline is privately owned, there is no camping along the river. However, camping is available a few miles north at the Bruce city park, and at the take-out (Flater's Resort).

Water levels are always adequate for good canoeing. Paddling can be dangerous under high-water conditions, however, and canoeists should be aware that water levels may increase rapidly when generators are started or spillways opened at the dam. For general information on current water conditions, call Flater's Resort (715-595-4771).

The average **GRADIENT** is 2.4 feet per mile.

The **shuttle route** is via County P and County E. Shuttle service and **canoe rental** are available at Flater's Resort (phone number above).

PUT IN below the Northern States Power Company **Thornapple Dam** on river-left. A gravel access road leads from County P to the **landing,** where there is room to park several vehicles.

From the beginning, paddlers see the same grassy, heavily wooded banks to which they've become accustomed on the upper Flambeau. The only real difference here is the frequency of houses and the lack of significant riffles and rapids. Not long after the County P bridge, County E runs close to the river. It will remain nearby for the rest of the trip.

A number of deep holes are apparent as the trip continues. Fishing for muskie, northern, walleye and catfish is popular.

Riffles precede the first big landmark on the stretch: Pine Island (3.6 miles). Occupying 23 acres, the island is three-quarters of a mile long. The scenery in this area of the river is especially attractive. After Pine Island, houses appear on the left.

At 5.7 miles, there is a public boat **landing** on the right, accessed from County E and located east of the Washington Creek Wildlife Area.

Another huge, wooded island—Barney's Island—signals the imminent end of the Flambeau.

TAKE OUT river-right at **Flater's Resort,** located at the tip of land at the Flambeau-Chippewa confluence.

View of the Flambeau from a campsite.

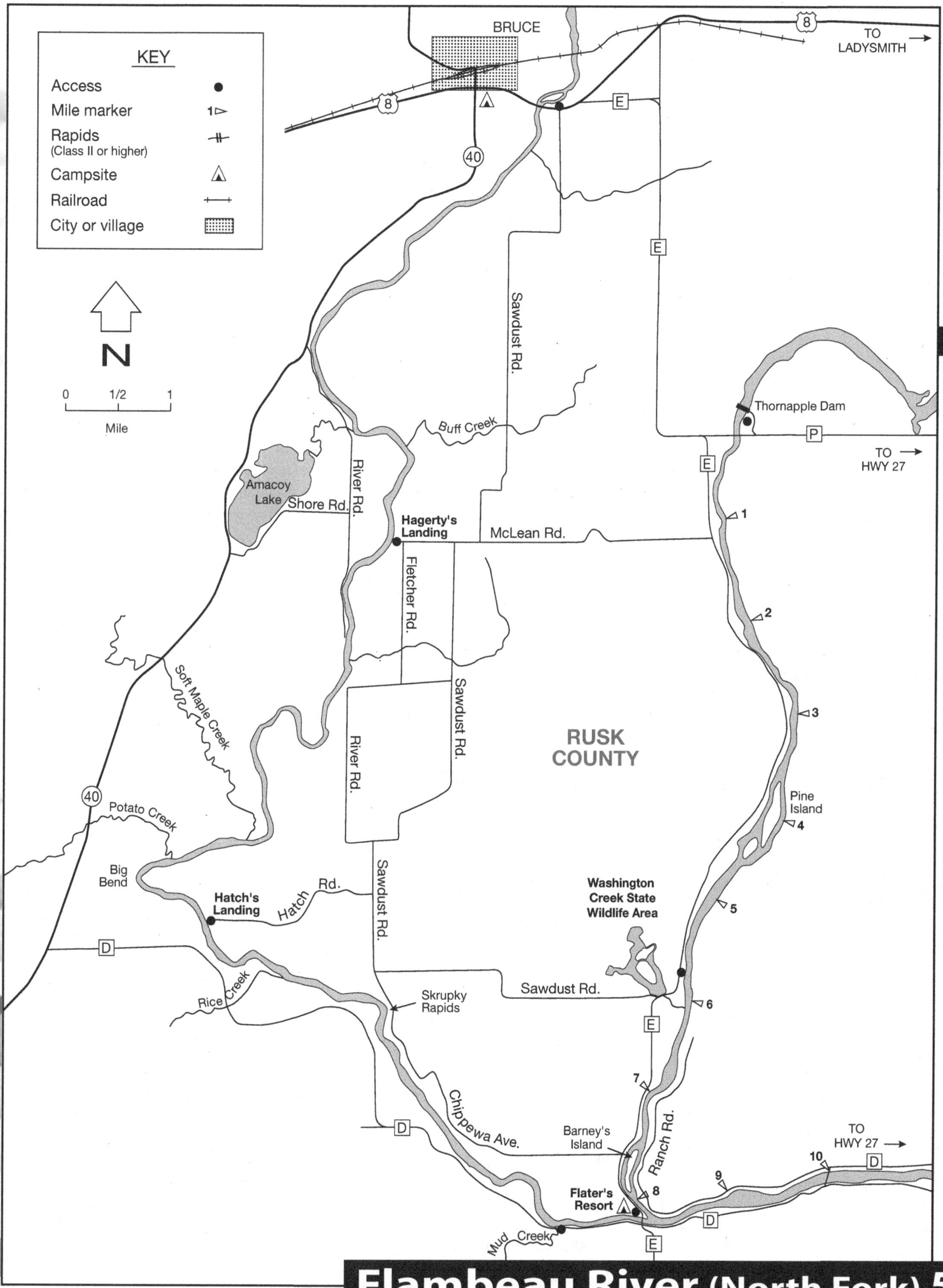

Flambeau River (North Fork) 5

Flambeau River (South Fork) 1

Fifield to Lugerville (12 Miles)

Less paddled than its better-known counterpart to the north, the South Fork of the Flambeau is a smaller stream, with numerous riffles, Class I–II rapids and even a Class III drop. Much of the adjoining land is privately owned. Not until the river crosses the Price/Sawyer county line (South Fork 33) do paddlers enter the Flambeau River State Forest. Consequently, you'll see a few more houses on the South Fork than on the larger North Fork.

It's still remote, however, and offers more varied scenery than its bigger brother. The tree-lined shores are home to many wildlife species, and the river produces good fishing for smallmouth, walleye, muskie, northern and panfish. Once you've paddled the South Fork, you'll agree that it lends itself to exciting day trips.

The first section described here, like the other two, is, for the most part, scenic quietwater, but there is a long rapids that can spell trouble for inexperienced paddlers.

Camping: Unlike the North Fork, there are no designated campsites along the river. Public campgrounds are available a few miles northwest at Connors Lake and Lake of the Pines, off County W.

Attention, Logging Buffs!

Logging-era enthusiasts who are paddling in this area have a great (and rare) opportunity to see close up what an authentic logging dam looked like.

Thanks to the efforts of the Chequamegon National Forest staff and many local volunteers, the original Round Lake log-driving dam at the source of the South Fork has been rebuilt. Originally constructed around 1880, the timber structure is flanked by earthen embankments and has sluice gates that were opened and closed with chain-driven gears operated from a deck. Last used in 1909 when the final log drive on the South Fork occurred, the dam is the only remaining one of its kind in Wisconsin.

To see it, drive east on Highway 70 16 miles from Fifield, then turn north on Forest Road 144 (Shady Knoll Road); follow the road for 2 miles to the parking lot.

Incidentally, the Smith Rapids Covered Bridge—another fascinating place to visit—is only 4 miles west of the dam on Forest Road 148, 2 miles north of Highway 70. One of only a few covered bridges in Wisconsin, this new wooden bridge was constructed in the old style and spans 90 feet of the South Fork.

Water levels are best in the spring (usually into June) and after sustained rainfall. When the water is low, canoeing can become unpleasantly scrapy as a result of the relatively high gradient and the absence of controlled-flow structures like the dams on the North Fork. In times of high water, some of the rapids develop big boat-swamping waves and can be hazardous. For information on water levels, call the Flambeau River State Forest headquarters (715-332-5271).

The average **GRADIENT** is 2.5 feet per mile.

The **shuttle route** is via Highway 13 and County F. **Boat rentals** and shuttle service are available at Flambeau Sports Outfitters (715-339-2012) and at other outfitters listed in North Fork 1.

PUT IN on river-right at **Movrich Memorial Community Park** in Fifield, between the Highway 70 bridge (upstream) and the old bridge on Balsam Street. An old rock dam is located here, with a tongue in the middle; you can put in either upstream or downstream from the old dam. Parking, picnic facilities, toilets and water are available at the park.

The river begins rather wide—about 125 feet—and continues that way for a considerable distance, flowing with moderate current between low, wooded banks. There are houses on the right for a while.

An attractive wayside at the Highway 13 bridge (2 miles) provides a good alternative **access,** downstream-left. Parking, picnic table, toilets and water are provided.

Patterson Creek enters on the right (3.8 miles), usually with signs of beaver activity. A long straightaway follows. After a left turn, a long succession of cabins begins. Near Simon Road, the river narrows to about 30 feet and drops over a small Class I ledge, with easy chutes. Avoid the big rock in the middle.

The river continues wide and deep, with a riffle at a small island. Farther downstream, a big island is followed by the mouth of Rock Creek on the left (7 miles).

A swampy area precedes **Boars Rapids** (7.5 miles), a Class I–II boulder garden that begins in a left turn, constricts and drops a few feet in 75 yards, with some good-sized waves.

A couple of big sweeping bends follow, then a shallow Class I boulder garden that is preceded by large boulders on the right, a pretty pine bluff on the left and an S-curve.

A mile later, the biggest rapids on the trip begins at an island: **Rocky Carry** (11 miles). Scout and/or portage on the left, if necessary, but remember that you're on private property; ask permission of the owner. Paddle to the right of the island, where the rapids begins moderately, then bends several hundred yards through Class II boulder gardens with steady gradient. Be careful as you weave your way between the boulders and over the waves, but have fun on Rocky Carry's long roller-coaster ride.

Downstream from the rapids, a few old wooden pilings remain from the mill dam built in the early 1900s by the Luger brothers.

TAKE OUT at the public landing at the end of Rocky Carry Road in Lugerville, on river-left immediately after the rapids, or at the County F bridge, downstream-left. A maze of small islands precedes the bridge.

Other trips: When water levels are sufficient, mostly in the spring, the South Fork is canoeable for 30 miles upstream, all the way from its source at Round Lake. Except for the last few miles before Fifield, all of this section lies in the Chequamegon National Forest, with occasional private property along the shoreline. Fishtrap and Smith Rapids campgrounds are located on the river, and there are several other federal campgrounds in the area. Flowing mostly through wilderness surroundings, this part of the river offers everything from marshland and eagles' nests to rapids and rock dams. For a map and description of this section, see Gary F. Kulibert, *A Visitor's Guide to Chequamegon National Forest* (Rhinelander, 1995).

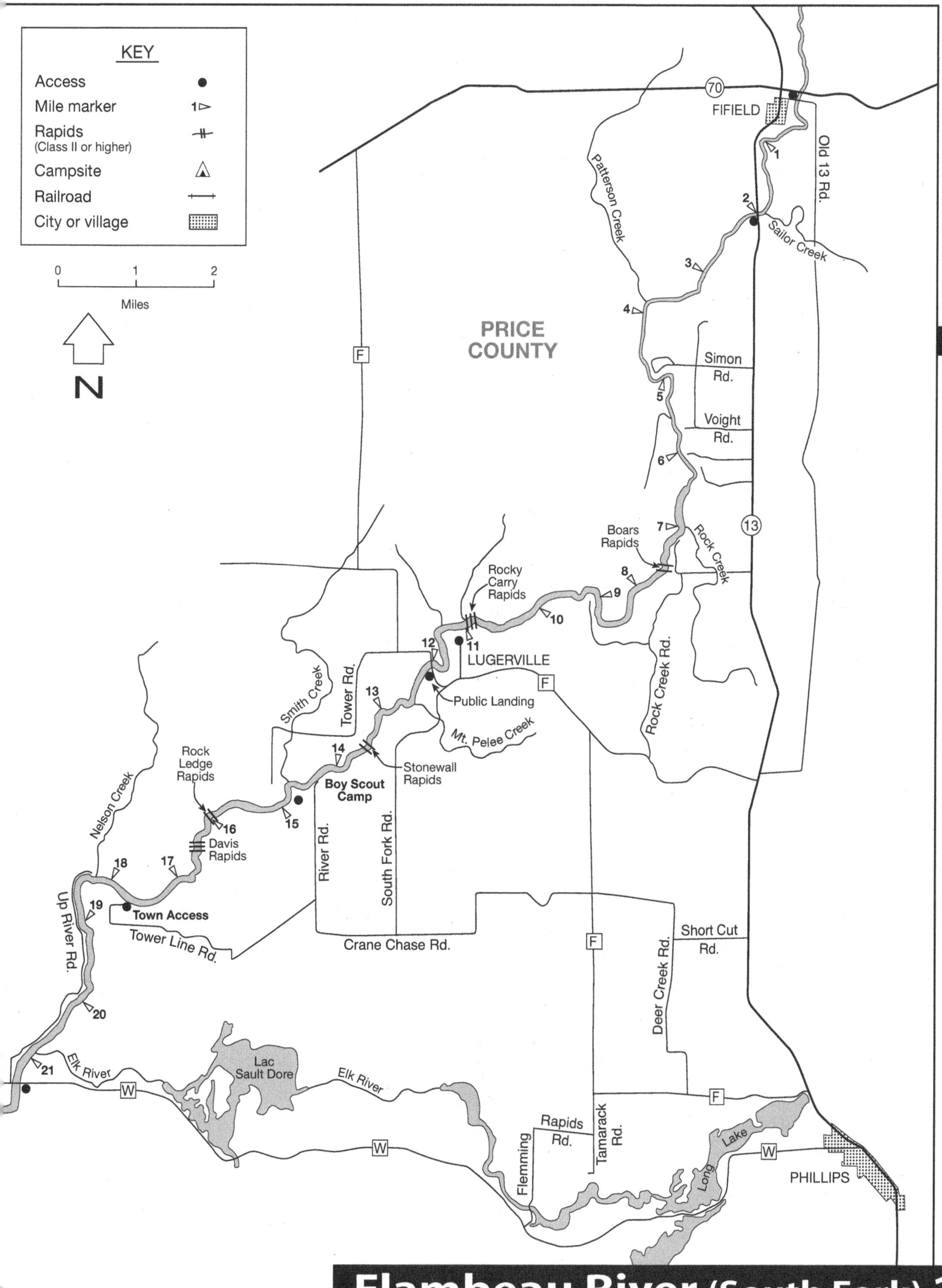

Flambeau River (South Fork) 1

Flambeau River (South Fork) 2

Lugerville to County W (9 Miles)

This section of the South Fork is comparable to the previous one. The countryside is beautiful and varied, the fishing good, and the riffles and rapids enjoyable and usually nonthreatening. You'll also pass a number of very attractive homes.

There is no designated **camping** along the river. Public campgrounds are available at Connors Lake and Lake of the Pines a few miles northwest of the take-out, off County W.

Water levels are best in the spring and after sustained rainfall, but high water can be dangerous. For sources of information on current water conditions, see South Fork 1.

The average **GRADIENT** is 4.4 feet per mile.

Heading toward some rapids on the South Fork.

The **shuttle route** is via County F, Tamarack Road, Rapids Road, Flemming Road and County W. For shuttle service and **boat rental,** see South Fork 1.

PUT IN at the village of Lugerville at the public landing at the end of Rocky Carry Road, or at the County F bridge, downstream-left.

After the bridge, the river is fairly wide, straight and deep, but a Class I rapids follows the first right bend. Named Kashinski after an early settler, the rapids occurs where the river splits around a small island after Mt. Pelee Creek. Nice riffles follow.

Stonewall Rapids is a short Class I–II rapids, immediately followed by a low rocky wall on the left (thus, the name).

Just downstream, a sign on the left indicates the location of a **Boy Scout campground.**

In a left bend, Smith Creek enters on the right alongside a beautifully landscaped property. After Smith Creek, a public access is found on river-left (reached from nearby River Road). Farther downstream, immediately after a large stone outcropping on the right, the river bends right, then left; **Rock Ledge Rapids** (Class I–II) is located in this S-curve.

Within half a mile, the river narrows and falls over a Class I–II boulder garden, **Davis Rapids.** There are several large rocks to avoid in this 50-yard rapids, and a big wave near the bottom. The last whitewater on the trip, a Class I boulder garden, follows downstream.

The remaining 4.5 miles are slow, wide and flat all the way to County W. Only two riffles interrupt the quiet-water. If you wish to eliminate some of the flat-water, you can take out at the public access on river-left at the end of Tower Line Road.

In the approach to County W, the Elk River enters on the left. The section's final riffle is found here.

TAKE OUT at the public **landing** at the County W bridge, downstream-left. There is room for a few cars.

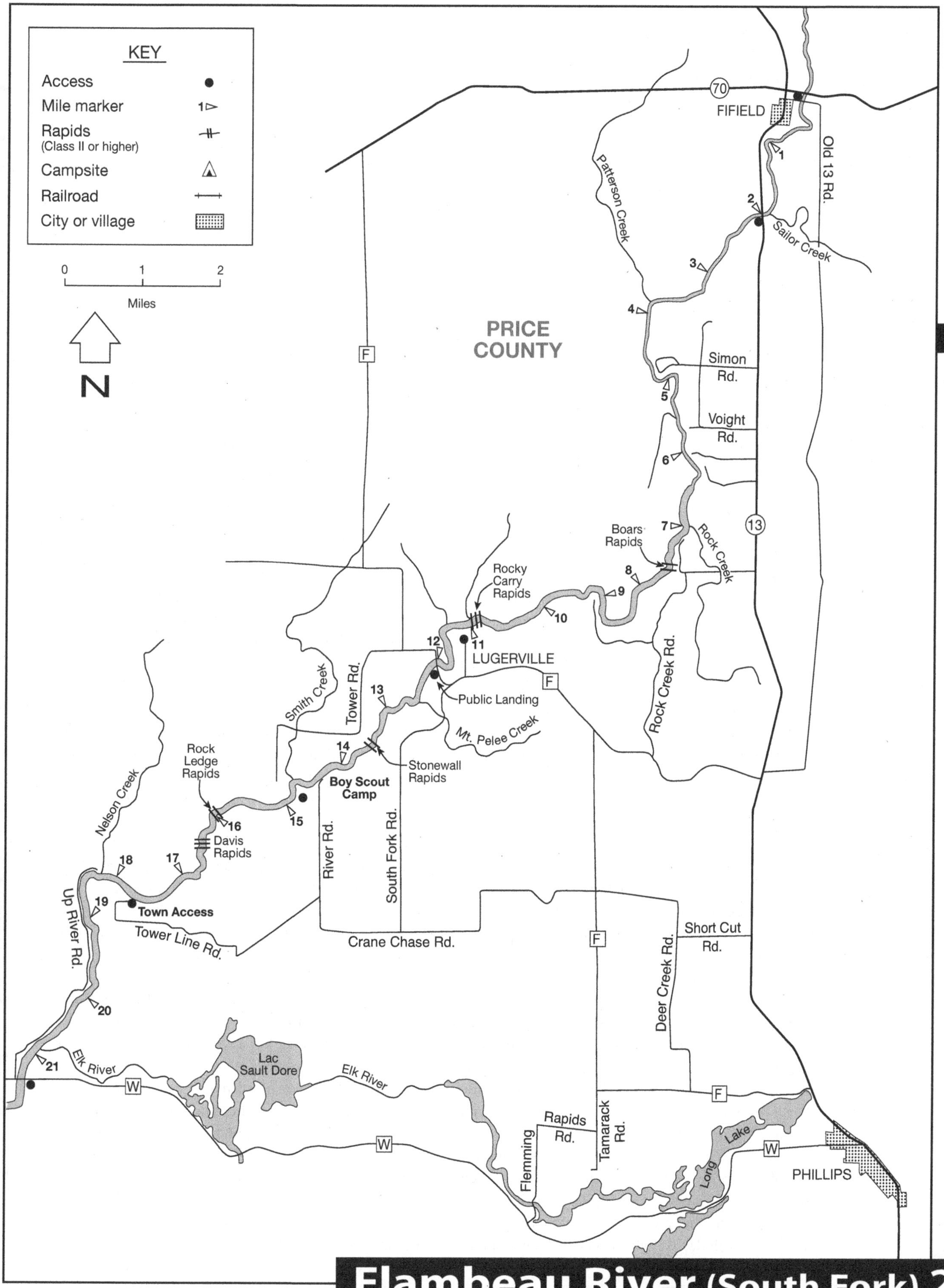
KEY
Access
Mile marker
Rapids
(Class II or higher)
Campsite
Railroad
City or village
0 1 2
Miles
N
PRICE COUNTY
FIFIELD
70
Old 13 Rd.
Patterson Creek
Sailor Creek
Simon Rd.
Voight Rd.
13
Boars Rapids
Rock Creek
Rock Creek Rd.
Rocky Carry Rapids
LUGERVILLE
Public Landing
F
Mt. Pelee Creek
Smith Creek
Tower Rd.
Stonewall Rapids
Boy Scout Camp
River Rd.
South Fork Rd.
Rock Ledge Rapids
Davis Rapids
Nelson Creek
Town Access
Tower Line Rd.
Up River Rd.
Crane Chase Rd.
Short Cut Rd.
Deer Creek Rd.
Elk River
Lac Sault Dore
W
Rapids Rd.
Flemming
Tamarack Rd.
Long Lake
PHILLIPS
1 2 3 4 5 6 7 8 9 10 11 12 13 14 15 16 17 18 19 20 21

Flambeau River (South Fork) 3

County W to Otter Slide Landing (10.2 Miles)

Perhaps the most popular canoeing stretch on the South Fork, this section provides some of the best whitewater on the river for experienced paddlers. The countryside continues to be wild and scenic, and the Flambeau River State Forest begins within a few miles of the put-in. Picturesque rock formations appear frequently on this section, sometimes coupled with exciting rapids. For paddlers and nonpaddlers alike, the Slough Gundy/Little Falls area is one of the prettiest places in the Flambeau River system. Readily accessible parking and walking paths make it a relaxing stop before or after a canoe trip.

There are no designated **campsites** on the South Fork. Paddlers who wish to continue past the confluence with the North Fork will find a beautiful riverside campsite on the left at "the Forks," and several additional campsites downstream. USFS campgrounds are located to the north at Connors Lake and Lake of the Pines, off County W.

Water levels are best in the spring and after sustained rainfall. In the summer, the river is often very scratchy. High water, on the other hand, creates big waves in some of the rapids—especially Slough Gundy. For sources of information on water levels, see South Fork 1.

Average **GRADIENT** is 6.9 feet per mile.

The **shuttle route** is via County W (northwest), County M (south), and Skinner Creek Road. For shuttle service and **boat rental,** see South Fork 1.

PUT IN at County W, downstream-left. There is a good **landing** here, with room to park several cars.

At the beginning, the river flows quietly through private land. The river is about 125 feet wide, with low wooded banks, a number of islands and occasional homes.

The two Class I pitches of **Carpenter Rapids** begin in a little bend in the river (1.5 miles). A long, flat stretch of deep water follows, with good current. Downstream from the rapids, there is a small concrete dam on the left, impounding a creek. A couple of big islands lie downstream.

Class II **Cornsheller Rapids** (4 miles) requires care; avoid the big boulders about halfway through this 300-yard-long rapids. Most paddlers start their run on the left, then work their way to the chute right of center. The Flambeau River State Forest begins about one-quarter mile upstream.

There is a series of Class I rapids downstream from the mouth of Price Creek, then a big island. **Bull Rapids** (a short, easy Class II) begins immediately after the island with a rocky, wavy constriction. Another easier pitch of Bull Rapids follows. The rock outcroppings in this part of the river are quite attractive, and good

Class III Little Falls on the South Fork.

lunch spots are plentiful. Minor rapids precede the County M bridge.

Another excellent **access** is found at County M, upstream-left. "Fisherman's Landing" has picnic tables and good parking. Located just below the bridge, on the right, is a prison camp. A sign warns paddlers not to take out here.

After curving left, the river heads toward a huge rock wall that turns out to be the upstream end of a big island; this area is known as **Slough Gundy** (7.5 miles). The left channel is usually little more than a trickle. After a short Class I rapids preceding the island, the main (right) channel loops around the island. Four Class II boulder gardens occupy the channel; the third pitch is generally the most challenging. Big waves often swamp open boats, especially at medium-to-high water levels. Slough Gundy should be scouted from the island, to the left of the main channel.

A short distance downstream is **Little Falls** (misnamed!). Here the river suddenly drops about 7 feet on both sides of a small rocky island; the main drop is on the right side, but both sides are tough Class IIIs. Portage along the trail on the left; portaging on the right shore or over the island is more difficult.

There is a DNR parking area off County M just south of the County M bridge, with short paths leading back to Slough Gundy and Little Falls.

Not far downstream from Little Falls, **Scratch Rapids** should not be taken lightly. Rocky on the left, this Class II often has big waves. The rest of the trip to the take-out is flatwater.

TAKE OUT on the left just before Otter Slide Rapids (within view of the **landing**). There are big boulders in the river at the undeveloped landing, which has room for a few cars. The Otter Slide access is 1.8 miles southwest of County M, on Skinner Creek Road.

Another 3 miles of quietwater leads to the Forks, where the South Fork and North Fork join. The next landing is Hervas Camp, on the left. For a description of the river downstream from the Forks, see North Fork 4.

Flambeau River (South Fork) 3

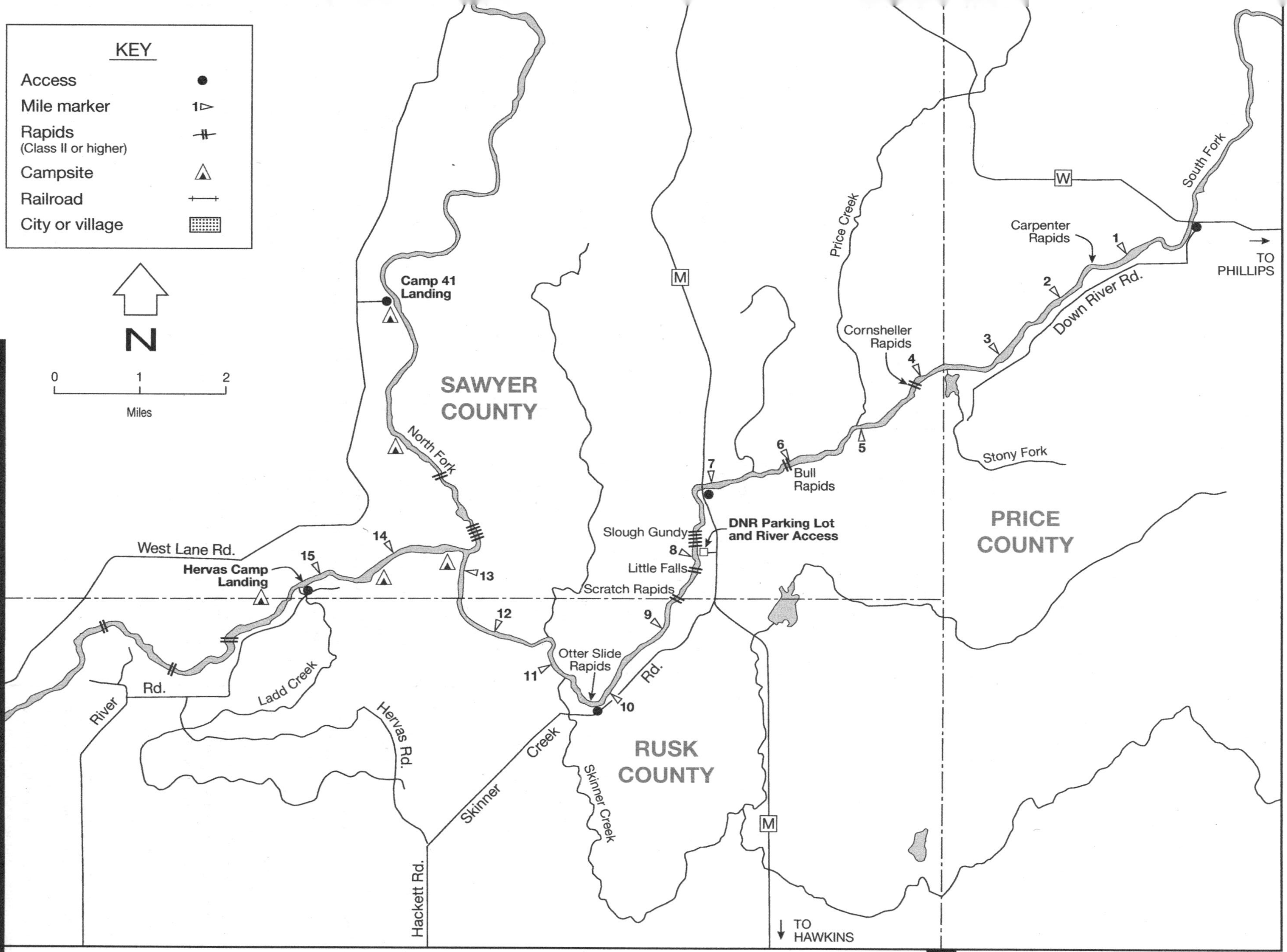

Jump River 1

Oxbow to Big Falls (9.2 Miles)

If you are unfamiliar with the Jump, this stretch of river will be a pleasant surprise. It has a little of everything, including high banks, pine groves, quiet-water sections and a couple of difficult rapids. Less venturesome and less experienced boaters can enjoy the trip by carrying their boats around Little Falls and taking out before Big Falls. Skilled kayakers and canoeists, on the other hand, can drive directly to one or both of these rapids and run them repeatedly.

Riverside **camping** is available at the take-out (Big Falls County Park), and downstream at the Jump River village park. There are several campgrounds to the south in the Chequamegon National Forest (for example, Spearhead Point, Eastwood, West Point and Picnic Point at the Mondeaux Flowage).

Water levels are best in the spring—usually until mid-June—and after sustained rainfall. The riffles and rapids sections are often unrunnable in the summer, but hazardous in high water. One way to judge whether there's enough water to paddle is to examine Little Falls from the nearby road (see below). Also check the downstream gauge at Sheldon (#05362000) on the USGS website; see "Water Levels" in the introduction.

The average **GRADIENT** is 8.7 feet per mile.

The **shuttle route** is via County I, Big Falls Road and County N to the park road. **Canoe rentals** and shuttle service are available at Flambeau Adventures near Ladysmith (715-532-7733, www.flambeauadventures.com).

PUT IN river-right along County I at the oxbow, 10 miles west of Highway 13. (The Highway 13/County I intersection is l6 miles north of Medford). There is an unimproved **landing** alongside County I, with very little room for parking.

The river is about 100 feet wide at the beginning, with high banks and a rocky bottom. Maple, cedar and birch line the shore, but the highlight of the foliage on this trip is the big, beautiful white pines that are found all the way to the take-out.

Fun for Nonpaddlers, Too

Most of the stretches of river described in this book feature attractions on or near the river that nonboaters can enjoy while their companions are out paddling. Goodman Park on the Peshtigo, the Dells of the St. Croix, and Dave's Falls on the Pike come readily to mind.

The Jump River is no exception. Among the places near it where you might spend an hour or a weekend is Big Falls County Park. Located just north of the Chequamegon National Forest in the southwest corner of Price County, the park surrounds a lovely dells where the river plunges through a series of exciting and difficult drops. Hikers can view the dells from riverside paths.

Big Falls Park provides some rugged scenery too. Here, the Jump has carved its way through ancient bedrock and pushed gigantic boulders aside. Picnic facilities, toilets, water and camping are available for those who want to tarry.

Big Falls, a long series of Class III drops.

Big boulders soon appear in the stream bed, together with many shallow riffles. Just below a riffle, and upstream from a couple of islands, are the remains of an old logging-era driving dam (1.7 miles).

Downstream, in a big right-hand bend, is a good **landing,** with picnic shelter and toilets. Many riffles follow in the straightaway that parallels the Price/Taylor county line.

You'll encounter high banks of clay and sand in the next two big left bends. The steep embankments in the second bend are close to Big Falls Road, on the right, and are known as Yellow Banks (5.5 miles). Downstream, big boulders and rock formations become more numerous. About a mile after Yellow Banks, in a sharp right-hand bend, are a couple of Class I rapids.

Little Falls, a 200-yard Class II boulder garden, is preceded by a northwest straightaway, then a mass of big boulders. Because Big Falls Road runs alongside the whole rapids, on the right, Little Falls is easy to scout.

The river widens somewhat after the County N bridge. After a couple of big bends, a northwest straightaway leads toward Big Falls. As you paddle across a big, placid pool, you can hear the roar of the falls.

TAKE OUT at the **county park** on the right, upstream from the falls. A picnic shelter is located atop the attractive knoll here, and can be seen from upstream.

Big Falls (Class III) is a 400-yard dells with huge boulders on both sides. Making an S-curve, the river falls dramatically over several big drops.

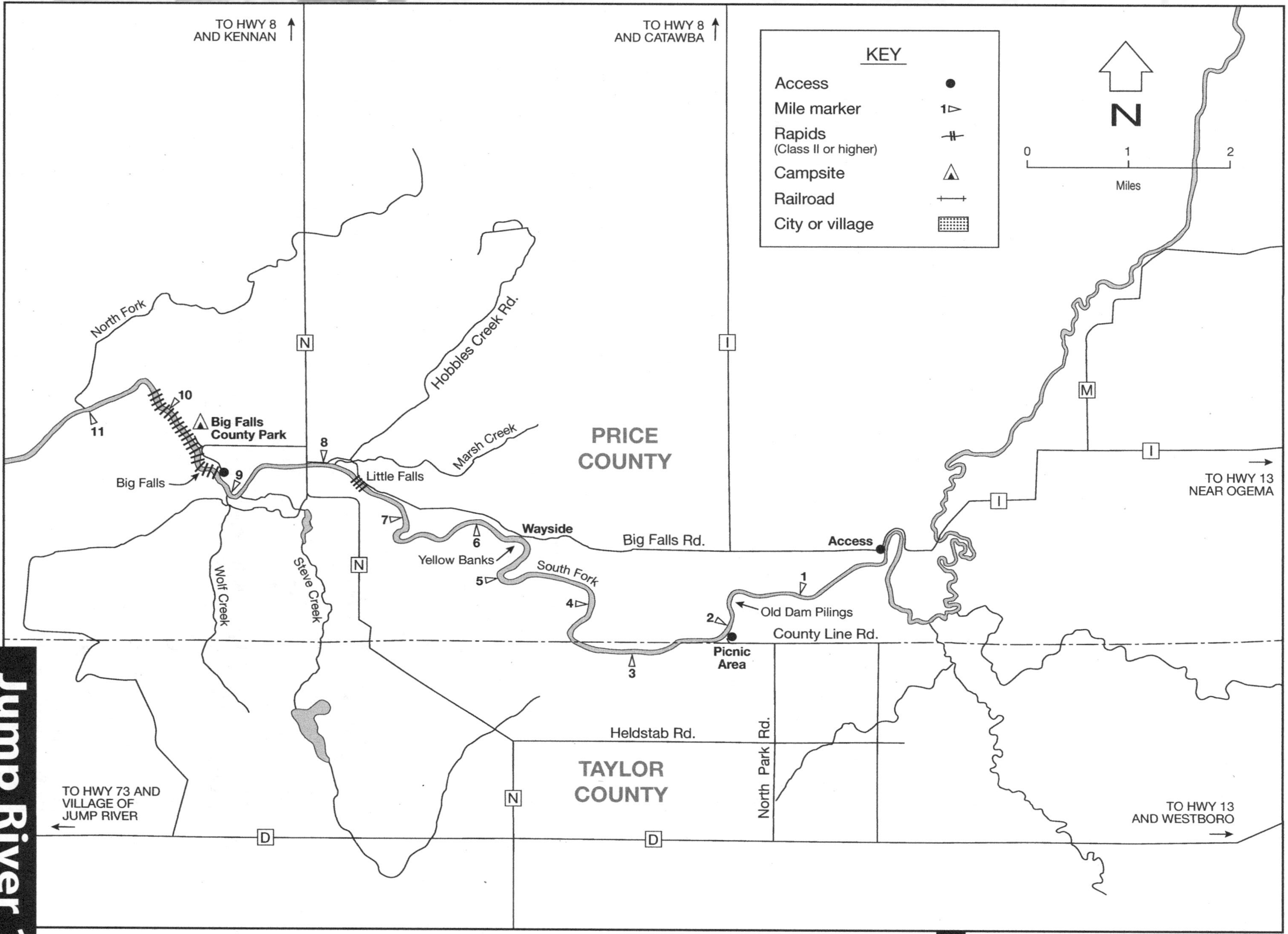

TO HWY 8
AND KENNAN
TO HWY 8
AND CATAWBA
KEY
Access
Mile marker
Rapids
(Class II or higher)
Campsite
Railroad
City or village
N
0
1
2
Miles
North Fork
Hobbles Creek Rd.
Marsh Creek
PRICE
COUNTY
10
11
Big Falls
County Park
8
Little Falls
Big Falls
9
7
6
Wayside
Big Falls Rd.
Yellow Banks
5
South Fork
4
Wolf Creek
Steve Creek
Access
1
Old Dam Pilings
2
Picnic
Area
County Line Rd.
3
TO HWY 13
NEAR OGEMA
Heldstab Rd.
North Park Rd.
TAYLOR
COUNTY
TO HWY 73 AND
VILLAGE OF
JUMP RIVER
TO HWY 13
AND WESTBORO

Jump River 1

Jump River 2

Big Falls to Highway 73 (10 Miles)

Flowing through three counties, this stretch of the Jump begins with a mile of continuous Class II rapids, then alternates for the rest of the trip between quiet sections and gentle whitewater. There are several wide, slow areas, especially during the last few miles, but riffles and Class I rapids are found throughout the trip. Generally, the shoreline is grassy and heavily wooded, although high banks of sand and gravel occasionally appear. The surroundings are undeveloped, with few houses visible. Like the upstream stretch, this section is fished mostly for smallmouth bass, muskie and panfish.

Riverside **camping** is available at the put-in (Big Falls County Park) and downstream at the Jump River village park. There are also several campgrounds to the south in the Chequamegon National Forest.

Water levels are best in the spring and after extended rainfall. The riffles and rapids are often too shallow for paddling in the summer, but can be hazardous in high water. For gauge information, see Jump 1.

The **GRADIENT** averages 6.7 feet per mile.

The **shuttle route** is via Big Falls County Park Road, County N, County D and Highway 73. For information on shuttle service and **canoe rentals,** see Jump 1.

PUT IN at Big Falls County Park, well below the falls; take the access road to the right, and launch your boat from the bank. The river at this point is filled with huge boulders and fast water. Class II rapids will continue uninterrupted for almost a mile, providing a wonderful stretch of whitewater for experienced paddlers.

Numerous rock outcroppings appear along the shore. One on the left has a spring that forms a miniwaterfall. After the North Fork of the Jump enters on the right, the river widens (1.3 miles). There are high sand and gravel banks in the area of the Price/Rusk county line.

At 4.8 miles, a slough on the right is followed by a Class I rapids in a left bend. In the next big left bend, there is another Class I rapids, and County M comes close on the right. A path leads up the steep bank to the road. Soon thereafter, the river splits around a big island.

From here to the take-out, the river is fairly wide with good current and occasional riffles. When you come across some old bridge pilings, you know that Highway 73 isn't far downstream.

TAKE OUT at the Highway 73 bridge, downstream-left. There is an excellent wayside **landing** here, with toilets, picnic facilities and good parking.

An alternate **take-out,** the village of Jump River, adds about a half mile to the trip. The **village park landing,** a pleasant grassy bank, is on the right, upstream from the bridge.

Other trips. Downstream, the 9-mile section from Highway 73 to the village of Sheldon is another popular day trip. Roads are close by (but unobtrusive) throughout the trip. The stretch is rather wide, with wooded, grassy banks, occasional rock outcroppings and many shallow riffles. Fishing is good in the many deep pools. The only real rapids—a Class I—comes just before the County H bridge. Put in at the wayside landing at the Highway 73 bridge, or downstream at the Jump River village park; and take out at Haley Park in Sheldon, after the railroad bridge.

A mile of boulder gardens begins below Big Falls.

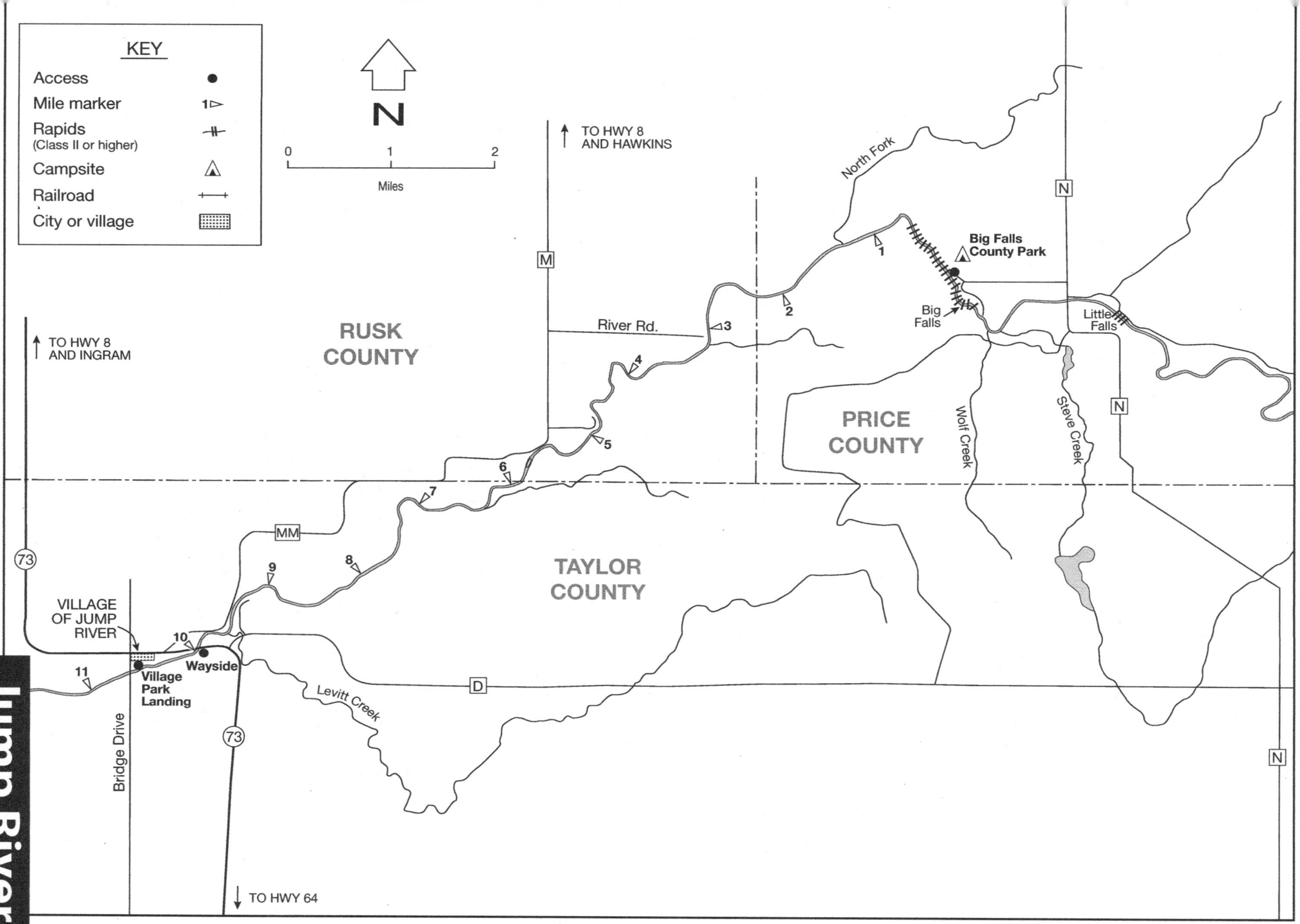
KEY
Access
Mile marker
Rapids
(Class II or higher)
Campsite
Railroad
City or village
N
0
1
2
Miles
TO HWY 8
AND HAWKINS
TO HWY 8
AND INGRAM
M
N
North Fork
Big Falls
County Park
Big
Falls
Little
Falls
River Rd.
RUSK
COUNTY
PRICE
COUNTY
Wolf Creek
Steve Creek
TAYLOR
COUNTY
MM
73
VILLAGE
OF JUMP
RIVER
Wayside
Village
Park
Landing
Bridge Drive
Levitt Creek
D
TO HWY 64
1
2
3
4
5
6
7
8
9
10
11

Jump River 2

Kinnickinnic River

River Falls to County F (7 Miles)

Almost within the shadow of Eau Claire/Chippewa Falls and the populous Twin Cities of Minneapolis/St. Paul, there exists a marvelously unspoiled stretch of wild river. Its clear water, aerated by innumerable riffles and small rapids, and protected from shoreline development, makes it one of the premium trout streams in the Midwest, and an increasingly popular destination for canoeists and kayakers. In its final 10 miles it flows through a gorgeous, narrow valley—known locally as the "lower canyon" where there is scarcely a sign of human activity.

Originating in St. Croix County a few miles north of Interstate 94, the Kinnickinnic twists and turns toward the southwest, with many public access points where fisherman can pursue the river's plentiful brook and brown trout. In River Falls, 2 hydroelectric dams block its path. From there, the "Kinni" begins a densely wooded, habitation-free stretch of 7 miles in a 200-foot-deep valley. Finally, two miles later, the river joins the St. Croix between Hudson and Prescott, forming a huge sandy delta at the mouth. Altogether, this splendid little river is only 22 miles long.

Because of the high incidence of minor rapids, rocks to dodge, and occasional limbs to avoid, the section described here is best suited for paddlers who have "advanced beginner" and intermediate experience and skills.

Incidentally, the name of the river is derived from an Ojibwa (Chippewa) word for "that which is mixed," referring to the custom of mixing willow or dogwood bark with native tobacco in order to make it taste and smell better.

Public **camping** in the area is available in River Falls at Hoffman Park (715-425-0924), and 10 miles to the northwest at Willow River State Park (715-386-5931).

Water levels are fairly constant throughout the paddling season, with a normal flow of approximately 90–120 cfs. There is a gauge just upstream from the take-out bridge. Check gauge #05342000 on the USGS website; see "Water Levels" in the introduction.

The **shuttle route** is via Park Street, Main Street (Highway 29), County FF, and County F. **Canoe/kayak rental** and shuttle service are available in River Falls at Kinni Creek Lodge and Outfitters, which is located on the river (877-504-9705 or www.kinnicreek.com).

PUT IN downstream-left from the lower (Powell Falls) dam on the south side of River Falls. Drive to the end of Park Street, where a trail leads from the Glen Park tennis courts down to the river bank. Launch your boat as far away from the dam as you can; a canoeist drowned in the turbulence below the dam some years ago.

Right away, you're likely to see trout fishermen wading in the river. Low-level riffles and rapids—the first of many—begin immediately as the river bends to the right.

Limestone outcroppings at the put-in are a preview of the rocky cliffs that you'll pass throughout the trip. Some of these formations are stunningly beautiful, including occasional "weeping cliffs" where water-seeps nourish lush vegetation.

No roads cross the river until the end—only a powerline at one point. Unlike the "Upper Kinni" (the part between I-94 and River Falls, where roads are never far away), silence reigns on this part of the river.

There are numerous stands of white pine along the scenic bluffs and atop cliffs. Because of the remoteness and the peaceful environs, wildlife sightings are not uncommon, including deer, eagles, herons, wild turkey, and a profusion of birds.

The current is brisk, and several tributaries augment the volume of the river—especially the Rocky Branch in this section. Something is always drawing your attention as you make your way down the river on this typically 3-hour trip: scenic bluffs and cliffs to gawk at, Class I rapids to negotiate, flora and fauna to observe, streambed boulders to steer clear of, and absolute tranquility to enjoy.

The trip ends at County F bridge. **TAKE OUT** upstream-right and carry your boat under the bridge to the downstream-right Kinnickinnic State Park parking area, where there's a day-use fee. The park entrance is located at the top of the hill north of the bridge. It's a beautiful place, with hiking trails that provide breathtaking views of the Kinnickinnic "gorge" and the river delta.

For a map of the public access points on the Kinnickinnic (principally upstream froom River Falls and on the South Fork), see the website (www.kinniriver.org) of the Kinnickinnic River Land Trust, an organization whose mission is "to protect the rare and beautiful Kinnickinnic and its watershed forever."

Kinnickinnic River

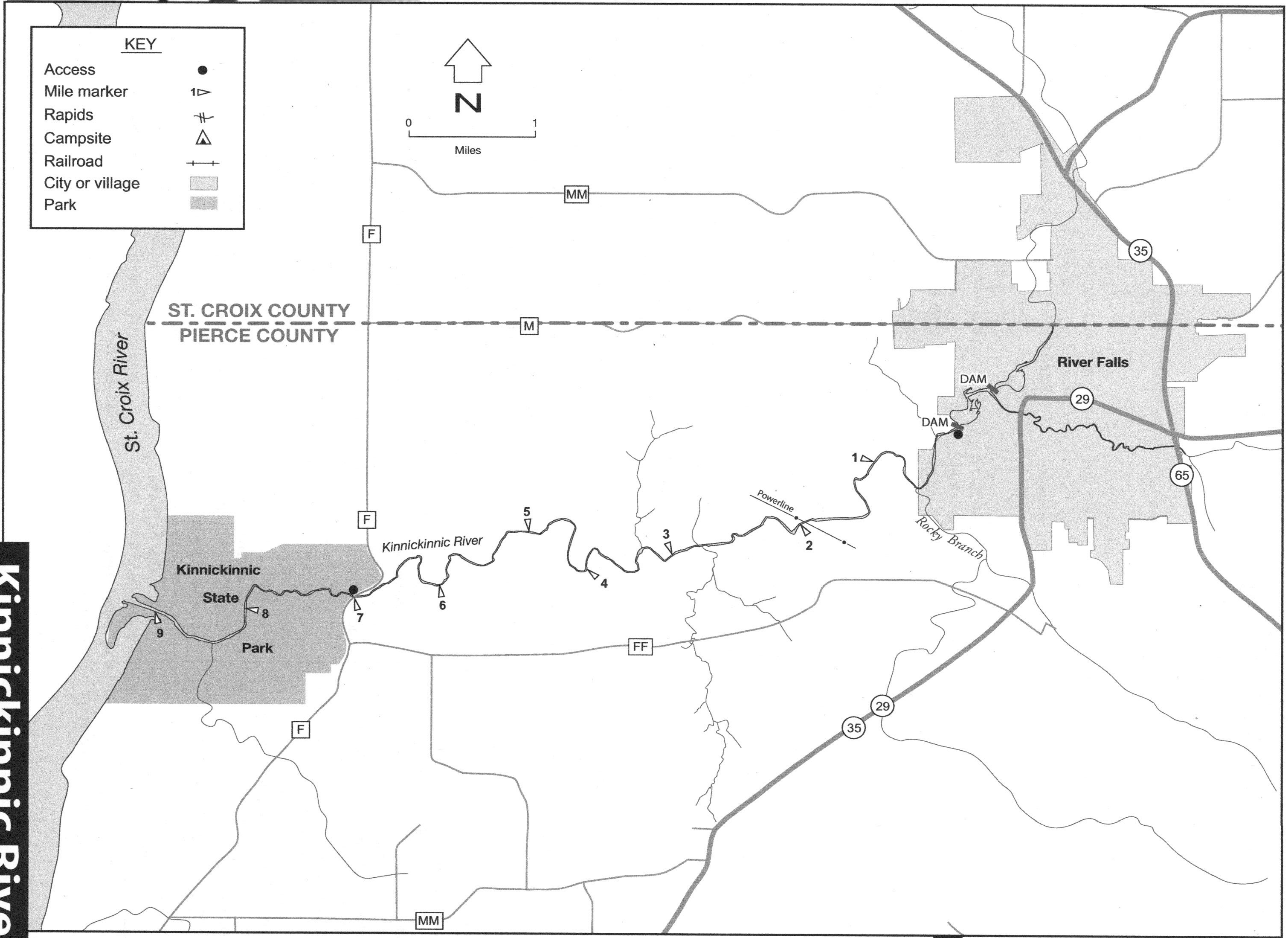

Manitowish River 1

Highway 51 to Highway 47 (7.5 Miles)

The Manitowish is a perfect river for quietwater canoeists who like to combine lake and river paddling. Originating at High Lake a few miles northeast of Boulder Junction, it flows through one lake after another as it courses westward toward the Turtle-Flambeau Flowage. Forty-four miles from its source, the Manitowish joins with the Bear River to form the Flambeau.

Uniquely, 85 percent of the frontage along the Manitowish is state owned, and most of the area through which it flows is wild. Ideal for novice canoeists and for anyone who relishes wilderness, the Manitowish is entirely flatwater, with only a few riffles. Its name comes from an Ojibwe word meaning "spirit," a possible reference to the mist that commonly hangs over the river.

The Manitowish is one of the best rivers in Wisconsin for observing wildlife. Be on the lookout here for eagles, deer, beaver lodges, wood ducks, mergansers, heron, muskrat, mink, cliff swallows and songbirds (especially common are yellowthroats and yellow warblers). Game fish include smallmouth, northern, muskie, walleye and panfish. Because the river passes through a great deal of marshland, you'll see a lot of lowland vegetation, such as willow, cattails, water lilies and arrowhead.

The two-day trips described here are on the Manitowish's longest river stretch, and involve very little lake paddling. Paddlers can canoe-camp and make a two- or three-day trip out of the 17 miles.

There are seven **campsites** along the river. Many canoe campsites are also located on the flowage. Sandy Beach Lake State Campground is a few miles to the south, off Highway 47.

Water levels are dependable for canoeing most of the time, thanks to releases from the Rest Lake dam. For general information on water conditions, call Hawk's Nest Turtle-Flambeau Outfitters near Manitowish (715-543-8585 or 800-688-7471).

The **GRADIENT** is only 1.3 feet per mile.

The **shuttle route** is via Highway 51 and Highway 47. Shuttle service and **canoe rental** are available at Hawk's Nest Turtle-Flambeau Outfiters (phone number above), located near the take-out for the first section. Canoes may also be rented at Chequamegon Adventure Company in Minocqua (715-356-1618 or www.paddlerama.com) and at Ruggers Landing Resort in Mercer (715-476-2530).

PUT IN at the **Highway 51 bridge,** downstream-left or -right. There is room for several cars. The river is quite scenic here, with heavily wooded banks, rocks in the stream bed, and clear water flowing over a sandy bottom. The stretch begins narrow, looping to the right with pleasant riffles that end at a cut bank on the right shore, where a deep hole is located.

Moderate current flows between high wooded banks, along with some marsh grass, bulrushes and cattails. After widening, the river enters Benson Lake, a small body of water; bear to the right toward the outlet. Cottages line the river for a while, mostly on the right. After the lake, woods again close in on both sides. There are many big, beautiful pines, together with oak, birch, shrubby alder, popple and hemlock. The setting is quite peaceful, with many attractive high banks.

After the river touches Highway 51 on the right, white numbered signposts appear. These correspond to a field guide published by the DNR, highlighting various characteristics of the river. You can request a copy at the DNR ranger station in Mercer.

After a lovely pine-studded bank on the right alongside Highway 51, Circle Lily Creek enters on the right. The first of several canoe-access campsites is found downstream in another pine grove (river-right). Downstream, in a big right turn, the woods are farther back and marsh grass borders the river. Frogs, damselflies and songbirds abound in this more marshy environment.

After a straightaway, the river bends toward the Highway 51 wayside **landing** (4.2 miles). Deep holes are found in the short bends before the wayside, which lies opposite an old concrete bridge abutment.

Highway 51 is close by for a while. After a couple of long, wide straightaways, several beaver lodges and occasional sloughs on both sides, another campsite appears on the right.

The river becomes increasingly marshy, with many meanders. Trees retreat from the shore, and sometimes are barely seen. Woods and road traffic appear again on the right shore as the Highway 47 bridge approaches.

TAKE OUT downstream-right at the **Highway 47 bridge,** near a restaurant.

Lakes, Lakes, Lakes

The density of lakes in Oneida, Vilas and Iron counties is one of the highest in the world. Much of the area of these three counties lies in the largest tract of land owned by the state, the 220,000-acre Northern Highland–American Legion State Forest, which contains more than 900 lakes.

In addition to the Upper Wisconsin River (north of McNaughton), the forest is home to the Turtle, Bear, Trout and Manitowish rivers, and features a network of marked hiking trails. Campgrounds and campsites (often located on lakes or rivers) are located throughout the forest; you'll find canoe-access-only campsites on the Manitowish.

Manitowish River 1

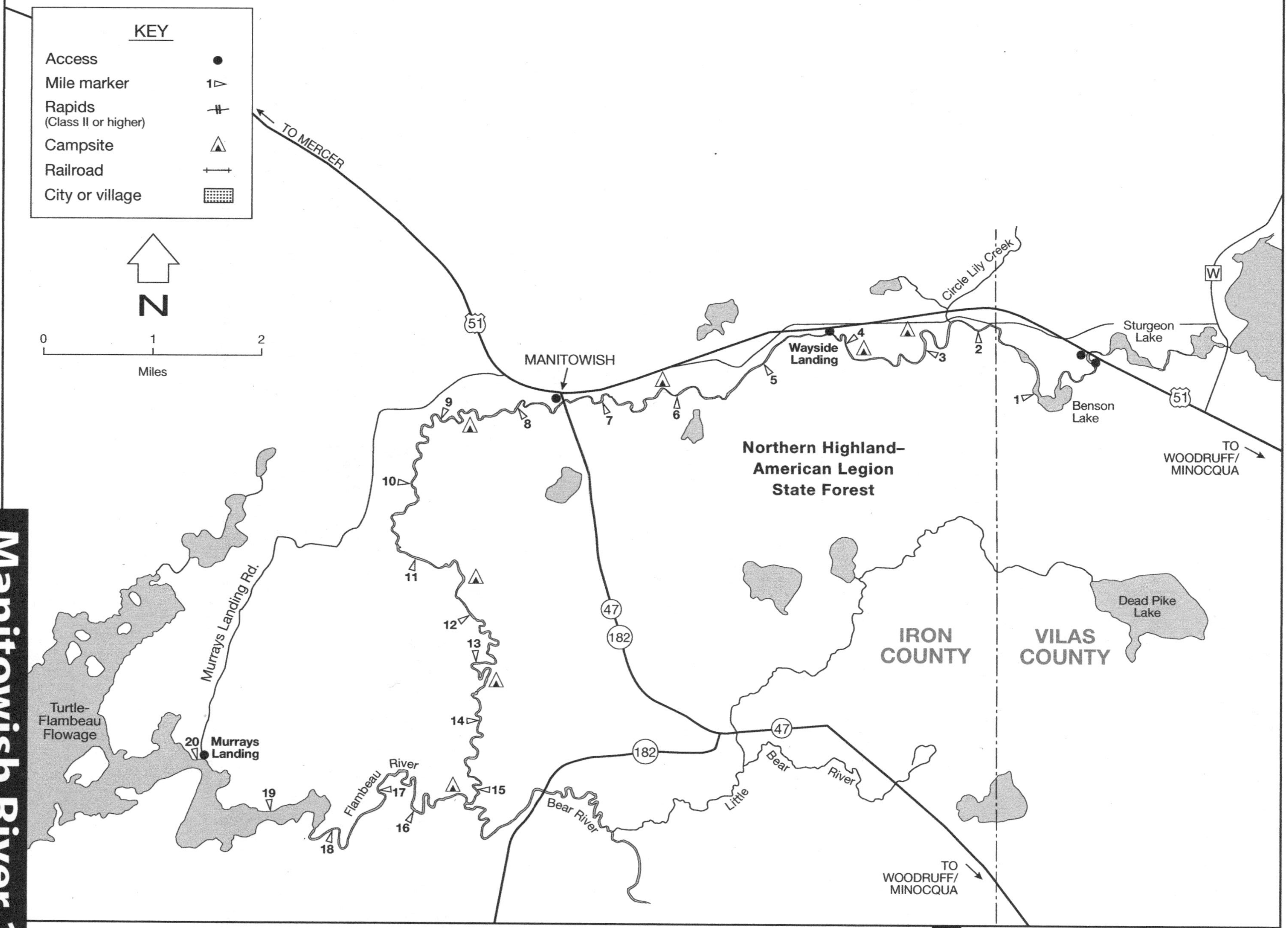

Manitowish River 2

Highway 47 to Murrays Landing (12.5 Miles)

If you liked the remoteness and seclusion of the previous section of the Manitowish, you'll enjoy this section even more. Both stretches lie within the Northern Highland–American Legion State Forest, a 220,000-acre region that has one of the highest concentrations of lakes in the world. Not only the Manitowish but also the Wisconsin and Chippewa-Flambeau rivers have their sources in this wilderness area.

While most of the river trips described in this book have access points between the put-in and take-out, this one does not. Once you have paddled away from the Highway 47 bridge, you will encounter no landings until the end.

Camping is available at several primitive sites along the river, and at numerous sites on the flowage. A few miles southeast is the Sandy Beach Lake State Campground, off Highway 47.

Water levels are fairly constant. For general information on water conditions, call Hawk's Nest Turtle-Flambeau Outfitters near Manitowish (715-543-8585 or 800-688-7471).

The **GRADIENT** of this section is only 0.8 feet per mile.

A typical combination of forest and marshland on the Manitowish.

The **shuttle route** is via Highway 51 and Murrays Landing Road. Shuttle service and **canoe rentals** are available at Hawk's Nest Turtle-Flambeau Outfitters (phone number above), located near the put-in at the intersection of Highways 51 and 47; at Chequamegon Adventure Company in Minocqua (715-356-1618 or www.paddlerama.com); and at Ruggers Landing Resort in Mercer (715-476-2530).

PUT IN at the **Highway 47 bridge,** downstream-right.

A few houses appear near the beginning, but you'll see no more signs of human habitation for the rest of the trip.

Soon after the put-in, the river moves away from Highway 51, henceforth flowing through an uninterrupted wilderness setting. From now on, the only people you'll see are fishermen and other canoeists.

Mixed woods and marsh are found throughout the section, as in the upstream stretch. Periodically, sloughs make "doglegs" off the main channel. In a number of places, the river bends so sharply back upon itself ("cutbacks") that you can see it flowing in the opposite direction just a few feet away. Tree blockages are rare.

Four primitive campsites are evenly distributed over the section; one is difficult to access because of steep banks. At 15.2 miles, the Bear River enters on the left. At this point, the Manitowish ends and the Flambeau begins.

The river now goes through a series of big bends toward the west, eventually widening as it enters the Turtle-Flambeau Flowage.

The flowage is a huge body of water and can be confusing for boaters who are not accustomed to Boundary Waters–type paddling. This trip, however, obliges you to canoe only across the relatively small eastern lobe of the lake. Bear right as you paddle toward the narrow neck of water where the landing is located. There's a prominent landmark called Baptism Rock that some canoeists aim for when paddling toward the landing. An excellent map of the flowage ("Turtle-Flambeau Scenic Waters Area") is available from the DNR ranger station at Mercer.

TAKE OUT at **Murrays Landing,** a sandy beach on the right where the flowage narrows.

Manitowish River 2

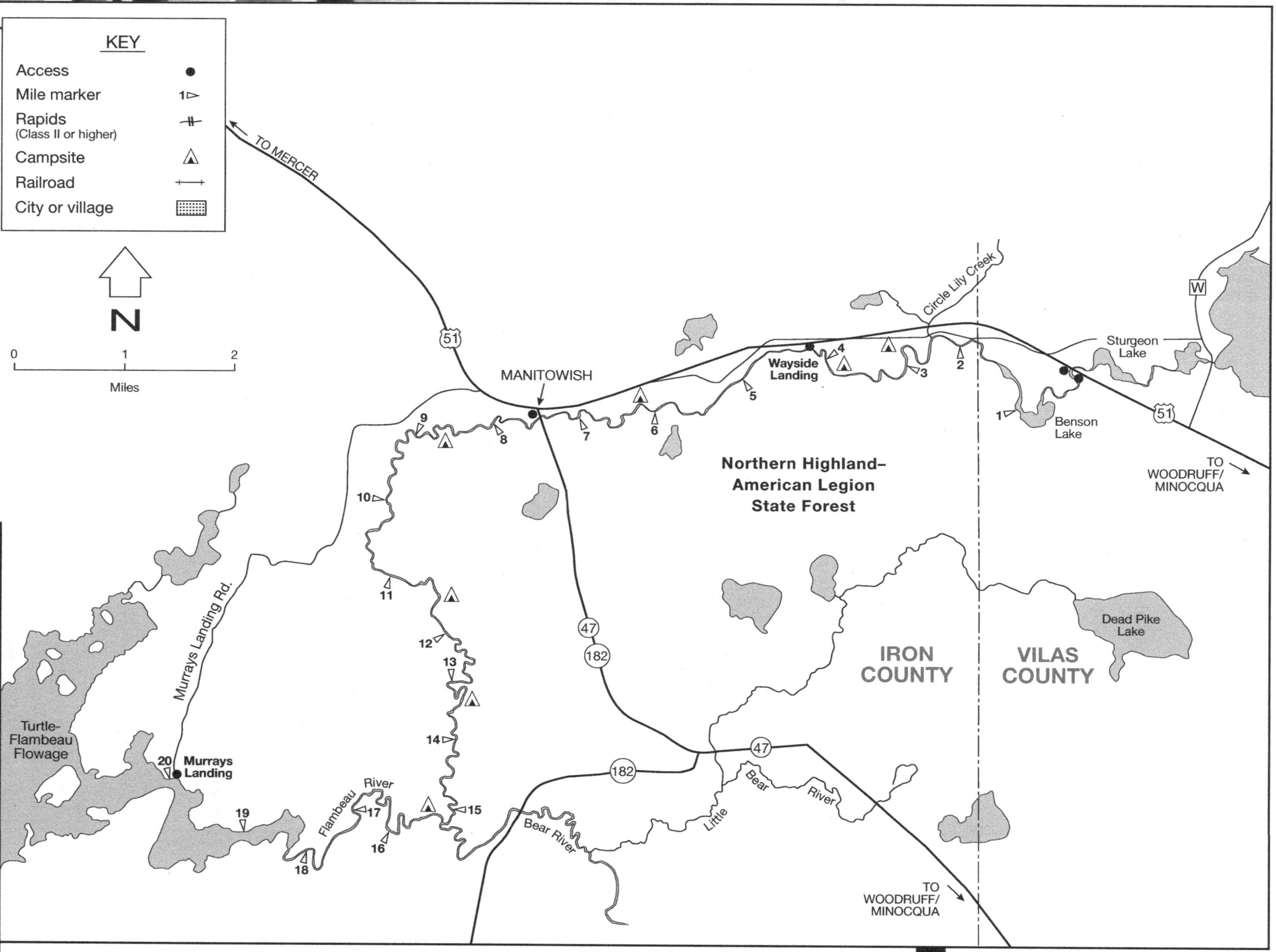

Menominee River

Niagara to Piers Gorge Landing (3.2 Miles)

Wide and often dammed, the Menominee has a couple of short stretches that are popular with highly skilled whitewater paddlers. Its high volume makes it unlike any other Wisconsin whitewater river; in fact, it is often compared to some of the big—and dangerous—rivers of the western and eastern United States.

The stretch downstream from the city of Niagara is definitely a Class III+ (and sometimes more) run, and is appropriate only for advanced and expert kayakers and canoeists. Less skilled boaters can enjoy the stretch by signing up for a guided raft trip. (This is also a good way to scout the river before paddling it.) The surroundings are beautiful, especially the second half of the trip, which can be accessed by a walking trail along the left shore. Boaters are advised to walk this trail before paddling to get an idea of what to expect in Piers Gorge.

Public **camping** is available at the Lake Antoine Park and Campground near Iron Mountain. There are also several private campgrounds in the area.

Water levels are dependent upon releases from the Little Quinnesec Dam at Niagara, and are unpredictable. The river tends to be "flashy" (that is, it quickly gets high, turbulent and hazardous when a lot of water is being released). Levels range from 1,200 cubic feet per second to 20,000. At lower flows, the river demands caution but is doable by advanced whitewater boaters (there is always enough water to paddle). At high flows, however, huge holes and waves develop, and paddlers should content themselves with a scenic walk along the shore. For current flows, contact Kosir's Rapid Rafts (715-757-3431 or www.kosirs.com) or Wildman's Whitewater Ranch (888-813-8254 or www.wildmanranch.com). Both Kosir's and Wildman's offer exciting **raft trips** on the Menominee.

The average **GRADIENT** is a deceptive 12.5 feet per mile.

The **shuttle route** is via Mill Street and Pine Street (in Niagara), then Highway 141, Highway 8 and Piers Gorge Road.

PUT IN on river-right downstream from the **Little Quinnesec Dam** in the city of Niagara. The convenient landing has a paved parking lot and toilets. From River Street (Highway 141), turn onto Pine Street, then turn left on Mill Street.

After the put-in, there are big stone cliffs on the left for a while. Good current flows briskly down to the first rapids.

At Class II+ **Sand Portage Falls** (1.6 miles), the river splits around an island; most of the flow and the biggest rapids are on the right. Because the water here is pushy but relatively nonthreatening, Sand Portage is a wonderful play spot for practicing fast-water ferries and surfing.

Another wide flatwater stretch follows. When you see a sandy **landing** on the left and a horizon line downstream, head for the landing in order to scout the big drops ahead.

Some riffles and Class I rapids precede the intimidating 10-foot drop of Class IV **Missicot Falls** (2.4 miles). The main chute is a tongue about 35 feet from the right shore, with big waves at the bottom. A few yards downstream from the slot lies a huge boulder known as Volkswagen Rock. At higher levels, the rock is covered with water; "Hell Hole" forms just below Volkswagen Rock at lower levels. Paddlers who don't wish to run the falls can portage and re-enter the river on the left.

After Missicot, the river bends sharply to the right into a rocky gorge; the water is very fast here. Within 150 yards, a small rocky island splits the river, with most of the water going left in big waves. One surfing wave here is called Chicken Surfer because it pulls in reluctant kayakers.

The river now bends left through the narrow, rocky gorge and drops several feet in the **Twin Sisters** (Class II–III). There is a highly irregular configuration in the middle, with difficult holes and counter-currents. The best run is on the far right, down a tongue into big waves.

After some tame Class I rapids, the river relents a little before the last drop, **Terminal Surfer.** This doesn't look like much from upstream, but its name is appropriate: There is a huge hole in the middle of a ledge that spans most of the river. The hole is very sticky, and has shredded many an errant raft. After Twin Sisters, work your way to the right so that you can sneak past Terminal Surfer on the far right.

TAKE OUT at the gravel **landing** on the left about 400 yards below Terminal Surfer, alongside a paper-mill pumping station. The landing is off Piers Gorge Road. Paddlers can also take out at the **Highway 8 bridge,** upstream-right, where a parking lot is located.

Piers Gorge Road is 1.1 miles long, ending at a trail head. From here the Piers Gorge Trail runs alongside the river as far upstream as Sand Portage Falls. The gorge is quite beautiful and attracts many tourists. Incidentally, the term "pier" refers to structures built from the shorelines in the 1800s to enable loggers to guide logs downriver.

Other Trips. Another whitewater trip covers about 4 miles at the very beginning of the Menominee. Putting in from Camelback Road near the confluence of the Brule and Michigamme rivers (river-right), paddlers come to a big island after 1.2 miles. On the left of the island is Bull Falls, a long Class II+ rapids that can be run again and again by carrying one's boat back up the island to the head of the rapids. The rest of the trip is flatwater. Take out on the right at the Spread Eagle Boat Landing.

For information about several pleasant quitewater trips on the Menominee (and **canoe/kayak rental**), contact Northwoods Wilderness Outfitters in Iron Mountain, Michigan (906-774-9009 or www.northwoods outfitters.com).

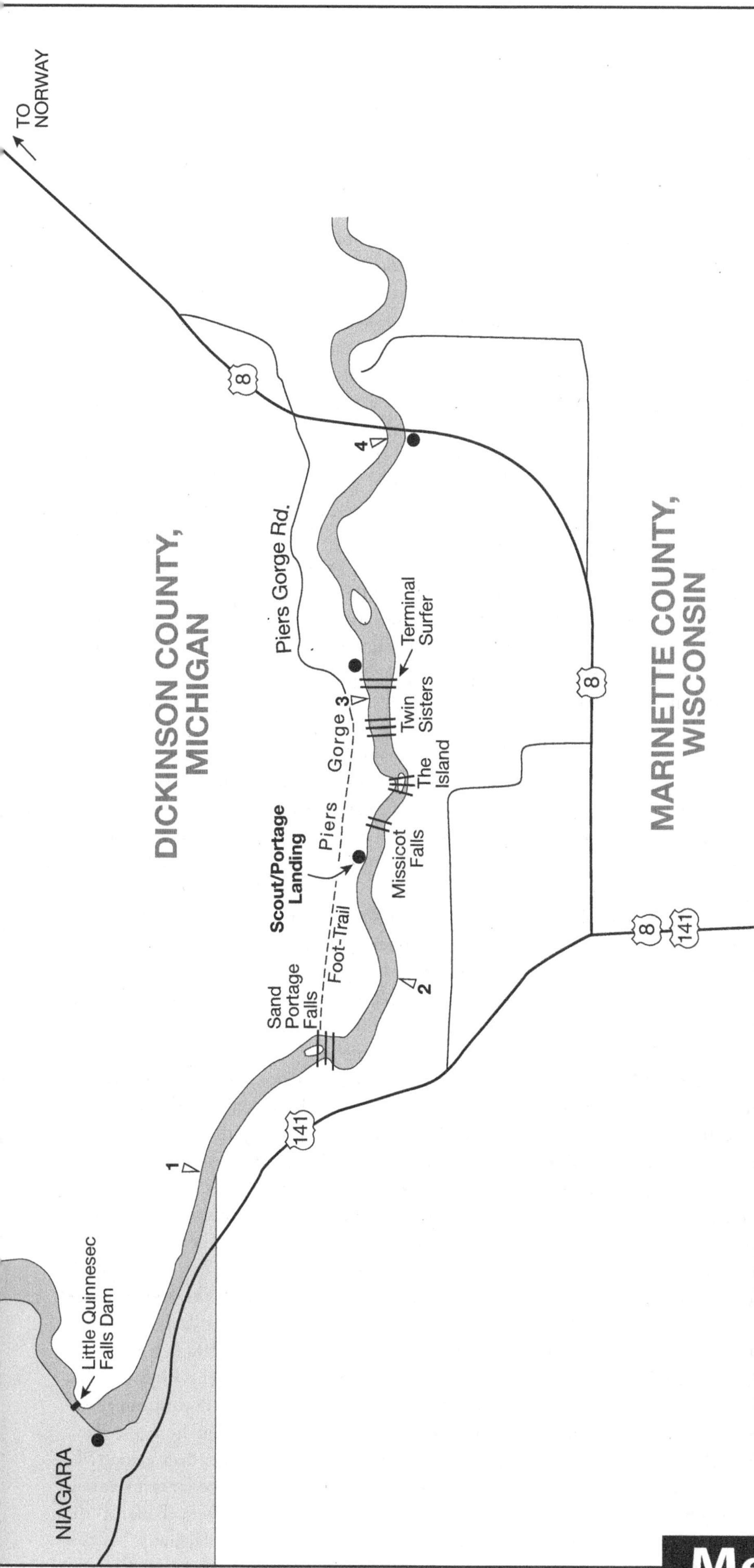

Cliffs along the Menominee below Niagara.

Menominee River

Montreal River

Saxon Falls to Highway 122 (3.2 Miles)

Everything about the Montreal is spectacular—from the uniquely intimidating access at the put-in, through breathtaking canyons and awesome waterfalls both before and after the paddling section. No other stretch of river in the state is as likely to generate such wonderment and delight as this 3.2-miler. Suitable only for physically fit, skilled boaters with whitewater experience, the section is normally a solid Class II run, but it quickly rises in hazard level when the river gets high.

A geologist's dream, the stretch begins in an area of hard, black volcanic basalt. In its course northwestward to Lake Superior, the Montreal has carved its way through the Penokee Range that parallels the shore. Just upstream from the put-in, the river drops tortuously over the many slots carved by Saxon Falls in the ancient rock. Downstream, walls as high as 200 feet are composed of sandstone and conglomerate, and form a sinuous, 2.5-mile canyon where low sloping banks are often found opposite tall cliffs. Rapids predictably occur wherever a cliff rises, as a result of rock periodically falling into the river. You frequently find ledges where hard rock resists the water erosion that has carried away softer adjacent stone.

You can get a good view of the canyon from the rim by walking a path that begins alongside County B three-quarters of a mile east of Highway 122. Be careful: It's a long way down!

Public **camping** is available near the take-out at Saxon Harbor County Park, off Highway 122.

Water-level information may be obtained by calling the Northern States Power Company canoe/kayak line at (715) 893-2213; this is a recorded message that is updated as conditions change. There is usually enough water to run the upper part of the stretch, but in the last mile or so (that is, after the canyon), the river gets wider and the boulder gardens become quite scrapy when the river is low. Thus, it is recommended that paddling be limited to 250 to 300 cfs or higher—unless you don't mind dragging your boat once you leave the canyon. Above 500 cfs, the stretch gets pushy. Some paddlers judge canoeability by the number of fingers of water coming over the last drop of Saxon Falls, just upstream from the put-in: One finger means low (Class II drops in the canyon, scratchy Class I–II boulder gardens thereafter), two means high (Class III), and three means a very wild ride.

Wisconsin's Border Rivers

Except for a short stretch of the St. Louis River in the northwest corner of the state, all the rivers that form part of the northern border of Wisconsin are represented here.

The St. Croix and Menominee are big, wide rivers, while the Montreal and Brule are much narrower and less powerful. Each has its own distinctive character.

- The St. Croix runs through a protected natural setting, with splendid canoe-camping opportunities.
- The Menominee is known for its big drops (popular with rafters and highly skilled paddlers), as well as its many slow impoundments.
- The Brule is isolated, a mostly flatwater habitat for trout.
- The Montreal features spectacular canyon scenery and challenging whitewater.

In addition, several rivers in this book flow into the huge bodies of water that also border Wisconsin: the Bois Brule into Lake Superior (what a view!), and the Oconto, Peshtigo and Menominee into Green Bay.

There are no intermediate accesses, so you must be sure when you begin the trip that your skills are adequate for the entire stretch.

The average **GRADIENT** is 21.8 feet per mile.

The **shuttle route** is via the powerhouse/dam access road, County B and Highway 122.

PUT IN on river-left, just downstream from the **powerhouse.** (**Saxon Falls,** with a total drop of 78 feet—lies just upstream, between the powerhouse and dam. A walk along the top of the bluff to view the falls is well worth the effort.) The 146-step steel staircase that descends the steep bluff to the put-in requires caution. It is cut off from a small parking area by a metal fence and locked gate. It is recommended that long ropes be used to gradually lower canoes down (or alongside) the staircase. Some canoeists indicate that they take along a couple hundred feet of rope and belay their boats down the hillside from a tree on top of the bluff. Once their boats are safely at the bottom, they negotiate the stairs to the put-in. In any case, if you're not careful, your trip can end here before it begins; the put-in is strictly an at-your-own-risk scenario.

The river is only about 40 feet wide at the beginning, and remains that width for the next 2 miles. Canyon walls appear quickly, on the right, in the first bend to the left. Here is located the first of many Class II **drops:** Whenever you see a cliff face ahead, expect a rapids, usually in the form of an irregular ledge. The upper part of the river is basically of a pool/drop nature, with many drops and short, fast pools in between.

Cedar, birch, maple, pine, spruce and hemlock abound on cliff tops and on lower banks. Cliffs are generally of sandstone or conglomerate (with many big boulders mixed in), and assume many shapes: sheer, hollowed-out, sometimes overhanging. Many gravel bars invite a lunch or rest stop, and eagles are a common sight. You're not likely to be fishing on this stretch, but there are trout in the river.

For skilled boaters, the canyon is a joyous experience—one of the most beautiful boat trips imaginable. Eventually, however, the walls disappear, the river doubles in width, and ledge drops are succeeded by a series of long, shallow boulder gardens. The wooded banks become lower and lower, and near the end there are several sizable islands. Finally, current slackens, and the small flowage of the Superior Falls dam begins.

TAKE OUT upstream-left at the **Highway 122 bridge,** where the dam is within view downstream. Awesome **Superior Falls** lies downstream from the dam. With a drop of 90 feet, it's even higher than Saxon Falls, and is certainly worth a visit. Lake Superior isn't far away.

Other trips. Upstream, the West Fork of the Montreal from the Giles Flowage to Highway 2 is narrow, fast, turbulent and dangerous—often solid Class III.

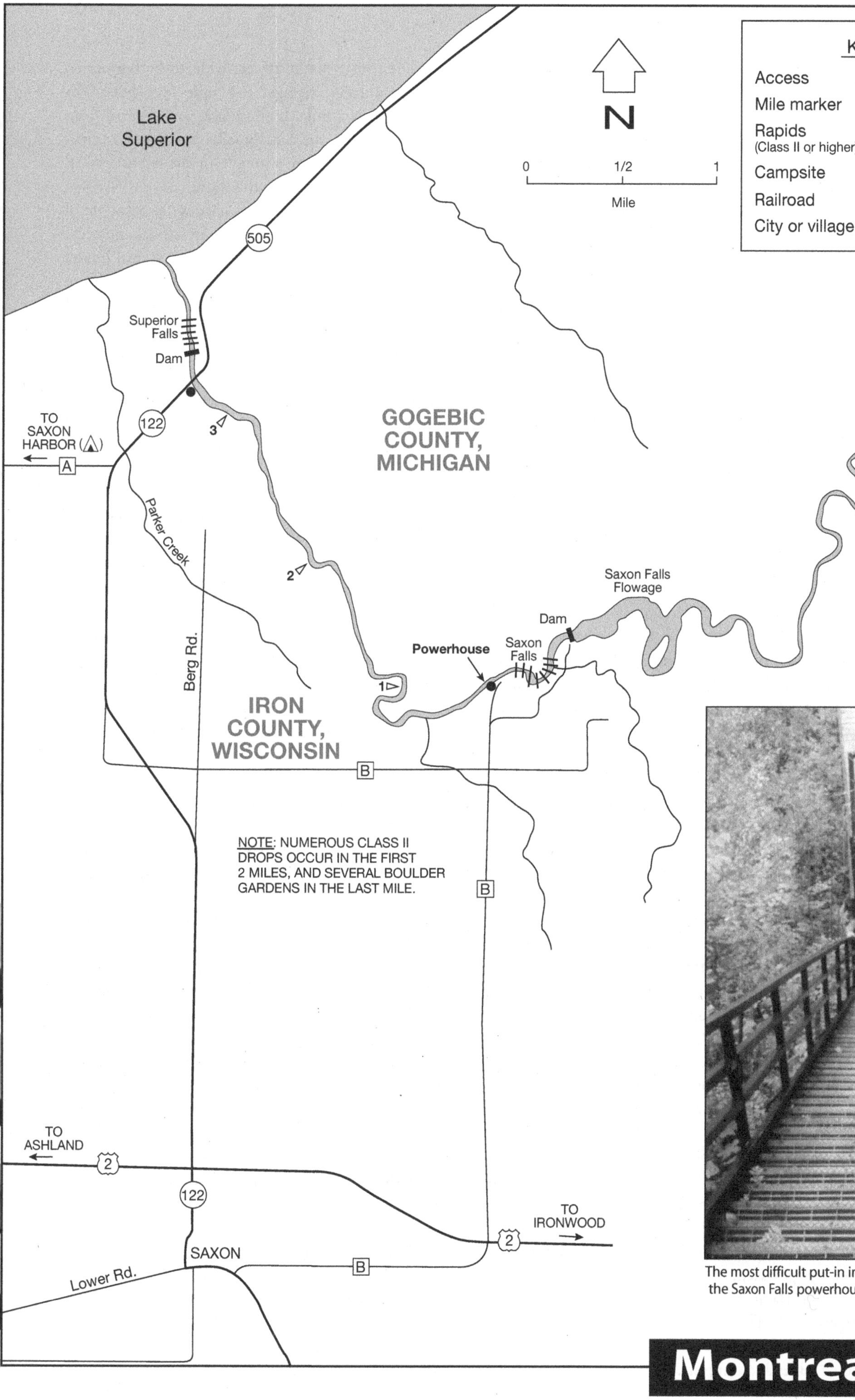

The most difficult put-in in Wisconsin: stairs to the Saxon Falls powerhouse.

Montreal River

Namekagon River 1

Hayward to Springbrook Landing (15.7 Miles)

If the weather and company are good, you are certain to have a fine time on the Namekagon. Despite the nearness of highways and the presence of several dams, the river has a consistently wild character. Numerous campsites along the Namekagon are accessible only to canoeists and make the river ideal for longer, overnight trips. Most of the river is winding and narrow, and many riffles and Class I rapids add a bit of excitement for novices and experienced paddlers alike. The Namekagon invites dawdling—enjoy the scenery and wildlife, and perhaps do some fishing.

Beginning at Namekagon Lake east of Cable, the Namekagon flows 98 miles to its confluence with the St. Croix near Danbury. The river is part of the 252-mile St. Croix National Scenic Riverway, which includes both the St. Croix and Namekagon rivers. The riverway was established in 1968, one of the original eight to be so designated under the National Wild and Scenic Rivers Act.

Visitor centers in Trego and St. Croix Falls provide a wealth of information on the riverway, including helpful maps that indicate current locations of campsites and landings. Downloadable maps are available on the St. Croix National Scenic Riverway website: www.nps.gov/sacn.

Camping: On this first section of the river, a dozen riverside campsites are marked with brown teepee signs; please limit your camping to these designated locations.

Water levels from Hayward downstream are usually adequate for good canoeing all summer. For information on river conditions, call or visit the Namekagon Visitor Center at Trego (715-635-8346). Outfitters in the Hayward and Trego areas also can be contacted.

Average **GRADIENT** is 3.1 feet per mile

The **shuttle route** is via Highway 27 and Highway 63. Several excellent landings on this stretch make it easy for paddlers to vary the length of their trip.

Shuttle service and **canoe/kayak rentals** can be obtained from many outfitters in the area, including the Wild River Inn, Hayward (715-634-2631); Jack's Canoe Rental, Trego (715-635-3300); Log Cabin Resort, Trego (715-635-2959); Pappy's Canoe Rental, Trego (715-466-2568); Pardun's Canoe Rental, Danbury (715-656-7881); and Wild River Outfitters, Grantsburg (715-463-2254). For additional outfitters, see the St. Croix National Scenic Riverway website: www.nps.gov/sacn.

PUT IN at the Hayward DNR ranger station on Highway 27. The landing is on river-left, just across the highway from the station, with parking, toilets, picnic tables and camping.

The river is about 50 feet wide at the beginning, and the current averages 3.5 miles per hour. For approximately a mile, traffic noise can be heard from Highway 27 on the left. Small islands appear right away and are common throughout the section. You'll see signed campsites along the shore.

The river is winding and narrow for a couple of miles, with many riffles (primarily in curves) and occasional rocks that must be dodged. After several houses on the left, the river widens. Fiddlers Creek enters from the right, and Spring Lake Creek from the left. The river passes through a mixed forest and lowland environment, with many high banks.

On the left amid some lowland vegetation, you will see a sign identifying the western end of the Namekagon-Court Oreilles Portage (4 miles). Indians and fur traders once carried their canoes across this 2½ mile trail, which joined the St. Croix and Chippewa river systems. There is a wooden **landing** and walkway near the portage sign. Farther downstream, the mouth of Hurley Creek appears on the left.

Many low islands punctuate the river in the long, wide stretch to **Stinnett Landing** (8.3 miles). At Stinnett the river narrows to about 30 feet at the site of the old bridge and drops a couple of feet with a nice wavy tongue of water down the middle. Nearby is a good fishing hole for muskies and northerns.

Downstream from Stinnett, the river narrows and quickens, with lots of riffles. After the County E bridge, you pass under two impressively designed railroad bridges.

Both upstream and downstream from the bridge at **Groat Landing** (11 miles), there are numerous curves with pleasant riffles and Class I rapids. Select the rock-free routes and ride the wave-trains. In medium to high water, paddlers should be especially cautious here. There are many islands downstream from Groat, and the current is excellent.

Highway 63 is close by on the right for several miles; occasionally, you will see vehicles through the vegetation. Despite the proximity of roads, however, you will encounter only a few houses on the entire stretch.

There is a short, easy boulder garden just downstream from the **North Springbrook Landing** (left, at 13 miles), and several enjoyable riffles and Class I rapids for the next 2.5 miles, especially before and after the Highway 63 bridge.

TAKE OUT at the **Springbrook Landing** (15.7 miles) on the left, or continue downstream toward Trego if you're canoe-camping.

Other trips. The 33 miles of river upstream from Hayward are interrupted at 16.5 and 26.5 miles by the Pacwawong and Phipps dams and their flowages. When water levels are sufficient, most of the stretch has excellent current, tight turns, wild shorelines, many riffles and Class I rapids, and trout.

Namekagon River 1

An inviting campsite on the Namekagon

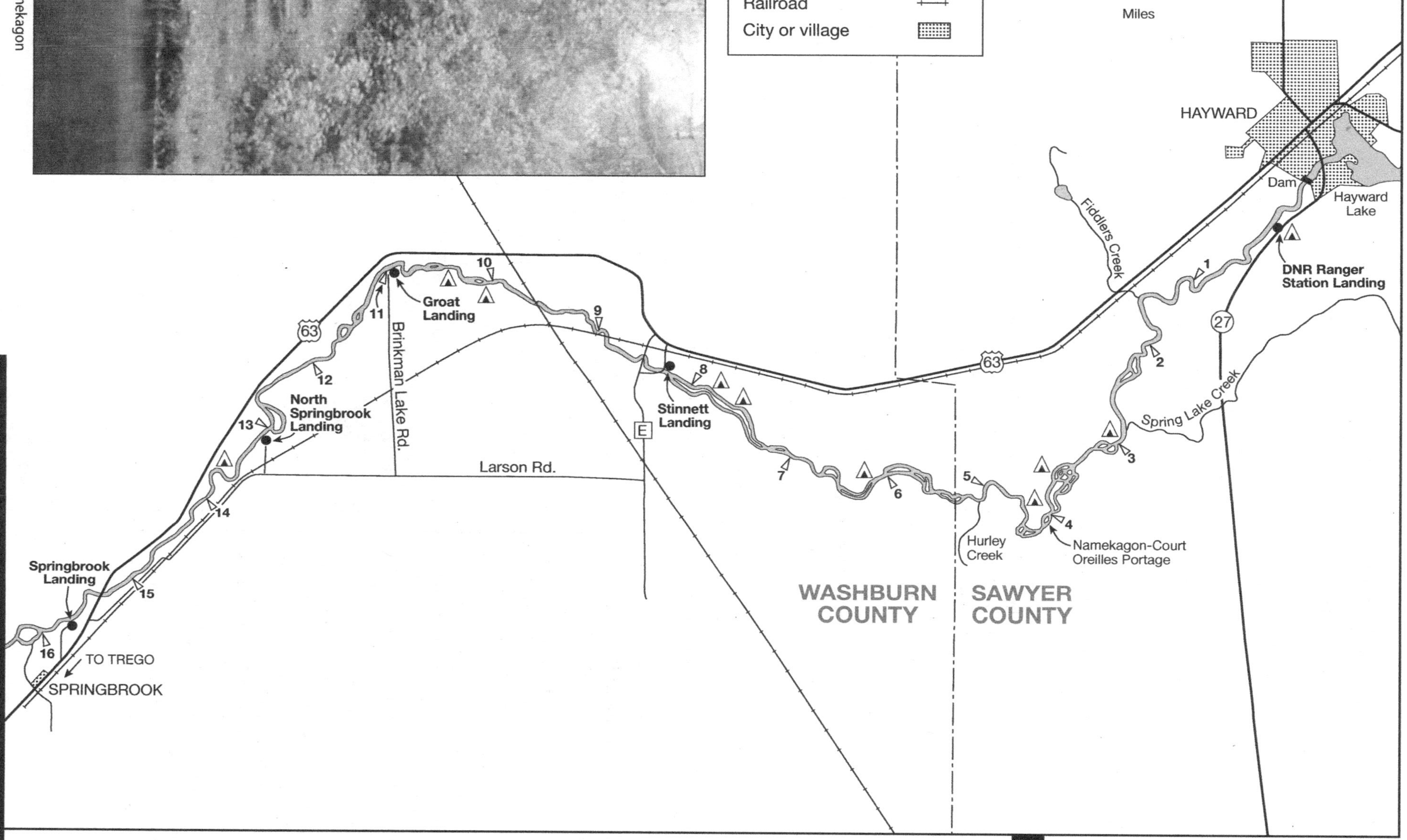

Namekagon River 2

Springbrook Landing to Trego Visitor Center (12 Miles)

The river continues to be paralleled and occasionally crossed by Highway 63, but the road doesn't detract from the tranquillity of this trip. Paddled in conjunction with the 15.7 miles below Hayward, this section makes a great two- or three-day canoe-camping venture. Fast water running through narrow stretches alternates with slower water in wider spots, and high banks are common. Dwellings are infrequent. One of the more popular fishing areas is found on this stretch.

Camping: At least half a dozen primitive campsites maintained by the Park Service are located along the shoreline between Springbrook and the take-out. As on the rest of the river, federal and state governments and private individuals own the shoreline property.

Water levels are almost always adequate for good paddling. For information on current river conditions, call the Namekagon Visitor Center at Trego (715-635-8346).

The average **GRADIENT** is 1.6 feet per mile.

The **shuttle route** is simplicity itself: Highway 63. For a list of outfitters that provide shuttle service and **canoe rental,** see Namekagon 1.

PUT IN at **Springbrook Landing,** on river-left, accessed from Highway 63.

Within the first 4 miles, a half-dozen creeks enter on both sides of the river, alternating between left and right. One of them, Bean Brook, is a good trout stream.

Occasional riffles and rapids continue all the way to the big oxbow. Two houses on the left precede the beginning of the oxbow, with a wide right-hand bend. As the river widens and slows, the Big Bend Landing appears on river left. Finally, a house on the right signals the halfway point of the oxbow, and the river swings back to the left. Fishermen are fond of the oxbow area.

The river swings west and passes under the North Road bridge near Earl. The **Earl Park Landing** and campsite are located downstream-right from the bridge.

After Earl, the river gets narrower and more circuitous again, with riffles and islands. A Class I rapids precedes the Highway 63 bridge a mile downstream from Earl.

After the Highway 63 bridge, the river makes another big bend, and you will see railroad tracks on the left. After a series of sand banks on the right, the river passes under Highway 63 again.

TAKE-OUT: Not long after the Highway 63 bridge, the Namekagon Visitor Center at Trego appears on the left at a wayside **landing** (12 miles). The head of the Trego flowage (and the virtual end of current) begins nearby. Take the time to stop by the visitor center to talk with the staff and to look over the displays, books, postcards, maps and other items of interest.

If you wish to continue paddling, you will pass under several more bridges in short order. Immediately upstream from the Highway 53 bridges, on the right, is the **landing** for Trego Town Park (12.5 miles), a very quiet campground. Paddling all the way to the dam at the end of the flowage adds 5 miles of very slow water.

Canoeists who wish to continue paddling on the Lower Namekagon without the tedium of the flowage may do so by taking out at the visitor center and putting back in at County K below the dam.

Biggest Fish in the World?

You can't help but be impressed by the sheer size of Hayward's huge muskie—143 feet long and 4½ stories high—poised in mid-leap. Constructed of fiberglass, it's part of the Fishing Hall of Fame and Museum located at the junction of Highway 27 and County B, near the Namekagon River.

Inside the behemoth is a collection of 400 mounted trophy fish. The best part of a climb through the huge muskie, however, is the observation deck in its mouth. It's a great place for photos.

Avid fishermen will love the collection of 300 antique outboard motors, thousands of lures, hundreds of vintage rods and reels, and many other fishing-related items, which are housed in the five other buildings on the site.

The nonprofit museum is open from April 15 through November 1. An admission fee is charged to maintain the enterprise.

The Namekagon: winding and riffly.

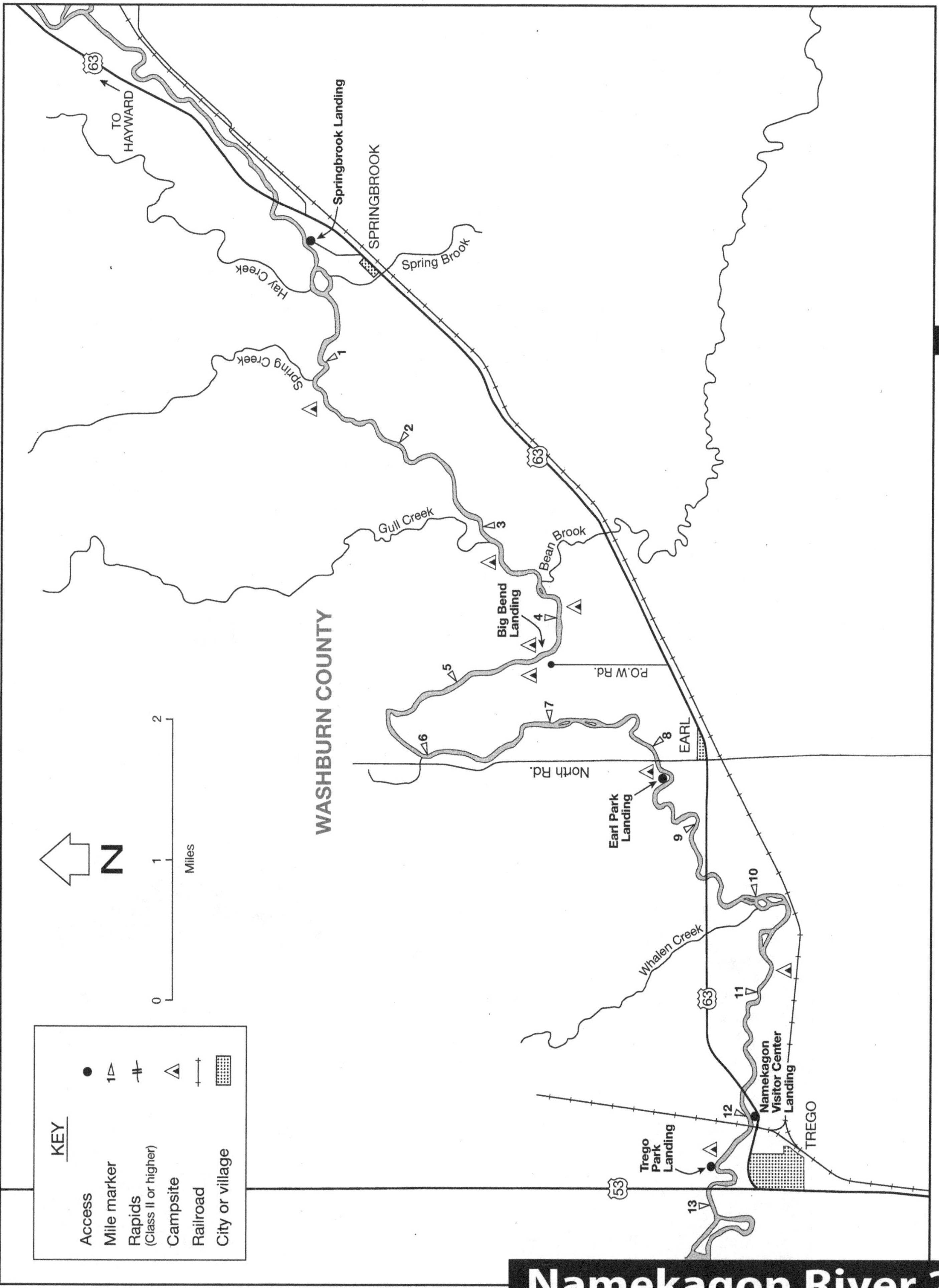

Namekagon River 2

Namekagon River 3

County K to McDowell Bridge Landing (20 Miles)

Below the Trego Flowage, the wild Lower Namekagon flows through 31 miles of remote, undeveloped countryside before joining the St. Croix. The landscape is varied and includes many high sand banks topped with pines. Lowland areas that abound in willow and ash alternate with upland forest where maple, oak, birch and aspen grow. This area of the river is rich in birds—especially eagles, osprey, herons and ducks—and you are almost sure to encounter deer, turtles and other animals. Many fishermen insist that this is the best part of the river for catching muskie, northern, walleye, bass and even sturgeon. (The name Namekagon comes from an Indian word meaning "place where sturgeon are abundant.")

Many designated **campsites** are situated along the river. Camping is also available at the Trego Town Park.

Water levels downstream from Trego are almost always adequate for good paddling. For specific information, call the visitor center at Trego (715-635-8346).

The average **GRADIENT** is 3.5 feet per mile.

The best **shuttle route** is via County K, Highway 77, Bridge Road and River Road. Whispering Pines, Howell and Fritz Landings can all be used to vary trip length. For a list of outfitters that provide shuttle service and **canoe/kayak rental,** see Namekagon 1.

PUT IN at the **landing** alongside County K, not far downstream from the Trego Flowage dam. Good parking is provided.

The river starts out narrow, winding and riffly. The shoreline is heavily wooded, and islands and sand banks are frequent. (Canoeists are asked to stay off sand banks in order to prevent erosion and to protect the nesting places of turtles.) Rocks in the stream bed are easy to avoid if you watch where you're going.

After 1.5 miles, a stream comes in on the left (in the middle of a bend), followed by a big island. McKenzie Creek comes in from the right a mile after the island.

Farther downstream, Christensen Creek enters from the right (with a house near the mouth), followed half a mile later by the **Whispering Pines Landing** on the right (9.5 miles).

The river widens and slows a little after Whispering Pines, goes through a lowland area for a while, then returns to higher wooded banks.

In a right-hand bend (12.2 miles), Casey Creek and another McKenzie Creek enter from the left; a house appears on the bluff between the creek mouths.

A mile downstream, deer trails can be seen on both sides of the river, and canoeists often surprise deer fording the stream bed.

Howell Landing, which has campsites and water, appears at 14.2 miles, followed by the Highway 77 bridge (17 miles) and **Fritz Landing** (18.1 miles). Fritz is on the left after a small island and is reached from River Landing Road.

TAKE OUT on the right at the **McDowell Bridge Landing** (20 miles). There are a couple of cabins on the right a half mile upstream from the bridge.

High sandy bluffs are a common sight on the Namekagon after Trego.

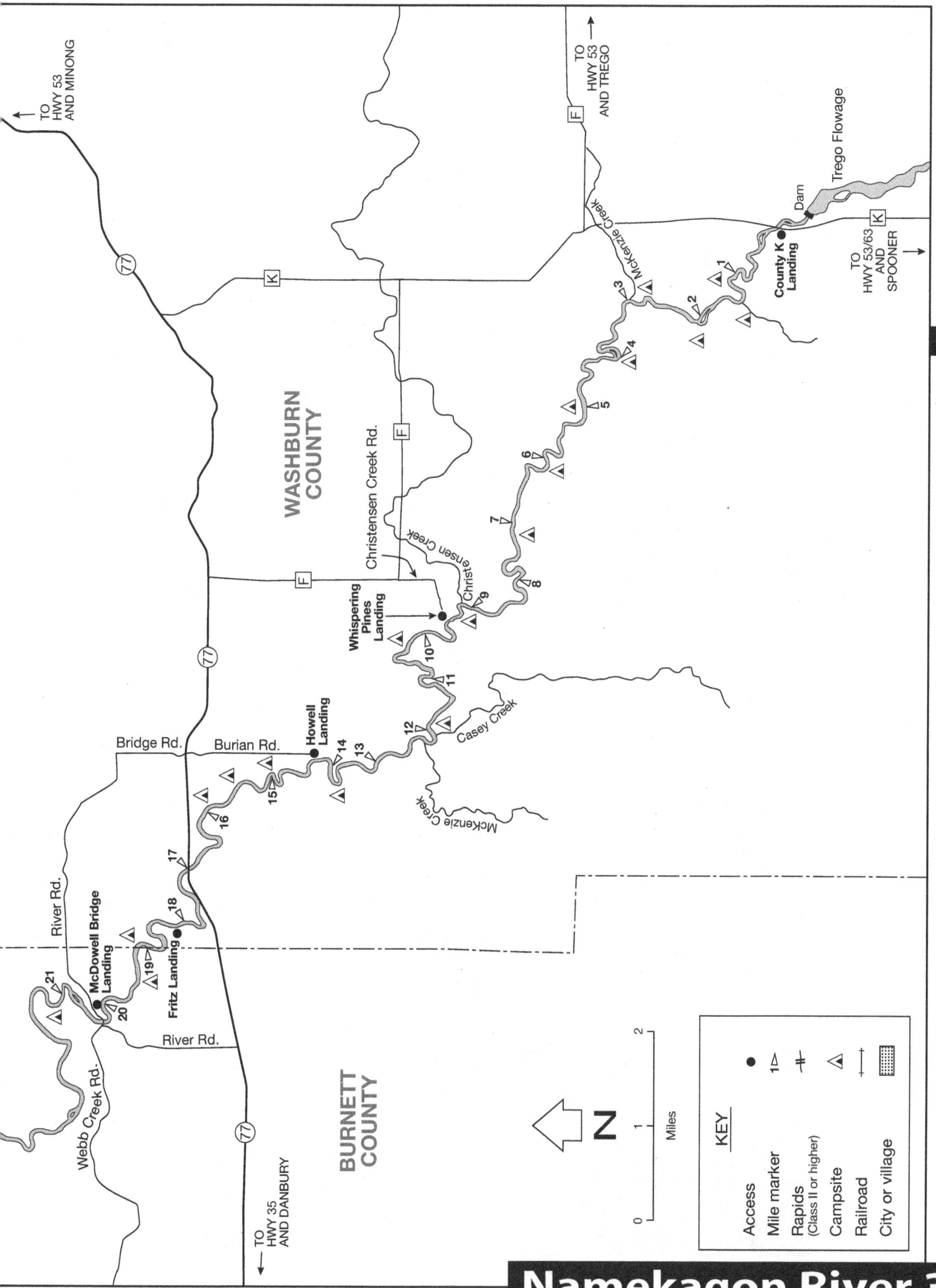

Namekagon River 3

Namekagon River 4

McDowell Bridge Landing to Riverside Landing (15 Miles)

The final leg of the Namekagon provides a sample of all it has to offer, including high banks and lowlands, quietwater and rapids. The final portion of the river tends to be wider than the upstream parts, but it is still wild, remote and curvy, with lovely sand banks and stands of pine. At its widest, it is still smaller than the broad expanses of the St. Croix. Pines and mixed hardwoods are dominant in the woods, fishing remains good, and some of the best rapids on the river are found near the end.

Twenty-two **campsites** are situated along this stretch, providing a choice of settings.

Water levels are almost always adequate for enjoyable paddling. For information on current water conditions, call the Namekagon Visitor Center at Trego (715-635-8346).

The **GRADIENT** averages 2 feet per mile.

The best **shuttle route** is via River Road, Highway 77, Riverside Cutoff, Springbrook Trail and Highway 35. For a list of outfitters that provide shuttle service and **canoe rental,** see Namekagon 1.

PUT IN at the **McDowell Bridge Landing,** river-right. Buildings appear on both sides just downstream from the bridge.

The river widens and slows after McDowell, forming a couple of big bends with large islands. Webb Creek enters from the left.

A major tributary—the Totogatic River—appears on the right, followed by a couple of cabins. Shortly thereafter, the river flows under the Namekagon Trail Bridge (6.5 miles); a **landing** is located 150 feet downstream-left from the bridge.

There are some pleasant riffles after the bridge, especially in the long bootlike bend. The river continues to widen gradually as it approaches the St. Croix.

In the last 1.5 miles before the confluence, the gradient increases in pitches, resulting in several long, shallow riffles and Class I rapids, especially after the mouth of Dogtown Creek on the left.

There are several cabins on the left as the St. Croix draws nearer. Finally, the Namekagon merges into the St. Croix at 11.3 miles.

In the remaining 3.5 miles before the take-out, there are several long Class I rapids on the St. Croix, especially in the main (left) channel around Big Island.

Not long after the end of Big Island and the mouth of Hay Creek (on the right), the Highway 35 bridge appears (15 miles).

TAKE OUT at the **Riverside Landing** upstream-right from the bridge. A county wayside with toilets, water and picnic facilities is located here. There is also a USFS landing downstream-right with a campsite.

The Namekagon has a consistently wild character that invites exploration.

Namekagon River 4

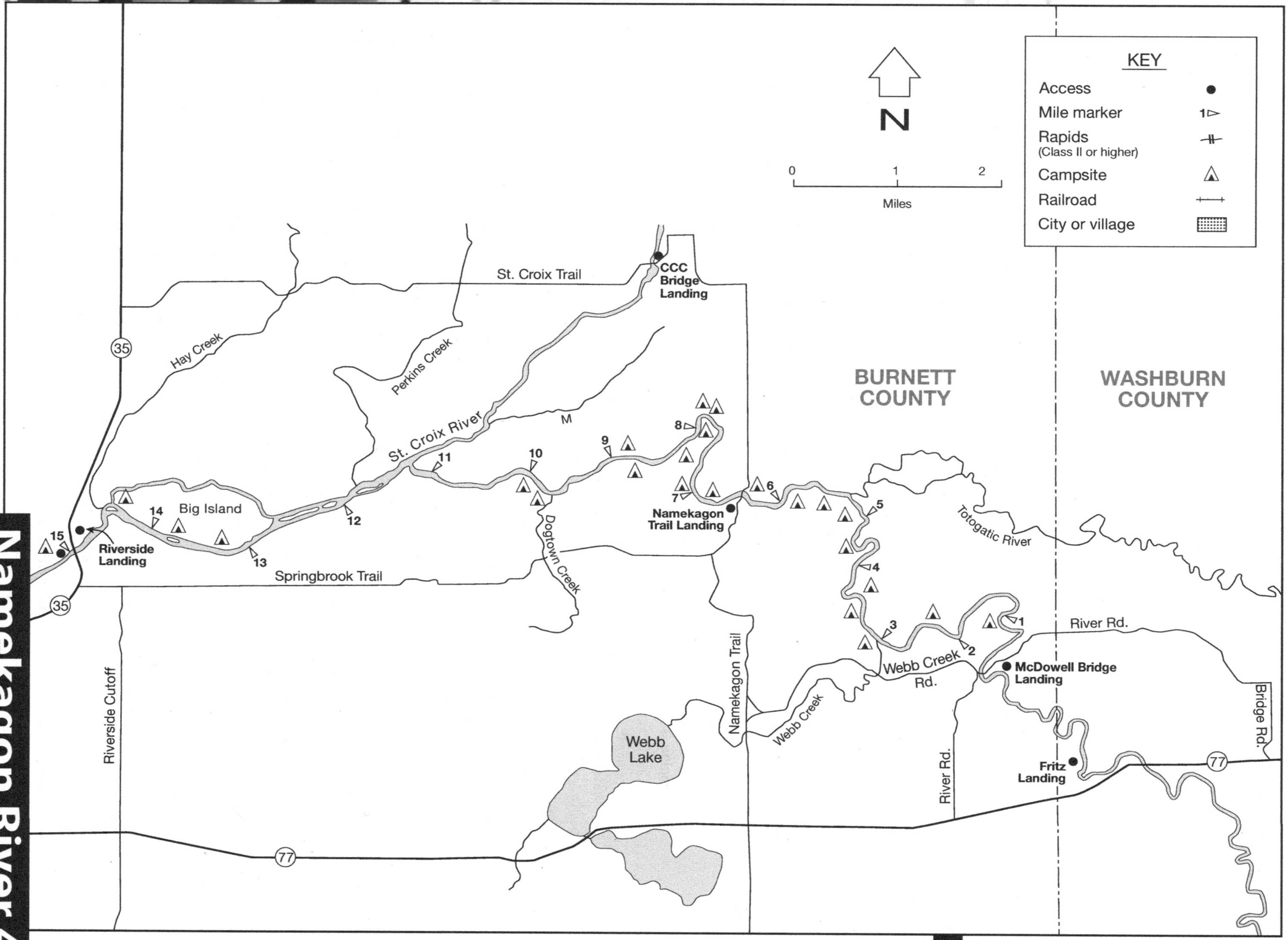

Oconto River 1

Tar Dam Road to Bagley Rapids (9.5 Miles)

Originating in northern Oconto County near Lakewood, the Oconto River flows through varied countryside—lowland swamp, upland forest, agricultural fields and even an urban setting—before emptying into Green Bay near the city of Oconto. Most of the upper portion of the river is too brushy for pleasant paddling, and much of the stretch from Chute Pond to Underwood meanders through bottomland where fallen trees are common. The remaining stretches, however, are highly recommended for both whitewater paddlers (Tar Dam Road to Bagley Rapids) and quietwater boaters (Underhill to the Bay).

When the water level is sufficient, the stretch beginning at Tar Dam Road offers a joyous succession of Class II boulder gardens, sometimes nonstop for as much as 20 minutes at a time. Definitely not for novices, this section has a consistently high gradient. Thus, the rapids are frequent, but the river gets "bony" when the weather has been dry.

Fallen trees blocking the river can sometimes be a hazard or annoyance; be alert for strainers and scout all locations where downed trees are a possibility (for example, at the Krammer Dam site). High water raises the danger level. Most of the land on this stretch is privately owned.

Camping is available near the take-out at the Bagley Rapids Campground, and farther downstream at Chute Pond County Park.

Water levels are not easy to assess since there is no nearby gauging system. Two rules of thumb are useful, however: If the Wolf River is running at moderate to high levels, the Oconto probably has enough water for an enjoyable paddle; or if plenty of water is flowing over the river ledges at the Bagley Rapids Campground, the water is high enough to paddle.

The average **GRADIENT** is a vigorous 21 feet per mile.

The best **shuttle route** is via Tar Dam Road (Forest Road 2104), Highway 32, Bagley Rapids Campground Road and Lower Bagley Road. (Note the alternate put-in described below).

PUT IN downstream right from the **Tar Dam Road bridge** (named after the tarred log-driving dam that used to be located here). This is private property, so ask permission from the nearby owner. There are a number of homes and cabins in the area of the bridge; dwellings continue throughout the stretch but don't detract from the wilderness quality. The river starts off narrow and intimate. The shoreline is mostly covered with deciduous hardwoods.

A boulder-strewn **rapids** (easy Class II) starts a few hundred yards downstream from the bridge, winding around a few curves. Then a stretch of flatwater leads down to the Forest Road 2310 bridge, an **alternate put-in** with good access upstream-right (1.1 miles).

After another Class II **boulder garden,** a flatwater stretch leads to **Loon Rapids** (2 miles), which begins on a left-hand turn with a cabin on the right. There are a couple of curving pitches, a little more difficult than previous rapids. Loon Rapids Road may be seen on the right. Flatwater takes you to a railroad bridge and beyond, except for a short rapids just before the bridge.

As the Highway 32 bridge approaches, there is a long, winding, high-gradient Class II rapids that finally ends after a right-hand bend down to the bridge. An **access** is located at the bridge, upstream-left, with a small parking area. After a brief quietwater respite, rapids resume under the bridge.

Another brief calm spot comes before the iron bridge just downstream from Highway 32. Then a very long, continuous Class II **boulder garden** begins with no let-up for a long time. Houses are fairly common along the rapids.

Finally, there's another short spell of quietwater, signaling the approach of the old **Krammer Dam** site (5.5 miles). After the river constricts and rapids resume, the dam site appears—a large rock outcropping comes out from the right, with boulders on the left, a narrow channel and a turbulent drop. Get out on river-right to scout. This solid Class II **rapids** has big waves, curlers and boulders to avoid. An easy boulder garden follows.

A long stretch of flatwater takes you underneath the County W bridge, past a number of islands, under a railroad bridge and down toward **Bagley Rapids Campground.** There are no homes for a while after County W.

As you approach the campground (9.5 miles), riffles and rapids resume. Campers and trout fishermen may be seen walking the paths along the river, especially on the left (this trail can be used for scouting/portaging). Not long after the beginning of the rapids, there is a difficult **constriction and ledge** (solid Class II), with a total drop of about 7 feet. The first part has a clearly defined tongue of water, but the ledge that immediately follows is more difficult; it is usually best run on a diagonal to the left.

TAKE OUT at the **campground** on the left if you are a registered camper, or a couple hundred yards downstream on river-left, where a 400-foot path comes down to the river from a **river-access** parking lot off Lower Bagley Road. After the ledge at Bagley Rapids Campground, the river bends right, then left past four tiny islands alongside the left bank; the take-out path comes immediately after the fourth island, before the river begins bending back to the right again. (The take-out opening is not easy to spot from the river, so you might want to hang a bandanna or other marker from a limb before beginning your trip.) Be sure to get out at this point because a Class III drop lies ahead.

Other trips: Class I–II rapids continue for a half-mile below the campground ledge, coming eventually to a spot where the river-left trail ends at several private homes. Here there is a very irregular and complex 4-foot ledge (Class III) with a loud roar that can be heard upstream. Because the drop is so difficult, only advanced paddlers should consider running it. The property owner on the left has indicated that paddlers may scout and/or portage the drop; if you do so, please be considerate. Rapids continue several hundred yards downstream, and shortly thereafter the flowage for Chute Pond begins. There are **take-outs** at the Kingston Road bridge (upstream-left) and the Chute Pond dam (upstream-left).

Upstream from Tar Dam Road, the U.S. Forest Service occasionally removes obstructive brush in the stretch from County T to Sullivan Springs Road (Forest Road 2330)—a slow, meandering lowland-hardwood section that includes a couple of small rapids. According to the USFS, a good short trip is from Smyth Road (FR 2101) to Sullivan Springs Road. There's an attractive covered bridge on Smyth Road.

Good action at the Krammer Dam site.

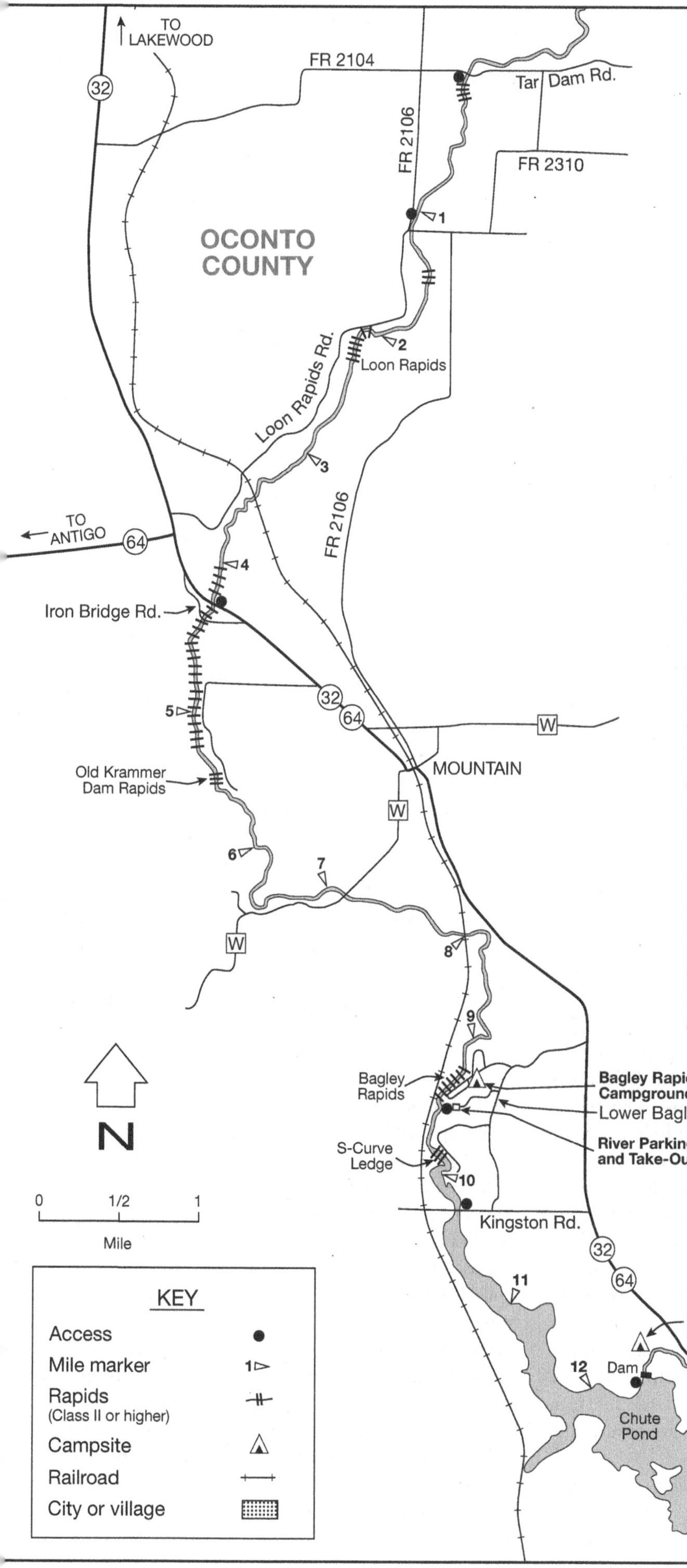

Oconto River 2

Underhill to Oconto Falls (16.8 Miles)

This section of the Oconto, an excellent stretch for novices and quietwater paddlers, can readily be broken into smaller portions because of the many good access points. The river is heavily wooded on both sides (hemlock, birch, maple, cedar, alder, elm, etc.), and there are many pleasant riffles to add a bit of excitement. Homes and cabins dot the shoreline here and there, but are not plentiful enough to take away the feeling of isolation. Fishermen are frequently encountered, angling for bass, northerns and panfish. On hot, humid days, boaters and inner-tubers enjoy swimming in the deeper pools.

Water levels are usually adequate for enjoyable paddling. If the riffle underneath the Pulcifer bridge (County C) is too shallow to be canoeable, you will find yourself scraping in other riffle areas between Underhill and County BB. After Highway 32 there is always plenty of water because of the back-up from the dam at Oconto Falls. Stay off the river when the water is high. Check the gauge near Gillett (#04071000) on the USGS website; see "Water Levels" in the introduction.

The **GRADIENT** averages 1.7 feet per mile.

The best **shuttle route** for the whole 16.8 miles is via County V, County U and Highway 22. Shorter trips are from Underhill to Pulcifer, 5 miles; Pulcifer to County BB, 3.5 miles; Pulcifer to Highway 32, 6.3 miles; and Highway 32 to Oconto Falls, 5.5 miles.

PUT IN at the **city park** in Underhill, several hundred yards upstream from the County V bridge. The park (located next to the Underhill baseball field) has a concrete boat ramp, picnic facilities and toilets.

Mud banks line the river, which flows with a steady current for the next 11 miles. Occasional sand and gravel banks appear about a mile downstream from the bridge, along with the first of many riffles. You'll encounter the first houses after Underhill in a left-hand bend at the Shawano/Oconto county line (2.2 miles).

The Highway 22 bridge (3.9 miles) comes into view soon after a couple of big bends in the river and some houses on the right shore. Between the Highway 22 bridge and Pulcifer, several gravel bars jut out from the right shore, and Highway 22 parallels the river on the left. Approaching Pulcifer (5 miles), the river is fairly wide and deep, and a high sand bank precedes the S-curve leading to the County C bridge. There are pleasant riffles upstream from the bridge and directly under it.

Short Jaunts in the Fall

Two short hiking trails near the upper Oconto are fun any time of the year but are especially so when the leaves are turning in the fall. Both are easily accessed from Highway 32.

The next time you see the sign for the Quartz Hill Trail, a mile south of Carter, take a few minutes to stop and walk one or both of its two sections. The half-mile eastern section leads to the top of McCaslin Mountain. Interpretive signs along the way explain how Indians used the quartz here for making tools. (McCaslin Mountain, incidentally, is a monadnock, like Rib Mountain in the Wausau area.) The three-quarter-mile western section of the trail leads to the site of an old fire tower.

Farther south, the Chute Pond Overlook Trail (3.5 miles south of Mountain) is less than a mile long, winding through heavily wooded hills and providing an occasional view of the flowage below.

A quiet afternoon on the Oconto Falls flowage.

An excellent **access** is located at Pulcifer Sportsman's Park immediately after the bridge on the left, with picnic facilities and parking. This is a good place to put in, take out or have lunch. Fortunately, the dangerous old low-head dam that used to be found just downstream has been removed.

For the next 3.5 miles, all the way to County BB, the river is consistently about 75 feet wide, and there are many wavy riffles; here and there a rock needs to be avoided. Homes and cottages are sparse. The current continues to be steady to County BB, but then begins to slow. There is an excellent **access** upstream-left at the County BB bridge, with good parking. The grassy area at the bridge makes this a good place for lunch or a relaxation break.

Between County BB and Highway 32 the river passes beneath a beautiful railroad bridge—very high and supported by elaborate stone piers.

A pleasant wayside **landing** is located upstream-right at the Highway 32 bridge, with toilets, picnic tables, water and a sandy boat landing. From here, paddlers have to provide most of the momentum by themselves; the 5.5 miles from Highway 32 to Oconto Falls have virtually no current. Homes, cabins and motorboat docks become more frequent as Oconto Falls approaches. After Larson Bridge (on Larson Bridge Road) the river widens considerably, and it becomes obvious that you're in a flowage.

If you choose to paddle all the way to Oconto Falls, the best **TAKE-OUT** is at the public **landing** on the left side of the lake, alongside Highway 22, upstream from the dam. Another **landing** (Waterside Park and Boat Landing) is located upstream a short distance, on the right side of the flowage.

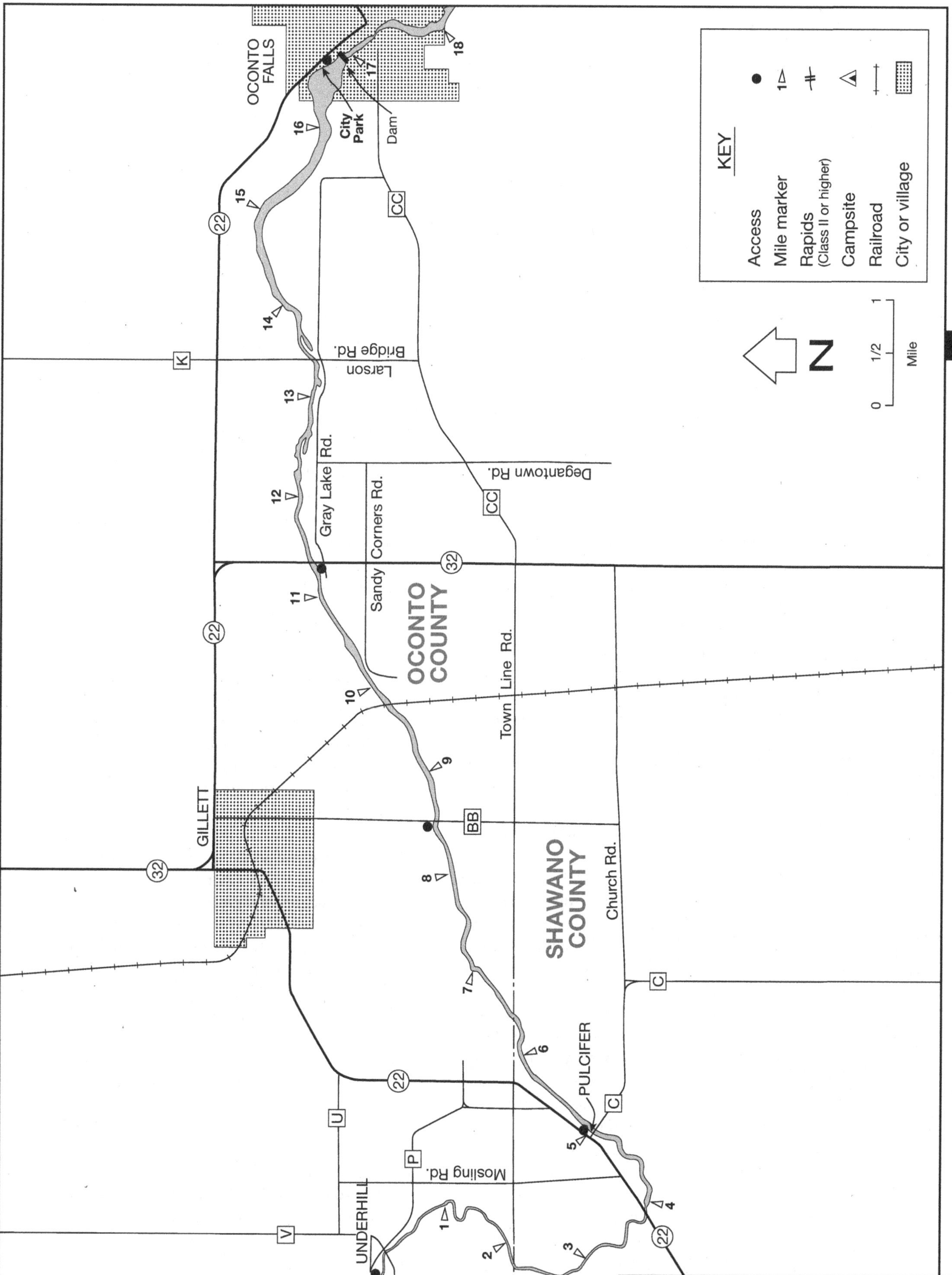

Oconto River 2

Oconto River 3

Highway 141 to the Bay (12 Miles)

The final leg of the Oconto includes a pleasant mix of wooded shoreline and developed surroundings. Designated the Lower Oconto River by the DNR, this once-polluted stretch was cleaned up in the 1980s and now supports a thriving population of steelhead, salmon, rainbows, brown trout, smallmouth, walleye, northern, bluegills, perch and crappies. Most of the 12 miles flow through relatively undeveloped countryside, and the half-hour of paddling through the city of Oconto is an interesting contrast to the rest of the trip.

You will find excellent riverside **camping** in the city of Oconto at Holtwood Park, a unique area that is almost completely surrounded by the river. Oconto County's North Bay Shore Recreation Area—about 10 miles north of the take-out—also has camping facilities.

Water levels are largely dependent upon the volume of release from the Machickanee Flowage dam at Stiles. Thanks to licensing agreements, Oconto Electric Cooperative now provides constant "run of the river" releases from the Stiles dam, assuring stable fish habitat and dependable paddling downstream. Don't paddle, however, when the river is high and swift. Check the gauge near Oconto (#0407 1765) on the USGS website; see "Water Levels" in the introduction.

The average **GRADIENT** is 1.2 feet per mile.

The best **shuttle route** for the complete trip is via Highway 141, Stiles Road/North River Road, Mott Street/Main Street through Oconto, Harbor Road and Bayshore Road. The trip can be shortened by using the access at the County J bridge, the North River Road Landing or the landing in Oconto.

PUT IN upstream-right at the **Machickanee Public Boat Landing** at the Highway 141 bridge near the village of Stiles, not far downstream from the dam (locals call the flowage Stiles Pond). Excellent parking is provided. Wading fishermen are fond of this part of the river.

The river begins fairly narrow, with good current. The current continues throughout the stretch, but gets progressively weaker as you approach Green Bay. There are many gentle bends and occasional small islands and riffles in the first couple of miles, and the mud banks are heavily wooded. During the spring and late-fall runs of steelhead and the mid-summer runs of rainbow, you are likely to spot many fish in the water; sightings of huge salmon are frequent also.

Farther downstream, the river straightens somewhat and becomes wider and shallower. Power lines cross overhead just before several islands, followed by the mouth of the Little River (a good trout stream) on the left (2.6 miles). A bridge crosses the Little River near its mouth.

The County J bridge (3.5 miles) crosses the river not long afterward, with an **access** on the left downstream. Under the bridge a gravel-bar constriction speeds up the flow. Nearby you'll see the Couillardville Town Hall, named after a pioneer family that settled in the area. A road runs along the river on the right for a while, and more houses come into view.

Downstream from the County J bridge, the **North River Road Landing** is found on the left (good parking). A long, rather straight stretch follows.

Old wooden pilings on the right and a rocky wing on the left mark the location of an old logging-era railroad grade and bridge (6 miles). A big slough appears on the right (7 miles) where an old oxbow has been cut off; the new channel goes straight ahead, toward a log home on the left shore, then bends to the right.

Suzie's Rapid (named after a Stockbridge Indian woman who once lived near here) appears downstream at 7.6 miles—a Class I S-curve with rocks and gravel bars. Afterward, the river becomes deeper and slower.

Soon, **Copper Culture Park** appears on the left at the west edge of Oconto. A museum at the site commemorates the prehistoric people who left copper artifacts here.

In the city of Oconto, there is a large promontory of land surrounded by the right-bending river. Inside this promontory is **Holtwood Park,** which offers camping and a boat landing. Oconto is a very historic city. Here you will find the prehistoric burial grounds of the Copper Culture people, together with the world's first building of the First Church of Christ Scientist and historic structures of the logging era, when Oconto had seven saw mills. The river now passes alongside motels, etc., then bends back to the left under the Highway 41 bridge; a city boat **landing** is located on the right where this left-hand bend begins.

Just downstream from the Highway 41 bridge is an old railroad bridge with a geared turntable. Houses appear on the right for a while. On the left, along the lowland woods, are some old wooden pilings.

Two more bridges appear downstream, followed by the huge Ajax Island (10.5 miles). Immediately after the island, there is a sewage treatment plant on the left, then a yacht club and marina, and many houses

TAKE-OUT: Just before the mouth of the river, there's an excellent public boat **landing** on the left at Breakwater Park, with a shelter, toilets, picnic tables and plenty of parking. A breakwater and a causeway extend into the bay from the banks of the river—a popular spot for fishermen.

Wisconsin's First Copper Craftsmen

As you approach the city of Oconto on the Oconto River, you pass a fascinating archaeological site: Copper Culture Park, a 4,500-year-old site where Indians of the Archaic Period buried their dead.

The people of this culture fished, hunted and gathered their food. They also fashioned ornaments, tools and weapons from copper—and were perhaps the first Americans to do so. They found the raw material for these artifacts in the copper country of northern Michigan near Lake Superior, and then heated and hammered it into useful objects. The center of the old Copper Culture is thought to have been in Wisconsin and the Upper Peninsula, but its copper products have been found in Minnesota, Ontario and elsewhere—suggesting a propensity for trade.

A museum on the grounds of the small park contains dioramas and displays about the Copper Culture people. Parking, toilets and picnic facilities are available. The park is also accessible by car from Highway 22.

Oconto River 3

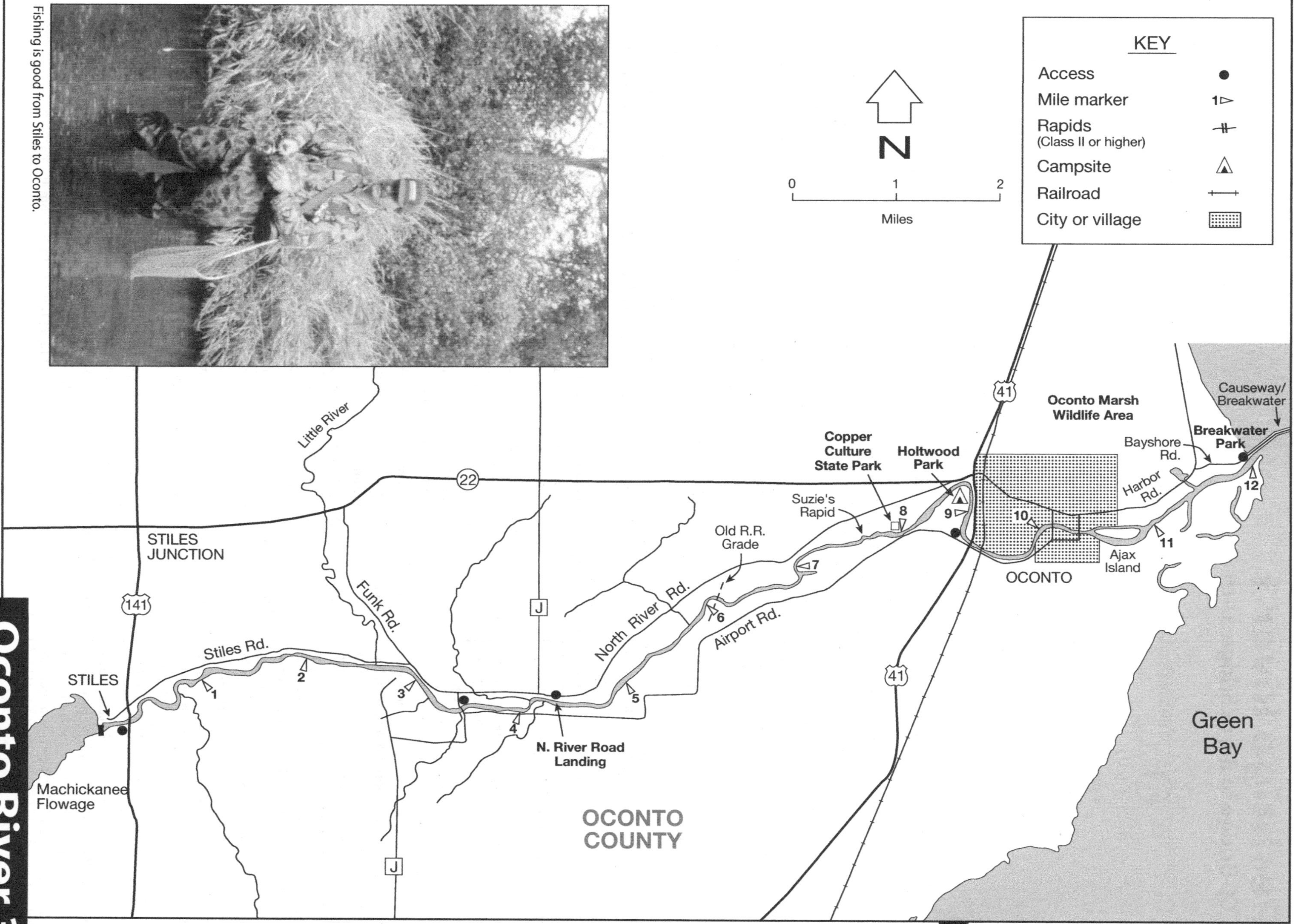

Fishing is good from Stiles to Oconto.

Peshtigo River 1

CCC Bridge to Burnt Bridge (8.9 Miles)

One of the great paddling rivers of Wisconsin, the Peshtigo provides enjoyable boating over most of its length. Originating north of Crandon, near the source of the Wolf River, the Peshtigo courses through Forest and Marinette counties before emptying into Green Bay. De-spite several large dams, the river is a delight for both flat-water and whitewater paddlers, offering some of the most challenging whitewater rapids in the Midwest. The "Pesh" is a popular fishing river, too, and features many lovely riverside parks for picnickers, campers and nature lovers.

West of Cavour, the upper reaches of the river tend to be too swampy and brushy to be enjoyable. In recent years, moreover, the once-popular stretch from Big Joe Landing to the CCC Bridge (shown on the map for Peshtigo River 1) has been blocked by so many fallen trees that it is no longer recommended. Recent paddlers on this section have reported long, miserable days trying to get over and around the numerous obstructions. Thus, the first recommended put-in on the river is at the CCC Bridge.

A good trip for intermediate paddlers, this narrow and wild stretch of the upper Peshtigo has great scenery, good current, trout fishing and plenty of Class I and II rapids. Most of the 8.9 miles passes between heavily wooded banks, but there is some lowland paddling as well. Land along the shoreline is both publicly and privately owned. Fallen trees are not usually a problem in this section, but paddlers should always be on the lookout for strainers. The Peshtigo is a small river here, but it can get dangerous in high water. Be careful.

Riverside **camping** is available at the take-out (Burnt Bridge Landing). USFS campgrounds at Bear Lake and Laura Lake are located nearby.

The section has been run enjoyably when the downstream gauge at Kosir's Rapid Rafts (715-757-3431) was as low as two inches. To get an idea of the relative **water level,** check the USGS gauge near Wabeno (#04067958) on the USGS website; see "Water Levels" in the introduction.

The **GRADIENT** averages 8.9 feet per mile.

The **shuttle route** is via Forest Roads 2131 and 2134.

PUT IN at the **CCC bridge**, upstream-right, where there is room for four to five cars. Across the river from the landing is an informative self-guided nature trail. The Dendro-Eco Trail has numerous stations explaining tree and animal species in the area, processes of growth and decay in the forest, and principles of forest management. This short hike (two-thirds of a mile) is very pleasant and informative—a good way to end a day of paddling.

The river is narrow here, about 40 feet wide. **Camp 12 Rapids** (Class II) begins after the first right-hand bend below the bridge. The first two pitches are rocky constrictions, and the third is a long boulder garden.

After a couple of bends, **Little Camp 12 Rapids** (8.8 miles) begins in a beautiful area where the river narrows, trees form a canopy, and conifers line both sides. This Class II rapids isn't very long; follow the chute down the middle. Continue to be vigilant for strainers.

A beautiful wooded stretch, with several creeks coming in on both sides, precedes **Coldwater Rapids** (11.2 miles). This is a Class I riffle/rapid, but be careful of the boulder cluster at the bottom.

Preserve Rapids (11.6 miles) begins with two short Class II boulder gardens, followed by a long pool, then a long, narrow rapids with easy-to-follow chutes. After another pool, the fourth pitch is long and winding, a solid Class II with a steep gradient. The Bill Gensmen Memorial Bridge (close to FR 2131 but on private property) is in the middle of the following pool. Another pool, with a house on the right, follows the fifth pitch, an easy Class II. The long sixth pitch is another solid Class II. Finally, the series ends with a short Class I.

After Preserve Rapids, the river widens and slows through a mile of lowland. The quietwater is briefly interrupted by a short Class I rapids caused by a boulder constriction; more flatwater follows. Whirlpool Creek, a good trout stream, enters from the right at 13.3 miles.

The three pitches of **Smiley Rapids** (14.6 miles) are an easy Class I. Forest Road 2131 is close by on the left; a short path leads to the river.

Big Rock Rapids (15.9 miles)—named after a huge boulder on the left bank near the end—is a long, curving Class II. Again, a short path leads to the river from FR 2131. Almost continuous riffles and one small boulder garden cover the rest of the stretch to Burnt Bridge.

TAKE OUT at **Burnt Bridge landing,** downstream-right (16.8 miles). A small primitive camping area is located here, but has little room for parking.

A Glimpse Into What Might Have Been

It's difficult to imagine what northern Wisconsin must have looked like a century and a half ago when giant white pine trees covered the land. Fortunately, there is a place where you can go to see a bit of this once magnificent landscape.

The next time you're paddling on the upper Peshtigo or Oconto and you find yourself in the Lakewood area, be sure to make a side trip to the Cathedral of the Pines. You'll never forget it. While the rest of northern Wisconsin was being stripped of its pine forest, lumbermen spared a tract so that future generations could see how the land once looked. Today, giant pines tower overhead, whistling in the wind. Herons nest in the treetops, their screeching lending an eerie prehistoric quality. Walking through the area is an incredibly peaceful and satisfying experience, filling you with regret that such beauty has been lost but grateful that this reminder of it has been preserved.

To get there, take Archibald Lake Road southwest off Highway 32 north of Lakewood, then turn right (north) onto Cathedral Drive, a narrow gravel road. You can also get to Archibald Lake Road from the south, via Highway 64 and County T.

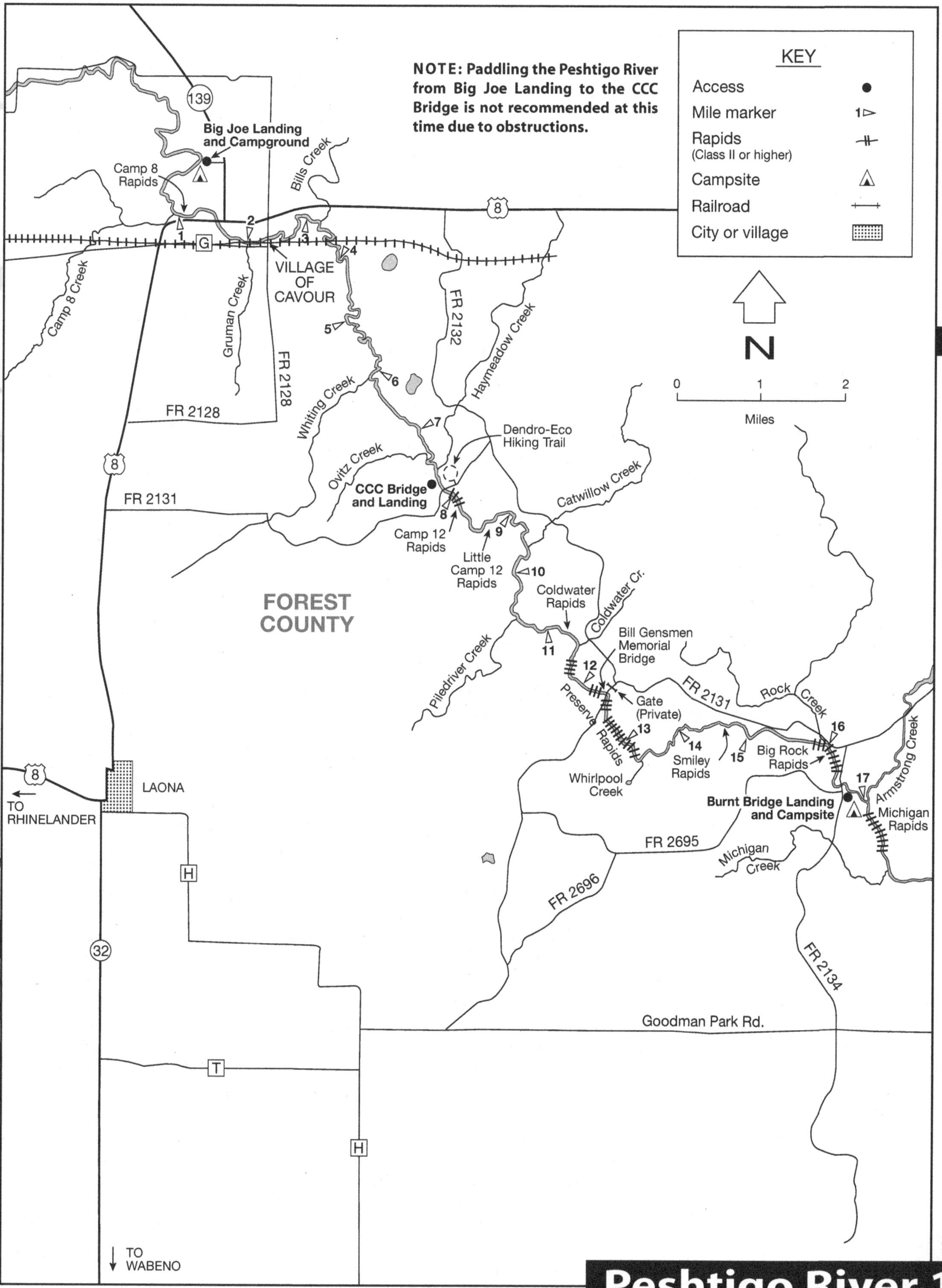
NOTE: Paddling the Peshtigo River from Big Joe Landing to the CCC Bridge is not recommended at this time due to obstructions.
KEY
Access
Mile marker
Rapids
(Class II or higher)
Campsite
Railroad
City or village
N
0
1
2
Miles
Big Joe Landing and Campground
Camp 8 Rapids
Bills Creek
VILLAGE OF CAVOUR
Camp 8 Creek
Gruman Creek
FR 2128
FR 2132
Haymeadow Creek
Whiting Creek
Dendro-Eco Hiking Trail
Ovitz Creek
CCC Bridge and Landing
Camp 12 Rapids
Little Camp 12 Rapids
Catwillow Creek
FR 2131
FOREST COUNTY
Coldwater Rapids
Coldwater Cr.
Bill Gensmen Memorial Bridge
Piledriver Creek
Preserve Rapids
Gate (Private)
Rock Creek
Smiley Rapids
Big Rock Rapids
Whirlpool Creek
Burnt Bridge Landing and Campsite
Armstrong Creek
Michigan Rapids
FR 2695
Michigan Creek
FR 2696
FR 2134
Goodman Park Rd.
LAONA
TO RHINELANDER
TO WABENO

Peshtigo River 2

Burnt Bridge to Goodman Park (11.8 Miles)

This section of the upper Peshtigo is a delight for intermediate and advanced whitewater paddlers. There are many difficult rapids, including two Class IIIs. When whitewater enthusiasts think of the Peshtigo, they usually have the downstream "Roaring Rapids" stretch in mind; a day on this section will expand their appreciation of the river. Most of the land along the shoreline is publicly owned, so the whole stretch is wild and undeveloped. Much of the section is narrow: Check for strainers as you go.

The trip can be cut in half by taking out at an intermediate access (noted below), which avoids 5 miles of flatwater and the two Class III drops.

There are small riverside **campsites** at Burnt Bridge and Burton Wells Bridge, and a beautiful campground at Goodman County Park. The federal campground at Bear Lake is nearby.

Water levels: The section has been run enjoyably when the downstream gauge at Kosir's Rapid Rafts (715-757-3431) was as low as two inches, but boaters should exercise great care when the river is high. Michigan Rapids, the Dells and other rapids become intimidating under high-water conditions.

The **GRADIENT** is a steep 15.6 feet per mile.

The **shuttle route** is via Forest Road 2134 and Goodman Park/Benson Lake Road (FR 2136).

PUT IN at **Burnt Bridge,** downstream-right, where there is room for only a few cars. The bridge is named after an earlier structure that was partially burned.

About a quarter mile downstream there is a short boulder garden with a big rock on the left. Several hundred yards of calm water follow. After Armstrong Creek enters on the left, Michigan Rapids begins in a right-hand turn. Take out on the right and walk the trail to scout the entry pitch (the most difficult part). Incidentally, this trail leads all the way back to Burnt Bridge.

The main pitch of **Michigan Rapids** comes at the beginning of this solid Class II rapids: a hundred-yard S-curve with big boulders and holes to dodge. River-reading and maneuvering skills are required for a successful run. Class II boulder gardens continue for half a mile, and Michigan Creek enters on the right at the end of the rapids. Both the creek and rapids are named after an early settler.

Strong Falls at Goodman Park requires a portage.

After a mile and a quarter of flatwater, a small rapids follows a river-right cabin.

More flatwater precedes the **Upper Dells** (2.9 miles), another long Class II boulder garden. These rapids begin with a small, constricted drop just left of a little island. The drop has a big boulder in the middle of it.

The **Dells** (solid Class II+) begin a short distance downstream. This is a very narrow, circuitous rapids with numerous drops, running along the right side of a long island. Take the right channel of the island, then get out on the island (left) before the rapids to walk along a rocky scout trail. The entrance to the Dells is very tight and prone to strainers; be sure to take a good look at the entire rapids, and portage if prudence dictates. Like many of the rapids on this section, the Dells can get very mean when the water is high.

There are many small rapids and riffles for a mile and a half after the Dells, but mostly quietwater.

Roaring Rapids (4.8 miles)—nothing like the downstream section with the same name—is a half-mile Class II boulder garden.

At **Burton Wells Bridge** (6 miles), the Peshtigo is crossed by Goodman Park/Benson Lake Road, making this a good place for a trip-shortening take-out. **Access** is downstream-right, with a primitive campsite and room for a few cars.

Halley Creek, a good trout stream, enters on the right downstream (6.2 miles). For most of the next 5 miles the river slows. Benson Lake Road (FR 2136) runs along the left shore, where two **landing** sites are visible. Only **Cooper Rapids** (an easy Class II, at 9 miles) and a second boulder garden (9.4 miles) break up the flatwater. The second rapids precedes the Hoosier Hole, a popular fishing spot. Two wicked drops remain downstream.

Taylor Rapids (10.8 miles) begins with two short Class II boulder gardens, followed by a large island, then Class III **Taylor Falls.** The falls can be scouted and/or portaged from the right shore, but you must be careful to take out well upstream from the drop. At the falls, the river constricts, with an irregular stone outcropping and a main drop of several feet on the far right. The current is swift and boulders are located in awkward spots, requiring perfect boat control. Many boaters have miscalculated the drop and experienced nasty swims or injuries.

The falls are followed by a long Class II rapids that ends just short of **Swede John Bridge** (11.5 miles). **TAKE OUT** at the bridge, upstream-left. If you continue past the bridge (not recommended), be sure to take out on the left bank as soon as you come to a sharp left-hand turn in the river; from there there's a short trail to Goodman Park. Do not paddle beyond this point because steep rapids begin after the river bend, leading down to Class II–IV Strong Falls. Take some time to walk around Goodman Park, a beautiful 240-acre area operated by Marinette County, and admire the impressive drop of Strong Falls from the shoreline and a footbridge.

Peshtigo River 2

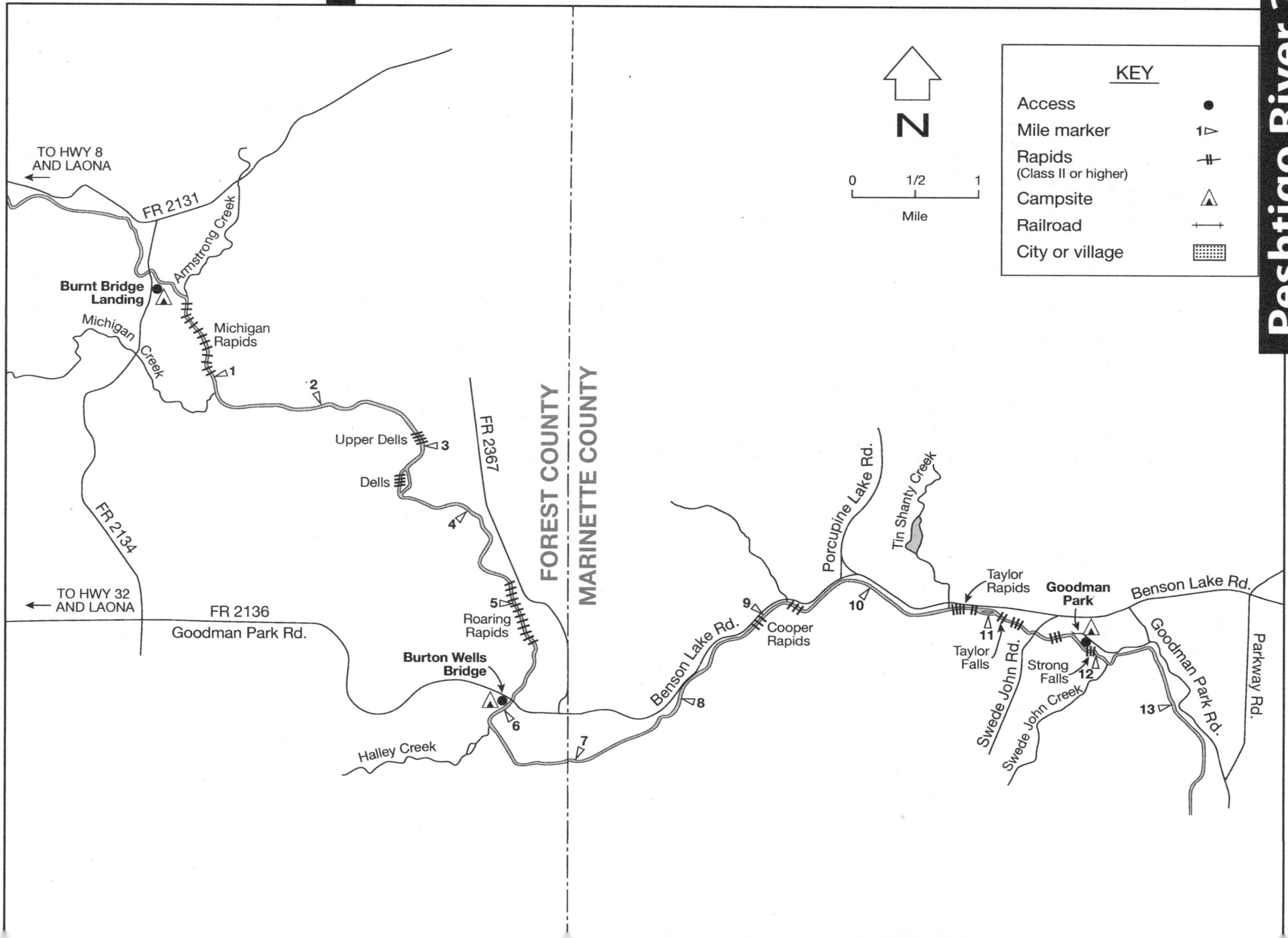

Peshtigo River 3

Goodman Park to Farm Dam Landing (8.6 Miles)

For almost 9 miles, the Peshtigo provides a relatively placid breather from the heavy-duty whitewater that runs upstream and downstream. Only two rapids occur on this section, breaking the quietwater roughly into three parts. Much of the stretch is wider and slower than previous sections, especially near the end. The river continues to be brownish in color, due to organic acids that form as water drains through wetlands. Most of the land along the river is publicly owned and includes two county parks, one at the beginning and another in the middle of the stretch.

Two beautiful **campgrounds** are located on the river: Goodman Park and McClintock Park.

Water levels: The section has been run enjoyably when the downstream gauge at Kosir's Rapid Rafts (715-757-3431) reads as low as two inches.

The **GRADIENT** averages 4.6 feet per mile.

The **shuttle route** is via Goodman Park Road, Parkway Road, Camp 5 Road, Harper Road, Old J, County C and Farm Dam Lane.

Scenic Bridges of Northern Wisconsin

There's something about a charming old bridge that strikes a chord in the heart of every paddler. And anyone who does a lot of paddling in northern Wisconsin has passed under many memorable bridges.

They come in every shape and size: massive and metallic, like the historic old railroad "swing bridge" on the St. Croix (St. Croix 8), and small and seemingly fragile, like the suspension footbridges over the Wolf at Boy Scout Rapids (Wolf 4). Some intricate old stone bridges, such as the one on the Oconto upstream from Highway 32 (Oconto 2), are wonders of design and engineering. Covered bridges are represented by the Smith Rapids Bridge, over the South Fork of the Flambeau: a glue-laminated re-creation of the wooden bridges of the past. Small, handsome wooden bridges are fairly common; several are encountered on the first section of the Bois Brule (Bois Brule 1).

Some bridges can raise the hair on the back of your neck. The unimposing little metal and wood "Yellow Bridge" on the Pike, for instance, signals the approach of Class III Yellow Bridge Falls. The rickety footbridge on the left channel of Big Smoky Falls on the Wolf hovers over a Class V cataract (Wolf 5).

Perhaps the most graceful and appealing of all are the four bridges over the Peshtigo at McClintock Park (Peshtigo 3). These gorgeous timber structures arching over the rapids are the visual high point of a beautiful roadside park.

PUT IN at **Goodman Park,** river-left. Near the entrance to the park, a short path leads from the parking area to the river downstream from Strong Falls. Before starting out, walk up to the falls and look them over. The park has excellent camping and day-use areas, with drinking water and lots of parking.

A riffle follows a river bend just downstream from the put-in. Thereafter, the river widens and slows for 3 miles, with thick forest on both sides. An occasional tree has fallen into the river, but the stream bed is so wide that getting around is no problem.

For a long time, the road is close by on the left; a few access points are apparent.

At 3 miles, a right-hand bend with a few boulders in the river and an island on the left signal the beginning of **Skinner's Elbow.** This series of Class I–II rapids begins with a boulder constriction and continues through several curves for half a mile.

The river widens and slows again, but not for long. More boulder fields begin as you approach **McClintock Park** (3.6 miles). Two beautiful wooden footbridges come into view. Take out on the left at the bridges to get to the park, which provides picnicking facilities, water, parking and an alternative put-in or take-out.

Not far downstream from the park are some attractive hemlock-covered high banks; the **McClintock Park Campground** is located here.

The Camp 5 Road bridge (4.7 miles) comes into view after a log home on the left. The river runs quite deep, wide and slow again.

After another 1.5 miles of flatwater, **Wilson Rapids** begins on a right-hand turn, with a river-wide row of boulders at the entrance. The rapids, a solid Class II, forms a big S-curve a couple hundred yards long, and gets progressively more intense. Definitely the toughest rapids on this section, Wilson can be scouted or portaged on either side. It is very pushy in higher water.

From here to the take-out, the river moves slowly. There are houses on both sides of the Peshtigo as the mouth of the Rat River enters on the right (7.5 miles). Power lines pass overhead soon afterward. After the Rat River, marshy vegetation increases, especially on the right shore.

TAKE-OUT: Look for the outlet of Otter Creek on the right (within view of a couple of big boulders downstream). Paddle a short distance up the creek to the public **landing** on the left, accessed from County C. There is a turnaround at the landing, with some parking. The river landing just downstream from Otter Creek is for commercial and private purposes only.

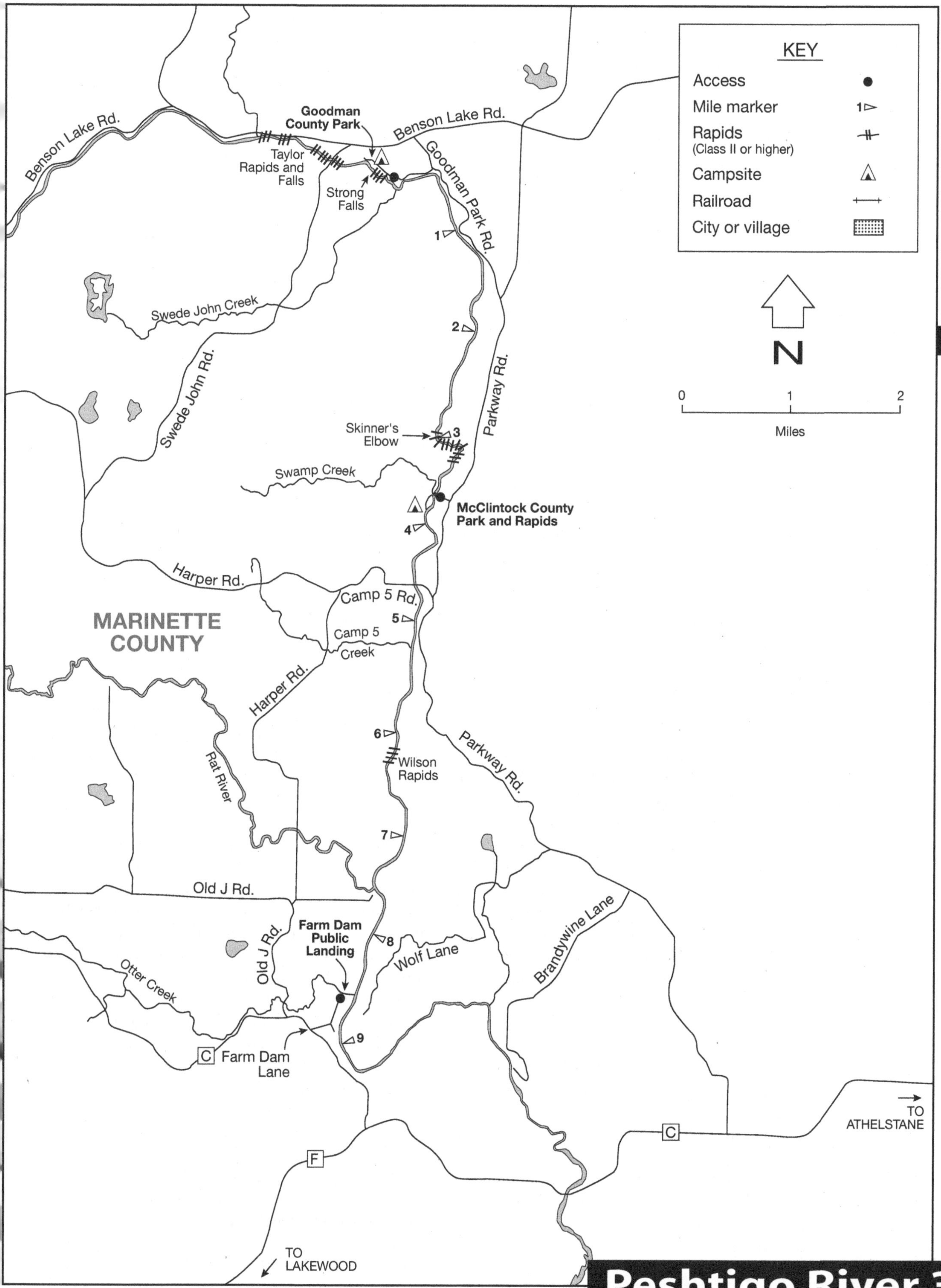

Peshtigo River 3

Peshtigo River 4

Farm Dam Landing to Landing #12 (5.5 Miles)

Definitely not for unskilled paddlers, this short section of the Peshtigo offers some of the most intense whitewater in the Midwest. You won't see many fishermen here, just kayakers, canoeists and rafters enjoying the almost continuous rapids. Six complex Class II–III drops are sandwiched between two very long Class II boulder gardens.

Paddlers are advised to make their first run of this section in the company of experienced boaters who are familiar with it. Most of the land along the stretch is privately owned; please respect property rights.

Public **camping** is available upstream at Goodman Park and McClintock Park. Several private campgrounds are also located in the area, including Kosir's Rapid Rafts on the river near the take-out, and Wildman's Whitewater Ranch alongside Horserace Rapids.

Water levels are measured by the gauge painted on the County C bridge near the take-out. The stretch is runnable when the gauge reads 0 inches or higher; at 10 inches and above, big holes develop in the drops, and the river demands a high level of skill. For the latest gauge reading, call Kosir's Rapid Rafts (715-757-3431), located at the County C bridge, or check the reading at www.kosirs.com (updated daily). Current river conditions are also available on the American Whitewater website: www.americanwhitewater.org.

The average **GRADIENT** of this section is an impressive 29 feet per mile.

The **shuttle route** is via Farm Dam Lane, County C and Landing 12 Lane. **Raft and inflatable kayak rentals** and shuttles are provided by Kosir's Rapids Rafts (number above), Thornton's Whitewater Rafts (715-757-3311) and Wildman's Whitewater Ranch (888-813-8254).

PUT IN at the public access at Farm Dam Landing (not the commercial/private access); there is room for several cars at the turnaround. (The landing is named after a logging-era structure that was located here.) Paddle a short distance down Otter Creek into the Peshtigo.

The trip begins with a long Class II **boulder garden** around a left-hand curve, followed by several more boulder gardens with short flat areas in between. In low water, this part of the trip can be miserably scrapy.

First Drop (2.1 miles) follows the boulder gardens, after a right-hand turn. Scout on the left shore—also an excellent vantage point for taking photographs. This Class II+ rapids is usually run on the left, down the chute; be on guard for the curler wave that often develops here. In the fast jet at the bottom you'll often find kayakers ferrying, surfing and doing enders. Like all the other drops on this section, First Drop has big eddies at the bottom.

Second Drop is within sight of First Drop, on another right-hand turn. Follow the wave-train down the center of this Class II rapids. Brandywine Creek enters on the left.

Not far downstream, after a little island in the middle of the river, **Third Drop** is usually a bit pushier than Second Drop. Run the big waves down the center. Just downstream from the main chute, a big back-roller **(Joey's Hole)** develops in medium to high water; run it straight-on with momentum to avoid being held by the hydraulic. Be careful, because a major drop is just a few yards away.

Five-Foot Falls, a Class II+ river-wide ledge at 2.9 miles, comes immediately after Third Drop. Unfortunately, the scouting and portage clearing on the left is posted "No Trespassing." The safest place to run Five-Foot is down the center: Line up on a small rocky island just downstream from the drop, and ride down an often-bumpy rock cascade. For advanced boaters, there is a chute on the left, not far from shore. This must be run very precisely, with a slight angle to the left; get ready to make a quick maneuver to the right to avoid the huge boulder at the bottom of the chute. Relax for a while in the eddies below Five-Foot. The toughest rapids on the river is just around the corner.

Horserace Rapids (Class III) begins with a couple hundred yards of fast boulder gardens that run into a small, narrow, high-gradient canyon. Get out on the right and walk along the rocky path to scout; portaging is a good idea for many paddlers. From beginning to end, Horserace increases in intensity. "Endless eddy" is on the left just before the final drop, which is usually run on a diagonal to the right. Watch out for "Diamond Splitter," a rock in the fast water at the bottom. Grab an eddy before proceeding farther.

Don't let down your guard, because **S-Curve Rapids** (Class II) begins several hundred yards downstream from Horserace. After a left-hand turn at a fork around a big island, the river runs swift and narrow, and you must maneuver carefully in order not to get slammed up against the rock wall on the left. Do not go to the right at the fork; a small drop lies there, followed by a very scratchy rock garden.

S-Curve is followed by more than a mile of continuous Class II **rapids,** bordered by many cabins. Then flatwater takes you to the County C bridge where a gauge is painted on the left abutment. Downstream-left is a private landing for Kosir's Rapid Rafts.

TAKE OUT half a mile downstream on the left at **Wisconsin Public Service Co. Public Landing #12,** where there's plenty of parking. The water is quite slow here because the head of the Caldron Falls Flowage is nearby.

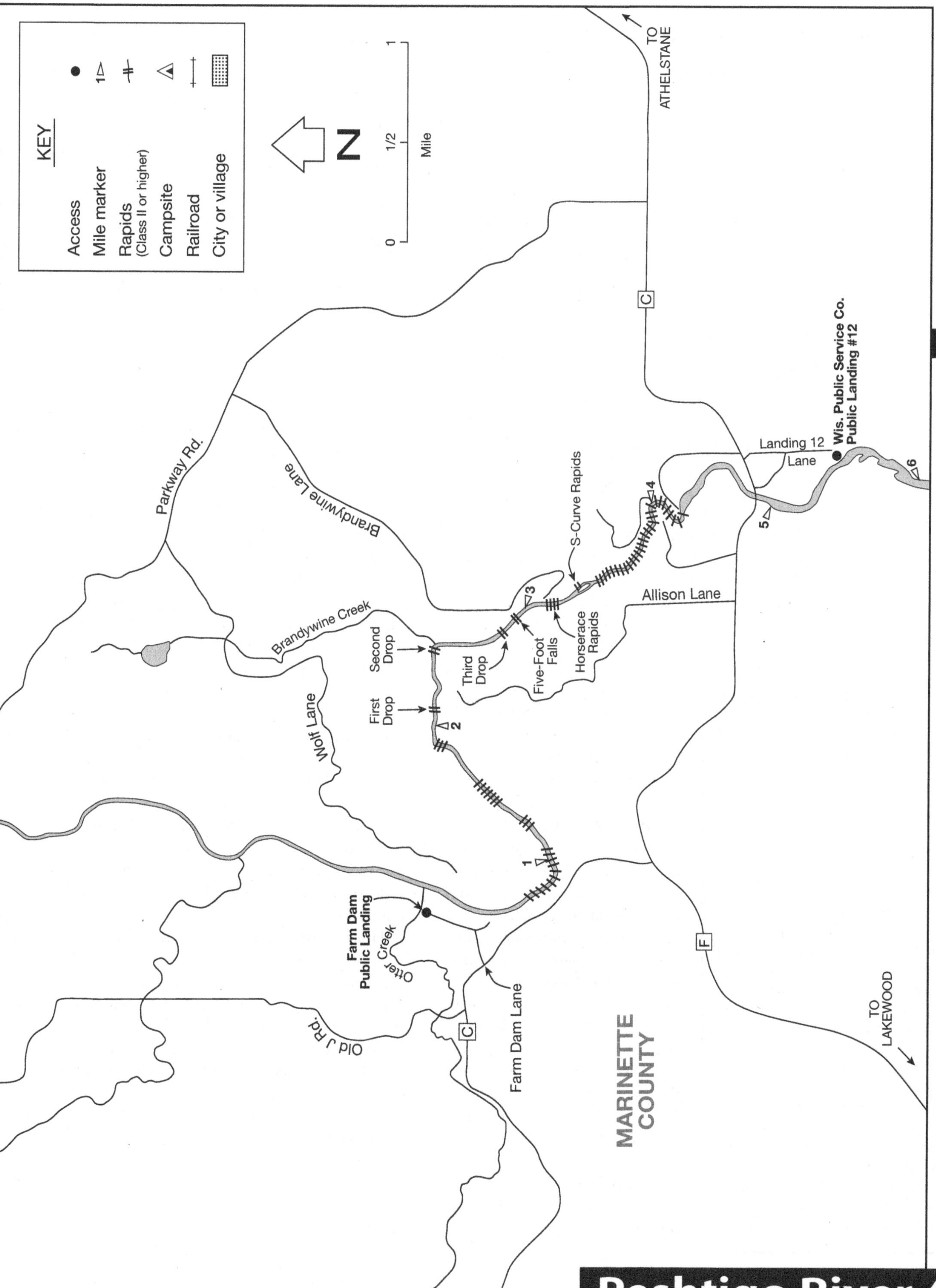

Peshtigo River 4

Peshtigo River 5

Johnson Falls Dam to Shaffer Road (8 Miles)

Downstream from the famous Roaring Rapids section (Peshtigo 4), three dams create the Caldron Falls, High Falls, and Johnson Falls flowages.

Most of the 8 miles of shoreline below Johnson Falls Dam is owned by the Wisconsin Public Service Company, which manages the property for conservation and recreation. Cooperatively, the DNR and WPS maintain the section as a trout fishery; fishermen are a common sight wading the river and walking the shoreline paths. They find not only trout but also northerns, walleye and smallmouth.

Most of the stretch has been kept in a wild state, with no development until near the end. On the average, the river is only about 80 feet wide until the last rapids; from there, it widens and slows. There are numerous riffles and Class I–II rapids, and thick stands of pine, hemlock, cedar and oak.

Water levels are largely dependent upon dam releases, but there is usually enough water for enjoyable paddling. Information on water releases from Johnson Falls Dam is available daily on a recorded message (800-236-7341) and on the WPS website (www.wisconsinpublicservice.com/news/hydro/hydrodata.asp). Wisconsin Public Service signs at the dam and elsewhere warn that "Water levels change rapidly due to hydro plant operations."

The average **GRADIENT** is 6.2 feet per mile.

The **shuttle route** is via Johnson Falls Road, Kostreva Road, County W and Shaffer Road.

PUT IN just below the **Johnson Falls Dam** on the right. Do not put in near the dam. There is a canoe trail leading down through the woods to a **landing** a safe distance below the dam, with ample parking nearby. An **alternate put-in** is located 1.1 miles downstream on the left (accessed from Medicine Brook Road, Newton Lake Road and County A).

After 1.2 miles of quietwater, the river bends right and Medicine Brook enters from the left. Just around the bend is a short Class II **rapids** with a big rock outcropping in the middle; there is a clear chute on the left side, with boulders on the right.

Mild rapids below Johnson Falls Dam.

Winding flatwater follows, with good current. There are numerous high banks along the forested shoreline. At 3 miles, a sharp right-hand turn, numerous boulders on the right and a high sand bank topped by a road indicate the approach of **Seymour Rapids,** a solid Class II. Seymour is a long, curving series of boulder gardens, with short flatwater pools in between. All along the right side is a fisherman's path, accessed by Forest Road 1634 from Kostreva Road. The rapids requires a lot of maneuvering, but includes many eddies and surfing waves for playing.

The current is brisk after Seymour, with numerous riffles and Class I–II rapids. **Spring Rapids** (4.7 miles) is the end of the whitewater; on the right at the end of this rapids is a dirt **landing** accessed from Kirby Lake Road off County W. This makes a good alternative take-out that shortens the trip to about 5.5 miles; the dirt road off Kirby Lake Road has a circle turnaround and room for several cars.

From Spring Rapids to Shaffer Road there are no more riffles or rapids, and the river widens and slows for 2.5 miles as it enters the comparatively narrow Sandstone Flowage. Many houses and cabins come into view on both sides.

TAKE OUT on the right immediately downstream from the **Shaffer Road bridge.** Be sure to ask the management of the supper club there if you can take out on their property. Farther down the flowage, another **landing** is located on the right at the end of Hideaway Lane.

Real-Life Gingerbread Houses

The next time you're in the Lakewood area, a short side trip will take you to the realm of the gingerbread houses.

Just south of Lakewood, turn west off Highway 32 onto North Maiden Lake Road and keepbearing to the right for about 3 miles. Suddenly, on your right, you'll spot a charming little house straight out of Hans Christian Anderson's fairy tales.

Lovingly and painstakingly constructed of thousands of small stones, mortar and wood, the gingerbread house is as whimsical a cottage as you're likely to see. Painted rocks festoon the roof and other parts of the house, and other clever touches manifest the imagination of the creator, Wilmot Swanson.

Drive a little farther down the road and you'll see more of Swanson's cobblestone creations, dating back as far as the 1930s, including an interesting Scandinavian-style open-loft barn. Today, all of these buildings are part of the Camp Lake Resort.

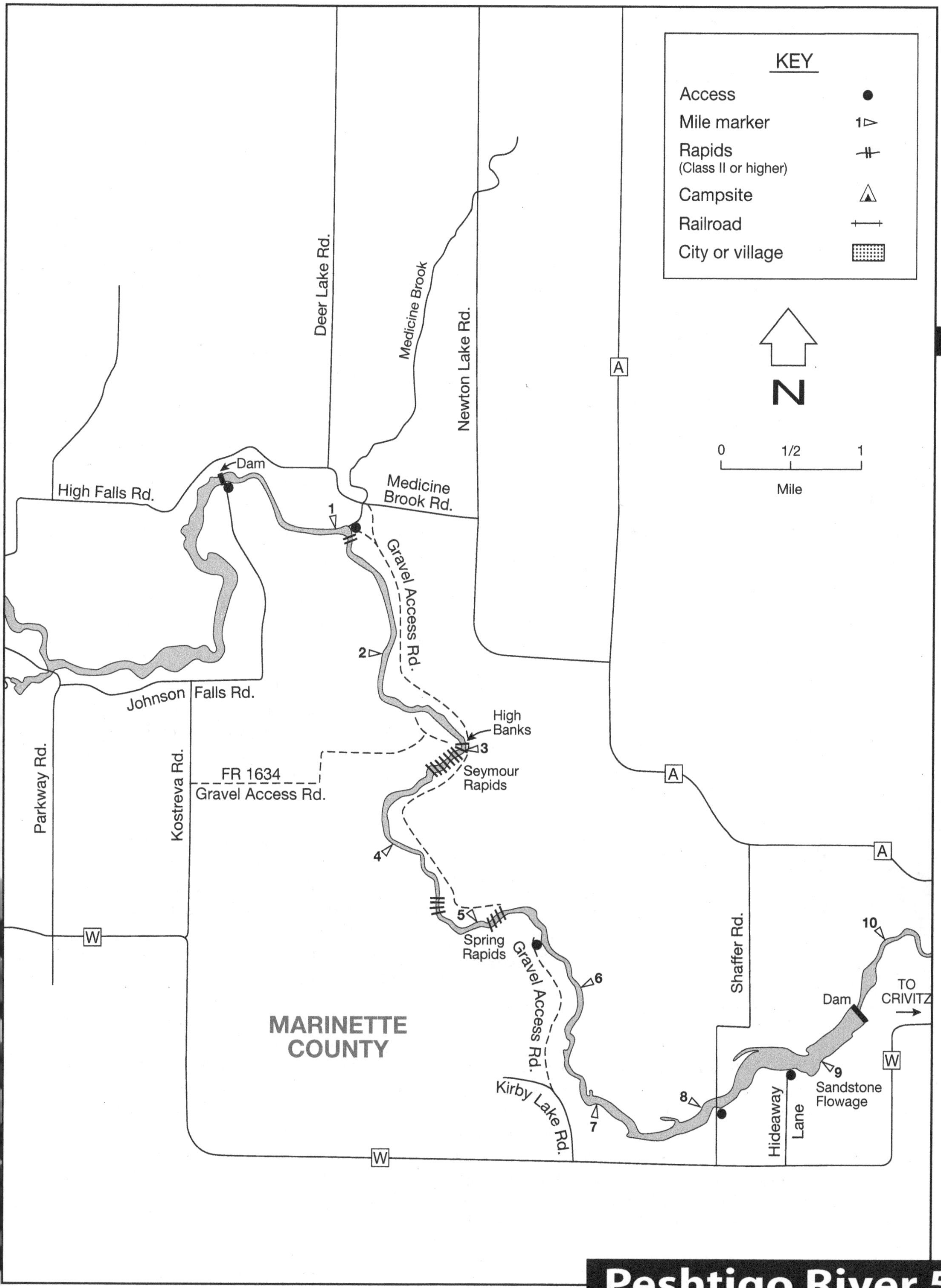
KEY
Access
Mile marker
Rapids
(Class II or higher)
Campsite
Railroad
City or village
N
0
1/2
1
Mile
Deer Lake Rd.
Medicine Brook
Newton Lake Rd.
A
Dam
High Falls Rd.
Medicine
Brook Rd.
1
Gravel Access Rd.
2
Johnson
Falls Rd.
High
Banks
3
Seymour
Rapids
FR 1634
Gravel Access Rd.
Parkway Rd.
Kostreva Rd.
4
5
Spring
Rapids
Gravel Access Rd.
6
W
Shaffer Rd.
10
TO
CRIVITZ
Dam
MARINETTE
COUNTY
9
Sandstone
Flowage
Kirby Lake Rd.
8
7
Hideaway
Lane

Peshtigo River 6

Sandstone Dam to Highway 141 (8.3 Miles)

By the time the Peshtigo leaves the Sandstone Flowage near Crivitz, it has had almost all of the whitewater impounded out of it. For 48 miles from here to Green Bay, the river grows progressively wider and calmer. Except for the village of Crivitz and the city of Peshtigo, however, it continues to flow through countryside that feels remote. The section from the Sandstone Dam to Highway 141 (easily cut in half by using Crivitz as a put-in or take-out) is popular with both fishermen and canoeists.

A private **campground** is located on the river just upstream from Highway 141 (see below).

Water levels are partly dependent upon dam releases, but there is usually enough water for enjoyable paddling. Information on daily water releases from the Sandstone Dam is available on the Wisconsin Public Service website: www.wisconsinpublicservice.com/news/hydro/hydrodata.asp.

The average **GRADIENT** is 2.4 feet per mile.

The **shuttle route** is via County W and Highway 141. **Canoe rental** and shuttle service for this section are available from the Peshtigo River Campground 2 miles south of Crivitz (715-854-2986).

The lower Peshtigo is placid and scenic.

The **PUT-IN** is on **Wisconsin Public Service Corporation property:** 2.3 miles west of the Crivitz bridge, a gravel road off County W goes 0.3 mile north to a riverside parking lot. Follow the upstream trail from the parking lot to the put-in, which is on the right bank far downstream from the dam. When you begin the trip, you're in the right channel alongside an island. The channel is narrow and fairly fast, with some rocks.

After the island, the river widens to 100 to 125 feet, and remains at that width for the rest of the trip. There is an enjoyable Class I rapids in the first bend to the right, with good waves.

For the first 5 miles (that is, to Crivitz), the shoreline consists mostly of high banks, many of them sandy. Birch, maple, pine, spruce, oak and popple are plentiful. You'll occasionally find trees that have fallen into the river, but they are usually easy to avoid. A fence runs along the left side for much of the first mile.

There are only a few islands on the whole stretch. A private concrete landing lies on the left shore upstream from one of the larger islands. There are no houses until one appears on the left in a right-hand bend after the island.

County A is fairly close on the left, and can eventually be seen from the river.

Sandstone Lodge (reached from County W west of Crivitz) is seen on the right after a big right-hand bend.

Several buildings appear on the left just upstream from the Crivitz bridge.

There is an excellent **alternate access** downstream-right at the County W bridge (4.8 miles). **Don Brooks Memorial Park** provides good parking, with picnic facilities.

The river turns left after the bridge, then continues to bend back and forth, with some big oxbows. There are more strainers on this part of the trip; be careful not to drift into them. After a couple of houses just downstream from County W, there are no buildings for a long time.

Much of the 3-plus miles from Crivitz to Highway 141 goes through an isolated lowland setting, although you will occasionally encounter high banks.

At 6.2 miles the river passes under an old railroad bridge. A creek enters from the right in a big left-hand bend at 7.1 miles.

Several homes appear on the left as the river makes a sharp right bend (7.6 miles). The river widens at this point as it approaches Highway 141.

The **Peshtigo River Campground landing** is on the right as the river bends back to the left (8.1 miles). This private campground offers camping, **canoe rental** and shuttle service; the campground is accessed by vehicle from Highway 141, south of the bridge.

TAKE-OUT: The Highway 141 bridge is a short distance downstream from the campground, after a sharp turn to the right. Take out upstream-right. A short spur road leads to the **landing,** with good parking.

Peshtigo River 6

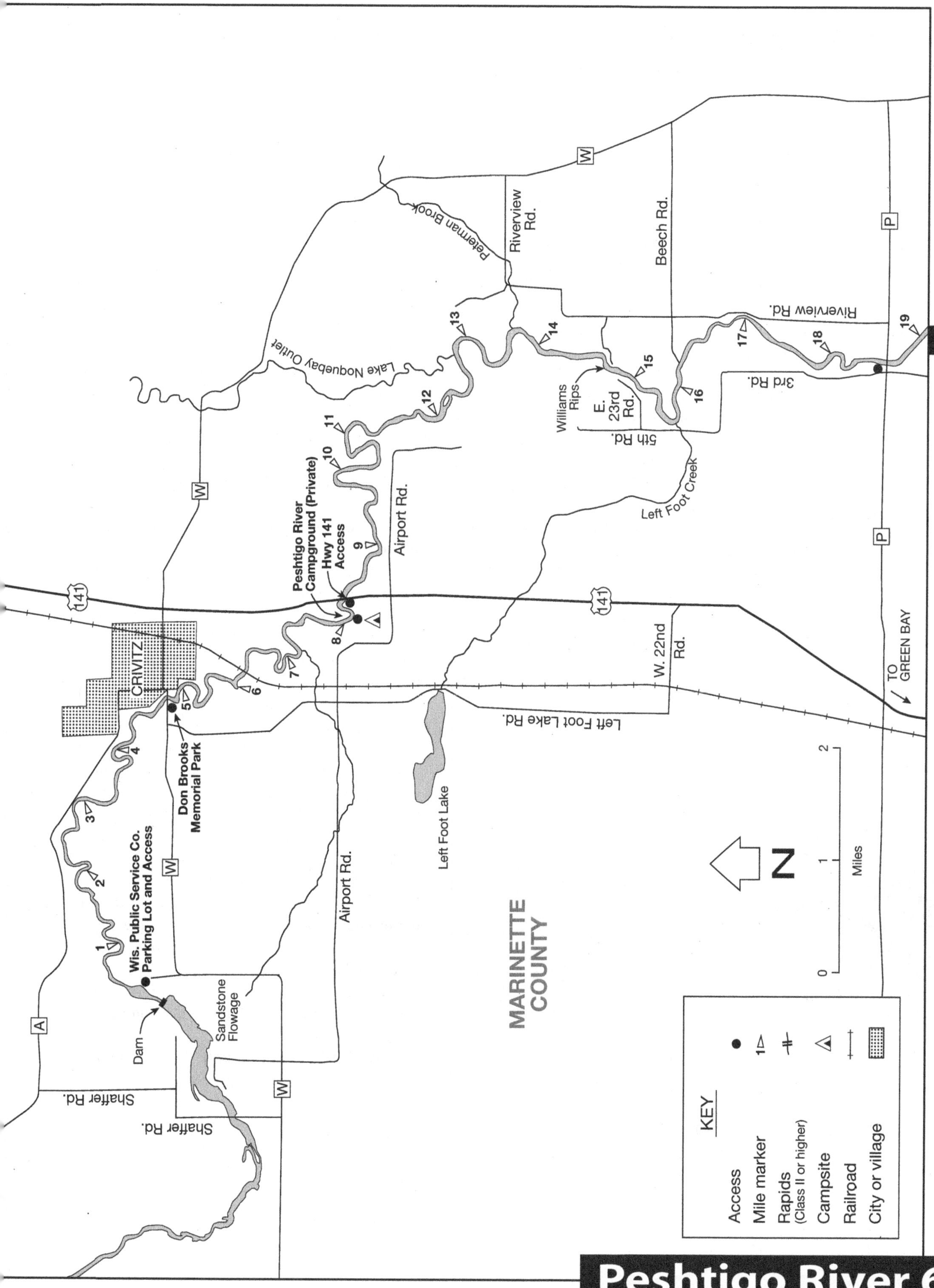

Peshtigo River 7

Highway 141 to County P (10.4 Miles)

A good stretch for beginners, this section of the Peshtigo winds through wooded lowlands and farmland. During the second half of the trip, the river gets rather wide but is still small compared to rivers like the Wisconsin and St. Croix. As an added bonus, the next-to-the-last rapids on the Peshtigo occurs on this stretch, a noisy but short and easy waker-upper. Houses appear here and there, but the area through which the river flows is clearly undeveloped. A roadside marker on Highway 141 indicates that this stretch of river crosses a geographical line halfway between the north pole and the equator. (Paddlers on the Red Cedar River will find a comparable sign in Colfax.)

Riverside **camping** is available at the private Peshtigo River Campground just upstream from the Highway 141 bridge. The campground is accessed by vehicle from Highway 141 south of the bridge.

Water levels: There is almost always enough water for enjoyable paddling. Although it is considerably downstream, you can check the gauge at Porterfield (#04069416) on the USGS website; see "Water Levels" in the introduction.

The average **GRADIENT** is 1.9 feet per mile.

The **shuttle route** is via Highway 141 and County P.

A calm section of river, with a remote feel.

PUT IN at the **Highway 141 bridge** south of Crivitz, upstream-right. There is a parking area on the short spur road off the highway.

Beginning with a right-hand bend, the river tends to be shallow at the start but deepens soon. The bottom is sandy throughout the stretch, and the mud and sand banks are heavily wooded until the last couple of miles. The river is consistently 100 to 125 feet wide for a while.

Several tiny creeks enter on both sides in the first few miles. Farm buildings appear on the right atop a high bank in the first sharp curve to the left, and there are several cabins in the next big left-hand bend. Occasionally, you'll come upon sandbars in the river, along with attractive sand banks and large wooded islands. Pine, hemlock, birch and cedar are abundant.

The mouth of Lake Noquebay Outlet enters on the left near the end of a big wide spot in the river; after the outlet, the river bends right, and a house appears not far downstream.

Peterman Brook comes in on the left in the middle of a right-hand bend. There is a private access on the left in the long straightaway after Peterman Brook.

Trees are sparse on the right because of farm cultivation, a setting you will encounter off and on for the rest of the trip.

Just downstream from a log cabin on a right-hand bend, Class I **Williams Rips** is followed by several houses on the right. You can hear the noise from the rapids from upstream. It has some big waves, but the main tongue is easy to find. As always, make sure there are no strainers in the fast water. All landings on the right are private.

Left Foot Creek enters from the right at the next sharp turn to the left. Fifth Road is close by on the right.

A big home on a high pine-covered bank on the left indicates the approach of Riverview Road; a number of houses follow. A grassy bank on the left is an **access,** but there is no room for parking alongside Riverview Road.

When the river makes its last right turn before the take-out, there is a beautiful pine bluff on the left. A sharp left turn follows.

TAKE OUT at the **County P bridge,** upstream-right, at the ruins of an old cheese factory.

Peshtigo River 7

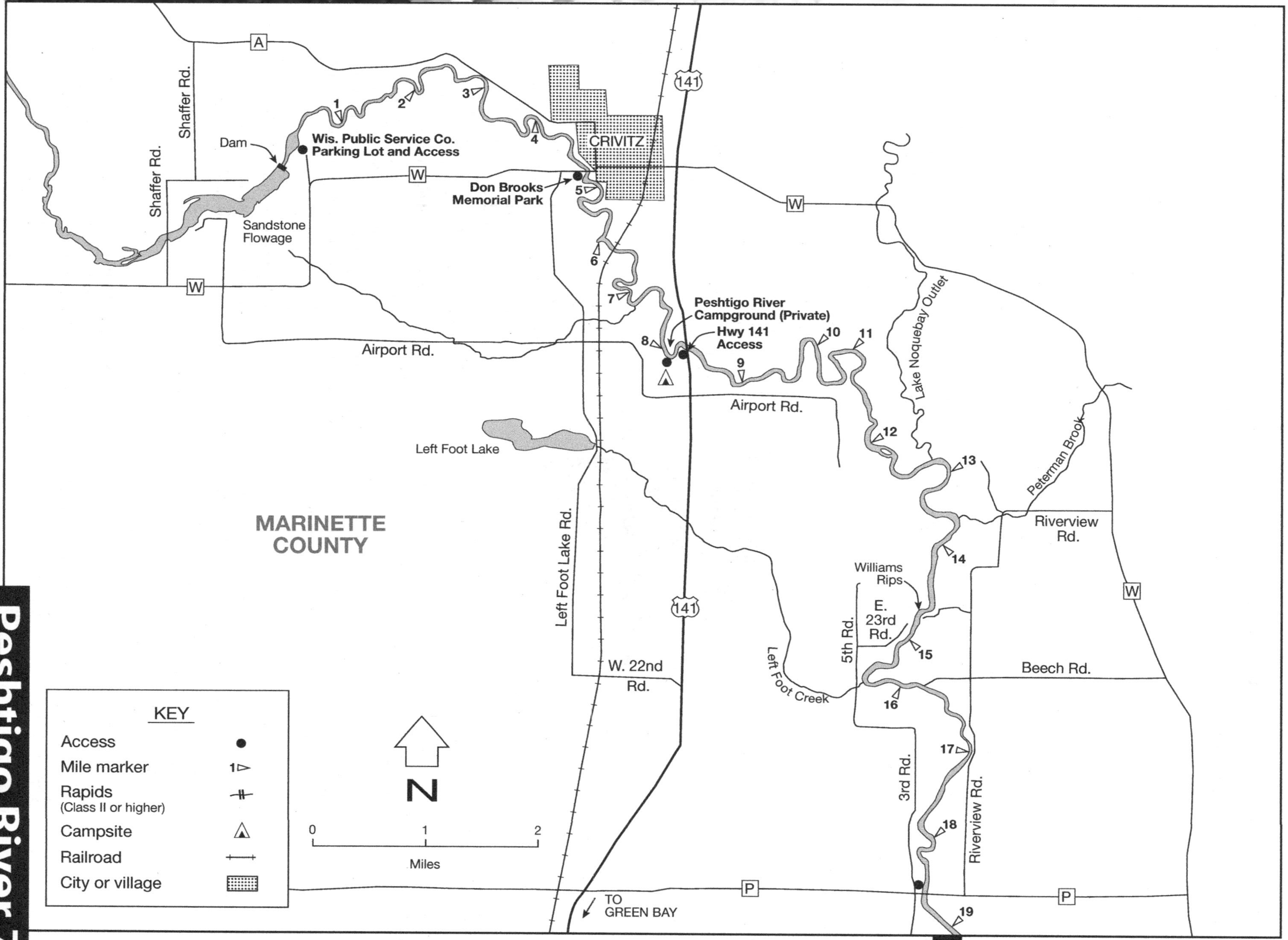

Peshtigo River 8

County P to County E (10.4 Miles)

The next-to-the-last section of the Peshtigo is a very pleasant paddle, with dependable current, a winding course, a mixed upland/lowland setting, a few glimpses of interesting marshy sloughs and an exciting but not very difficult rapids. Appropriate for novices, the stretch can nevertheless be tiring if the wind is out of the east. Paddlers often see deer and eagle, and anglers catch northerns, smallmouth and panfish along the stretch.

Public **camping** is available a few miles south of the take-out at Badger Park in the city of Peshtigo.

Water levels are almost always adequate for good paddling. High water demands special caution, and may require staying away altogether. Check the Porterfield gauge (#04069416)—located near the County E bridge on this section—on the USGS website; see "Water Levels" in the introduction.

The average **GRADIENT** is only 0.9 feet per mile.

A suitable trip for novices, with dependable current.

The **shuttle route** is via County P, 3rd Road, Highway 64 and County E.

PUT IN at the **County P bridge,** upstream-right, near the old cheese factory.

The section begins fairly wide and deep, with a left-hand bend. A house with a big grassy yard appears on the left around the bend. Cedar trees are plentiful at the beginning. Later, pines, maples and birches are abundant.

Before long, the river becomes shallow as you approach a Class I rapids, located in a curve alongside a river-right house. Waves are created as the river drops a little, but the route is easy to find. High and low banks alternate downstream.

Shortly after a house on the right, the river sharply bends left, then right (1.5 miles). There is an island at the next left-hand bend (2 miles). Attractive wooded banks line the river for a while, including a high bluff on the left midway through a big right-hand loop. As soon as the loop ends and the river swings to the left (3.2 miles), Fawn Lane parallels the river on the right; there are many cabins here.

A big island precedes the County W bridge (4.2 miles); the right channel is narrow, shallow and choked with deadfall. There is no good access at the bridge. After County W, the banks are generally low and grassy, but trees line the river all the way to the take-out. You will spot an occasional deer stand.

Downstream from the bridge, the Little Peshtigo River (4.5 miles) enters on the right, opposite a cabin. After a small, grassy island (5 miles), the river bends right, then left, with several houses along the bank in the curve. There is a slough on the left where the river bends back to the left. Several times on the rest of the stretch, you will see sloughs in the midst of bends.

Another slough on the right, then Gravelly Brook on the left (5.9 miles) follow the next right-hand bend. Other sloughs follow.

The Ferndale Road bridge (7.3 miles) is an **alternate access;** the put-in or take-out is downstream-right or left, but with little room for parking. Downstream, the river continues wide, with moderate current and low shoreline. Swampy sloughs appear in the first loops after the bridge, then a straightaway that ends at a wooded island and a right turn. There are a few farm buildings and wooded bluffs in the remainder of the section, but most of the last miles flow between low banks, with sloughs in the bends.

TAKE OUT at the County E bridge (10.4 miles), upstream-right or downstream-left. Because of the large rocks used for rip-rap at the bridge, this is not an easy **access.** There is room for a few cars alongside the road.

Another possible take-out is 2.5 miles farther downstream at the unimproved **landing** alongside Bagley Road. By the time you reach this landing, which is next to the railroad tracks where the river swings right, you are already into the backup of the Potato Rapids Flowage. There is still a little current at Bagley Junction, and room for a couple of cars.

Downstream a mile from the Bagley Road landing is the public boat **landing** owned by the Wisconsin Public Service Corporation. This landing, on river left, is well into the flowage and is tucked away behind some islands.

■ ■ ■

Two dams lie downstream from this section: Potato Rapids Dam, upstream from the Highway 64 bridge 4 miles north of the city of Peshtigo; and the paper-mill dam located in the city just south of Highway 41. The final trip on the Peshtigo begins well below the paper-mill dam.

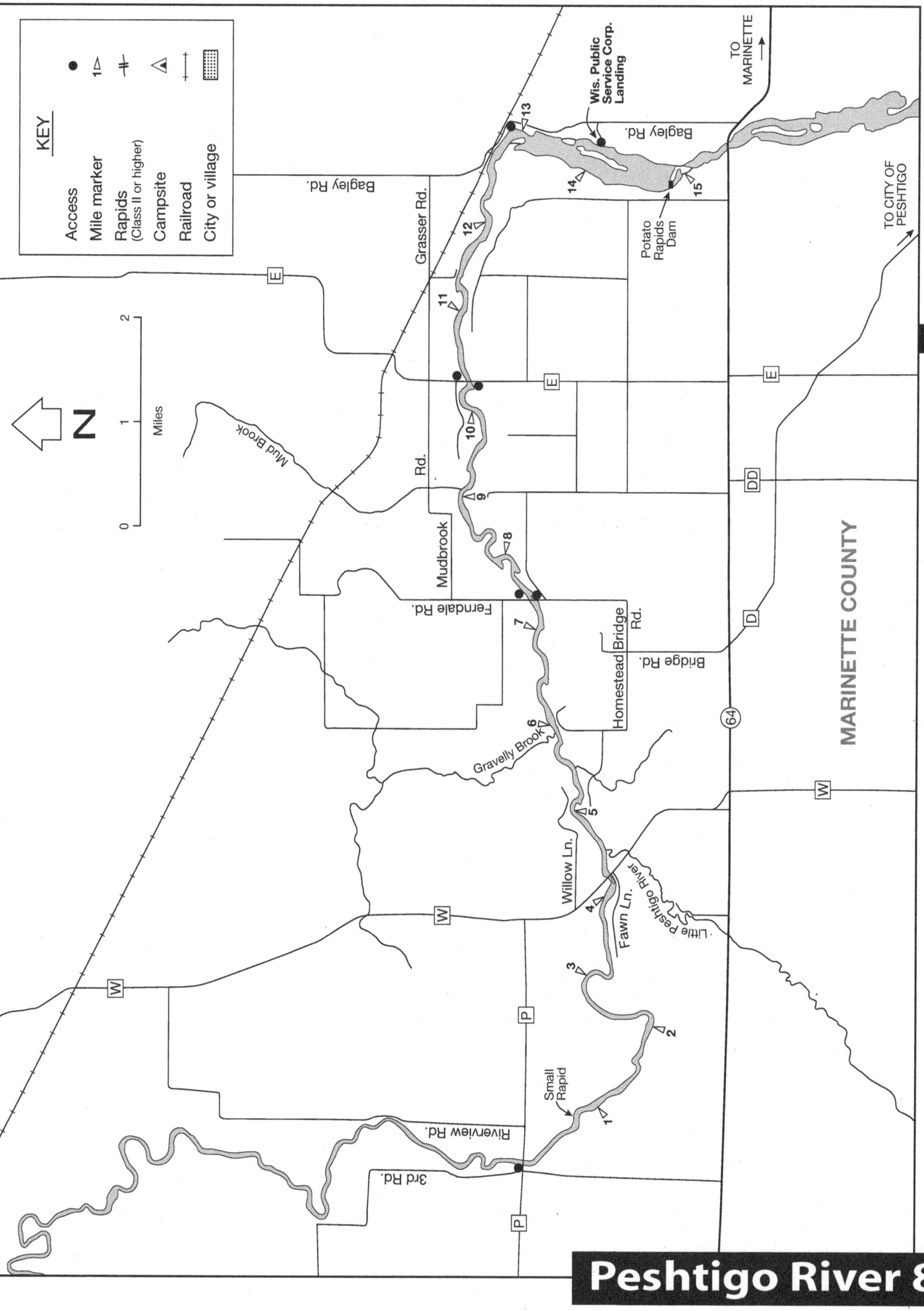

Peshtigo River 8

Peshtigo River 9

City of Peshtigo to Klingsporn Public Landing (10.3 Miles)

The Peshtigo ends the way it begins—in a low, marshy area. But in addition to marshland, this section gives paddlers the opportunity to experience some wild, wooded stretches, a huge island, imposing sand banks and a historic city. The trip begins on the south edge of the city of Peshtigo, which lost hundreds of citizens in the disastrous forest fire of 1871. Waterfowl and other birds are plentiful on this trip, especially in the large wildlife area near the end.

Riverside **camping** is provided by the city of Peshtigo at Badger Park, upstream from the dam.

Water levels are almost always adequate for good paddling. For water flow informtation, check the daily readings for the Potato Rapids and Peshtigo dams on the Wisconsin Public Service website: www.wisconsinpublicservice.com/news/hydro/hydrodata.asp.

The average **GRADIENT** is only 0.5 feet per mile.

The **shuttle route** is via County B and County BB.

PUT IN river-left at the **East Side Boat Landing** in the city of Peshtigo off County B, downstream from the railroad bridge and the paper-mill dam. Good parking is provided. Do *not* put in at the designated canoe-portage just below the dam: The water is often quite swift here.

The stretch begins with a wide, deep straightaway in a wooded lowland setting. Dam outflow usually produces good current.

The straightaway ends at a high sand bank on the right, then turns left. Here, and elsewhere along this section, "boils" are encountered in the water, caused by underwater configurations and currents. From this point, the banks are higher on the right for a while. You'll see many nesting boxes for wood ducks in the woods.

Sand banks and concrete rip-rap appear on the right at the apex of the first big oxbow (2.2 miles). At the end of the oxbow, when the river heads back to the right, a high wooded bank and house appear on the left. County BB is close by on the left for a while, with many houses. Twice more, big oxbows take the river close to County BB. A creek enters on the left in the third of these approaches, followed by several houses (5 miles). Small sloughs appear on both sides here and there.

Sand bluffs along the Peshtigo as it nears Green Bay.

There is a large slough on the right where the river sharply bends left (6.4 miles). Harbor Road is fairly close on the right, and you will often hear traffic. (In the logging era, a railroad track ran from the city of Peshtigo to the port at the mouth of the river, following the route taken by Harbor Road.) The low banks remain wooded, but vegetation becomes progressively more marshlike.

When the river bends right just before a huge island (7.8 miles), there are very attractive high sand banks on the left, topped with conifers. Take the left channel at the island, especially when the water is low. Soon after the left channel begins, there are sheer sand banks, 15 feet high, with numerous swallow nests. This was once the site of an Indian camp. Avoid the occasional fallen tree.

A home appears on the right where the two channels join after the island, and the river bends left. From this point on, the river environment becomes quite marshy, with fewer trees and many islands. Deer stands and duck blinds are occasionally visible. Almost 5,000 acres near the mouth of the river comprise the Peshtigo Harbor Wildlife Area, a haven for waterfowl and other wild animals.

TAKE-OUT: After some houses on the left, the river makes one last bend to the left before the public **landing** on river-left. Klingsporn Landing is not conspicuous, so be on the look-out for it. It is accessed by a short signed road from County BB south of Peshtigo where BB turns east. Some parking is available. A landing farther downstream on river-left is no longer accessible.

Klingsporn is still almost two miles of marsh paddling from the mouth. If you wish to get a little closer to the mouth, you can continue to the **Harbor Road Landing** on the right. (To drive to the landing, take West Front Street out of Peshtigo, then Hale Road.)

Fire in Peshtigo

Almost everyone knows that a terrible forest fire once consumed the city of Peshtigo, but few are aware of how bad it really was.

During the dry fall of 1871, the inhabitants of Peshtigo had gotten used to small fires burning almost constantly in the forests of the northeast, so on October 8 they had no idea of what was in store for them. That night, winds whipped the flames into a firestorm that swept through the little logging town, then up the coast of Green Bay. At least 1,200 people lost their lives—800 in Peshtigo alone—and 1,250,000 acres of forest were devastated.

In terms of lives lost, it was the most catastrophic forest fire in American history. Ironically, the Peshtigo fire was relegated to page-two status in the newspapers because it occurred on the same night as the famous (but less disastrous) Chicago fire.

Today, a dramatic mural in downtown Peshtigo commemorates the fire, and a museum displays objects that survived the conflagration. This book's final day trip on the river begins near the spot where many of the citizens of Peshtigo saved their lives by immersing themselves in the water.

For a very engaging account of the fire, see Robert W. Wells' Fire at Peshtigo (NorthWord, 1983).

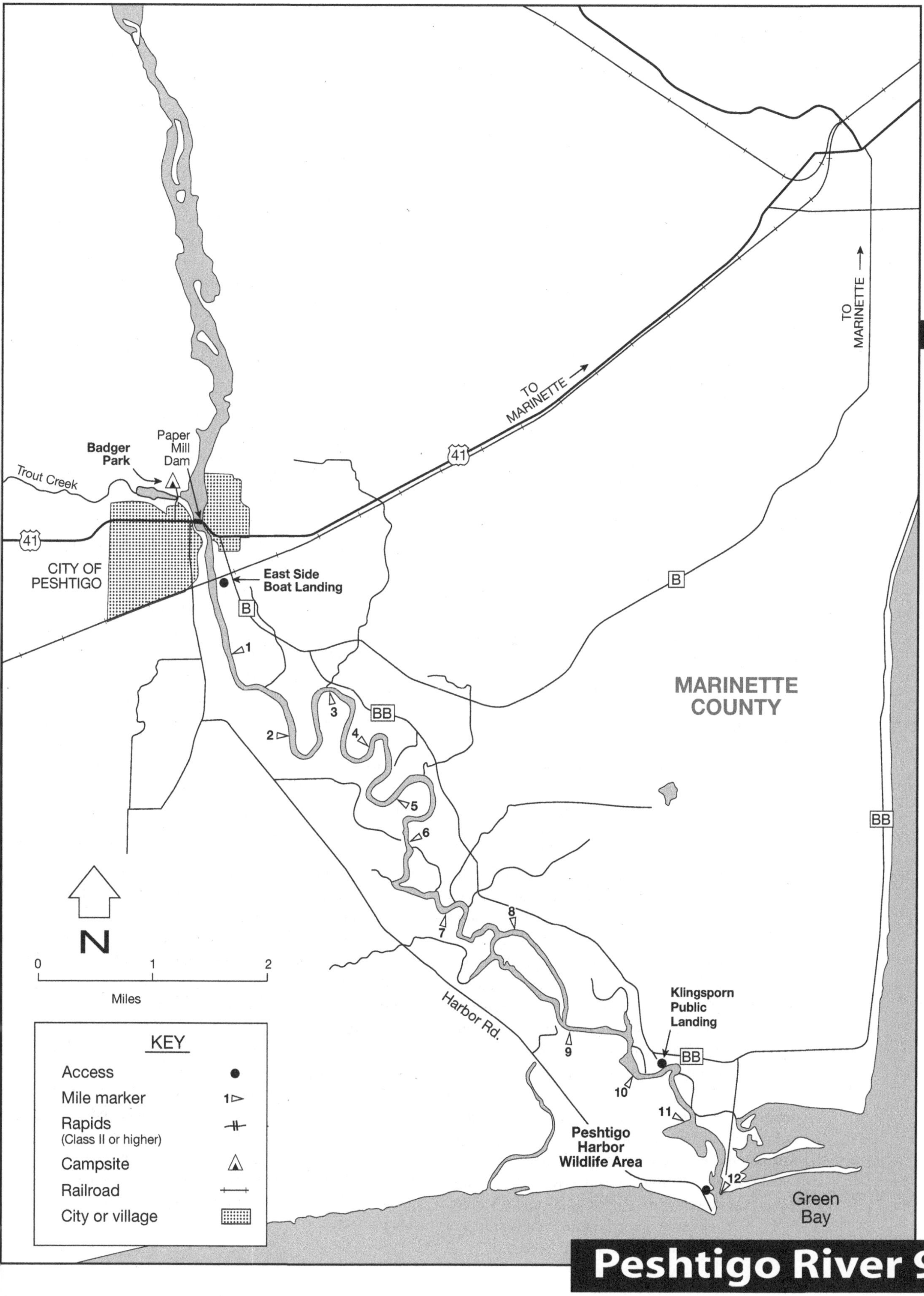

Peshtigo River 9

Pike River

Highway 141 to Yellow Bridge Falls (9.5 Miles)

One of the prettiest and most unspoiled rivers in Wisconsin, the Pike (along with the Pine and Popple) was given special protection by the Wisconsin Wild Rivers Act of 1965. The three rivers are to "receive special management to assure their preservation, protection, and enhancement of their natural beauty, unique recreational, and other inherent values." Paddlers will see little development along the Pike, while encountering mixed forest, good current, pleasant flatwater, frequent riffles and rapids, attractive rock formations, fishing opportunities and peacefulness.

The section is often broken into two parts: Highway 141 to County K (6.4 miles), which, except for Powerline Rapids, is suitable for novices; and County K to Yellow Bridge Falls (3.1 miles), which is for experienced whitewater paddlers.

The nearest public **camping** is at two Marinette County parks, both about 10 miles away: Twelve-Foot Falls Park to the north, and Old Veterans Lake Campground to the northwest. Goodman Park and McClintock Park are farther to the west.

Water levels are fairly dependable year-round, but the section downstream from County K can get scratchy after prolonged rainless periods. Check the Amberg gauge (#04066500) on the USGS website; see "Water Levels" in the introduction.

The average **GRADIENT** is 10.5 feet per mile.

The best **shuttle route** is via Highway 141, County K and Pike River Road.

PUT IN at the **Highway 141 bridge** near Amberg, downstream-left or upstream-right.

The river begins with attractive wooded scenery, dependable current and a consistent width of about 90 feet.

Powerline Rapids (also known as Bull Falls) appears about a mile downstream. A Class II rapids (more difficult in high water), this drop falls through a small canyon and is only about 50 yards long. There are several large boulders to avoid; most paddlers enter the rapids on the left, then maneuver through the rest of the drop. As you near the rapids, be sure to take out on the right and walk along the scout/portage path. Only experienced paddlers should run Powerline Rapids.

The rest of the stretch to County K is mostly flatwater, but with a number of pleasant riffles, rapids, and small drops. Downed trees are sometimes encountered, so be wary of strainers. Attractive rock outcroppings are common, and a few houses appear on the shoreline.

A couple of trout streams—K.C. Creek and Slough Creek—enter on the left at 3.8 and 4.3 miles. At 4.8 miles, the river abruptly turns right (south) at a huge stone bluff; there is a house on the left.

In the remaining 1.5 miles before County K, several riffles and minor rapids are encountered, with interesting ledges and boulder constrictions.

The County K bridge has a good **access** and parking area on the upstream left side. After County K, the river gets narrower and rockier, with more gradient and frequent rapids. There are three curving Class I rapids downstream from the bridge, with rocky shorelines.

Scrounge Canyon, a Class II rapids two hundred yards long, is located about a mile from County K. The rapids is filled with boulders, but has some nice eddies along the sides.

Flatwater and a couple of small rapids follow Scrounge. Then, at 8.8 miles, **Horseshoe Falls** (Class II) appears after a right-hand turn. A curved ledge, Horseshoe is usually run in the center where there's a tongue. Most paddlers get out on the right to scout. At medium and high water levels, a backroller can develop here. Note the access road (private) on the left upstream from Horseshoe. A small drop follows Horseshoe Falls.

After half a mile of flatwater, Yellow Bridge (over Barker Road) comes into view. Just upstream from the bridge is an irregular river-wide **ledge** that can be scouted from a river-left landing. Boaters can take out at this **landing** (which has good parking), or can run the ledge, then take out on the left just below the ledge and upstream from the bridge. This ledge can be run in several places; sometimes it is difficult to make an elegant run, especially when the water is low. Only advanced paddlers should consider continuing beyond this point, because the following rapids is quite difficult and can involve a very mean swim.

Yellow Bridge Falls (Class II–III) comes right after the bridge and involves two pitches. Run the first, rocky pitch angled toward the right in order to hit the river-right eddy before the next drop. Carefully look over the main drop from this eddy; you will see a distinct horizon line, followed by a sheer 5-foot drop. Generally it is best to run this main drop to the right or right of center, angled a little to the left. A couple hundred yards of boulder garden follow, so be careful. Please respect the property rights and no-trespassing signs of the owner of the adjacent property.

The **TAKE-OUT** is an easy-to-miss clearing on the left at the end of the boulder garden. There is some room for parking at the take-out, which is **accessed** from Pike River Road a short distance from Barker Road.

Below Yellow Bridge Falls, the Pike continues for four miles (mostly fast-flowing, with a class II boulder garden and a 2-foot drop) to its confluence with the Menominee.

Horseshoe Falls: a popular play spot on the Pike.

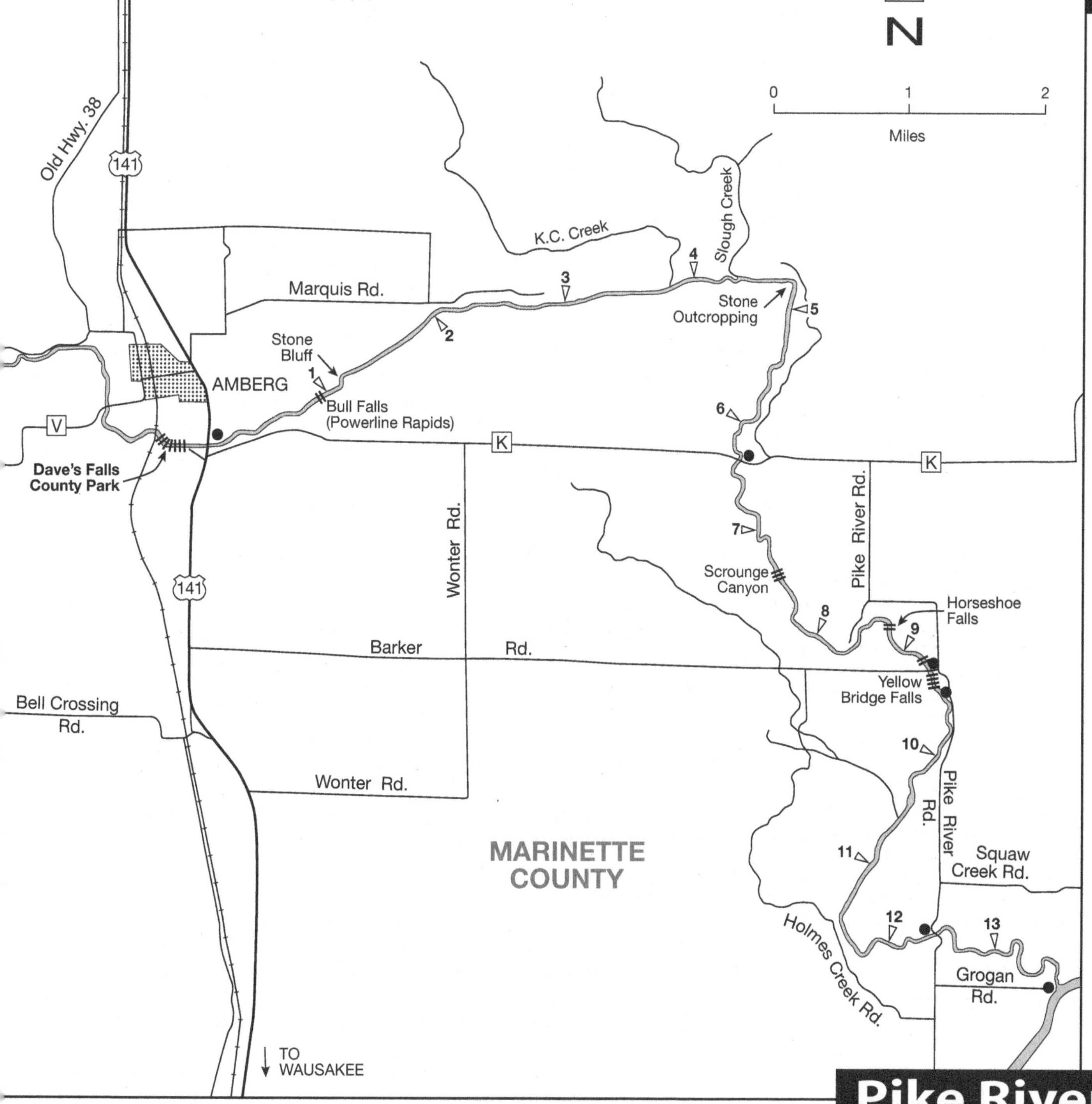

Pine River 1

Highway 55 to Highway 139 (15.5 Miles)

Beaver lodge on the Pine.

A delightfully small river, the Pine mixes long, quiet stretches with riffles and rapids, often becoming quite narrow as it winds along through a wild environment. Much of the river flows through remote areas of the Nicolet National Forest.

The Pine was protected as a "wild river" by the Wisconsin Wild Rivers Act of 1965, along with the Pike and Popple. A trout stream periodically stocked with browns and rainbows, it is heavily forested, and there's plenty of wildlife.

Riverside **camping** is permitted on National Forest land along the river, at a few primitive sites on state-owned land, and on Florence County forest land bordering the river, but much of the shoreline is privately owned. A detailed canoe-trail map designating specific areas of public ownership is available upon request at the Wild Rivers Interpretive Center in Florence (715-528-5377 or 888-889-0049).

One popular unimproved campsite is located a mile from the take-out near the mouth of Stevens Creek (upstream-left). National Forest campgrounds are located nearby at Windsor Dam, Stevens Lake, Chipmunk Rapids, Lost Lake and Lauterman Lake.

Cradle of Rivers

Six of the rivers in this book (the Brule, Oconto, Peshtigo, Pine, Popple and Wisconsin) have their origin within the Nicolet National Forest, and another (the Wolf) runs alongside it. Thus, the Nicolet has been called the "Cradle of Rivers."

Named after Jean Nicolet, the French explorer who "discovered" Wisconsin in 1634, the forest is an irregularly shaped tract of 656,000 acres in the northeast part of the state. Paddlers on the upper stretches of the rivers mentioned above will enjoy a wild setting and numerous camping opportunities. Campsites range from primitive clearings along the river to fully developed campgrounds.

The forest was created during the Depression—in 1933—in an effort to recover the woodlands that had been devastated during the logging era. In addition to great canoeing rivers, it contains 1,200 lakes, more than a thousand miles of trout streams and a dozen hiking trails. Several interpretive trails feature signs that convey information about the geology, history, wildlife and vegetation of the forest.

Water levels are usually best for canoeing and kayaking in April, May and early June, and after periods of rainfall in the summer and fall. The riffles and rapids can be intolerably scrapy when the water is too low. For general water conditions (high, medium or low), call the Wild Rivers Interpretive Center in Florence (see number above).

The average **GRADIENT** is 3.8 feet per mile.

The **shuttle route** is via Highway 55, Long Lake Road (Forest Road 2168) and Highway 139. Trip length can be varied by using accesses at Lotto Road and/or Forest Road 2169. **Canoe and kayak rentals** are available at Wild Rivers Adventure Company in Florence (715-952-8027).

PUT IN downstream-left at the **Highway 55 bridge,** where there is room to park several cars alongside the shoulder. The river is only about 30 feet wide here; at times, it gets wider than this downstream but not by much. Near the beginning, you may encounter a beaver dam or two, but they usually don't pose a significant obstacle. For the first few miles the moderate current flows through a series of winding constrictions with easy riffles and Class I rapids, alternating with quiet stretches.

There are a few houses where FR 2170 approaches the river on the right. After a series of oxbows, the **access** from Lotto Road appears on the right: a bare spot on the bank in a left-hand turn. Although this access is on private land, it is often used as an alternate put-in. There is a locked gate at the end of Lotto Road.

For the next few miles there are many riffles and Class I–II **rapids,** interspersed with slow-moving pools of water. Most are easily handled and nameless, but two have names.

Downstream from the mouth of Kingstone Creek, 10 miles from the put-in, is a short but tricky Class II rapids, called **Dam Rapids** because it is formed by the remnants of an old logging dam. The right side, around a little island, is usually the best place to make the run, but watch out for strainers. Scout/portage on the left. This rapids requires maneuvering, and should be "carried around" by inexperienced boaters.

The two brief pitches of the **CCC Camp Rapids** (Class I–II), named after the Civilian Conservation Corps camp that was once located on the right, occur 1¼ miles later. An old bridgeless road crossing is found just below the rapids. Most of the river from here to Forest Road 2169 is flatwater, but there are riffles here and there. The FR 2169 bridge, **accessed** downstream-left, has room for very little parking along the shoulder.

You'll see several houses downstream from FR 2169. The river continues to be narrow and winding, mostly with low banks.

A couple hundred yards of curving Class I–II **rapids** begin near the mouth of Stevens Creek on the left. The rapids begin immediately after a huge boulder on the right shore, where the river narrows. A long Class I–II rapids starts a half mile below Stevens Creek, with high bluffs on the right. Riffles and Class I rapids continue all the way to Highway 139.

TAKE OUT downstream-left at the **Highway 139 bridge.** Parking is available nearby on state land.

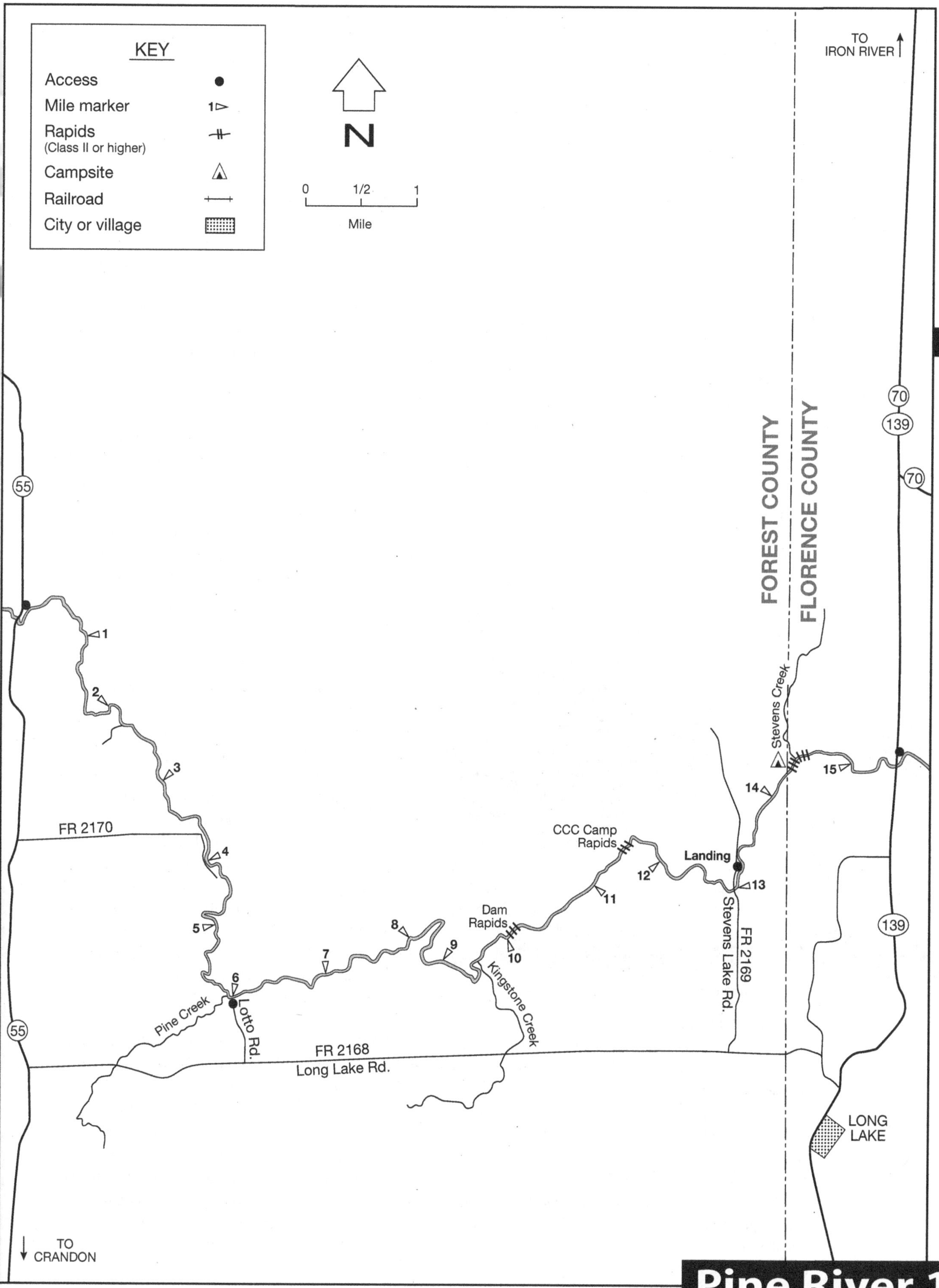
KEY
Access
Mile marker
Rapids
(Class II or higher)
Campsite
Railroad
City or village
N
0
1/2
1
Mile
TO IRON RIVER
70
139
70
55
FOREST COUNTY
FLORENCE COUNTY
Stevens Creek
1
2
3
4
5
6
7
8
9
10
11
12
13
14
15
FR 2170
CCC Camp Rapids
Landing
Dam Rapids
Kingstone Creek
Stevens Lake Rd.
FR 2169
139
Pine Creek
Lotto Rd.
55
FR 2168
Long Lake Rd.
LONG LAKE
TO CRANDON

Pine River 2

Highway 139 to Goodman Grade (17 Miles)

The Pine gains more volume and width in this stretch but still has the feel of a small, remote stream. Near the end, a major drop requires portaging by many canoeists.

Camping: A streamside campground at Chipmunk Rapids invites canoe-campers. Camping is permitted along the river on Nicolet National Forest land, but much of this section is privately owned, especially the part beginning at Snake Tail Rapids. National Park campgrounds are available nearby at Stevens Lake, Lost Lake, Lauterman Lake and Perch Lake.

Water levels are best in the springtime, usually through early June and after sustained rainfall in the summer and fall. For general water conditions (high, medium or low), call the Wild Rivers Interpretive Center in Florence (715-528-5377 or 888-889-0049). You can get a rough idea of canoeability by looking at the roadside rapids just upstream from Chipmunk Rapids Campground. Also, there is a DNR staff gauge located downstream-left from the highway 101 bridge; it should read at least "1" for an enjoyable trip.

Approaching Meyers Falls, from a kayaker's perspective.

The **GRADIENT** averages 7 feet per mile.

The **shuttle route** is via Highway 139, Highway 70 and Goodman Grade. Other trips are possible, of course (for example, Forest Road 2169 to Chipmunk Rapids, or Chipmunk Rapids to Highway 101), by using alternate landings (see Pine 1 and Pine 3). The Goodman Grade access road is short (1 mile), but can get muddy in spots.

PUT IN downstream-left at **Highway 139.** After the bridge, the river is fairly wide and slow, with occasional riffles. There is an old railroad bridge upstream from the Forest Road 2133 bridge. Cottages appear on the right before FR 2133 (access downstream-left), which is immediately followed by a Class I rapids.

The next few miles provide beautiful wilderness paddling: winding, wooded and relatively uninhabited. Eventually, an attractive cabin appears on a high bluff on the left, together with several overhead power lines, in an area where lowland is dominant. After the woods draw close to the river again, a few cottages line the left shore, and **Chipmunk Rapids** begins. These Class I–II rapids run alongside Forest Road 2156 in two pitches.

The access for the **Chipmunk Rapids Campground** (7.4 miles) is located on the right a few yards below the FR 2156 bridge, near an artesian well. This small campground (six sites) makes for a good put-in, take-out, campsite or rest stop. An excellent walking path—the Lauterman Trail—begins on the north side of the bridge. The river continues flat, slow and heavily wooded after FR 2156.

Shortly after a creek enters on the right, **Snake Tail Rapids** begins on a left turn (11.1 miles). Get out on the left to scout (and perhaps portage) this drop along the well-established trail that goes past a small cabin. The first pitch (about 150 yards long) is the most difficult, a solid Class II series of ledges with big boulders to avoid. Two short Class I–II pitches follow, also curving.

Snake Tail marks the eastern boundary of the National Forest and the beginning of the Wild Rivers section of the Pine. Flatwater is followed by a long stretch with many riffles and easy rapids. Lauterman and Kieper creeks successively enter from the left.

After a sharp right bend, then a sharp left followed by a straightaway, Class III **Meyers Falls** lies ahead (16 miles). There is a large island at this point, with a tiny (often unnoticed) channel on the right side and the main channel on the left. After a short rapids, the river narrows in a mini-canyon to about 30 feet and drops about 10 feet in a few yards. Take out on the right at least a hundred yards upstream from the falls to scout/portage; you can usually hear the roar well in advance. Quietwater and small islands follow the falls all the way to the take-out.

TAKE OUT on river-left at **Goodman Grade,** the remnant of an old logging railroad (easy to miss, so be on the lookout). Old pilings in the middle of the river here can be mistaken for an island. Leading north from the river to Highway 70 is a mile-long dirt road. A logging road/trail leads west from Goodman Grade to Meyers Falls; another leads east to Bull Falls. The nondescript entrance to Goodman Grade from Highway 70 is located 8.8 miles east of the intersection of Highway 70 and Forest Road 2450 (Dream Lake Road).

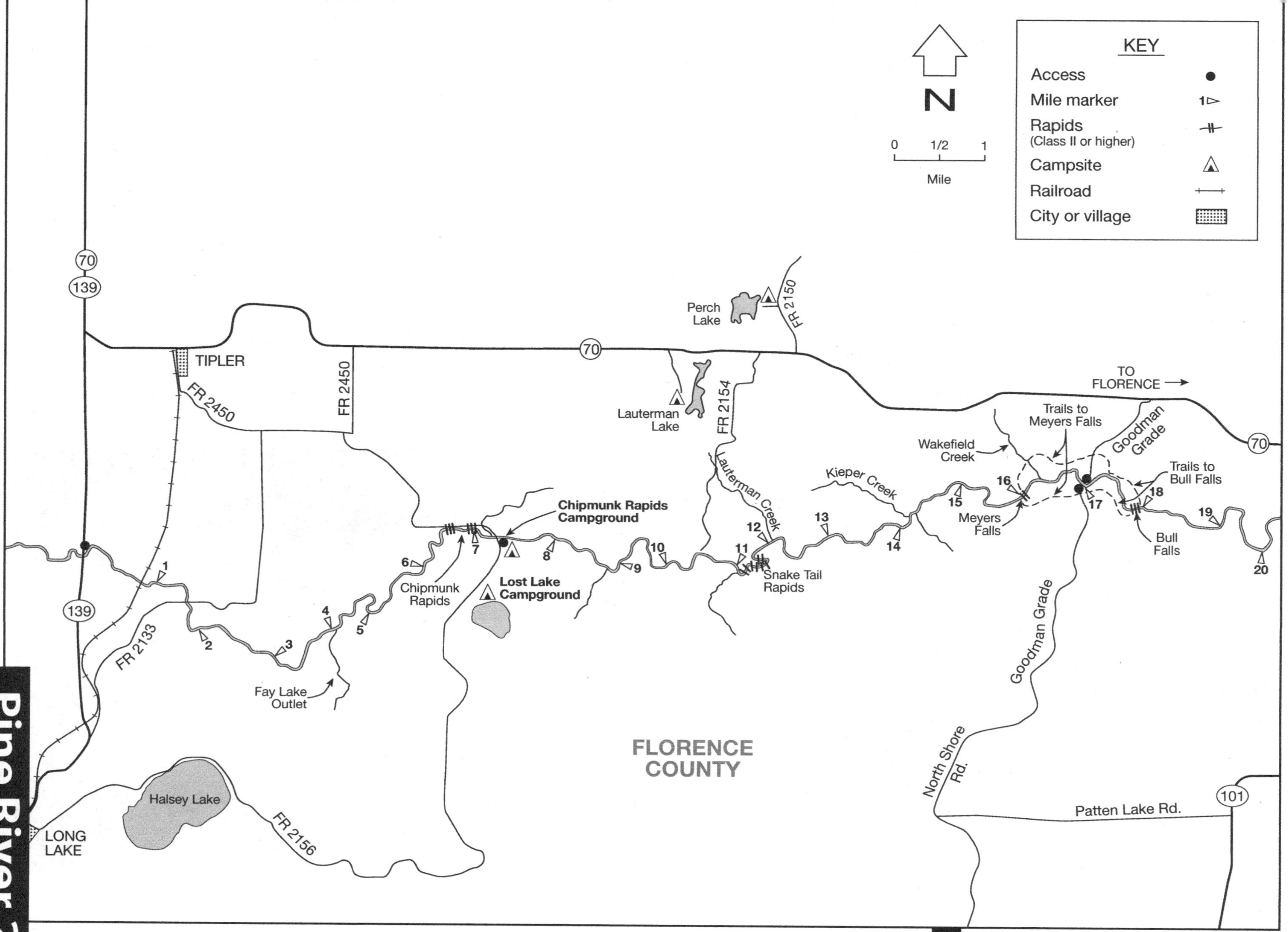

KEY
Access
Mile marker
Rapids
(Class II or higher)
Campsite
Railroad
City or village
N
0
1/2
1
Mile
70
139
TIPLER
FR 2450
FR 2450
70
Perch
Lake
FR 2150
Lauterman
Lake
FR 2154
TO
FLORENCE
Trails to
Meyers Falls
Goodman
Grade
Wakefield
Creek
70
Trails to
Bull Falls
Kieper Creek
Lauterman Creek
Chipmunk Rapids
Campground
Chipmunk
Rapids
Lost Lake
Campground
Snake Tail
Rapids
Meyers
Falls
Bull
Falls
1
2
3
4
5
6
7
8
9
10
11
12
13
14
15
16
17
18
19
20
139
FR 2133
Fay Lake
Outlet
Goodman Grade
FLORENCE
COUNTY
North Shore
Rd.
Patten Lake Rd.
101
Halsey Lake
FR 2156
LONG
LAKE

Pine River 2

Pine River 3

Goodman Grade to Highway 101 (8.8 Miles)

This section of the Pine offers a succession of different environments: first, a long, wooded upland area with numerous Class I and II rapids, then a stretch where the river makes its way between many islands, and finally a mile or so of slow water bordered by wooded swamps. There is one difficult rapids early in the trip, but it can easily be portaged, if necessary. Much of the surrounding land is private, but only a few cabins are to be seen. All of this section is protected by the Wisconsin Wild Rivers Act of 1965.

Public **campgrounds** are located nearby at Perch Lake, Lauterman Lake and Keyes Lake.

Water levels are best in April, May and early June and after periods of sustained rainfall in the summer and fall. For general water conditions (high, medium or low), call Wild Rivers Interpretive Center in Florence (715-528-5377 or 888-889-0049).

The **GRADIENT** averages 13.6 feet per mile.

The **shuttle route** is via Goodman Grade, Highway 70 and Highway 101.

PUT IN river-left at the Goodman Grade **landing,** a mile south of Highway 70. In the spring and after rainfall, this road can be difficult. Be careful not to get stuck.

About a mile downstream, **Bull Falls** comes immediately after a left-hand turn. You'll probably hear it well before you see it; get out on the left to scout along a rocky trail. The first pitch of Bull Falls (a solid Class II) is the most difficult part. Alongside a rock wall on the left, the river narrows and drops over several ledges, with big boulders to dodge; big waves form in high water. If portaging, you can carry your boat to the bottom of the first pitch and put in alongside a small rocky island. A mile of delightful, continuous Class I–II boulder gardens follows.

Paddlers will encounter lots of riffles on the Pine.

There is a long series of Class I rapids in a big left-hand bend where orange pipeline markers appear on both sides of the river (2.8 miles).

Seven-Mile Creek enters from the left in a sharp right turn (3.8 miles), and the river gets shallow and riffly downstream.

A cabin appears atop a high bluff on the left at the tip of a sharp right-hand bend (4.5 miles), the first building since Snake Tail Rapids. The Bessie Babbet Lake Outlet enters from the left at 5.1 miles.

The next section is quite unlike any place else on the river. For a long stretch, the river channel is populated with small islands. The right shore is lowland, while wooded bluffs rise on the left. Pick the main channel between the islands, and look out for deadfall.

After the islands, the current slows as the river loops around to the southwest toward Thompson Road. A swampy lowland dominates the last mile.

TAKE OUT at the **Highway 101 bridge,** upstream-right.

Other trips. From Highway 101, the Pine continues approximately 18 miles before flowing into the Menominee. After several miles of deep flatwater, LaSalle Falls drops vertically 20 feet; a half-mile gorge with solid Class II rapids follows. The falls is unrunnable and must be portaged on the right before a right-hand bend that follows a straightaway.

Soon after the gorge, a flowage begins, formed by the Pine River Dam. There is a long canoe-portage trail around the dam and powerhouse on the left. Below the powerhouse, 14.5 miles of river can be paddled to the Menominee, with accesses at the powerhouse, at the end of the portage trail (off Pine River Road), at County N, at Johnson Creek Road and at the end of Landing Road south of Lake Ellwood. A map of the lower Pine from the flowage to the Menominee may be obtained at the Wild Rivers Interpretive Center in Florence. Note that a portion of the Pine downstream from Highway 101 is shown in this book on the map for Popple 2.

In 1997, as part of a negotiated plan to relicense a number of hydroelectric plants in Wisconsin and Michigan, the Wisconsin Electric Power Company agreed to remove the Pine River Dam in the future. Thus, the Pine will again flow free and unrestricted.

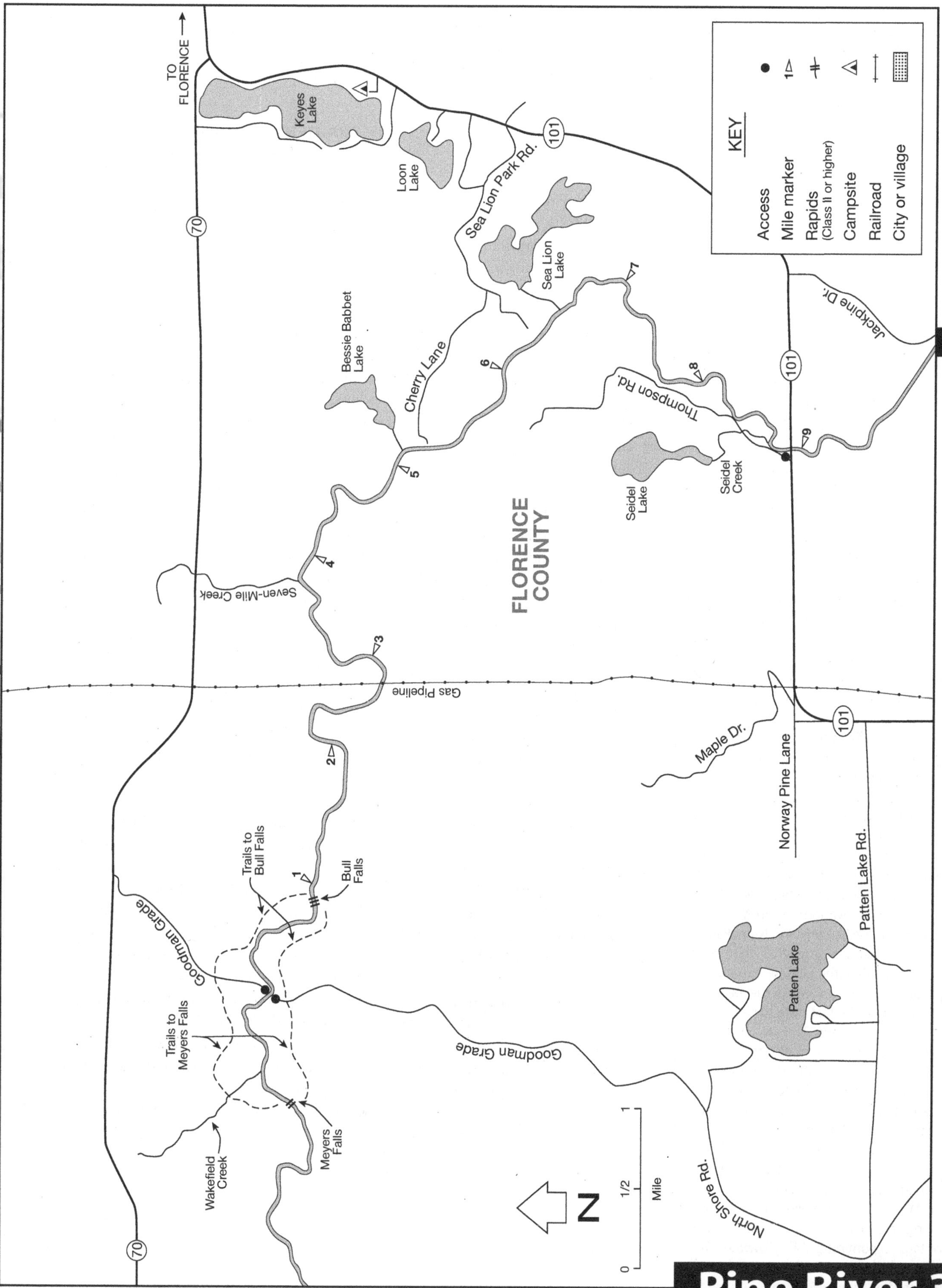
TO FLORENCE →
Keyes Lake
Loon Lake
101
70
Sea Lion Park Rd.
Sea Lion Lake
Bessie Babbet Lake
Cherry Lane
Thompson Rd.
Seidel Lake
Seidel Creek
Jackpine Dr.
FLORENCE COUNTY
Seven-Mile Creek
Gas Pipeline
Maple Dr.
Norway Pine Lane
Patten Lake Rd.
Patten Lake
Goodman Grade
Goodman Grade
Trails to Bull Falls
Bull Falls
Trails to Meyers Falls
Meyers Falls
Wakefield Creek
North Shore Rd.
1
2
3
4
5
6
7
8
9
N
0
1/2
1
Mile
KEY
Access
Mile marker
Rapids (Class II or higher)
Campsite
Railroad
City or village

Pine River 3

Popple River 1

Forest Road 2398 to Forest Road 2159 (10.8 Miles)

A small river that flows almost wholly through wild surroundings, the Popple River is protected from development by its location in the Nicolet National Forest and its inclusion (along with the Pine and Pike) in the Wisconsin Wild Rivers Act of 1965. It is so remote, winding and intimate that boaters often surprise deer, beaver, eagles and other wildlife. Trout are common, too.

The river is paddleable for 30 miles from Highway 139 to its confluence with the Pine River, but the first few miles pass through a lowland area that is subject to beaver dams and brush. Six miles downstream from Highway 139 is McDonald's Rapids (Class II). Because of the initial marshiness, the usual put-in is Forest Road 2398 (Twin Rivers Road). From here, the Popple gradually increases in intensity, culminating in four major drops in its last 10 miles. Thus, it is clearly not a river for beginners.

The first section, described below, is suitable for intermediate paddlers; only advanced paddlers should attempt the second section.

Camping: Much of the first section is in the Nicolet National Forest, where camping is permitted, but there is also considerable private property, especially after the first FR 2159 bridge. A detailed canoe-trail map designating specific areas of public ownership is available upon request from the Wild Rivers Interpretive Center in Florence. There is an undeveloped campsite on the river near the mouth of Morgan Creek, and a nearby USFS campground at Morgan Lake.

Water levels are usually best for canoeing and kayaking in April, May and early June, and after periods of sustained rainfall in the summer and fall. Shallow riffles and rapids necessitate scraping and carrying when the water is low. For general water conditions (high, medium or low), call the Wild Rivers Interpretive Center in Florence (715-528-5377 or 888-889-0049).

Protecting Our Wild Rivers

The 1960s were a great time for advocates of wild-river protection in Wisconsin. Beginning in the 1950s, controversy had raged between would-be developers and conservationists who wished to preserve at least part of the state's dwindling wilderness. In the 1960s, the battle came to a head with efforts to construct dams on the upper St. Croix and Wolf rivers—ostensibly for flood control and the enhancement of recreational activities.

Fortunately for future generations, the tireless efforts of conservationists paid off with the passage of the National Wild and Scenic Rivers Act by Congress in 1968. Two of the eight river systems included in this federal classification were in Wisconsin: 185 miles of the St. Croix and Namekagon, and the portion of the Wolf that flows through the Menominee Reservation.

Not so widely known is the fact that Wisconsin was the first state to pass a Wild Rivers Act of its own. The law, passed in 1965, called for a system of undeveloped, free-flowing rivers "to afford the citizens of this state an opportunity to enjoy natural streams, to attract out-of-state visitors, and to assure the well-being of our tourist industry." Selected for protection as part of the 1965 act were parts of three remote northern rivers located in or near national forest land: the Popple, Pine and Pike. Continuing controversy—some object to river frontage becoming publicly owned—has made it difficult to add other rivers to this protected system.

The **GRADIENT** averages 6.4 feet per mile.

The **shuttle route** is via FR 2398, FR 2162 and FR 2159. Note that the take-out is at the second FR 2159 bridge. To get to the put-in, go east on FR 2162 (Newald Road) from Highway 139, or north on FR 2159 (Newald Tower Road) from Highway 8. **Canoe and kayak rentals** are available at Wild Rivers Adventure Company in Florence (715-952-8027).

PUT IN at the **FR 2398 bridge** downstream-left, where there is room for a few cars alongside the road. The river begins fairly wide (about 50 feet) and deep, with plentiful pine, popple and alder, and occasional hay meadows.

Half a mile downstream, a long series of Class I–II **rocky pitches** begin. These are narrow, winding and enjoyable, but be on guard for deadfall. Many high, pine-covered banks follow the rapids, including one with a cottage on the left (one of only a few cabins you'll see on this trip). A lowland area follows; look for waterfowl and signs of beaver activity. Wood-duck boxes appear along the shore occasionally.

South of Morgan Lake, a cable pedestrian bridge spans the river near a home, followed by a couple of cabins.

A short, narrow boulder garden, **Burnt Dam Rapids** (Class I–II), begins near the mouth of Morgan Creek (5.3 miles). Look for the primitive campsite nearby.

A long, winding, more difficult boulder garden begins a quarter-mile upstream from the first FR 2159 bridge (5.8 miles).

The river becomes a little wider and deeper after the mouth of the South Branch, on the right (6 miles). From here, there is less lowland and more wooded banks.

Upstream from the mouth of Rock Creek (on the right, 8.2 miles), there is an island in the middle of a right-hand bend. In the main (left) channel around the island, a 600-yard Class II **rapids** has a fairly steep gradient, preceded by a shorter, easier boulder garden. The rapids mark the eastern boundary of the national forest and the beginning of the Wisconsin Wild River section.

The old abutments of the Goodman Railroad grade and several cabins are passed as the second FR 2159 bridge approaches.

TAKE OUT downstream-left at **FR 2159.** A small parking area is located here.

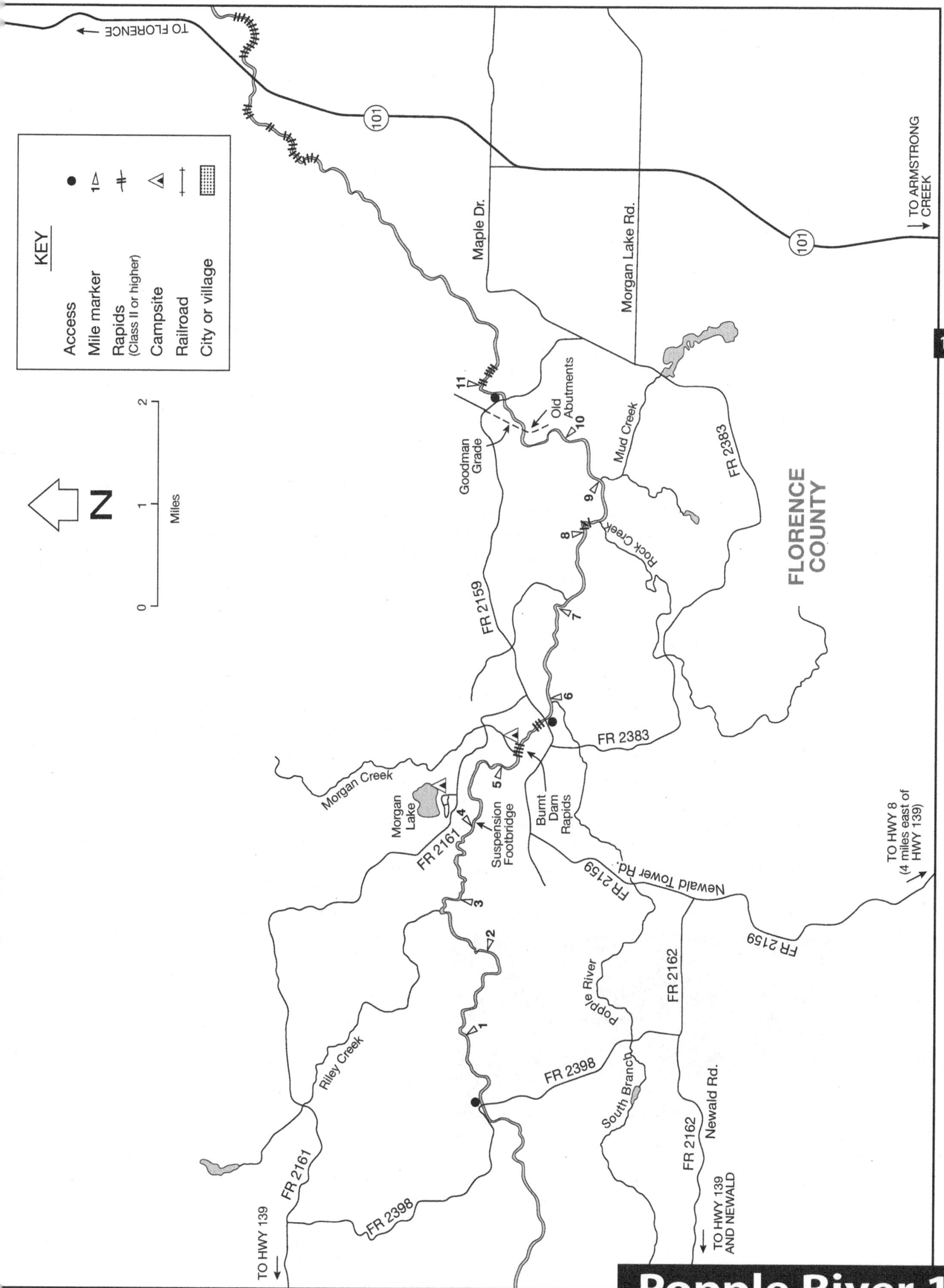

Popple River 1

Popple River 2

Forest Road 2159 to Highway 101 (12.2 Miles)

This is a marvelously varied section of the Popple River that includes wide, deep stretches, winding rapids, tall bluffs, alder swamps and rugged stone formations. The last 11 miles also present four impressive Class III drops that should be run only by advanced paddlers. The river is protected as a Wisconsin "Wild River," and the setting is quite remote, with only a few cabins. Pine, popple, balsam, birch, cedar, maple and alder grow thick along the shoreline.

The section can readily be shortened into 5.0- and 7.2-mile portions by using Highway 101 as an access.

Camping is available near the put-in at the USFS Morgan Lake Campground.

Water levels are usually best in April, May and early June, and after periods of sustained rainfall. For general water conditions (high, medium or low), call Wild Rivers Interpretive Center in Florence (715-528-5377 or 888-889-0049). Check the rapids under the FR 2159 bridge or downstream from the Highway 101 bridge to see whether there's enough water to paddle. This section of the Popple demands respect and caution when the water is high; big waves and grabby holes develop in the drops and rapids.

The average **GRADIENT** is a lively 14.7 feet per mile.

The **shuttle route** is via FR 2159, Maple Drive and Highway 101 to the Pine River bridge.

PUT IN at the second **FR 2159 bridge,** downstream-left. There is a small parking area here for a few cars.

A quarter mile of quietwater brings you to two cabins, one on each shore; these signal the approach of **Little Bull Falls,** which is preceded by a short rapids. Get out on the left and follow the path alongside this Class III drop to scout. The river narrows to about 30 feet and drops 4 feet over a ledge into an impressive hole. Several hundred yards of tight, winding Class II boulder gardens follow. The color of the water tends to be rather dark, making the rocks difficult to see.

Running Washburn Falls, one of the most difficult rapids on the Popple.

Almost a mile of flatwater follows, ending at another long set of Class II **rapids.**

After another stretch of quietwater, there is an almost continuous succession of Class II rapids for more than a mile, all the way to **Big Bull Falls** (4.3 miles). Be on the lookout for a rocky cedar island and obvious horizon lines; the river splits around this island, with 7-foot Class III drops on both sides. Both can be seen from the scout/portage path on the left, although the right drop is only partially visible. The view of the falls from downstream is quite beautiful. The left channel is narrow and boulder-laced, while the right drops over a couple of steep ledges with tricky holes. After a brief pool, Class II rapids continue. (Incidentally, nonpaddlers can easily view the falls by following a signed footpath from West River Road, off Highway 101.)

The Highway 101 **access** is downstream-left, where an attractive wayside with picnic tables and parking lot is located (5 miles). The long series of Class II boulder gardens that follow Highway 101 are the last on the Popple, but two big drops remain.

After a lengthy flatwater stretch and the mouth of Lamon-Tangue Creek on the right, a narrowing and quickening of the stream bed and the appearance of numerous huge boulders should alert you to the approach of Class III **Washburn Falls** (7.2 miles), which can be scouted from a trail on the right. The river narrows here, and drops dramatically over a series of ledges; the roar can be heard upstream, and there is a distinct horizon line.

The long flatwater stretch from here to **Jennings Falls** is quite interesting for its changes of setting, including a lowland heavily populated with cedars. The river grows wider after Woods Creek flows in from the left. After the creek mouth, the Popple turns right toward Jennings Falls (9.7 miles). A rock-faced wall on the right indicates that the falls are approaching. This Class II–III drop, which can be scouted on the right, necessitates maneuvering through a succession of big wave-trains.

After another 1.3 miles of flatwater, the Popple flows into the Pine River. At this point, **TAKE OUT** on the right bank at the confluence or about half a mile downstream. Both accesses are reached from the south by White Birch Road, which is often in poor condition during the spring. If you don't mind paddling a mile against the current, you can also head upstream on the Pine and take out at the Highway 101 bridge. Please note, if you continue downstream on the Pine, you MUST make a half-mile portage around the unrunnable La Salle Falls gorge!

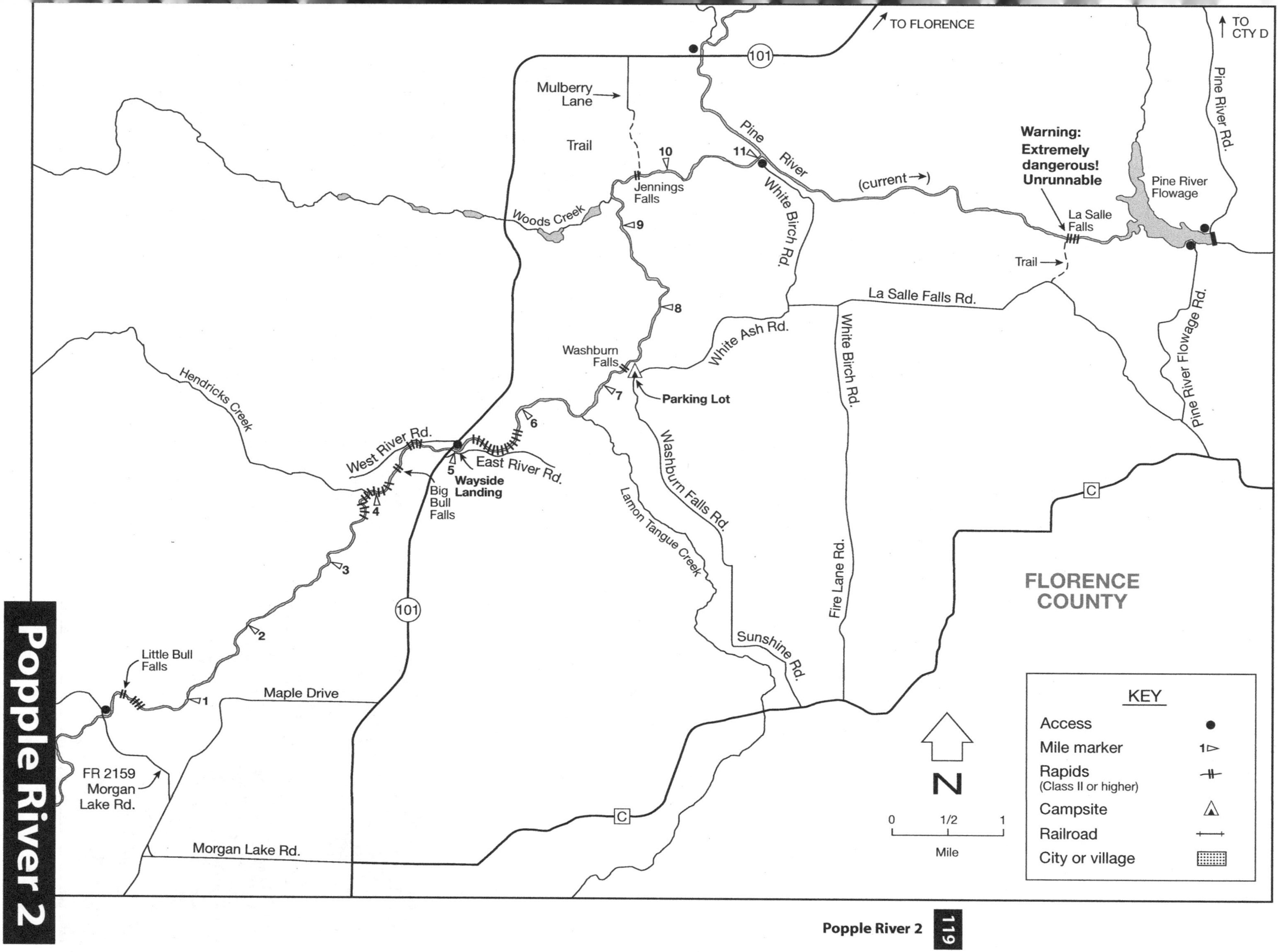
Popple River 2
TO FLORENCE
TO CTY D
101
Mulberry Lane
Trail
10
Jennings Falls
11
Pine River
White Birch Rd.
(current →)
Warning: Extremely dangerous! Unrunnable
Pine River Flowage
Pine River Rd.
La Salle Falls
Trail
La Salle Falls Rd.
Pine River Flowage Rd.
Woods Creek
9
8
Washburn Falls
White Ash Rd.
Parking Lot
7
White Birch Rd.
Hendricks Creek
West River Rd.
6
East River Rd.
5
Wayside Landing
Big Bull Falls
4
Washburn Falls Rd.
Lamon Tangue Creek
Fire Lane Rd.
C
FLORENCE COUNTY
3
101
2
Little Bull Falls
1
Maple Drive
Sunshine Rd.
FR 2159 Morgan Lake Rd.
C
Morgan Lake Rd.
N
0
1/2
1
Mile
KEY
Access
Mile marker
Rapids (Class II or higher)
Campsite
Railroad
City or village

Prairie River

County J to County C (9.5 Miles)

A lovely little stream that is very popular with trout fishermen, the Prairie River is paddleable for about 25 miles before joining the Wisconsin River at Merrill, near its confluence with the Wisconsin. Often only 40 to 50 feet wide—sometimes less—the river alternately winds through wooded bluffs and low banks, with many pine trees, small islands, riffles and plentiful wildlife along the way. Part of the shoreline is a state-designated fishing area, with DNR accesses.

One of the features of the river is the Prairie Dells, a beautiful gorge that in recent years has been returned to a natural state after the removal of the Dells Dam. Class II rapids are located in the dells and farther upstream at Dudley.

Camping is available a few miles southwest of the take-out at Council Grounds State Park near Merrill.

Water levels are best in the springtime and after sustained rainfall. Two good checkpoints to determine whether there is enough water to paddle are the downstream shoals at the first bridge below County J (Prairie Drive), and the dells themselves, accessed by a short spur road off Highway 17. Also, check the gauge northeast of Merrill (#05394500) on the USGS website: see "Water Levels" in the introduction.

The **GRADIENT** averages 8.4 feet per mile.

The **shuttle route** is via County J, Highway 17 and County C. Several convenient accesses are available (for example, Heineman Road, Haymeadow Creek County Park, Shady Lane and Prairie Road), making it possible to vary trip length.

The beautiful Prairie Dells.

PUT IN upstream-left at **County J,** west of Bloomville. The river begins narrow, with tag alder along the banks. Occasional shallow spots are encountered down to the Prairie Drive bridge, which is immediately followed by old wooden pilings.

Soon after the Heineman Road bridge at 1.5 miles (**access** upstream-right), an old abutment can be seen on the right shore—the site of the old Heineman Railroad grade. Just downstream is a small island that is commonly obstructed by deadfall; a path on the left circumvents the problem. Look for a big eagle's nest shortly afterward in a pine tree on the left shore.

No cottages are encountered from the put-in until the mouth of Haymeadow Creek (3 miles), which signals the approach of the **dells,** a very long, continuous Class II rapids in a small canyon. A trail runs alongside the dells for almost a mile, on river-left.

Scout at least part of the dells (it's a beautiful walk anyway) and portage if in doubt. Near the end of the gorge, you can see the sparse remnants of the old Dells Dam on the rocky walls.

Occasional riffles and Class I rapids follow the dells, together with a couple of cabins. The sandy DNR **access** at the end of Shady Lane (5.3 miles) appears on the left (good parking). The water is deep and wide in this stretch, with islands and pine groves.

Yankee Rapids is a series of easy Class I rapids between Shady Lane and the DNR Prairie Road access. Near the end of Prairie Road (6.6 miles), a short public-access lane leads to a parking area, from which a path goes down to the river; the hard-to-spot **landing** is on river-left alongside a couple of small islands. Downstream, the river runs alongside County C for awhile.

TAKE OUT upstream-left at the **County C bridge.**

Other trips: Below County C, the river gradually widens and slows, eventually flowing into the Wisconsin River at Merrill. Until recently, the Ward Mill Dam blocked the flow of the Prairie on the north side of the city.

Upstream from County J, especially before the mouth of the North Branch, the Prairie is quite narrow and winding, with a higher incidence of brush and deadfall obstructions. A half mile of Class I–II rapids (the Dudley Pines) lies just north of the Highway 17/County CC intersection, beginning near Bridge Road. Accesses for the 12 miles north of County J are available at R & H Road, Hackbarth Drive, the short lane opposite Echo Lake Road, Highway 17 at Dudley, Town Hall Road, Prairie Forks Road and Axen Road.

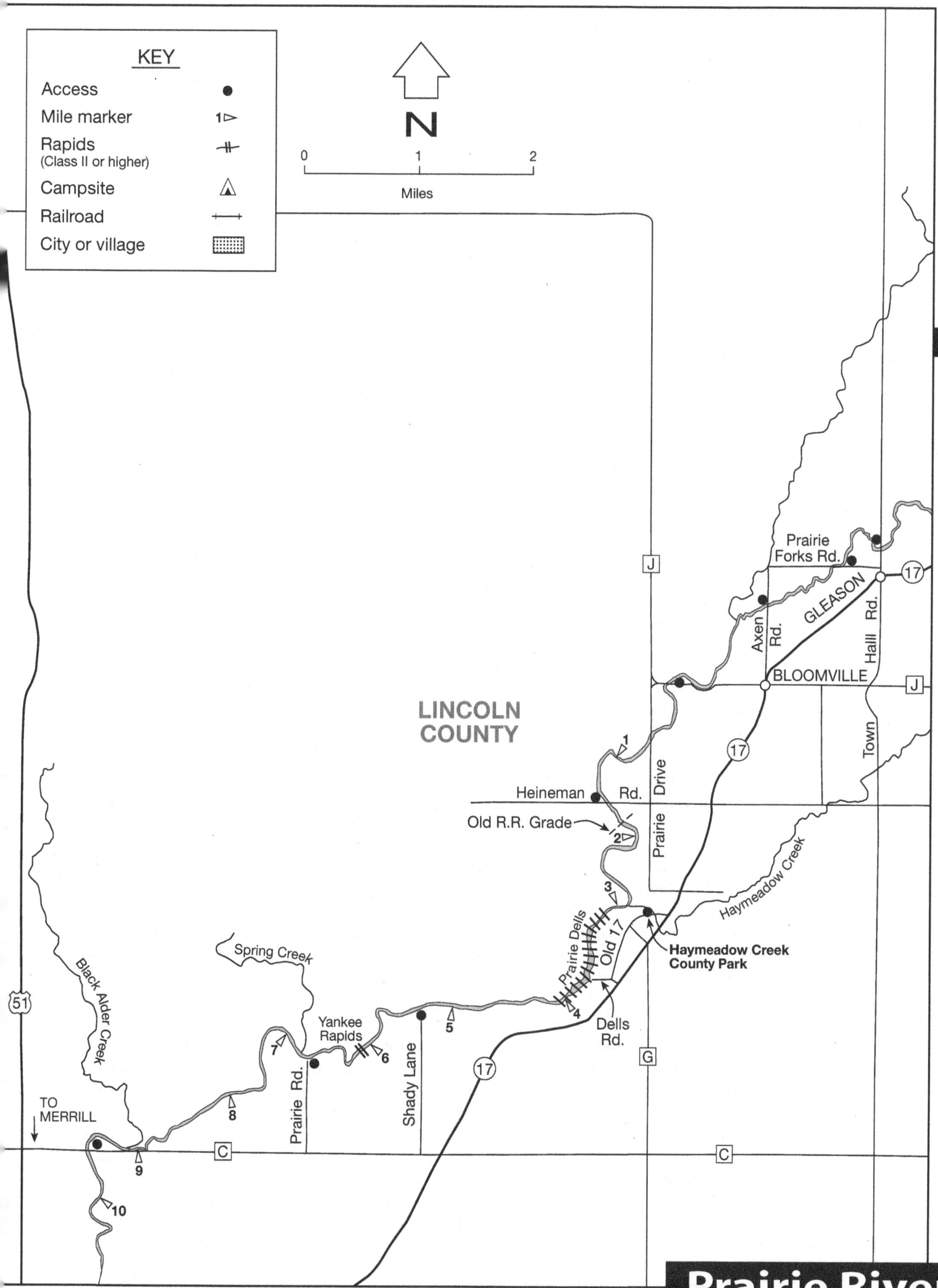

Prairie River

Red River

Lower Red Lake Powerhouse to Village of Red River (4.1 Miles)

Scarcely four miles long, this stretch of the Red River (a tributary of the Wolf) serves up two of the most popular and challenging whitewater rapids in Wisconsin. The trip is generally suitable for intermediate paddlers; occasional Class I–II rapids provide excellent playspots for surfing, eddying and ferrying. Deer flies can be pesky in the summer. Most of the land alongside the river is privately owned, so paddlers should limit their shoreline forays to the put-in, designated take-outs, scouting points and (if necessary) portages.

Water levels are quite variable, depending principally upon the amount of release from the powerhouse, but there is almost always enough water for comfortable paddling. The height of the river can be judged by the amount of air space showing in the slot at the base of the powerhouse wall: A completely open slot means low water, partial space means medium high, and no space indicates that the two big rapids downstream will be difficult. You also can check the midstream rocks 150 feet downstream from the powerhouse; the river is high if they're completely covered.

The **GRADIENT** averages 9.7 feet per mile.

The best **shuttle route** is via Lower Lake Road, Cherry Road and County A. If Ziemer's Falls is used as the take-out, the best shuttle route is via Lower Lake Road and Butternut Road.

The **PUT-IN** (approximately a mile southeast of the village of Gresham) is a small sandy beach just below the dam and powerhouse on **Lower Lake Road.** A parking area river-right has plenty of room for vehicles.

The stretch begins with a 40- to 50-foot-wide river bed, steady current and a mixed forest of maples, hemlocks, pines and cedars. Shells cover the river bottom.

Almost half a mile from the put-in, after a left-hand bend, is **First Drop,** a simple river-wide ledge (Class I–II). The backroller, fast water and downstream eddies make this a popular play spot. The beautiful home and outbuildings on the right serve as a reminder that this is private property. Gardner Creek enters from the left after First Drop.

Approximately half a mile later, there is a rock outcropping in the middle of the river; at lower levels, the left channel is too scrapy to be runnable. Usually, however, there is an excellent surfing wave in the right channel. The midriver rock makes a pleasant spot to relax or have lunch.

Double Drop (two small ledges), another good place to practice basic boating maneuvers, is encountered at 1.2 miles.

Just around the corner from Double Drop is **Monastery Falls** (also known as Alexian or Freeborn Falls), an impressive Class III series of drops in a constricted mini-canyon that ends alongside the ruined but still picturesque Alexian Monastery on the left. After Double Drop, make your way to river-right and take out to scout and/or portage. Walk along the shoreline, being careful not to fall on the slippery rocks; leave your PFD and helmet on.

The first drop, immediately after a 6-foot entry slot, is the most difficult part; a successful run requires plenty of momentum, boat control and sometimes a good brace. Many a boater is caught in the "stopper-hole" here and experiences a nasty swim. If you are unfortunate enough to have to swim Monastery, try to stay away from the left-hand side of the final drop: There are sharp rocks hidden there. Monastery is especially difficult at medium to high water levels, and should not be attempted by the inexperienced. Don't be afraid to walk your boat around this rapids. Many kayakers and canoeists carry their boats to the spot just below the first drop (carefully!), and run the rest of the rapids from there. The bottom of the rapids is a popular spot to practice fast-jet ferries and 360-degree turns; a large, quiet pool downstream makes mistakes inconsequential.

A bit downstream, there are two small Class I rock constrictions. At the second, the remains of a building from an old grist mill can still be seen in the woods on the right.

Half a mile downstream from Monastery, after a deep flatwater stretch, is **Ziemer's Falls** (solid Class II+). This complex set of rapids begins with a fairly easy ledge that drops into some waves; immediately after this initial drop, eddy-out on the left and get out to scout the rest of the rapids from the rocky shore. After the entrance drop, there is an S-curve of fast water ending with a final drop that can be run on the far right, down a narrow slot in the middle, or (in medium to high water) down the left. There are a number of eddies to hit throughout the rapids.

Ziemer's is a classic, technical rapids that requires a lot of maneuvering. Locals frequently come to sun themselves and party on the rocks alongside it. There is a public **access** road from Butternut Road; thus, many paddlers take out here, 2.1 miles downstream from the powerhouse.

Below Ziemer's are several rocky riffles and small, easy drops. After one such drop (**Finley Court Rapids,** about 0.3 mile downstream from Ziemer's), there is a public **take-out** on the left, owned and maintained by the Red River Paddlers. (Take Kathryn Road off Butternut Road, then Finley Court. The canoe-access parking area has big rocks alongside it. It's a short walk to the river, down a rocky, sandy hillside with steps cut into it.)

At 3.4 miles, there are concrete abutments on both sides. Another small, rocky constriction follows, with a nice wave-train. Just upstream from the take-out bridge, there is one more drop, with a curious configuration that usually requires that it be run from the left on a diagonal; there is usually a curler wave beneath the ledge on the left side of the drop.

TAKE OUT at the **County A bridge,** upstream-left, in the village of Red River. There is little room for parking here.

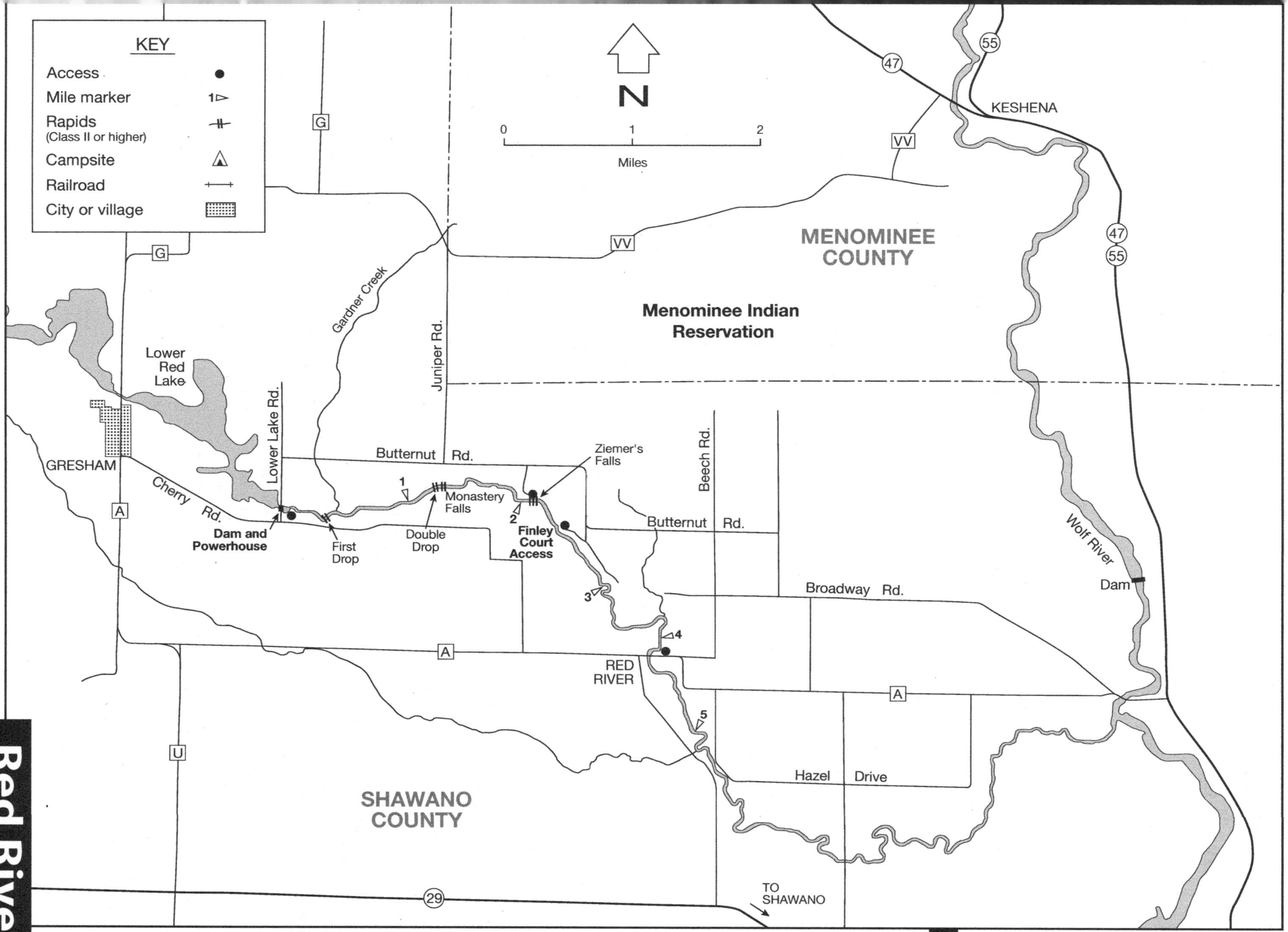
KEY
Access
Mile marker
Rapids
(Class II or higher)
Campsite
Railroad
City or village
N
0
1
2
Miles
KESHENA
MENOMINEE
COUNTY
Menominee Indian
Reservation
Lower
Red
Lake
GRESHAM
Gardner Creek
Juniper Rd.
Lower Lake Rd.
Butternut Rd.
Cherry Rd.
Dam and
Powerhouse
First
Drop
Double
Drop
Monastery
Falls
Ziemer's
Falls
Finley
Court
Access
Beech Rd.
Butternut Rd.
Broadway Rd.
Wolf River
Dam
RED
RIVER
Hazel Drive
SHAWANO
COUNTY
TO
SHAWANO

Red River

Red Cedar River 1

Rice Lake to County W (7.8 Miles)

A wonderful river for families, novice canoeists, anglers and anyone interested in tranquil surroundings, the Red Cedar is paddleable along its whole length. Originating at Red Cedar Lake, the river flows southward through Rice Lake, Cameron, Sand Creek, Colfax and Menomonie before joining the Chippewa west of Eau Claire. Roads are never far away, but they seldom diminish the sense of isolation experienced by boaters on the Red Cedar.

The river is located in beautiful, hilly countryside studded with dairy farms. There are no rapids for beginners to worry about, few riffles and infrequent deadfall—just plenty of grassy banks, terrific fishing holes and convenient accesses. Often spotted are heron, mallards, turtles, songbirds and eagles. The river has a good reputation for smallmouth and walleye fishing, but northern, perch and bullhead are also caught. In the summer, paddlers will notice occasional algae blooms, and underwater vegetation is sometimes profuse in the smaller channels of islands and in the slack water of bends.

In the first three sections, you'll find that Barron County does an outstanding job of providing comfortable, well-maintained landings along the river—a model for other counties in the state. Like the downstream stretches, section one begins and ends with excellent accesses.

Public **campgrounds** are located on Red Cedar Lake (Waldo Carlson Park), near Chetek (Southworth Memorial/Ten Mile Lake Park) and near Cameron on Prairie Lake (Veterans Memorial Park). Many private campgrounds are located in the Rice Lake, Cameron, Barron and Chetek areas.

Water levels are fairly dependable all year, and uncomfortably low only during droughty conditions. Only during high-water conditions does the river become threatening. The only USGS gauge on the river is located downstream from the dam in Menomonie and is thus not a good indicator of water levels on this part of the river.

The **GRADIENT** averages 5.1 feet per mile.

The **shuttle route** is via South Street, Main Street, County O, Highway 53 and County W.

PUT IN at the **Red Cedar River County Park** (river-left), at the west end of South Street in the city of Rice Lake. There is another **access** on river-right alongside River Road, 1 mile north of County O (near the sewage-treatment plant).

At the put-in, the river is about 70 feet wide and flows between grassy banks. The forest on both sides is primarily deciduous (oak, maple, popple, alder, birch, etc.), but pine is plentiful downstream. Moderate current carries boaters down to the first bridge, at County O. Look for swallow nests under all the bridges on this stretch.

After County O, the river winds peacefully for several miles toward Highway 53, passing the mouth of Meadows Creek on the left (1.8 miles), some islands, and a number of homes and cabins. After a cabin with an unusual dock (steel beams project several feet from the bank), there is a deep hole in a left bend; from here, the water is deep all the way to the Highway 53 bridges (3.2 miles).

The Sawyer Bridge, a short distance downstream, is within sight of Highway 53. There is an excellent county **landing** at the bridge, upstream-left. Houses appear as the river bends left after the bridge, and traffic noise from Highway 53 can be heard for a while. You'll find deep pools in the next couple of bends.

Current persists but slows occasionally in deeper areas. Pools continue to appear often in bends.

As the river heads south toward County W, the river splits around a couple of sizable islands. A short distance upstream from County W, an old iron railroad bridge crosses the river, followed by a lovely stand of red pine.

TAKE OUT at the County W bridge, downstream-right—another excellent **landing** provided by Barron County.

If you have the time, visit the Barron County Historical Society Museum, located just a few hundred feet east of the take-out on County W.

Other trips: Upstream from Rice Lake (that is, from the Red Cedar Lake dam at Mikana), the 11 miles of river tend to be shallower, with few of the deep holes that are common after Rice Lake.

Not Just Your Average Museum

Let's face it. Most county historical museums—filled, warehouse-fashion, with "old stuff"—aren't exactly scintillating experiences. You definitely won't yawn, however, if you spend an hour or two at the museum in Barron County.

This attraction is a fascinating village of 28 buildings, painstakingly moved to the site, that represent the way people used to live. The village includes an 1877 log home, a 1905 one-room schoolhouse, an old railroad depot, a blacksmith shop, a general store and many other authentic structures.

Located 1.5 miles west of Cameron on County W (near the Red Cedar River), the Barron County Historical Museum is open 1 to 5 p.m. on Thursday, Saturday and Sunday from June 1 through Labor Day.

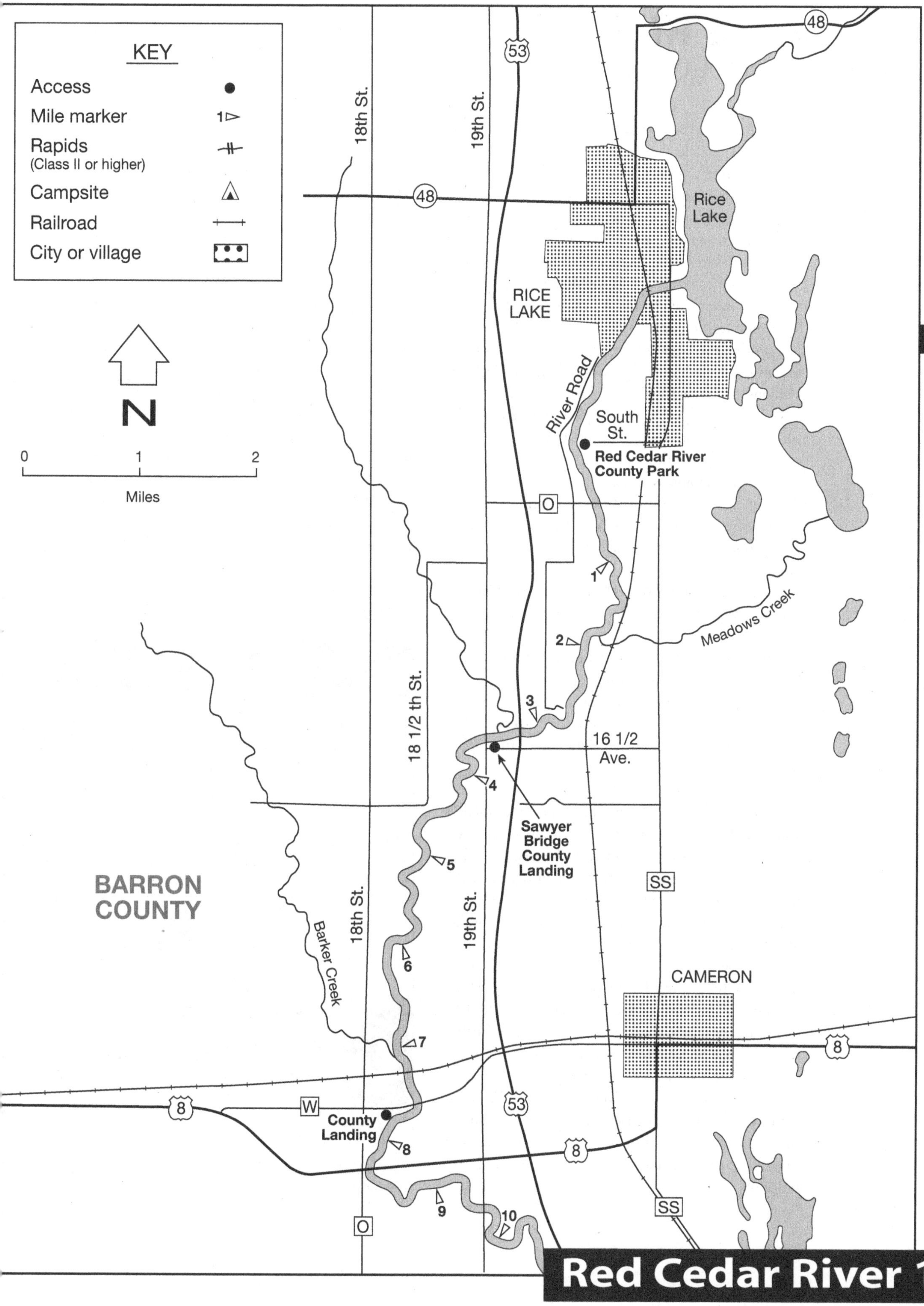

Red Cedar River 1

Red Cedar River 2

County W to County I (11.2 Miles)

Starting near Cameron, this stretch of the Red Cedar presents paddlers with several different environments. Beginning wide and deep, it flows around many islands, passes by high banks and attractive stone formations, narrows occasionally and traverses semi-marshy areas. You will pass under four bridges before the take-out, and sometimes paddle close beside roadways. Landings are convenient and well-maintained. Except when the water is high, this is another good day trip for beginning paddlers.

During the logging era, the Red Cedar was one of the most important tributaries of the Chippewa. Millions of logs were floated down the river to the mills of the Knapp-Stout Company in Menomonie, which at one time was the largest lumber-producing enterprise in the world.

Public **camping** is available at Veterans Memorial Park on Prairie Lake near Cameron; and at Southworth Memorial Park on Ten Mile Lake near Chetek.

Water levels are sufficient for good paddling most of the year.

The average **GRADIENT** is 3.5 feet per mile.

The **shuttle route** is via County W, Highway 53 and County I.

PUT IN at the Barron County **landing** at the County W bridge, downstream-right.

A short paddle takes you down to the Highway 8 bridge, where there is no good river access. After Highway 8, the banks on the right are a little higher than usual.

There is a large island where the river heads east, and some traffic noise is heard. Look out for deadfall if you take the narrow right channel. Houses appear on the left in the big right bend after the island; trailers follow on the right. The 19th Street bridge is in the next left bend (1.8 miles), immediately preceded by old concrete piers in the middle of the river. Bridge **access** is upstream-right.

Cranberry Creek enters on the left where the river begins to turn toward the southeast. For a while, Highway 53 and 20th Street run parallel on the left. Oak and pine trees grace the attractive left bank. Farther south, a big home on the right comes before the mouth of the Yellow River (4.1 miles).

On this part of the river (Cranberry Creek to County OO), there is a great deal of marsh grass along the shore, but the setting is still predominantly upland forest. The stretch is long, flat, straight, deep and very peaceful.

Five old concrete piers precede the County OO bridge, **accessed** upstream-left in an attractive grassy area. Marshy vegetation disappears after OO, and the bends are quite deep. After Brown Creek enters on the right, the river flows through another long, quiet stretch, until Highway 53 is heard again in the distance. You'll see homes on the left when 9th Avenue draws near. The water continues fairly deep all the way to County D (8.8 miles), with an especially deep hole in the bend before the bridge. The public **access** is downstream-right.

High, wooded banks and deep water follow the bridge, with stone formations in the left bluff. At 9.5 miles, high sand and gravel cutbanks appear on the left in a sharp right turn. After again approaching the road and some houses on the right, the river passes through a very pretty area with overhanging trees. Stone bluffs are found on the right where the river makes the final sharp turn toward County I. After a few small islands and an old bridge piling in the middle, the bridge comes into view.

TAKE OUT at County I (another Barron County **landing**), downstream-right.

Quietwater paddlers can relax on the Red Cedar.

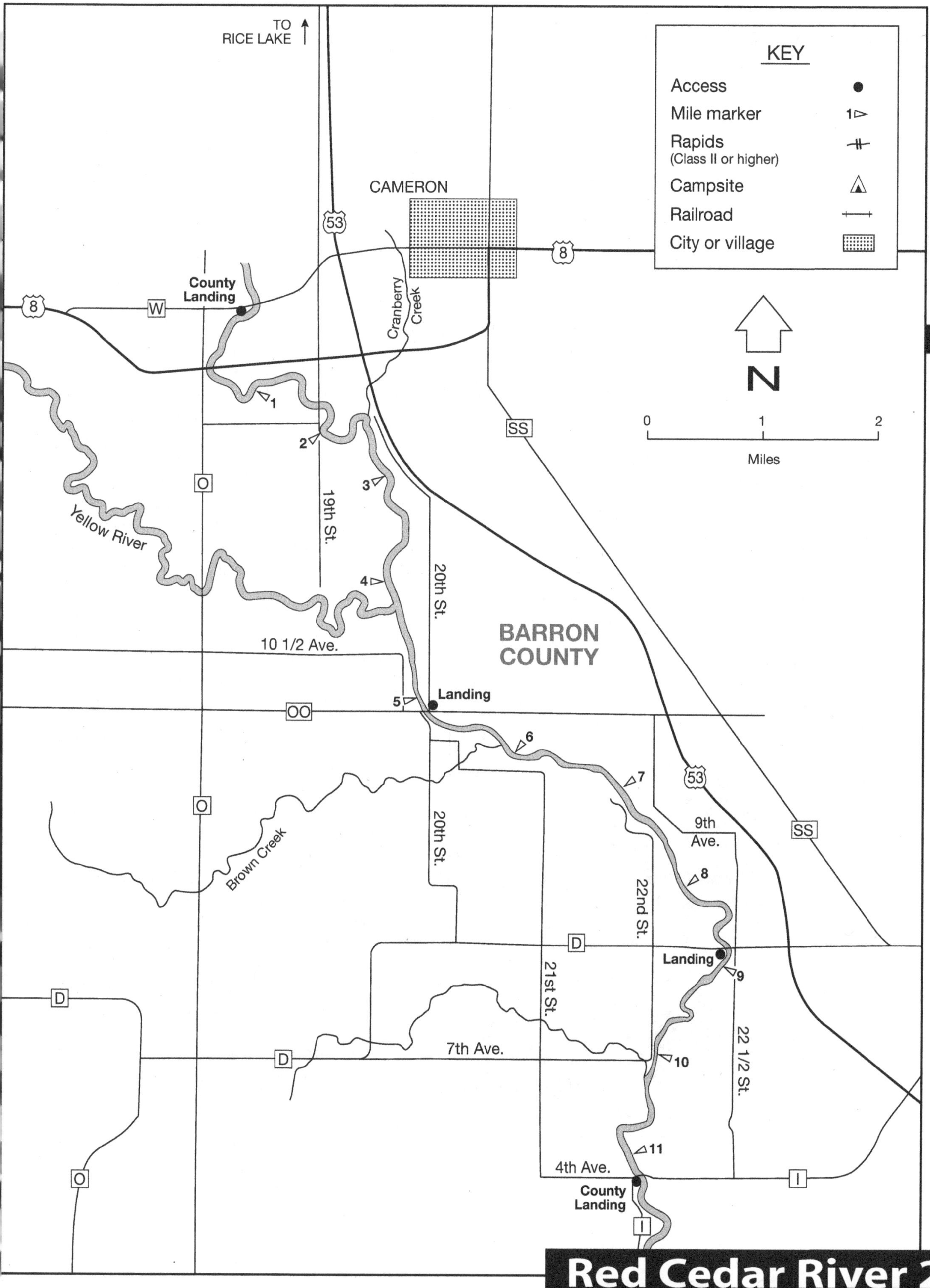

Red Cedar River 2

Red Cedar River 3

County I to Highway 64 (13.7 Miles)

This section is one of the most frequently paddled on the Red Cedar and another excellent day trip for quietwater canoeists. Its popularity is due not only to the good walleye and smallmouth fishing, but also to a couple of very pleasant stops along the way—Myron Park and Sand Creek. The riverside campground at Myron Park makes it possible for boaters to canoe-camp, stretching the trip into a leisurely weekend excursion. Houses and other buildings are relatively uncommon along the river, and much of the section is quite tranquil. It's a great stretch to float along on the moderate current.

Public **camping** is available on the river at Myron Park, and near Chetek at Southworth Memorial Park, on Ten Mile Lake.

Water levels are almost always adequate for enjoyable paddling.

The average **GRADIENT** is 3.6 feet per mile.

The **shuttle route** is via County I, County M and Highway 64.

PUT IN at the public boat **landing** at the County I bridge (downstream-right), a couple miles southwest of Chetek. There is plenty of parking space.

At the beginning, the river is fairly shallow, but it quickly becomes deeper at a bend to the right. From here all the way to Colfax, the water is often quite deep in bends, providing excellent places to stop and drop a fishing line. The water is fairly clear, and the banks are thick with maple trees. Current is moderate, sometimes quickening around islands.

Anglers will find good fishing on this stretch.

The first farm buildings appear after the right bend, along with the first of many islands. County I isn't far away on the right.

The Chetek River joins the Red Cedar on the left (2.2 miles). Incidentally, the Chetek is also a good paddling stream, and the stretch from Lake Chetek Dam to County I-A provides 7 miles of pleasant paddling.

The river comes close to County I again, followed by some big islands and a few farm buildings, and then becomes wide, deep and slow in the big left bend before Tiller and Sioux creeks. Big pine trees appear in the right bend after Tiller Creek, and are more numerous downstream. An excellent **landing** (with parking, toilets and water) appears on the left just before the river turns left to the County I-A bridge. An unimproved **access** is located downstream-right at the bridge (off West River Road). Once again, the river flows alongside the road on the right for a while.

Downstream from the I-A bridge, attractive sandstone cliffs appear on the left, preceded by exceptionally high banks on the right. The river widens to about 200 feet after the cliffs but is still fairly deep. From the cliffs to Myron Park, the setting is extremely peaceful, with many deep pools.

Myron Park comes at the end of a long straightaway, where buildings appear on the left. Dunn County provides a **landing** and campground here in a pleasant pine grove. After the park, some stone outcroppings are found on the right after the river straightens out. Many islands follow.

Houses on the left indicate the approach to the village of Sand Creek, where County V crosses the river. Upstream-right at the bridge is the **village park** (with **landing,** toilets, parking and picnic facilities). A restaurant and grocery store are a short walk from the park.

Below Sand Creek, the river is wide and slow, with many deep spots. In the approach to Highway 64, West River Road hugs the right bank.

TAKE OUT at the wayside (with parking, toilets and **landing**) at the Highway 64 bridge, downstream-left.

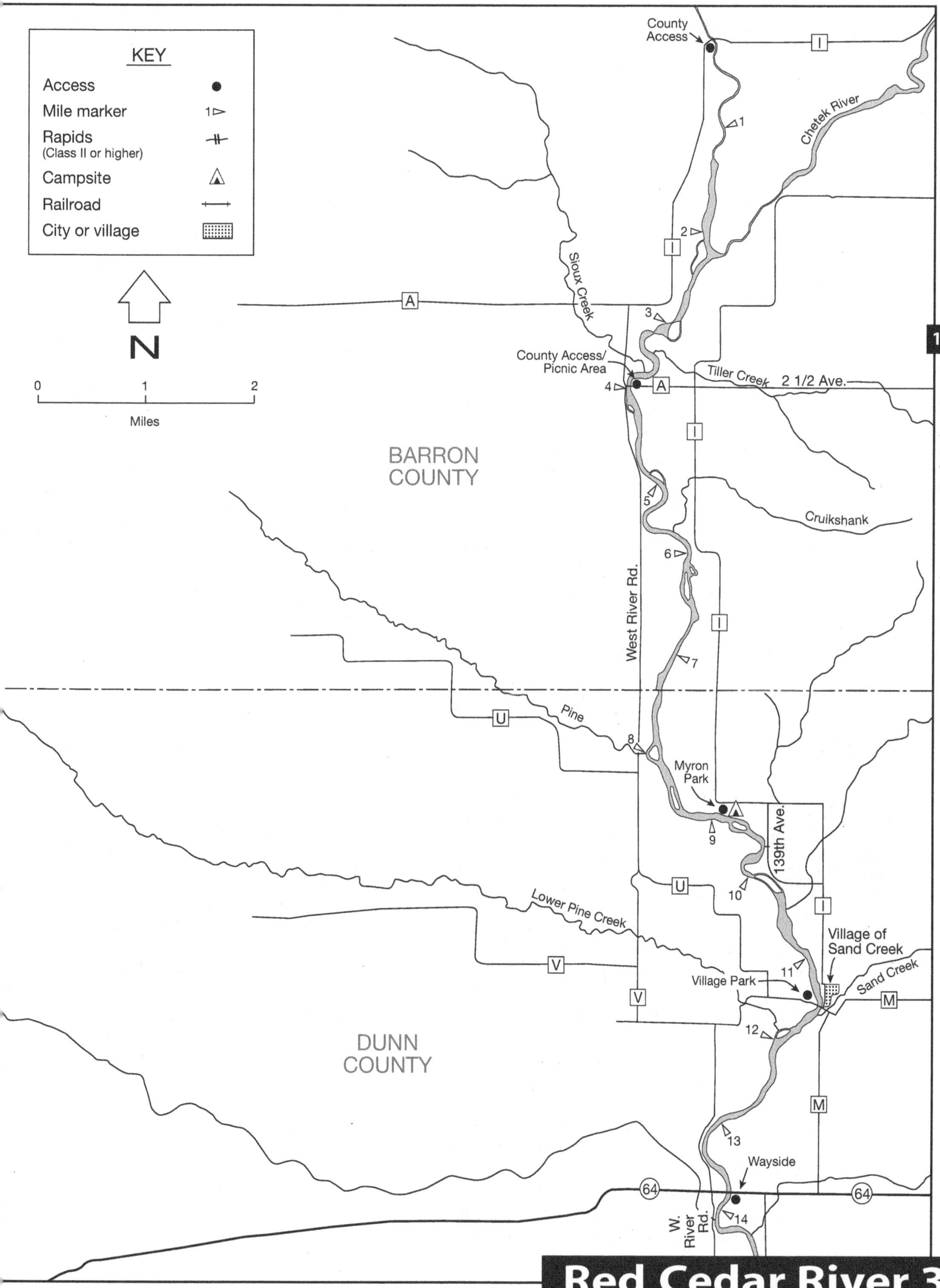

Red Cedar River 3

Red Cedar River 4

Highway 64 to Colfax (15.3 Miles)

Many devotees of the Red Cedar River say that this is its prettiest stretch. It certainly is the most tranquil. Deep all the way, the river passes few houses and flows to the constant accompaniment of birds calling and frogs croaking. Eagles are frequently sighted. Beautiful sandstone cliffs and other interesting rock formations line the shore during the second half of the trip. Because of the many deep holes, this is a particularly good place to fish for walleye; you may see a jon-boat or two while you're canoeing. During the last couple of miles, the river changes character, growing narrower and quicker. You will need to attend to occasional deadfall.

Public **camping** is available several miles upstream from the put-in at Myron Park, off County I (see Red Cedar River 3).

Water levels are almost always sufficient for enjoyable paddling.

The average **GRADIENT** is 3.9 feet per mile.

Families enjoy the Red Cedar's tranquillity.

The **shuttle route** is via Highway 64, County M, Highway 40 and Highway 170.

PUT IN at the well-maintained Highway 64 wayside (**landing,** toilets, picnic facilities, parking), downstream-left.

Soon after the landing, Hay Creek enters from the right, with West River Road visible on the shore. There is a deep fishing hole in the left bend after Hay Creek ("Cornfield Bend"). Low, grassy banks prevail, and deep pools are common. County M briefly comes close on the left.

Making a sharp elbow (2.2 miles), the river swings to the right, followed by a big island, then a left turn. There are high, sandy cutbacks in the left bend, plus power lines and houses. Long straightaways follow, first south, then west, with several big islands in between. You'll see thick aquatic vegetation growing on the bottom in some shallow areas.

After the river bends south again (left), there's a big wooded island (4.1 miles); Popple Creek enters from the right at the head of the island. An unimproved private **landing** comes down to the river on the right from County W, just south of County S and the Popple Creek bridge.

After the next big island, a couple of wooded bluffs appear. Eddies Creek enters in a sharp bend, and there are stone formations in a river-right bluff. A long southeast straightaway follows, and low banks resume. Downstream, power lines cross overhead near a big slough on the right.

Several big, sweeping bends take the river toward County W, then back alongside County M. Where County M touches the river, 25-foot stone mini-cliffs rise from the water.

After a big island, the river loops left past some sand and gravel cutbanks, to the bridge at **22-Mile Ford Park** (9.6 miles, with **access** downstream-right). County M then parallels the river for a while. The banks are high and wooded here, and the river wide and deep.

After a creek enters on the left, the river heads away from County M, encountering a big slough before turning south again. Many islands and gravelly shoals follow: Look out for deadfall in some of the narrow channels.

After the mouth of Bronken Creek on the right (11.6 miles), beautiful sandstone cliffs appear on the right as the river curves left, then right. A long south straightaway follows toward Colfax. Just downstream from some power lines, the river jogs around a big wooded hill on the right, with stone formations near the water. A clump of islands is met downstream. In the big bends that follow, another large "dogleg" slough is passed on the left, and traffic noise from roads in the Colfax area can be heard.

You'll encounter sandy bluffs and gravel bars during the last 2 miles, but most of the shoreline is low and wooded. The banks close in during the last mile, and the current accelerates. Be watchful for downed trees. Deer flies can be a nuisance here in the summer.

TAKE-OUT: Houses and a road on the right signal the approach of the **landing,** an easy-to-miss bare spot on the right bank within sight of the Highway 170 bridge downstream. The landing is at Tom Price Memorial Park, located alongside Highway 170 on the west side of Colfax.

Other trips: Below Colfax, the Red Cedar soon flows successively into two big impoundments, Tainter Lake and Lake Menomin. From the dam at the city of Menomonie, the river again flows unimpeded for about 16 miles to the Chippewa River. There are accesses at Downsville (Highway 25) and upstream from the mouth (County Y). For a detailed map and description of this part of the river, see *Paddling Southern Wisconsin.*

A highlight of this part of the river is the Red Cedar State Trail, which runs along the river for 14.5 miles from Menomonie to the Dunnville Wildlife Area. The trail is popular with bicyclists, skiers, hikers and snowshoers.

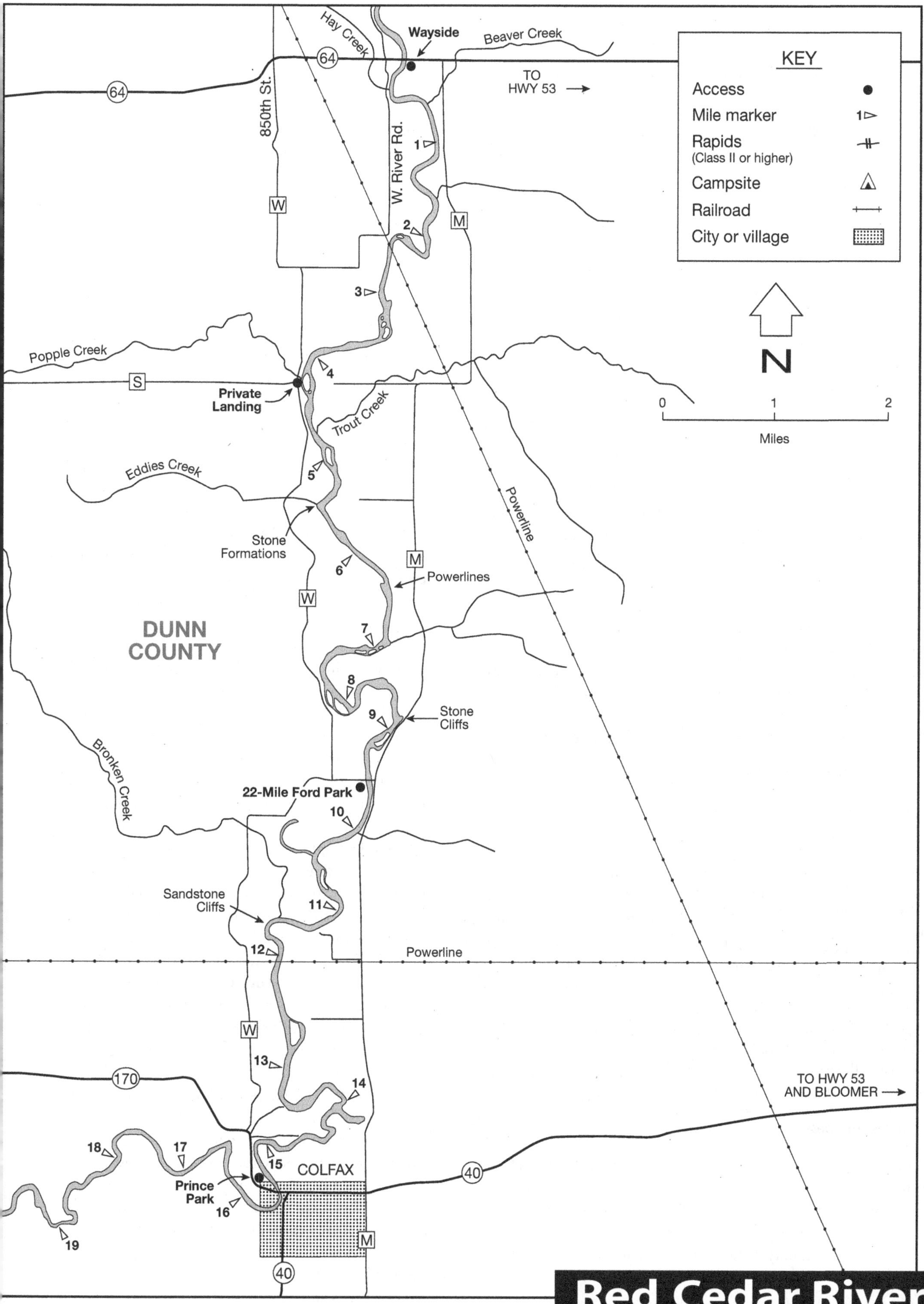

Red Cedar River 4

St. Croix River 1

Gordon Dam to Schoen Park Landing (11.7 Miles)

Part of the St. Croix National Scenic Riverway (which also includes the Namekagon), the St. Croix flows 154 miles from the dam near Gordon to its confluence with the Mississippi. The St. Croix was one of the original eight rivers to be protected under the National Wild and Scenic Rivers Act of 1968, and consequently has been preserved in a wonderfully wild state. Canoe landings and primitive campsites are provided all along the river, making it a popular canoe-camping destination.

Section maps of the St. Croix (and Namekagon), showing up-to-date locations of all campsites, are available at the St. Croix National Riverway website (www.nps.gov/sacn) or at one of the visitor centers: in Trego (715-635-8346), or in St. Croix Falls (715-483-2274).

During most of its course, the St. Croix flows through a wide, low-banked valley, but in the 20 miles below the Gordon dam, before the Namekagon adds its considerable volume, the river is narrower, with numerous riffles and Class I rapids. Except for landings, bridges and an old dam, canoeists see little evidence of human habitation; only a few cabins are passed along the way. Mixed forests of pine and hardwoods are thick along the shores, and eagles, ducks, herons, muskrats and other wildlife are plentiful.

Public **camping** is available at three parks along the way (Gordon Dam Park at the put-in, Louise Park at 10 miles and Schoen Park at 11.7 miles), and at several primitive sites on the river.

Water levels upstream from the CCC Bridge are best in the spring. Attempting these 15.4 miles when the water is low means walking your boat through many shallows. For water conditions, call the visitor information center at Trego (715-635-8346). Also consult "river levels" at the St. Croix National Scenic Riverway website (see above).

The **GRADIENT** of this first section is 6.8 feet per mile.

The **shuttle route** for this first section is via East County Y, Mail Road, County T, Rocky Brook Trail and Schoen Park Road.

A Great Place to Enjoy the Dells

Whenever you're near the St. Croix, consider visiting Interstate Park, through which it flows. It's a marvelous destination for anyone who loves fascinating geology and spectacular scenery. An excellent example of cooperation between adjacent states, the park was established in 1900 on both the Wisconsin and Minnesota sides of the river as a means of preserving the unique environment of the St. Croix Dells.

The rock that forms the dells—dark volcanic basalt—resulted from eruptions that occurred a billion years ago. More recently, about 10,000 years ago, meltwater from the last glacier poured south, carving out the wide valley of the St. Croix. When the torrent encountered hard basalt, it cut the deep and narrow gorge of the dells, along with a profusion of "potholes," formed when sand-laden whirlpools drilled deep depressions into the rock.

There's a great deal to see and do on either side of the river. Both parks have hiking trails, potholes (the best are on the Minnesota side), campgrounds, canoe landings, cliffs for rock climbing, interpretive centers and much more.

Canoe rentals and shuttle service for the first two sections of the river are available at Pardun's Canoe Rental, Danbury (715-656-7881).

PUT IN river-left at the pleasant **county park** below the **Gordon Dam;** there is plenty of parking.

At the beginning, the river is rather wide and shallow. Fishermen are often seen here, angling for muskie, northern, smallmouth and walleye. Islands occasionally appear.

Downstream about a mile, the river narrows and drops a little in the right channel of a large island, resulting in a Class I rapids.

Wide shallows and riffles follow. Then the river deepens before **Scott Rapids,** a 300-yard-long Class I–II boulder garden with many rocks to dodge. Scott Bridge (1.9 miles) immediately follows the rapids. The Moose River comes in from the right near the bridge.

The river deepens somewhat after Scott Bridge, with riffles here and there, and passes the mouths of several creeks before arriving at the old **Coppermine Dam** (6 miles). The roar can be heard upstream, and a sign on the right directs paddlers to portage past the dam on a short path. Most of this old logging-era dam is gone, but several large rock structures remain, resulting in wavy drops that require caution. Scout carefully if you are considering running it, and pick the chute with the most water and no obstructions. There have been reports of spikes sticking up from some of the underwater timbers.

There are many riffles and small rapids during the next few miles, especially in the right channel of a big island downstream from the mouth of Buckley Creek **(Shelldrake Rapids).**

The **access** at the County T bridge, upstream-left, is excellent, with picnic tables, toilets and parking. Fishing is said to be good downstream from County T. **Beartrap Rapids** (two short Class I pitches) follows the bridge, and you'll encounter many rocky Class I rapids all the way down to **Louise Park.** The **Louise Park Landing** (10 miles), on the right, provides camping, toilets and picnic facilities. The next 4.5 miles, from the park to Fishtrap Rapids, are flat, mostly straight and subject to wind.

TAKE OUT at **Schoen Park Landing** on the right (camping, toilets, picnic site and parking).

Other trips: Canoeists who wish to begin at the headwaters of the St. Croix can put in upstream at Upper St. Croix Lake in the Solon Springs area, then paddle a slow river stretch mostly dominated by wetlands, and finally enter the 2,500-acre St. Croix Flowage (impounded by Gordon Dam). A trip from the head of Upper St. Croix Lake to Gordon Dam covers about 19 river miles.

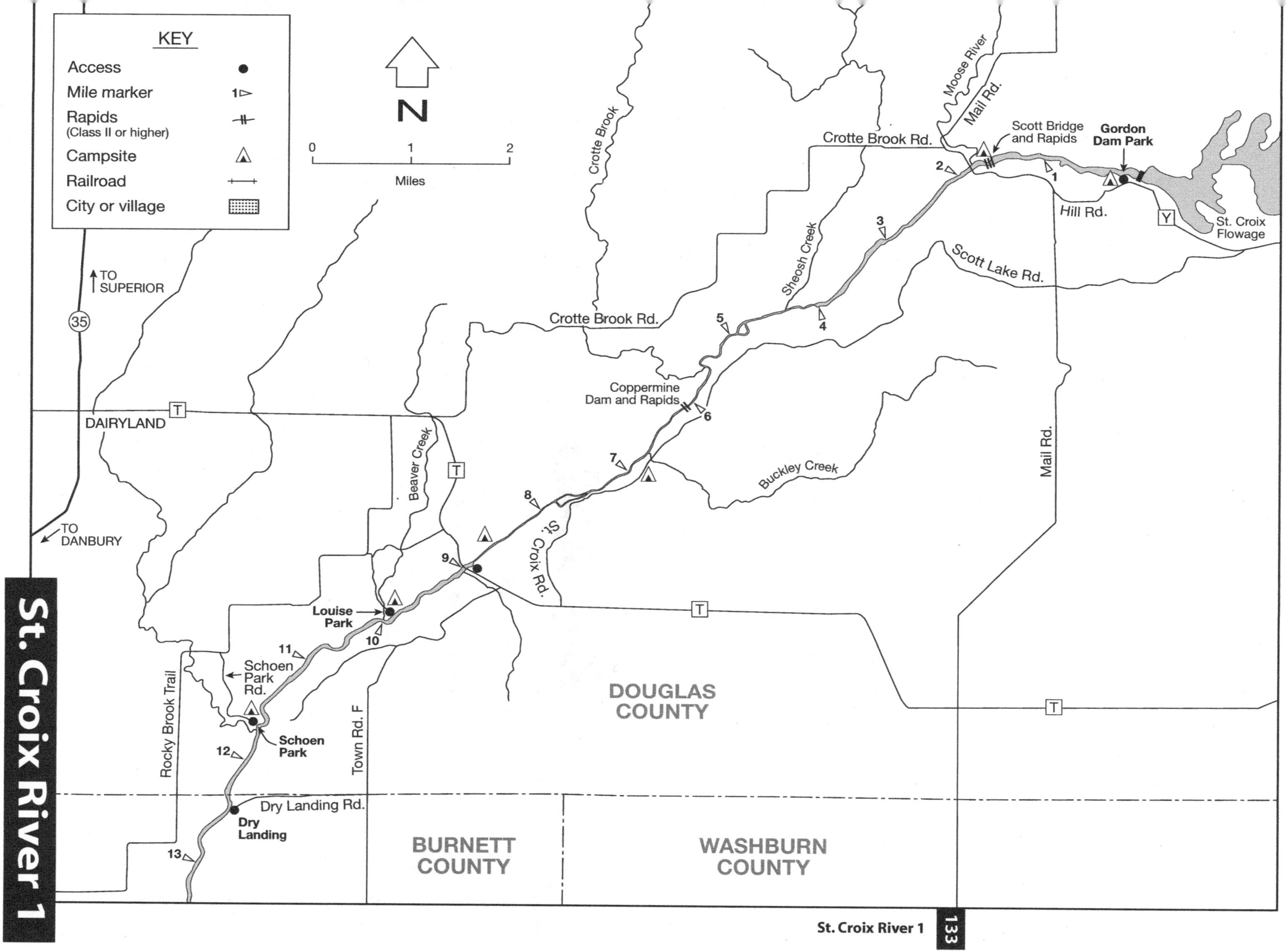

St. Croix River 1
KEY
Access
Mile marker
Rapids
(Class II or higher)
Campsite
Railroad
City or village
N
0
1
2
Miles
TO SUPERIOR
35
TO DANBURY
DAIRYLAND
T
Crotte Brook
Crotte Brook Rd.
Moose River
Mail Rd.
Crotte Brook Rd.
Scott Bridge and Rapids
Gordon Dam Park
Hill Rd.
Y
St. Croix Flowage
Scott Lake Rd.
Sheosh Creek
Coppermine Dam and Rapids
Buckley Creek
Mail Rd.
Beaver Creek
St. Croix Rd.
Louise Park
Schoen Park Rd.
Schoen Park
Rocky Brook Trail
Town Rd. F
Dry Landing Rd.
Dry Landing
DOUGLAS COUNTY
BURNETT COUNTY
WASHBURN COUNTY
1
2
3
4
5
6
7
8
9
10
11
12
13

St. Croix River 2

Schoen Park Landing to Highway 35 (11 Miles)

Most of this trip is on the relatively narrow upper St. Croix, but after meeting the Namekagon, the river widens to the dimensions that people associate with it. There is less whitewater here than on the previous stretch, but one set of rapids—Big Fishtrap—is the most difficult on the St. Croix. After about a third of the trip, gradient declines, and the rest of the river has only a few riffles and rapids. The St. Croix is still a fairly small river here—but not for long. Because of the excellent camping possibilities, this section is often part of multiday canoe-camping trips.

Public **camping** is available on the river at the put-in and take-out (Schoen Park and Riverside Landing), and at several shoreline campsites along the way.

Water levels are always adequate downstream from the CCC Bridge, but are generally scratchy upstream in the summer. The section from Gordon Dam to the CCC Bridge is regarded as a springtime run. For general information on water levels (high, medium or low), call the visitor center at Trego (715-635-8346).

The **GRADIENT** averages 3.6 feet per mile.

A relaxing river for family and friends.

The **shuttle route** is via Schoen Park Road, Rocky Brook Road, Big McGraw Road and Highway 35.

PUT IN river-right at the **Schoen Park landing,** where camping, picnic facilities, toilets and water are available.

Continuing its southwestward course after the landing, the river is flat and subject to wind.

About a mile downstream, **Dry Landing** is a little clearing on the left bank. The access road is not always in good condition.

The quietwater ends at 2.8 miles with a very long, winding Class I–II rapids—**Big Fishtrap,** the largest and most challenging on the St. Croix. At average flows, it's difficult not to scrape a little now and then. Fishtrap tends to be rather noisy.

Little Fishtrap Rapids (Class I) begins upstream from the CCC Bridge and continues beyond it. There are good-sized waves at the end.

The CCC Bridge (3.7 miles) is **accessed** upstream-left, where there's a good **landing** with toilets and picnic tables. From here to the confluence with the Namekagon, the river is deep and relatively slow; the only break in the flatwater is a riffle/rapids after the mouth of Moore Farm Creek on the left.

Cabins appear on the left at the mouth of the Namekagon River (7 miles). Although a tributary of the St. Croix, the Namekagon has greater volume at this point. Hence, the St. Croix is conspicuously bigger from now on.

You'll encounter many islands in the river, most notably the appropriately named Big Island. There are some pleasant riffles and Class I rapids in the main (left) channel of this island.

TAKE OUT on the right at the **Riverside Landing** near the Highway 35 bridge. The upstream landing is part of a very attractive county wayside, while the downstream landing is maintained by the National Park Service.

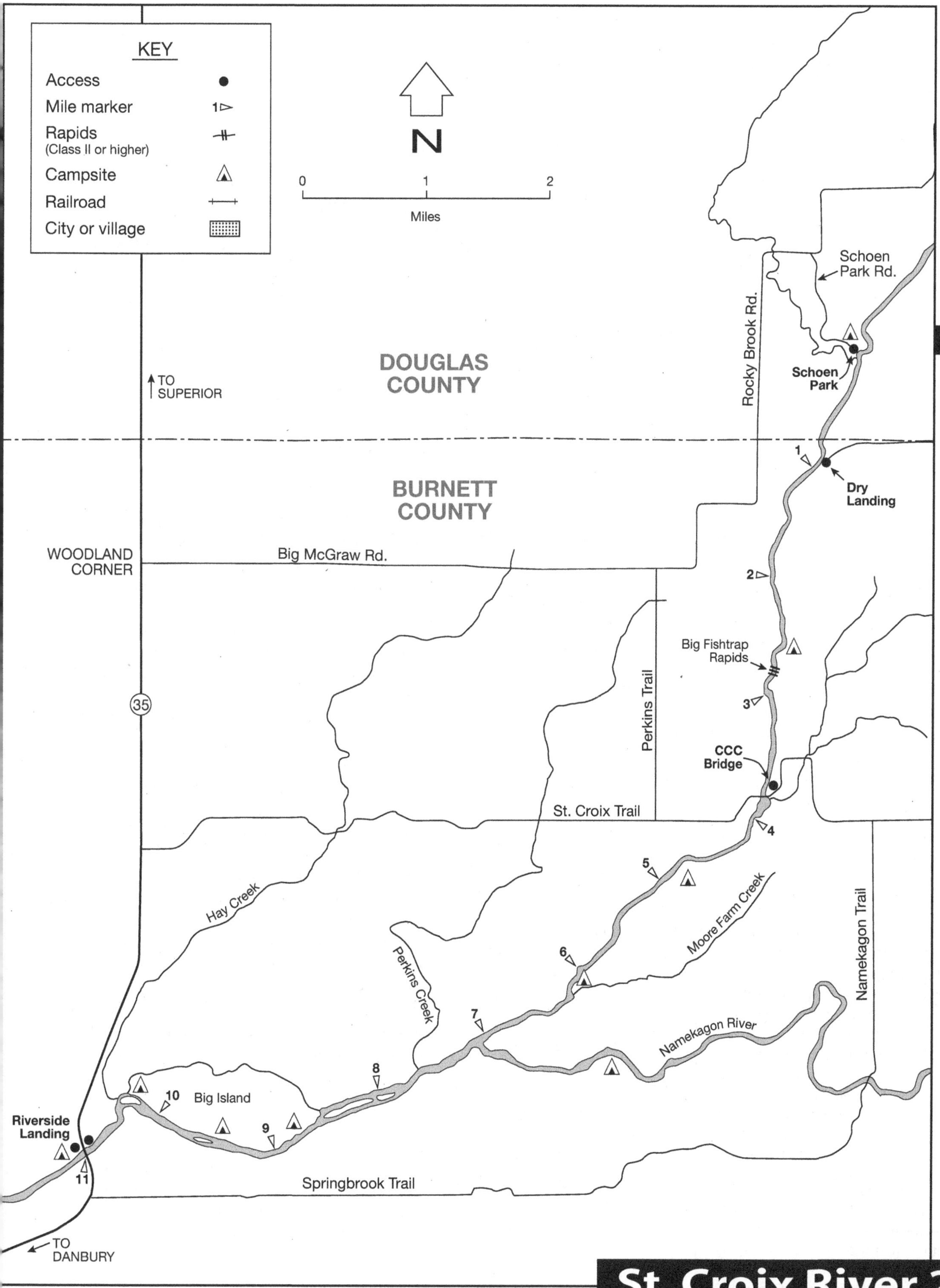
KEY
Access
Mile marker
Rapids
(Class II or higher)
Campsite
Railroad
City or village
N
0
1
2
Miles
DOUGLAS COUNTY
BURNETT COUNTY
TO SUPERIOR
WOODLAND CORNER
Big McGraw Rd.
35
Rocky Brook Rd.
Schoen Park Rd.
Schoen Park
Dry Landing
Big Fishtrap Rapids
CCC Bridge
Perkins Trail
St. Croix Trail
Hay Creek
Perkins Creek
Moore Farm Creek
Namekagon River
Namekagon Trail
Big Island
Riverside Landing
Springbrook Trail
TO DANBURY
1
2
3
4
5
6
7
8
9
10
11

St. Croix River 3

Highway 35 to Highway 77/48 (13 Miles)

Not far from the beginning of this third leg of the St. Croix, the river becomes the border between Wisconsin and Minnesota. (There's no mistaking where the border begins—the river presents paddlers with a rapids.) Now that it has been augmented by the sizable volume of the Namekagon, the St. Croix moves along briskly, making it possible to cover fairly long distances with only moderate paddling. Wind out of the southwest can slow progress considerably, however. The surroundings continue to be wild and heavily wooded, and you'll see more and more fishermen on the river. The trip begins and ends with excellent accesses, and has two intermediate landings that can be used to vary trip length.

Public **camping:** In addition to primitive campsites near the put-in and take-out, a couple of sites are located along the river. Downstream from this section, there is an excellent campground at St. Croix State Park on the Minnesota side, off Highway 22. On the Wisconsin side, there is a group camping area (reservations required) at the northern end of Governor Knowles State Forest, off Highway 77.

Water levels are almost always sufficient for enjoyable paddling. For general information on water conditions, call the visitor center at St. Croix Falls (715-483-3284).

In this section, the average **GRADIENT** has leveled out to 1.5 feet per mile.

The **shuttle route** is via Highway 35 and Highway 77. **Canoe rentals** and shuttle service on sections 3 through 8 are available as follows (arranged from north to south): Pardun's Canoe Rental, Danbury (715-656-7881); Campmasters Canoe Rental, Danbury (715-656-3219); Wild River Outfitters, Grantsburg (715-463-2254, www.wildriverpaddling.com); Ekdall Country Store & Canoe Rental, Grantsburg (877-469-9777 or 715-463-3686); Taylors Falls Canoe Rental, Taylors Falls, MN (800-447-4958 or 651-465-6315); and Eric's Canoe Rentals, St. Croix Falls (715-483-9007 or www.ericscanoerental.com).

PUT IN river-right at the **Riverside Landing** near the Highway 35 bridge, either upstream at the county park or downstream at the Park Service landing.

Downstream, on the left, are the first high bluffs on the St. Croix. These continue for a while as the river flows around many islands. The water is fairly deep, as it is in most of the river from this point on, with brief shallows occasionally encountered.

You're likely to see anglers in fishing boats on this part of the river, especially just downstream from Riverside.

Just before the Wisconsin/Minnesota border, **State Line Rapids** is found on both sides of a big island. The left channel is a little narrower and the rapids a bit more challenging (Class I+).

The St. Croix State Forest begins on the Minnesota side at the state line, and continues along the shoreline almost all the way to Highway 77.

Four miles after Riverside, **Pansy Landing** is an opening in the woods on the left. The access road is sometimes rough. A ferry and post office were once located nearby, and the postmaster's wife is said to have grown many pansies around the place.

Downstream, a huge hill comes into view, and remains prominent until it's passed on the left miles later.

After a long swing to the southwest, traffic noise from Highway 35/77 is heard. In a big right bend, the **Yellow River Landing** appears on the left behind an island (8.3 miles). The landing is on St. Croix Indian Reservation property, near Danbury, and a small fee is charged for its use. Danbury is a short walk away.

The Yellow River enters on the left just downstream from the landing, and is followed in turn by a railroad bridge.

The 5 miles between the Yellow River Landing and the take-out flow through wild countryside, passing the mouth of the Lower Tamarack River along the way.

TAKE OUT at the Highway 77/48 bridge **(Thayer's Landing),** downstream-left.

One of the many lovely islands on the St. Croix.

Why "St. Croix"?

Early maps and accounts of the St. Croix referred to it as the River Madeleine, but since the late 1600s it has been known by its present name. Where did the name come from?

The most obvious answer, of course, is that the river was named as an act of piety by early Christian missionaries, explorers or traders after the symbol of their faith, the "holy cross."

Another comes from a story told by an early voyageur of a Frenchman who was buried near the mouth of the river with a cross over his grave. Yet a third possibility is that the river was named after an early trader named Sainte Croix.

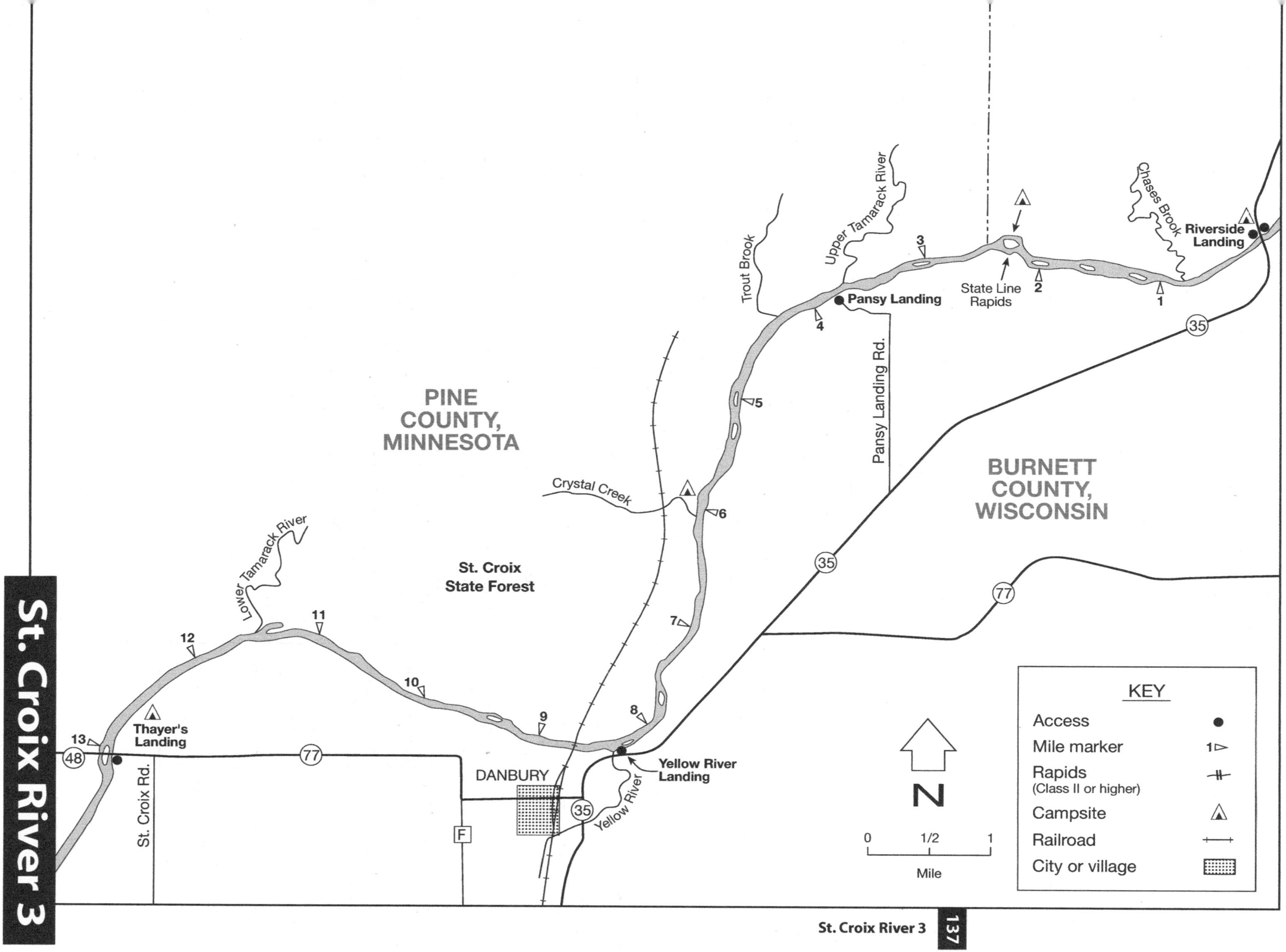
St. Croix River 3
Riverside Landing
Chases Brook
1
2
State Line Rapids
3
Pansy Landing
Upper Tamarack River
Trout Brook
4
Pansy Landing Rd.
35
5
PINE COUNTY, MINNESOTA
BURNETT COUNTY, WISCONSIN
Crystal Creek
6
7
8
Yellow River Landing
Yellow River
35
77
St. Croix State Forest
Lower Tamarack River
11
12
10
9
DANBURY
F
Thayer's Landing
13
48
77
St. Croix Rd.
N
0
1/2
1
Mile
KEY
Access
Mile marker
Rapids
(Class II or higher)
Campsite
Railroad
City or village

St. Croix River 4

Highway 77/48 to Norway Point (14 Miles)

Also part of the Wisconsin/Minnesota border, this stretch is ideal for novices and quietwater enthusiasts. The river is 150 to 200 feet wide, with a steady current averaging 3 miles per hour. The low banks are covered with maple, oak, popple, pine, spruce, fir and cedar. There are no private houses on the stretch—only a few canoe landings, campsites and park buildings. Deer, eagle, osprey, kingfishers, ducks, heron and songbirds are abundant, and bass, muskie and walleye are common on fishermen's stringers. Be forewarned that this part of the river is often windy.

Public **camping** is available at several primitive campsites maintained along the river by the Park Service, and at St. Croix State Park on the Minnesota side.

Water levels are usually adequate for enjoyable paddling. For general information on water conditions (high, medium or low), call the visitor center at St. Croix Falls (715-483-2274).

The **GRADIENT** averages 1.4 feet per mile in this section.

The **shuttle route** is via Highway 77, St. Croix Road, County F and Norway Point Landing Road. For **canoe rentals** and shuttle service, see St. Croix 3. Incidentally, the shuttle route will take you past the huge Crex Meadows Wildlife Area, where hundreds of species of animals are found.

PUT IN at the Highway 77 bridge, downstream-left **(Thayer's Landing).** Excellent parking is provided.

The river passes through a wide valley formed long ago by glacial activity, and a sandy bottom can be seen through its clear water, which is a bit shallow in wider places. During the first couple of miles, two creeks enter from the left—the second in the middle of a big right-hand bend.

Another creek enters from the left (3.5 miles), near the location of the old Sioux Portage Trail, once used by Indians and trappers to get to Yellow Lake. A large island soon appears downstream. Immediately after the island, you'll see a big hill on the left downstream, and "State Park" signs begin appearing on the Minnesota side. These signs mark the beginning of the 34,000 acres of **St. Croix State Park,** which continues all the way down to the take-out (and beyond). The park offers almost everything that outdoor enthusiasts could want. On the Wisconsin side lies the 18,700-acre **Governor Knowles State Forest.** A primitive campsite (the first of several) appears on the left.

St. John's Group Campsite (5 miles) is located on the right, downstream from the mouth of Crooked Creek, also on the right. Canoe-camping is not allowed at St. John's.

Downstream, **Little Yellow Banks Landing** (7 miles) appears on the right, at the head of a big island. Campsites and water are available at Little Yellow Banks. Go around the left side of the large island to avoid shallow water and deadfall.

The river bends sharply to the right, and the Clam River enters from the left, followed immediately by a campsite.

The **St. Croix State Park Interpretive Center** (at Big Yellow Banks) is on the right at 9.8 miles. The building and grounds are beautiful, with excellent exhibits on the river's history, flora and fauna. It's well worth your time to stop and visit.

After a long west-southwest stretch, Mouse Island comes into view just before a sharp left bend. **Sand Creek Landing** (13.4 miles) is located on the right at the bend.

TAKE-OUT: After a short paddle due south, **Norway Point Landing** is located on the left in a sharp right-hand turn. Like Little Yellow Banks, the St. Croix Park Center and Sand Creek, Norway Point has water and campsites. It also offers the Cedar Interpretive Trail, which gives a close-up view of the plants, animals and geology of the area.

A Surefire Way to See Wildlife

If you're interested in wildlife observation—and what paddler isn't?—you owe it to yourself to visit Crex Meadows, located near the St. Croix River just north of Grantsburg. Its 30,000 acres of woods, prairies and wetlands, which are owned and managed by the Wisconsin DNR, provide habitat for a huge variety of wildlife.

Back in the 1800s, settlers ill-advisedly drained the area, destroying the native shrub prairies and wetlands and causing many birds and animals to disappear. When the state purchased the area in 1946, however, the wetlands and prairies were restored by means of dikes and controlled burning, and wildlife is abundant again. There are healthy populations of grouse, prairie chickens, Canada geese, sandhill cranes, deer, muskrat, beaver and many other animal species.

Thousands of visitors come to Crex every year, especially during the spring and fall bird migrations. An excellent road system makes it easy to get close to the wildlife.

To get to Crex Meadows, take County F north from Grantsburg for a half mile.

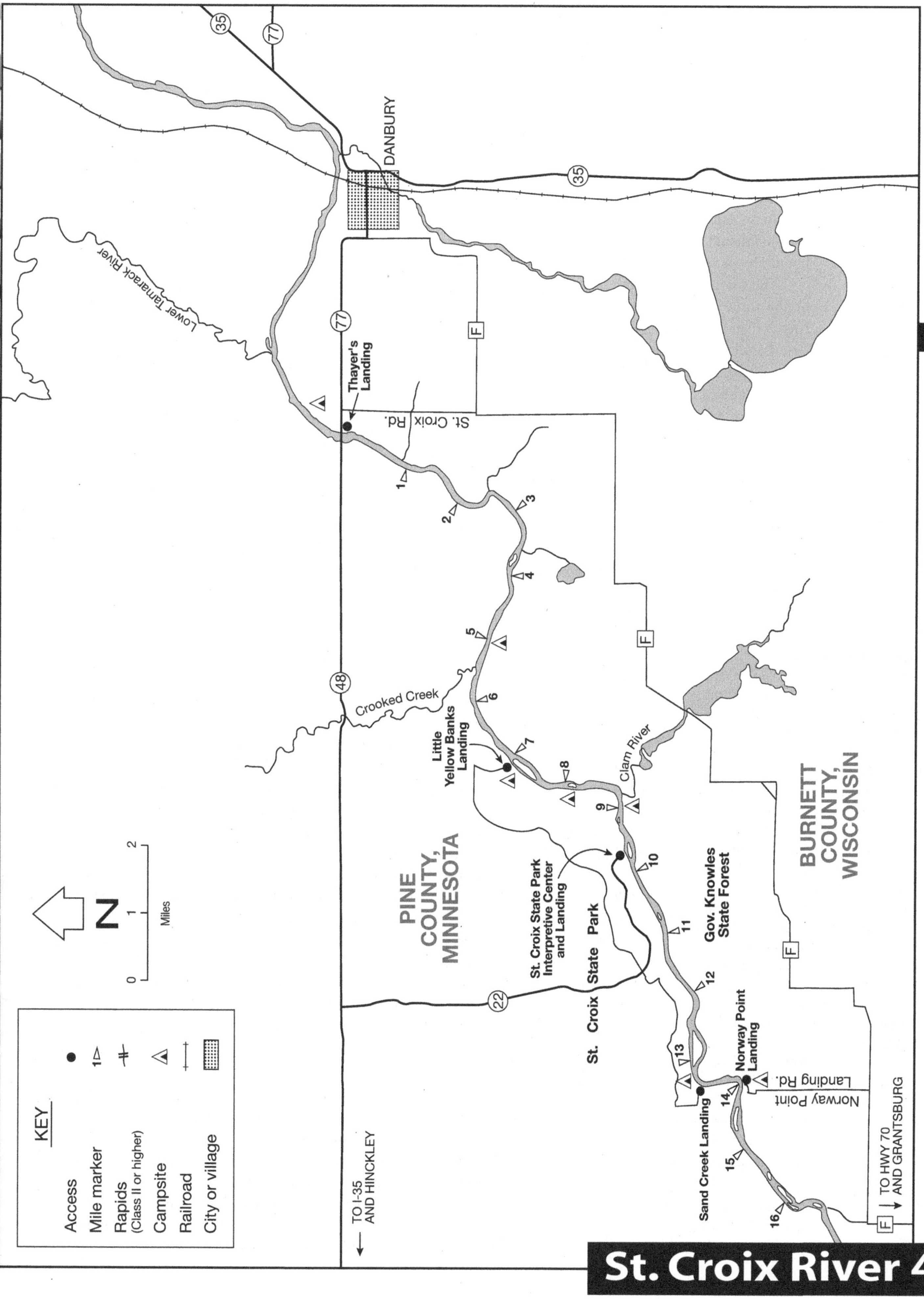

St. Croix River 4

St. Croix River 5

Norway Point to Highway 70 (14.5 Miles)

Unlike the previous stretch, this section of the St. Croix offers not only peaceful, scenic quietwater, but also some exciting riffles and rapids. Experienced paddlers will have no difficulty, but medium to high water conditions call for extra caution. The St. Croix is a big river and should be given a lot of respect when the water is up; stay home if in doubt. Wind is sometimes challenging.

The wooded banks continue to be rather low most of the time, but there are more high banks on this stretch than upstream. Private homes are nowhere to be found until Soderbeck Landing (10.4 miles). Fishermen are sometimes seen, in pursuit of muskie, northern, walleye and bass.

Because of the many excellent landings, trip length can easily be varied. This section and the previous one are often combined for a pleasant two-day trip.

Public camping: There are many scenic campsites along the shore and on islands, especially after Nelson's Landing. The James N. McNally Village Campground is located in nearby Grantsburg.

General information on **water levels** (high, medium or low) may be obtained by calling the visitor center at St. Croix Falls (715-483-2274).

The **GRADIENT** in this section is a more lively 4.1 feet per mile.

The **best shuttle** route is via Norway Point Landing Road, County F, Bistram Road, Soderbeck Road and Highway 70. For **canoe rentals** and shuttle service, see St. Criox 3.

PUT IN at **Norway Point Landing.** Less than 3 miles of paddling takes you to **Nelson's Landing,** which (like Norway Point) offers water and campsites. Be careful at Nelson's: Novices sometimes have trouble here when the water is medium to high. A series of riffles and rapids follows.

Not far downstream, immediately after a small island and a minor rapids, you can continue down the main (left) channel of the river or take the smaller, faster Kettle River channel to the right. (Most paddlers take the main channel.) This fork is known as **"Head of the Rapids."** When the river is low, the right channel involves a lot of scraping and walking, but at other times it provides a succession of Class I–II rapids as it flows past the mouth of the Kettle River (on the right) and eventually rejoins the main channel of the St. Croix. Usually, the best rapids occur at the confluence of the two channels; high water means big waves. Huge wooded islands separate the two channels. Many attractive campsites are found along the river here, often on islands; one particularly scenic site is located at the end of the promontory where the two channels join.

The river widens and becomes shallower after the confluence. Rock outcroppings appear on the right, and springs occasionally run down the banks. One such spring occurs just downstream from Fox Landing (5.5 miles). You will continue to encounter islands.

The Snake River enters from the right at 10.4 miles, followed by the **Snake River Landing** on the Minnesota side. Directly across the St. Croix is the **Soderbeck Landing**, a frequently used access point that was once the location of a ferry service. Several houses appear on the left after Soderbeck—the first you will have seen in a long time. Riffles occasionally appear.

Two miles below Soderbeck, there is a big right-hand bend; then when the river curves back to the left for the last leg before the Highway 70 bridge, Sandrock Cliffs appear on the left behind some islands (13 miles). A small channel takes you to the scenic cliffs and **campground;** if you have the time (and if there's enough water in the channel), be sure to stop at this beautiful spot. The cliff-top view is impressive.

TAKE-OUT: From Sandrock Cliffs, the Highway 70 bridge is only 1.5 miles downstream. The **landing** is upstream-left, with good parking.

The view from Sandrock Cliffs.

A Good River-Read

It would be fortunate if every river had as well-written a book about it as the St. Croix. James Taylor Dunn, a lifelong resident of the St. Croix Valley, has authored a fascinating account of the river from the days of the Chippewa and Sioux, through the logging era to modern times. A lively book, *The St. Croix: Midwest Border River* (Minnesota Historical Society Press, 1979) is also scholarly; Dunn once served as chief librarian of the Minnesota Historical Society.

Reading the book certainly makes canoeing the river all the more enjoyable, as the significance of place names, towns and natural features is made clear. In one particularly relevant chapter for paddlers—the last—Dunn recounts a canoe trip that he and a friend took from the headwaters to Stillwater.

The book is available at the four visitor centers of the St. Croix National Scenic Riverway.

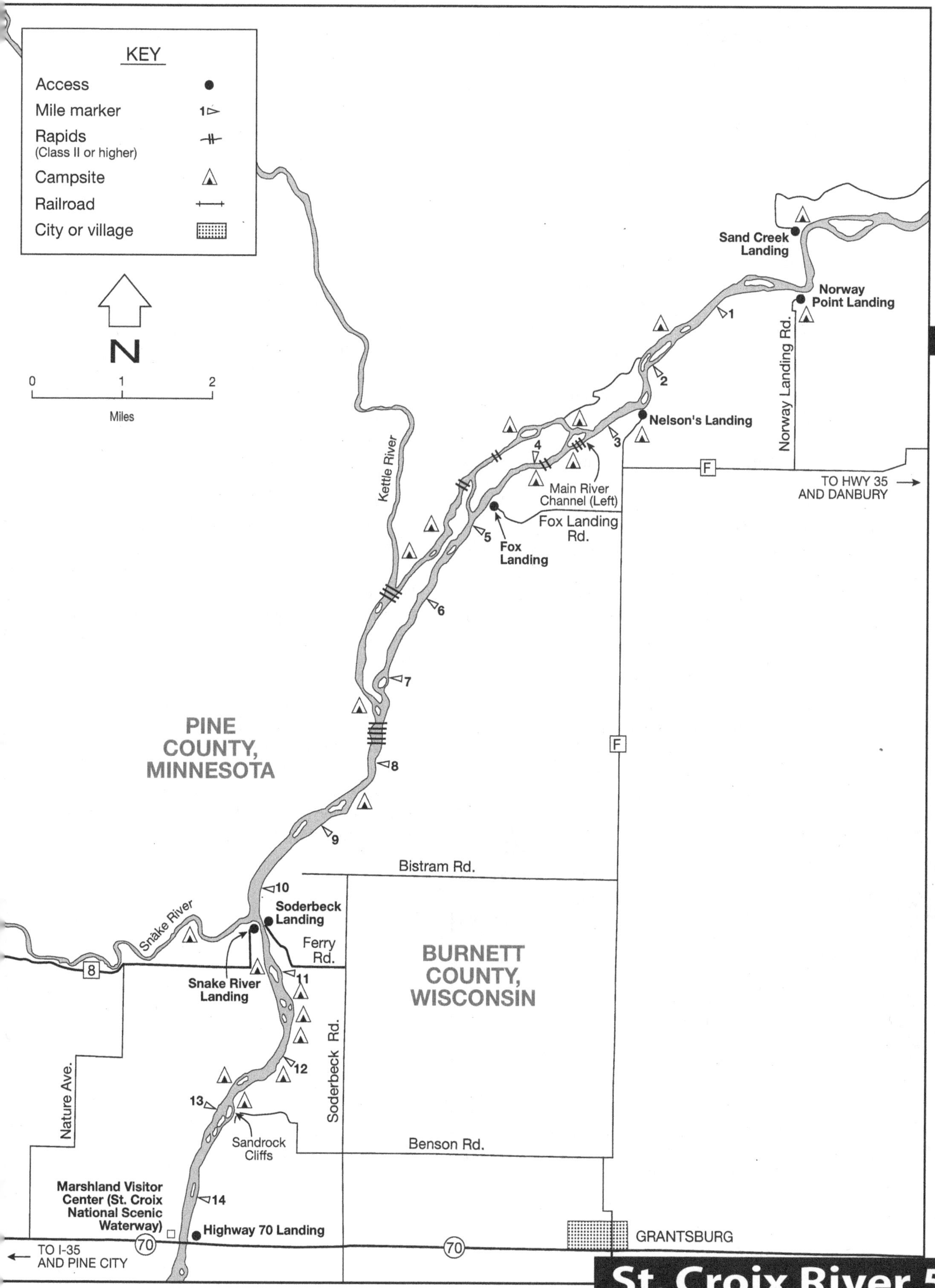

St. Croix River 5

St. Croix River 6

Highway 70 to County O (8.8 Miles)

Because roads run nearby, you'll see a few more cabins on this section than you've become accustomed to upstream, but most of the stretch is quite undeveloped. What's more, the wooded shoreline is often interrupted by lovely stone formations—a hint of what is to come after St. Croix Falls/Taylors Falls. A couple of riffles break up the flatwater, and current continues to be a significant aid to paddling. Fishing for northern, muskie, walleye, bass and catfish is popular all along the stretch. Paddlers who want a longer trip can continue downstream to the Sunrise Ferry Landing (17 miles), or farther, especially if canoe-camping.

A number of riverside **campsites,** maintained by the National Park Service, are found on both sides of the river.

Water levels are almost always adequate for enjoyable paddling. For general information on water levels (high, medium or low), call the visitor center at St. Croix Falls (715-483-2274).

The **GRADIENT** in this section averages only 1.1 feet per mile.

The **shuttle route** is via Highway 70, River Road, Fish Lake Road and County O. For **canoe rentals** and shuttle service, see St. Croix 3.

PUT IN at the Park Service **landing** at the Highway 70 bridge, upstream-left. The Marshland Center of the St. Croix National Scenic Riverway is located across the river on the Minnesota side, and Grantsburg isn't far away to the east. All of the Wisconsin shoreline during this trip is in the 55-mile-long Governor Knowles State Forest.

The St. Croix: wide, wild and peaceful.

The river begins in a typical St. Croix setting: wide, with low, grassy banks, profuse deciduous trees and several islands. The Wood River soon enters on the left, opposite a clearing on the Minnesota side.

About 1.5 miles downstream from Highway 70, **Raspberry Landing** appears on the left, soon after a noisy spring. After a house following the landing, the river continues wide and fairly slow, with gentle riffles in shallower spots. A series of large islands follows Raspberry Landing.

Attractive stone outcroppings and a long stand of red pines begin on the right after a river-right campsite. A cabin on the left, and a long, pleasant set of riffles precede the **Stevens Creek Landing** on the right (4.8 miles); the landing comes in a big left bend. Beautiful stone formations topped with pines are on the left after Stevens Creek Landing, and the river widens.

Three cabins in a left bend show the nearness of a road paralleling the river on the Minnesota side. Rock Creek enters on the right.

Downstream, bare banks on both sides indicate the former site of a bridge. On the right is the **Old Railroad Bridge Landing,** followed by campsites on both sides. Before long, there is a river-wide riffle at two islands.

In the long, straight stretch to the south, beginning around Rock Creek, springs can often be heard running down the bluffs on the left.

Immediately after several cabins on the right, landings come into view on both sides.

TAKE OUT on the Wisconsin side at the **County O Landing,** or on the right at the **Rush City Ferry Landing** (Rush City, Minn., is a few miles to the west).

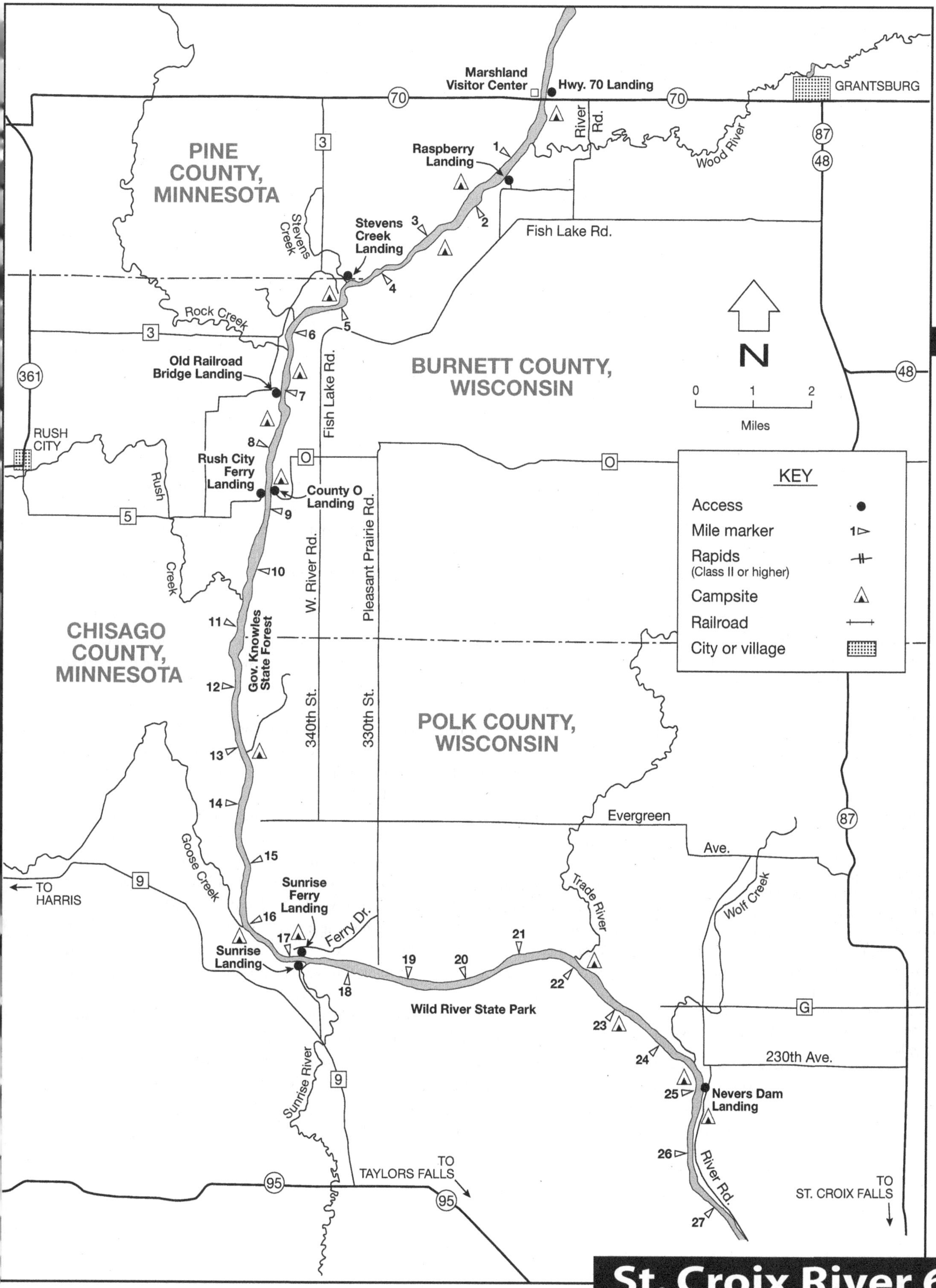
Marshland
Visitor Center
Hwy. 70 Landing
GRANTSBURG
70
River
Rd.
Wood River
87
48
PINE
COUNTY,
MINNESOTA
3
Raspberry
Landing
1
2
Fish Lake Rd.
Stevens
Creek
Landing
3
4
Stevens
Creek
Rock Creek
5
6
3
Old Railroad
Bridge Landing
7
361
Fish Lake Rd.
BURNETT COUNTY,
WISCONSIN
N
0
1
2
Miles
48
RUSH
CITY
8
O
O
Rush City
Ferry
Landing
County O
Landing
Rush
5
9
Pleasant Prairie Rd.
W. River Rd.
10
Creek
KEY
Access
Mile marker
Rapids
(Class II or higher)
Campsite
Railroad
City or village
CHISAGO
COUNTY,
MINNESOTA
11
Gov. Knowles
State Forest
12
340th St.
330th St.
POLK COUNTY,
WISCONSIN
13
14
Evergreen
Ave.
87
15
Goose Creek
9
TO
HARRIS
Trade River
Wolf Creek
Sunrise
Ferry
Landing
16
Ferry Dr.
17
21
Sunrise
Landing
19
20
22
18
Wild River State Park
G
23
230th Ave.
24
Sunrise River
9
25
Nevers Dam
Landing
26
River Rd.
TO
TAYLORS FALLS
95
95
TO
ST. CROIX FALLS
27

St. Croix River 7

County O to Nevers Dam Landing (16.2 Miles)

For 73 miles the St. Croix flows freely without a dam, except for the meager remnants of Coppermine. From County O, it still has 27 more miles before the big hydroelectric structure at St. Croix Falls/Taylors Falls, but already the current slows. By the time the river reaches the site of the famous old Nevers logging dam, it is wider, deeper and slower still. Moreover, its broader expanse and southward orientation can make it a "bear" when winds are strong out of the south.

The section from County O to Nevers is well worth paddling, however. There is one long stretch, for instance, that is as wild and unspoiled as anywhere on the river. It is also enjoyable to paddle along and watch the shoreline change from woods and grass to sand and clay banks. And for history buffs, there's the thrill of taking out at the site of one of the biggest logging dams ever built.

Camping is available at several primitive sites along the river, maintained by the National Park Service. Campgrounds are also located nearby at Wild River State Park in Minnesota, across the river from Nevers Dam, and to the south at Interstate Park, which lies in both Minnesota and Wisconsin.

Water levels are always adequate for canoeing. For information, call the St. Croix National Scenic Riverway Headquarters at St. Croix Falls (715-483-2274).

The **GRADIENT** of this stretch averages only 1.2 feet per mile.

The **shuttle route** is via County O, Highway 87, 230th Avenue and River Road. For **canoe rentals** and shuttle service, see St. Croix 3.

PUT IN on river-left (the Wisconsin side) at the **County O Landing**. There is plenty of parking.

The stretch begins like most of the St. Croix—wide, with heavily wooded banks. A couple of cabins appear a quarter-mile downstream, on the right. Current is slower than it was upstream, and the river is generally deeper.

Bottleneck at the Dells

Like most rivers in northern Wisconsin, the St. Croix once was filled with millions of logs. These were cut in winter and floated downriver in spring to the mills at Stillwater and Hudson. Because of the narrowness of the dells, however, and the sharp right turn at Angle Rock, colossal logjams were common on the St. Croix.

One jam that occurred in 1886 is especially notorious: The river was completely filled with logs for many miles upstream from the dells, piled as high as 50 feet. It took months of work by machines, horses and hundreds of men to get the logs moving again.

Finally, in 1890, the Nevers Dam was built upstream to control the flow of logs and to prevent such jams. Nevers was the largest dam of its kind in the world, and was used for log-driving for 22 years. Now, only its rock pilings remain.

Near the Burnett/Polk County line, there is a beautiful home, then a cabin on the right in a left bend, just after a couple of big islands. Downstream, after a river-left campsite on top of a bank, a very wild section of the river begins, with no sign of civilization except other boaters.

The river continues toward the south, making several gentle bends. At the Goose Creek campsite on the right, a big bend to the left (east) begins, and traffic noise from Highway 9 can be heard on the right.

Near the end of the big left bend, Sunrise Ferry campsite and **landing** appear on the left; the campsite has a big sandy beach. There is another landing on the Minnesota side. Both are named after the logging-era town located nearby. After a campsite, the Sunrise River enters on the right.

Downstream from Sunrise, the river gets wider and slower, and sand and clay banks become more numerous. The mouth of the Trade River is on the left—followed immediately by a campsite—as the St. Croix turns right toward the southeast. Sand beaches appear.

When you encounter eight regularly spaced piles of rock in the river, you know that you're about half a mile upstream from Nevers Dam. These piles once served to impede and break up massive ice floes so that they wouldn't crush the dam.

Downstream, four piles of rock mark the site of the old **Nevers Dam,** a huge structure built in 1890 to help regulate the flow of logs and to prevent logjams. The pilings are all that remains.

TAKE OUT at the river-left **landing** just after the rock pilings. There are big sandbars on both shores, and a sign on the Minnesota side warning of the danger of drop-offs and unpredictable currents. The 6,800-acre Wild River State Park lies on the right, with a landing 2.5 miles farther downstream.

Other trips: From Nevers Dam, it is 11 miles to the St. Croix Scenic Riverway Headquarters and Landing in St. Croix Falls, just upstream from a big hydroelectric dam. A 10-mile paddle from Nevers ends at Lions Park Landing, a lovely area alongside Highway 87 (parking, picnic facilities, water and toilets). River Road runs alongside the river most of the way from Nevers Dam to Lions Park. Some current persists all the way to the dam, but it's quite weak after Nevers. There are 17 riverside campsites between Nevers and St. Croix Falls.

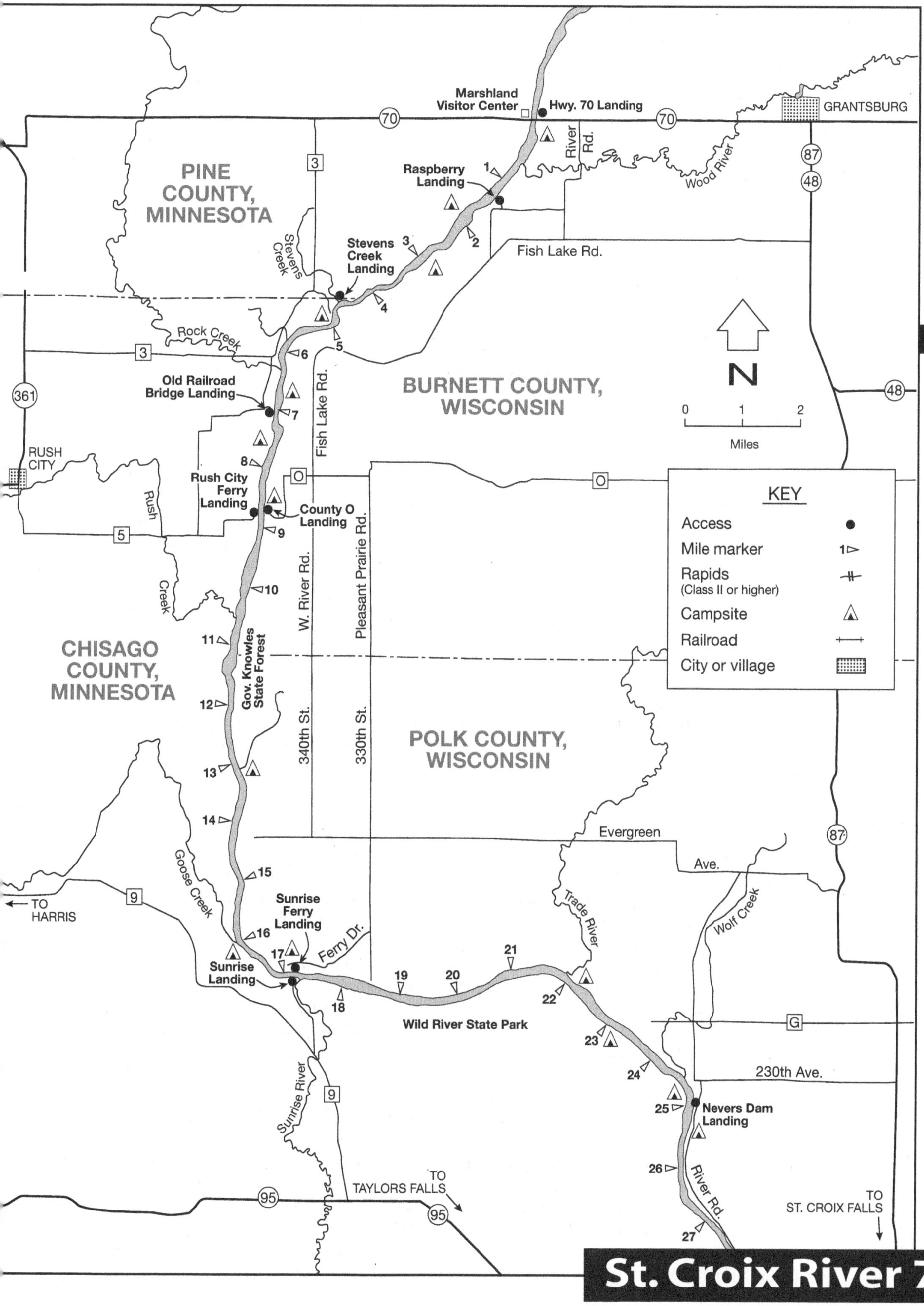
Marshland Visitor Center
Hwy. 70 Landing
GRANTSBURG
River Rd.
Wood River
PINE COUNTY, MINNESOTA
Raspberry Landing
Stevens Creek
Stevens Creek Landing
Fish Lake Rd.
Rock Creek
BURNETT COUNTY, WISCONSIN
N
0 1 2
Miles
Old Railroad Bridge Landing
RUSH CITY
Rush City Ferry Landing
County O Landing
Rush Creek
W. River Rd.
Pleasant Prairie Rd.
KEY
Access
Mile marker
Rapids (Class II or higher)
Campsite
Railroad
City or village
CHISAGO COUNTY, MINNESOTA
Gov. Knowles State Forest
340th St.
330th St.
POLK COUNTY, WISCONSIN
Evergreen Ave.
Goose Creek
TO HARRIS
Sunrise Ferry Landing
Ferry Dr.
Sunrise Landing
Trade River
Wolf Creek
Wild River State Park
230th Ave.
Nevers Dam Landing
Sunrise River
TO TAYLORS FALLS
River Rd.
TO ST. CROIX FALLS

St. Croix River 8

Interstate Park to William O'Brien State Park Landing (15.2 Miles)

This last section of the St. Croix may be the most enjoyable of all. Extremely popular with paddlers from the Minneapolis/St. Paul area, it has all the makings of a great trip. Perhaps the biggest draw is the magnificent dells, carved from dark basalt by the meltwater of the last glacier. The cliffs, potholes and other features of the dells can be enjoyed from Interstate Park, on both sides of the river. Nearby are wonderful towns like St. Croix Falls, Taylors Falls, Osceola and Marine on St. Croix, which are steeped in history and invite a stay by canoeists and nonboaters alike. And, of course, there's the river itself—mostly wide, sometimes windy, but always rewarding with its beautiful stone formations, many sandbars and campsites, and comfortable landings.

This trip can easily be shortened by using Osceola as a take-out or put-in.

A few **campsites** are located along the river, and large, developed campgrounds are available at Interstate Park, on both the Wisconsin and Minnesota sides, and at William O'Brien State Park in Minnesota.

Water levels fluctuate somewhat because of the dam, but are almost always adequate for good paddling. For general information on water conditions, call the St. Croix Scenic Riverway Headquarters at St. Croix Falls (715-483-2274). Also check "River Levels" at the St. Croix National Scenic Riverway website: www.nps.gov/sacn.

The average **GRADIENT** is only 0.6 feet per mile.

The **shuttle route** for a trip putting in and taking out on the Minnesota side is via Highway 8 and Highway 95. A trip on the Wisconsin side (Interstate Park to Somerset Landing) is via Highway 35, County Line Road and Marine Road. Of course, trips combining accesses on both sides are also possible. For canoe rentals and shuttle service, see St. Croix 3.

PUT IN just south of St. Croix Falls/Taylors Falls at **Interstate Park.** There are excellent canoe **landings** on both sides of the river; the Wisconsin landing is about half a mile upstream from the Minnesota access. Admission to both parks involves a day-use fee. (Mile markers on the accompanying map begin at the Wisconsin landing.)

Incidentally, kayakers and canoeists who want only to play in the Class II **rapids** below the Highway 8 bridge carry their boats under the bridge and put in upstream-right.

Trips begin below the dells with wooded, grassy shoreline and a wide river. Highway 8 hugs the right shore, atop stony bluffs. A short distance downstream from the put-in, an island on the right side is said to have been created accidentally when construction workers used too much dynamite to carve out room for the highway.

At a gas line clearing, the river turns right and narrows, passing through a lovely dells area, with a rocky island in the middle. On the high basalt cliff on the left, you can see a big white painted "X" that once served as a navigational aid for steamboats.

The river widens again after Rock Island, and you'll often see pontoon boats downriver. The **Franconia Public Landing** is on the right, 2.7 miles downstream from the Wisconsin Interstate Park put-in. Then, cabins and trailers line the right for about a quarter mile. After a long straightaway, the Eagle's Nest campsite is found on the right where the river bends left, with a small riffle. Nice sandbars appear. You won't see any more houses until Osceola.

A very long island precedes Osceola, and you'll hear the sound of traffic on Highway 35. High up on the bluffs, the Osceola water tower rises above the trees; then the Highway 243 bridge and some houses on the left appear. An excellent canoe **landing**—with picnic facilities, toilets, water and phone—is on the downstream-right side of the bridge (6.5 miles).

Osceola—a charming little town named after a Seminole chief—cannot be seen from the river but can be reached by a path that comes down to the river at the bridge, upstream-left.

Lovely wooded sandstone cliffs run alongside the left shore for some distance below the bridge. There are several shallow spots after Osceola, but it's easy to find the deep places to paddle. The railroad runs along the left shore for a while, and in a couple of locations springs can be heard and seen tumbling down the bluffs.

Two miles after Osceola the river makes a sharp left turn at Cedar Bend, cited as the boundary between the Sioux and Chippewa in the Treaty of 1837. From here to the old railroad swing bridge (10.8 miles), low sandstone cliffs line the right side.

Immediately following the bridge is a huge island. The right channel is deeper and used by motorboats, while the shallower left channel has some sandbars and is more suitable for canoes. Cabins and boat moorings are found on the right shore, where the **Log House Boat Landing** appears at 13.2 miles.

Suddenly, there are no more houses, and signs announce the beginning of **William O'Brien State Park** on the right. From here to the canoe landing in the park, a beautiful low sandstone wall forms the right shoreline, with many white pines.

TAKE-OUT: After the state park signs begin, stay to the right, especially at the head of Greenberg Island, and follow the right channel down to the park **landing** (15.2 miles).

Another mile of paddling leads to the **Somerset Public Landing** on the left.

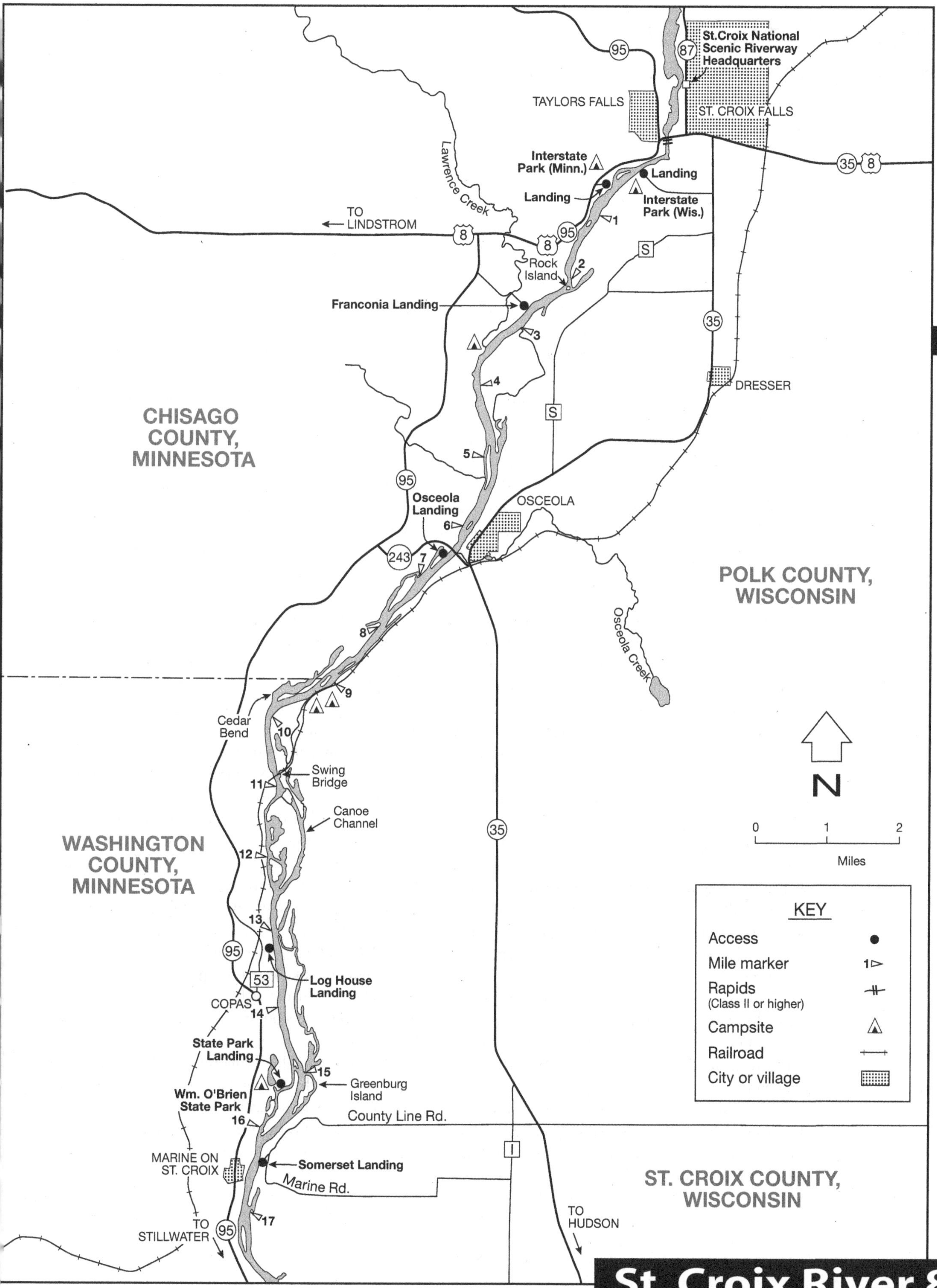
St.Croix National
Scenic Riverway
Headquarters
TAYLORS FALLS
ST. CROIX FALLS
Interstate
Park (Minn.)
Landing
Landing
Interstate
Park (Wis.)
Lawrence Creek
TO
LINDSTROM
Rock
Island
Franconia Landing
DRESSER
CHISAGO
COUNTY,
MINNESOTA
Osceola
Landing
OSCEOLA
POLK COUNTY,
WISCONSIN
Osceola Creek
Cedar
Bend
Swing
Bridge
Canoe
Channel
WASHINGTON
COUNTY,
MINNESOTA
N
0
1
2
Miles
Log House
Landing
COPAS
State Park
Landing
Wm. O'Brien
State Park
Greenburg
Island
County Line Rd.
Somerset Landing
MARINE ON
ST. CROIX
Marine Rd.
TO
STILLWATER
TO
HUDSON
ST. CROIX COUNTY,
WISCONSIN
KEY
Access
Mile marker
Rapids
(Class II or higher)
Campsite
Railroad
City or village

Tomahawk River 1

Willow Flowage Dam to Swamp Lake Road (11.5 Miles)

The 22 miles of river described in this section and the next constitute one of the least paddled but most attractive canoeing streams in the state. Located a few miles northwest of the city of Tomahawk, this portion of the river is beautiful, wild and varied, and includes a couple of exciting rapids. Except for these two rapids, the Tomahawk is suitable for novice paddlers. Much of the river has a remote feeling—be alert for eagles' nests—and local fishermen indicate that bass, trout, walleye, muskie and northern are to be found. Most of the shoreline is privately owned.

No public **camping** is available nearby, but there are many private resorts with campgrounds in the Willow Flowage and Tomahawk area.

Water levels vary according to the volume released from the Willow Reservoir Dam. If the water is low, the river can be quite scratchy at Halfbreed Rapids and Prairie Rapids, and in riffly areas. High water makes the river dangerous. Wisconsin Valley Improvement Company (715-848-2976 or www.wvic.com) will provide information on water releases from the dam.

The average **GRADIENT** is 2.6 feet per mile.

The **shuttle route** for the first stretch is via Willow Dam Road, County Y and Swamp Lake Road. **Canoe/kayak rental** is available at Chequamegon Adventure Company in Minocqua (715-356-1618 or www.paddlerama.com).

PUT IN downstream-left from the **Willow Flowage Dam,** off Willow Dam Road. Carry boats as far as possible on the path that leads from the parking lot, in order to get clear of the dam outflow. There are plenty of parking spaces in the lot, plus toilets.

Immediately after the dam, the river bends to the right; there are a few houses on the right until the river swings left away from Willow Dam Road. Occasionally, trees fall into the river on one side or the other, so be on the lookout for strainers. Pine, maple, alder, birch, popple and spruce are plentiful along this stretch. There are no houses for a long time.

Oelhafen Creek (2 miles) enters from the left in the midst of a big right-hand bend in a lowland area.

At 3 miles Bear Creek enters from the left; a tall, attractive sand bank topped with pines follows the creek mouth on the left.

The County Y bridge (3.5 miles) may be **accessed** downstream-right at the private campground (ask permission). A few houses appear on the right after the bridge, but none for a long time afterward.

In the middle of a right-hand bend, a small cabin appears high up on a river-left bank, followed immediately by a left-hand bend with an island in it. **Halfbreed Rapids** is directly ahead. A solid Class II rapids, Half-breed is a couple hundred yards long. The river narrows, falls several feet, and S-curves, with fast water, big waves and many boulders. Near the end, it splits around two small islands. Novices can easily get into trouble, particularly at the beginning (where there's a tricky curler wave) and at the end of the rapids, so only experienced whitewater paddlers should attempt it. Boat control is required all the way. Take out on the left just above the rapids and walk the well-defined scout/portage trail along a high wooded bank; the trail ends at several private trailers before going back downhill to the river just below the rapids. This is private property, so you should ask permission from the owner. If the river is low, boaters can also portage along the river on the right. There are a few cabins on the left after the rapids, as Rocky Run Road parallels the river for a while. The river begins moving away from the road after Swan Creek enters on the left.

Downstream, a beautiful pine-covered bank appears on the left in the middle of a big right-hand bend. For the next few miles, pine and maple dominate on the left, alders on the right, and the river is lovely and wild. There are very few houses, and the river becomes winding, fast and riffly.

Eventually, homes on the left are followed by a series of good-sized islands. Note the long fence on the left for a 900-acre game farm.

During the last 1.5 miles before the take-out bridge, the lowland disappears, the river narrows, and the banks are heavily wooded again—another beautiful section. Houses appear on the right as the river approaches Swamp Lake Road; there are a couple of sharp bends before the bridge.

TAKE OUT upstream-right or downstream-left at the **Swamp Lake Road bridge.** There is an **alternate take-out** on the right bank 0.2 mile upstream from the bridge, at a point where the road is only a few feet from the river.

Other trips: The Tomahawk is also paddleable upstream from the Willow Flowage, but for the most part passes through a marshy environment. There is an access at Camp 9 Road. Cedar Falls, a difficult rapids, is found just above the flowage.

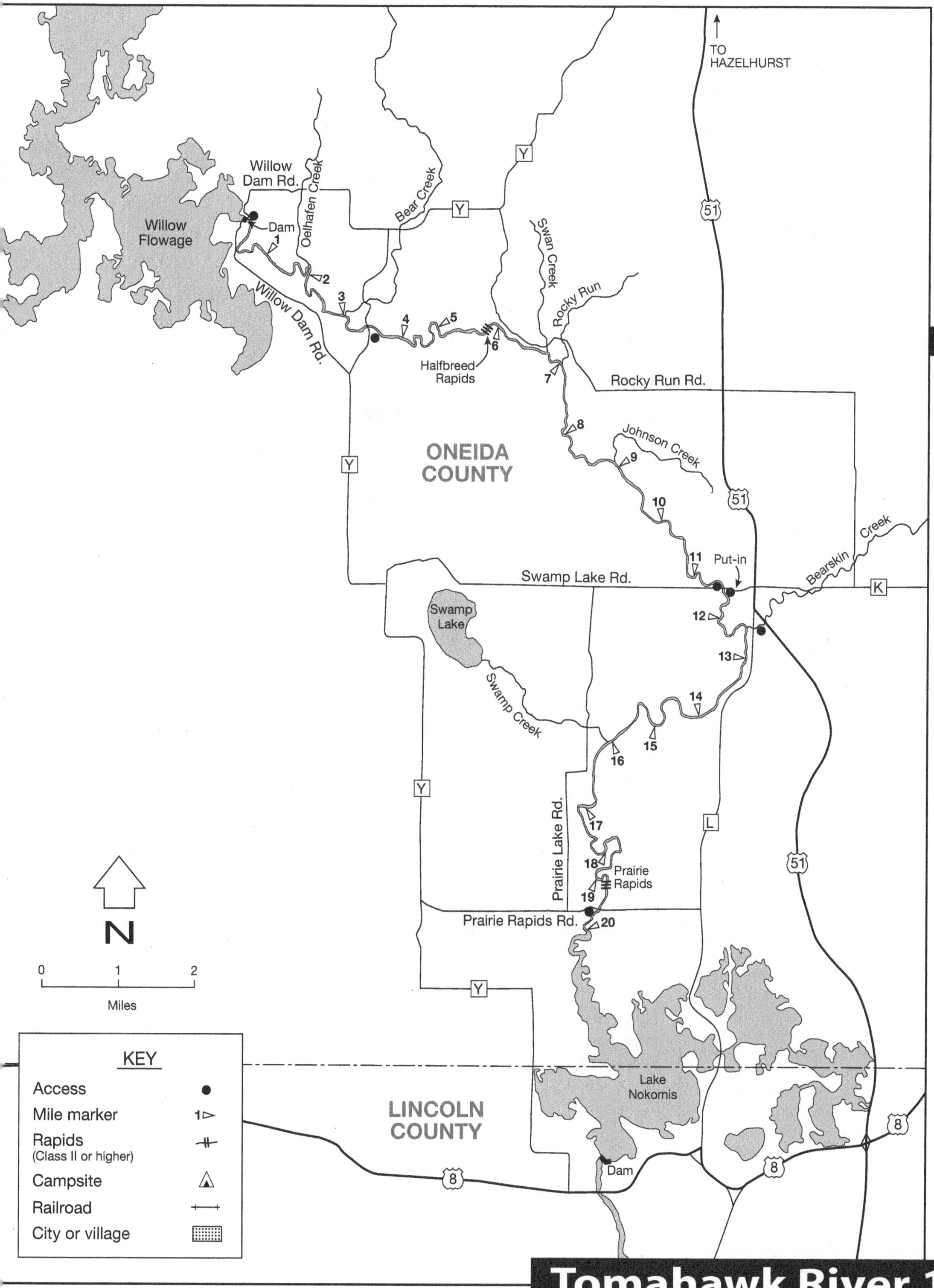

Tomahawk River 1

Tomahawk River 2

Swamp Lake Road to Prairie Rapids Road (8.2 Miles)

Like the upstream portion, this section of the Tomahawk provides a great deal of variety: many high, pine-covered sand banks, some lowland areas, heavily wooded shoreline, long stretches with no human habitation, and a challenging rapids. Except for the rapids, which is near the end, this section is suitable for novices. Be careful of strainers: Fallen trees do not usually block the entire waterway but pose a hazard for unwary paddlers. Your chances of observing wildlife (especially eagles) are quite good.

No public **camping** is available nearby, but there are many private resorts with campgrounds in the area.

Water levels: See Tomahawk 1.

The average **GRADIENT** is 1.2 feet per mile.

The **shuttle route** is via either Swamp Lake Road, Prairie Lake Road and Prairie Rapids Road; or Swamp Lake Road, County L and Prairie Rapids Road. For **canoe/kayak rental,** see Tomahawk 1.

PUT IN upstream-right or downstream-left at the **Swamp Lake Road bridge.** The first mile is winding and fairly narrow, about 60 feet wide (like most of the previous section), with many high pine-covered banks. There are a few houses on the left.

After a big right-hand bend, the river widens and approaches County L (Business 51), then runs alongside it for a while. Bearskin Creek enters from the left, immediately followed by a snowmobile bridge.

An **alternate put-in** is at the attractive little wayside on County L alongside the Bearskin Creek bridge. From here, it's a short paddle to the river. Bearskin Creek, incidentally, is a good trout stream.

The river narrows here, then widens again. There are very few dwellings for the next 6 miles.

Lowland vegetation dominates for about a mile. Then wooded banks reappear on the right as the river swings left. High sand banks appear on the right (topped by pines and maples) where the river swings sharply back to the left.

Preserving Wisconsin's Wilderness Areas

The state's decision in late 1997 to purchase 8,700 acres of the Willow Flowage was one of many steps to protect wild areas from development.

Formed by a dam built on the Tomahawk River in 1926, the Willow Flowage is popular with walleye fishermen, hunters, hikers and lovers of wildlife. Eagles abound, and wolves are known to inhabit the area. There are 93 miles of heavily-forested shoreline, surrounding a 6,400-acre lake.

Earlier, two comparable water systems were also acquired by the state: the Chippewa Flowage in 1988 and the Turtle-Flambeau Flowage in 1990. Paddlers are also well aware of the state's acquisition of shoreline on such premier rivers as the Wolf, Flambeau, Bois Brule, Wisconsin and St. Croix.

We all hope that Wisconsin will continue to be a national leader in protecting quiet, unspoiled places for future generations.

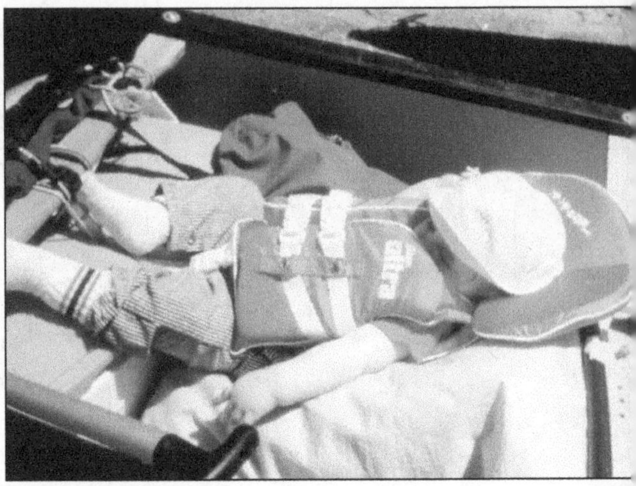

Enjoying a quiet float.

After a right-hand curve, the river moves into another lowland area. Swamp Creek enters from the right. A private landing comes in on the right (off Prairie Lake Road), not far downstream from Swamp Creek. The next couple of miles are often quite windy. High sand banks are plentiful, especially wherever the river bends sharply.

A couple of miles before the take-out the river bends left, then right, then left again to trace a pattern to which locals have given a graphic but unprintable name. The river narrows somewhat at this point, and woods begin to close in again on both sides.

Prairie Rapids follows a sharp left bend, then right. The sound can be heard upstream before the two bends. At the beginning of the rapids, the river narrows, then drops through two pitches with a short pool in between. Both pitches are solid Class II and require boat control. The first is a fairly straightforward boulder garden, but with a couple of rocks in bad spots near the bottom. After the brief pool, the second drop follows—a more complex S-curve with more boulders and bigger waves. One or more strainers are often found in the rapids, so be sure to get out and scout on either side. Inexperienced paddlers should portage.

You'll see the **TAKE-OUT (Prairie Rapids Road bridge)** from the bottom of the rapids. Take out downstream-right at the grassy area near the tavern (ask permission).

The Lake Nokomis flowage begins at the Prairie Rapids Road bridge. Then the Tomahawk joins the Wisconsin and Somo rivers at Lake Mohawksin.

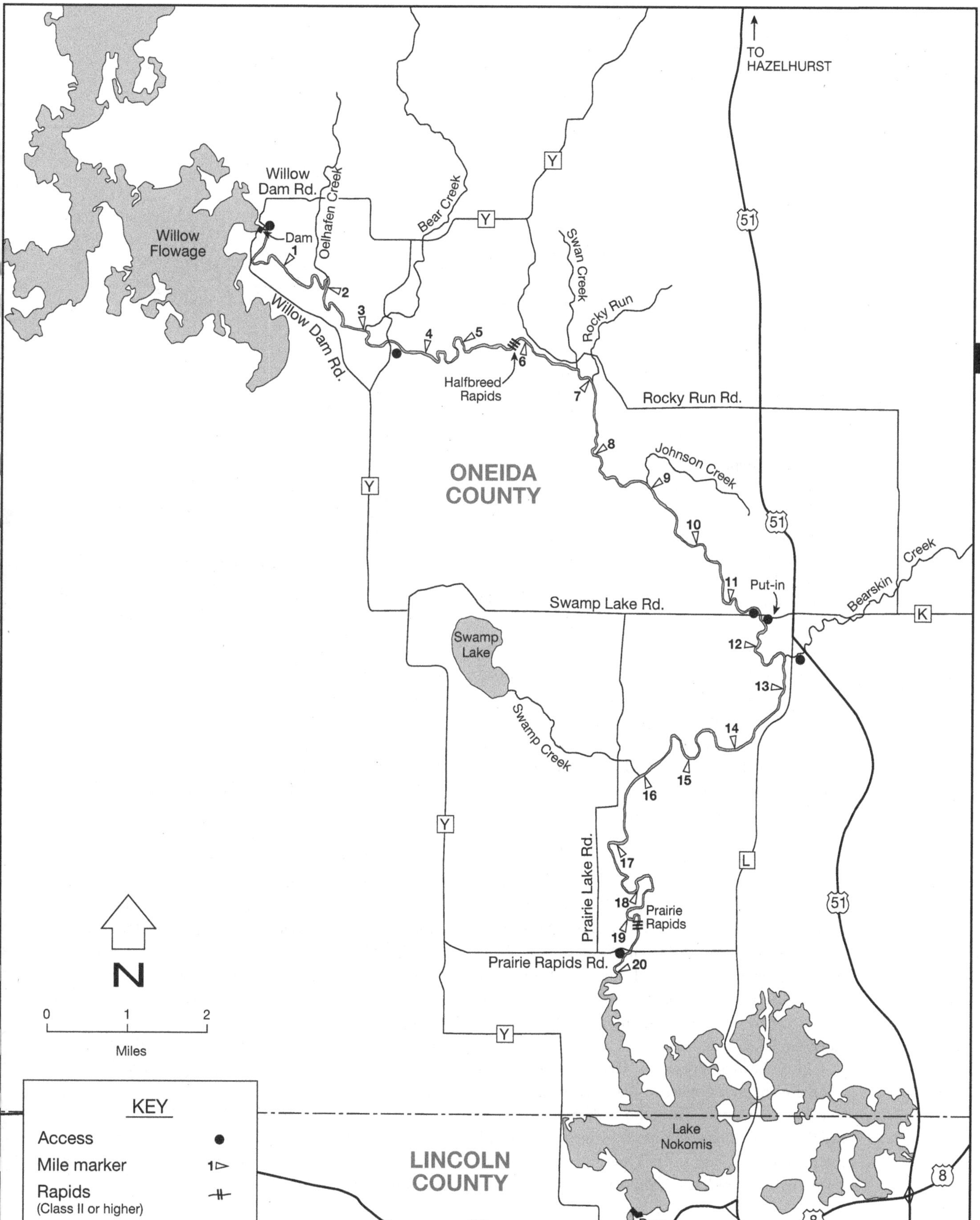

Tomahawk River 2

White River

Maple Ridge Road to Highway 112 (13 Miles)

A beautiful stretch of river with almost no development from beginning to end, this part of the White is a delight for experienced canoeists. About half of the trip consists of riffles and Class I–II rapids, but they are generally nonthreatening for paddlers with good boat control. This section is narrow, winding and densely wooded, with lots of wildflowers on the shoreline. Like the lower Bois Brule, the water is rather dark because of the clay that erodes from the high banks. Good current prevails all the way, and even the flowage is pleasant—relatively short and narrow compared to other flowages. According to fishing enthusiasts, the White is also an excellent trout stream. All things considered, this is definitely a go-back-again river!

Public **camping** is available at the village park in Mason, at Two Lakes Campground south of Drummond and at Perch Lake Campground north of Drummond.

Water levels are usually adequate for enjoyable paddling, but the river is dangerous when high. Because the White River USGS gauge is located downstream from the dam at Highway 112, it is not a reliable indicator of water levels on this section.

The **GRADIENT** averages 12.3 feet per mile.

The **shuttle route** is via Maple Ridge Road, Highway 63, Highway 118 and Highway 112.

PUT IN east of the village of Mason at the **Maple Ridge Road bridge (**1.1 miles from Highway 63), upstream-left. Putting in at the village park on the south side of Mason adds a few miles of flatwater paddling.

The river begins quite narrow (40 feet wide) and winding. Soon after the put-in, a long series of riffles and Class I rapids begins, continuing for several miles. You'll come upon rapids and riffles—too numerous to count—throughout the trip, especially in bends. Tall clay banks, sometimes as high as 90 feet, appear frequently.

There is occasional deadfall, but it can usually be paddled around. Be on guard, however, because the river is generally narrow and heavily wooded. You'll see a great variety of trees, including pine, cedar, maple, alder, birch, ash and spruce.

After the long, opening stretch of mild whitewater, there are several miles of flatwater, with an occasional riffle or rapids. Then, the gradient increases and **rapids** resume, becoming more frequent and a little more difficult (Class I–II). Typically, the rapids are short- or medium-length boulder gardens and wavy constrictions. They are fun to run, but occasionally have awkwardly placed boulders that can get inexperienced boaters in trouble.

High clay banks on the White.

From the midpoint of the trip on, gravel bars are fairly common and make excellent places to stop for lunch, relaxation and a swim. Occasionally, you'll see stone strata on the left.

Rapids are fewer as the river approaches Highway 112, and finally disappear. In the last mile, current slackens, and the river widens in the flowage.

TAKE OUT on the left side of the **dam** at the **Northern States Power Company canoe landing.** A sign here indicates that a buried pipeline runs to the powerhouse downstream from the dam.

Other trips: The section upstream from Mason is a popular flatwater run. A long trip puts in at Pike River Road (where there are no clay banks and the water is clear), and a shorter trip begins at Sutherland Road. Both trips go through the Bibon Swamp Natural Area, a huge marsh.

Canoe rentals for this quietwater section of the river are available at Bear Country Sporting Goods in Drummond (715-739-6645).

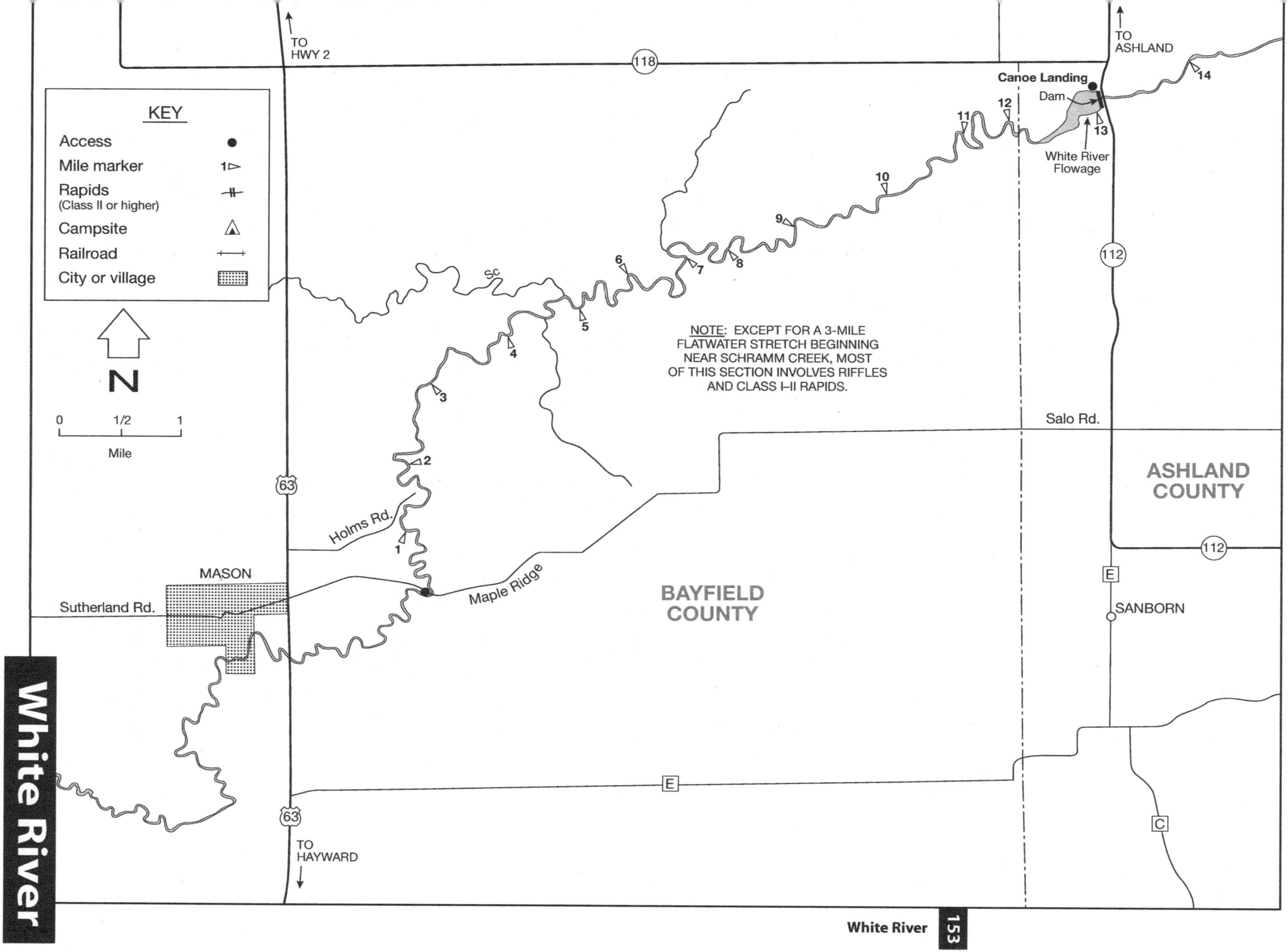
White River
KEY
Access
Mile marker
Rapids
(Class II or higher)
Campsite
Railroad
City or village
N
0
1/2
1
Mile
TO HWY 2
TO ASHLAND
TO HAYWARD
118
112
63
E
C
Canoe Landing
Dam
White River Flowage
NOTE: EXCEPT FOR A 3-MILE FLATWATER STRETCH BEGINNING NEAR SCHRAMM CREEK, MOST OF THIS SECTION INVOLVES RIFFLES AND CLASS I–II RAPIDS.
Sc
Salo Rd.
Holms Rd.
Maple Ridge
Sutherland Rd.
MASON
SANBORN
ASHLAND COUNTY
BAYFIELD COUNTY
1
2
3
4
5
6
7
8
9
10
11
12
13
14

Wisconsin River 1 & 2

Lac Vieux Desert to County K (17 miles)
County K to County G (16 miles)

Beginning as a tiny Northwoods stream at Lac Vieux Desert near the Michigan border, the Wisconsin River travels almost the entire length of the state before emptying into the Mississippi near Prairie du Chien. A dozen smaller rivers and innumerable creeks join it along the way, making it a major American river.

Twenty-six hydropower dams interrupt the course of its 430 miles. For this reason, the Wisconsin is called "The hardest working river in America," a situation that limits its canoeability to a certain extent. Canoeists not fond of flowage paddling (with accompanying powerboats, slack water, and wind) are limited to the headwaters area and stretches below dams. Fortunately, there are many attractive sections that lend themselves to enjoyable day-trips and multi-day camping trips. Eighteen beautiful sections are described in detail between this book and *Paddling Southern Wisconsin.*

Paddlers who have never ventured farther north than Eagle River, and who thus have an image of the Wisconsin as a big, wide river, will be shocked when they see its origin for the first time. Exiting Lac Vieux Desert from a small dam on the southwest side of the lake, the new river is very creek-like. Although it widens somewhat downstream, it remains a small stream almost all the way to its confluence with the Eagle River. This part of the river is a good choice for paddlers who prefer small, winding, remote streams in a wilderness setting.

All along its length, the headwaters section is a mixture of marshland and forest, often alternating. Occasionally the environs are reminiscent of Canada. The streambed consists of sand, pebbles, and rocks, and twists through a seemingly endless succession of meanders (much more than the accompanying map can convey). There are even some low-level rapids to liven things up a bit. Fishermen encounter smallmouth, brook trout (especially in the rapids), musky, and walleye (downstream from County K).

This part of the river is generally suitable for beginning paddlers, but a certain degree of boat-control is desirable for an enjoyable trip. For example, you're likely to encounter a few beaver dams, which occasionally require a carry-over. Limbs in or over the water sometimes make maneuvering necessary, and demand caution.

Please note that the County K access for the 2 trips described here is arbitrary. You can easily design your own trip (making it shorter or longer, for instance) by accessing the river at other put-ins and take-outs.

Camping: For paddlers who want to canoe camp, there are a number of primitive campsites along the river, especially north of County K. Also located on the river, on 40 acres at the mouth of Portage Creek, is Rohr's Wilderness Tours, which has a canoe landing and campground (715-547-3639 or www.rwtcanoe.com). Near the put-in is the federal Lac Vieux Desert Campground.

Water levels are adequate for paddling most of the year, especially downstream from Portage Creek. You can check the current flow from the Lac Vieux Desert dam by calling the Wisconsin Valley Improvement Company (715-848-2976).

The **GRADIENT** for the entire stretch is 1.7 feet per mile.

The **shuttle route** for trip one is via West Shore Road, County E, Highway 45, and County K. For trip two: County K, Highway 45, and County G.

Canoe/kayak rental and shuttle service are available at Rohr's Wilderness Tours, off Razorback Road north of Rummels Road (number above).

PUT IN: You can begin your headwaters adventure in several places: (1) at the public boat landing near the Park Service campground on Lac Vieux Desert, then paddling down the west shoreline and making the easy, marked portage at the dam; (2) parking at the lot alongside West Shore Road, then carrying your canoe up the path to the little park downstream-right from the dam; or (3) parking at the lot on West Shore Road, then carrying your canoe across the road and putting in downstream from the two 3-foot-diameter culverts that carry the river under the road. It all depends on how badly you want to paddle "from the very beginning of the river."

From the outset, the setting is quite wild as the river twists back and forth through marshland and forest. Here you're likely to see the handiwork of beavers and to spot deer and other wildlife. In the approach to Highway 45 (where there's an excellent **access,** downstream-left), the river widens considerably.

After Highway 45, the river narrows and the current accelerates. Some cabins appear in this stretch, and a long succession of switchbacks (Snake Meadows). As you approach the mouth of Portage Creek, there are a couple of miles of riffles and Class I Scratch Rapids. Look for Rohr's **canoe landing** on the right, downstream from the creek mouth. A major tributary, Portage Creek increases the volume of the river substantially.

Rummels Road is an **access** (downstream-left, between the vehicular and snowmobile bridges), and there is also an undeveloped **landing** on river-right alongside Heart Lake Road. Downstream from Tamarack Creek (on the right), the river widens. At County K, there is another good **access,** upstream-left.

River Road (which can get mushy in the spring) has a **landing** at the end, on river-left. Marshland is succeeded by forest (predominantly maples), where you should be on guard for deadfall. Many switchbacks slow your progress, but gradually the river begins to straighten out. Most paddlers on this part of the river **TAKE OUT** at the public boat **landing** at County G, downstream-left, where there's a small park.

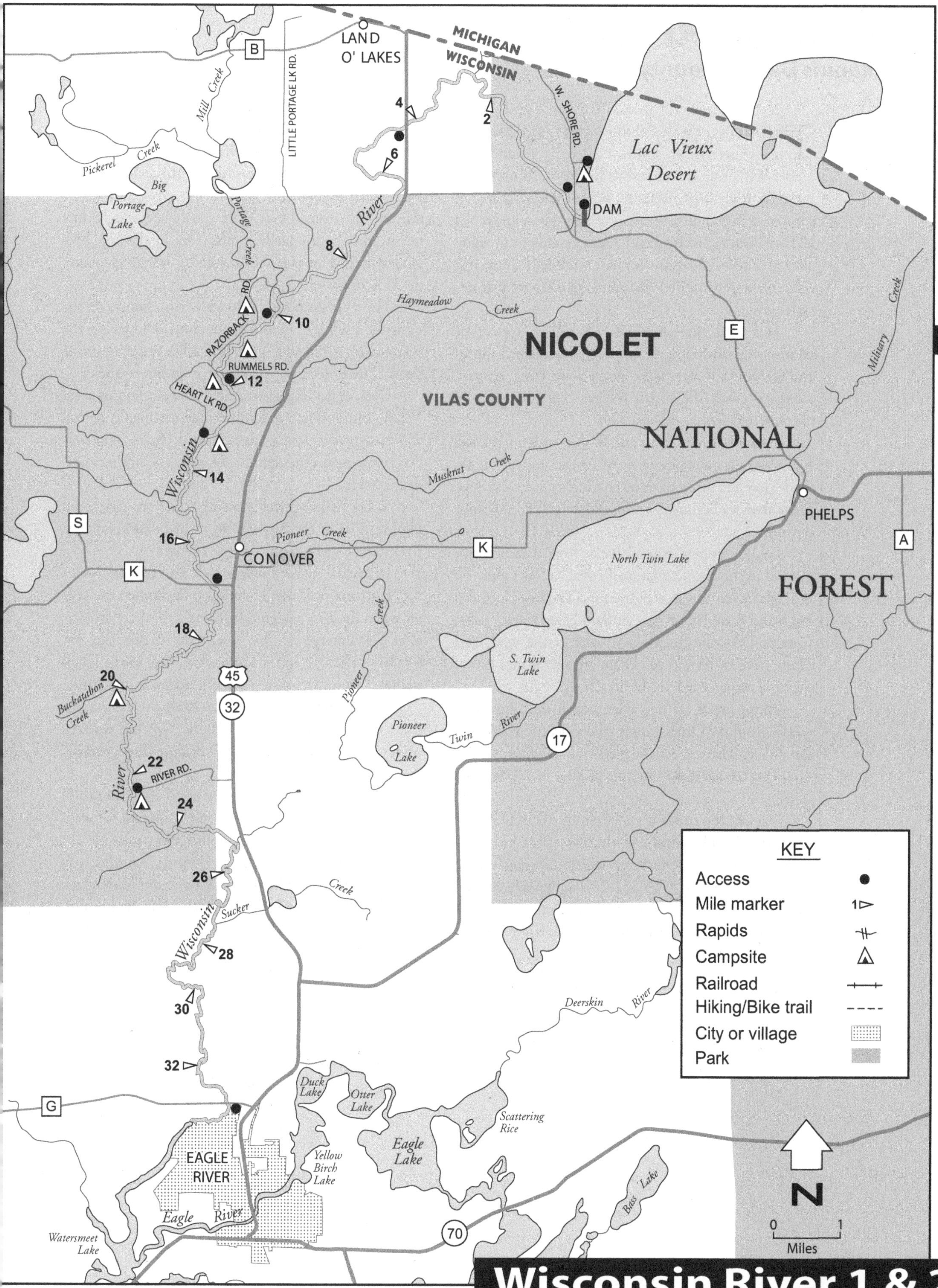

Wisconsin River 1 & 2

Wisconsin River 3

Otter Rapids Dam to County O (7.1 Miles)

The first day-trip after the headwaters section starts near Eagle River, where the gently meandering Upper Wisconsin encounters its first dam. At one time, the river from Eagle River to Wisconsin Dells roared through a 200-mile succession of awesome rapids, but all have been tamed by dams. Today's paddler can enjoy attractive scenery, steady current, wildlife, fishing and other pleasures, but the Wisconsin is no longer a white-water river.

This short stretch passes through a variety of countryside, including heavily wooded upland shores and lowlands. Parts of the section are fairly narrow, compared with the broad reaches that are typically encountered farther downstream.

Always remember that the Wisconsin is a big river: It can become quite powerful and dangerous when high. Under low and medium water conditions, it is an appropriate river for beginners—who take proper precautions, of course.

Public **camping** is available at Anvil Lake Campground in the Nicolet National Forest, a few miles east of Eagle River; and in the American Legion–Northern Highland State Forest near Buffalo Lake, Carrol Lake, Cunard Lake and Tomahawk Lake to the west, and Plum Lake to the north. There are also a number of private campgrounds in the area.

Water levels are dependent upon the amount of release from the Otter Rapids Hydroelectric Dam near the put-in. There is usually plenty of water to paddle.

The **GRADIENT** for this section is 1.4 feet per mile.

The **shuttle route** is via Highway 70 and County O. **Canoe-kayak rental** and shuttle service are available at Hawk's Nest Outfitters, which is located on the river near Eagle River (715-542-2300 or www.hawksnestcanoe.com) and at Chequamegon Adventure Company, Minocqua (715-356-1618 or www.paddlerama.com).

PUT IN downstream-right from the **Otter Rapids Dam,** alongside **Highway 70,** 3.5 miles west of Eagle River. From the parking area, follow the canoe-portage signs down the trail and launch your canoe well below the outflow from the dam. If you have enough time for it, the hydro facility offers an interesting self-guided tour. This is one of the oldest power plants on the Wisconsin.

The river starts out fairly wide, with houses on the right for a while. There are numerous boulders in the stream bed as the river goes through a series of gentle bends. You'll need to pay a little attention to rocks.

Deer, eagles, osprey and ducks are commonly seen. Maple, cedar, birch, alder and pine are plentiful; you will pass several lovely pine-covered banks. Highway 70 is close by on the right as the river goes into a wide, deep stretch.

There is a gravel landing on the right, off Highway 70, at the top of a big right-hand bend. The river narrows as it turns back to the left.

In a wide, marshy area, a dock and sign announce the Sportsman's Chalet (5 miles). Head down the center when the river widens into a marshy lake. Not long after you emerge on the other side of the lake, the County O bridge appears a few hundred yards downstream. Osprey nests are sometimes seen in this area.

TAKE OUT at the boat **landing** upstream-right from the County O bridge. There is an old wooden bridge just before the County O bridge. Good parking is provided.

Fishermen are often seen around the County O bridge and elsewhere on this stretch, fishing for walleye, northern, muskie, smallmouth and panfish.

By the time you reach the County O bridge, you can tell by the lack of current that you are nearing the huge (4,500-acre) Rainbow Flowage. The next recommended river stretch begins near the Rainbow Dam, eliminating 6 miles of flowage paddling.

Wisconsin River 3

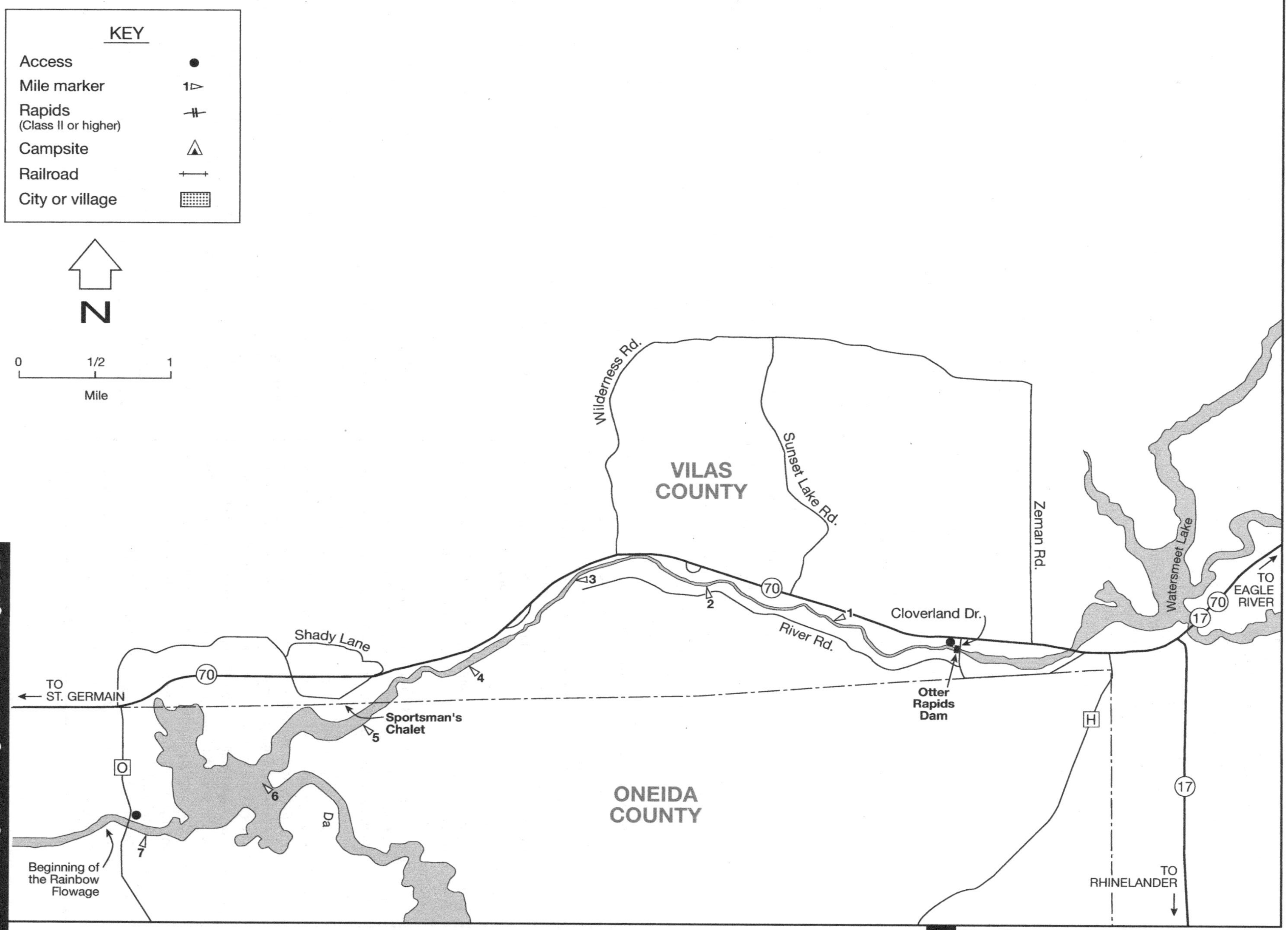

Wisconsin River 4

County D to McNaughton Bridge (10.1 Miles)

Another good trip for beginners, this section is consistently about a hundred feet wide, with attractive shorelines. The woods are mainly deciduous, but have occasional stands of white and red pine and other coniferous trees. Although houses appear here and there, the stretch has a remote feeling. Except for Rainbow Rapids, the whole trip is flatwater, with good current. You will encounter high sand banks, upland forest and lowland vegetation, and will likely see eagles, osprey, kingfishers, herons and ducks. Anglers fish along the shoreline and from boats.

Public **camping** is available in the American Legion–Northern Highland State Forest near Carrol Lake and Cunard Lake to the north, and Tomahawk Lake to the west. There are also a number of private campgrounds in the area.

Water levels, affected by the amount of release at Rainbow Dam, are usually adequate for good paddling. Check the "Rainbow Lake" gauge (#05391000) on the USGS website; see "Water Levels" in the introduction. This gauge is located near the put-in, downstream from the Rainbow Flowage dam.

The Most Perilous Falls on the Wisconsin

In its 430-mile journey from Lac Vieux Desert on the Michigan border to the Mississippi, the Wisconsin drops 1,050 feet. One indication of how fully the river has been tamed is the fact that 62 percent of this total drop (650 feet) is now captured behind power dams.

Before the river was tamed, however, it presented lumbermen with a long series of formidable rapids and falls, especially in the 150-mile stretch below Rhinelander. Many lives were lost every year in the prime logging days—approximately 1850 to 1900—as rivermen attempted to negotiate their logs through one intimidating drop after another.

Among the most notorious were Grandfather and Grandmother Falls north of Merrill, Jenny Falls at Merrill and Big Bull Falls at Wausau. (Bull, incidentally, is from a French-Canadian word, bulles, meaning "rapids.")

Most of the infamous falls of those days are now hidden beneath dams or flowages, but one remains to be marveled at. When the hydroelectric dam at Grandfather Falls was built a few miles north of Merrill, the falls themselves were bypassed by a diversion canal that rerouted water to a downstream powerhouse. Venturesome folks who don't mind a rugged walk can view the original channel (usually with very little water running through it) by following a segment of the Ice Age Trail that begins near the canal. It's a wonderful experience—especially when you realize that the falls drop more than 90 feet in less than a thousand yards.

For a free brochure and map describing the "Grandfather Falls Recreation Area," contact the Wisconsin Public Service Corporation (800-450-7260).

The average **GRADIENT** is 1.0 feet per mile.

The **shuttle route** is via County D, Highway 47 and Bridge Road. **Canoe/kayak rental** is available at Chequamegon Adventure Company in Minocqua (715-356-1618 or www.paddlerama.com).

PUT IN at the public boat **landing** on County D, downstream from the Rainbow Flowage Dam. Good parking is provided.

The medium-high wooded banks at the put-in are typical of this stretch. A couple of houses are visible on the right at the first right-hand bend. Most of this stretch is without houses, but you will see some on roads approaching the river (Rapids Road, River Road, Riverview Drive).

A group of boulders in the river bed, a river constriction and water noise precede **Rainbow Rapids** (1.8 miles)—two curving pitches of Class I fast, wavy water. Stay in the main chute and avoid rocks.

Immediately after the rapids, opposite a creek entering from the right, there's a lunch spot on the left bank.

Rainbow Rapids Bridge (2.8 miles), on River Road, is a relatively low wooden bridge on wooden pilings. Clearance can be a problem in high water. No matter what the water conditions, be careful to stay clear of the pilings.

Downstream from the bridge, River Road touches the river on the left just after the mouth of a creek, and many high sand banks appear.

Gradually, the river widens and slows, flanked by low banks and lowland vegetation. Current persists, however.

Upstream from the mouth of Horsehead Creek, there is an abrupt crook in the river (first right, then left); three houses are located here.

A series of oxbows occupies most of the final portion of the trip.

TAKE-OUT: McNaughton Bridge appears after a long straightaway and two sharp bends. Take out upstream-left from the old bridge, which is situated just upstream from the new one. The grassy **landing** has room for several cars.

Other trips: Downstream from McNaughton Bridge, the river continues to wind through a lowland environment, including several miles of wild-rice marshes, before flowing into another flowage near Rhinelander. Five miles below Rhinelander is the Hat Rapids Dam, where the next recommended canoe stretch begins.

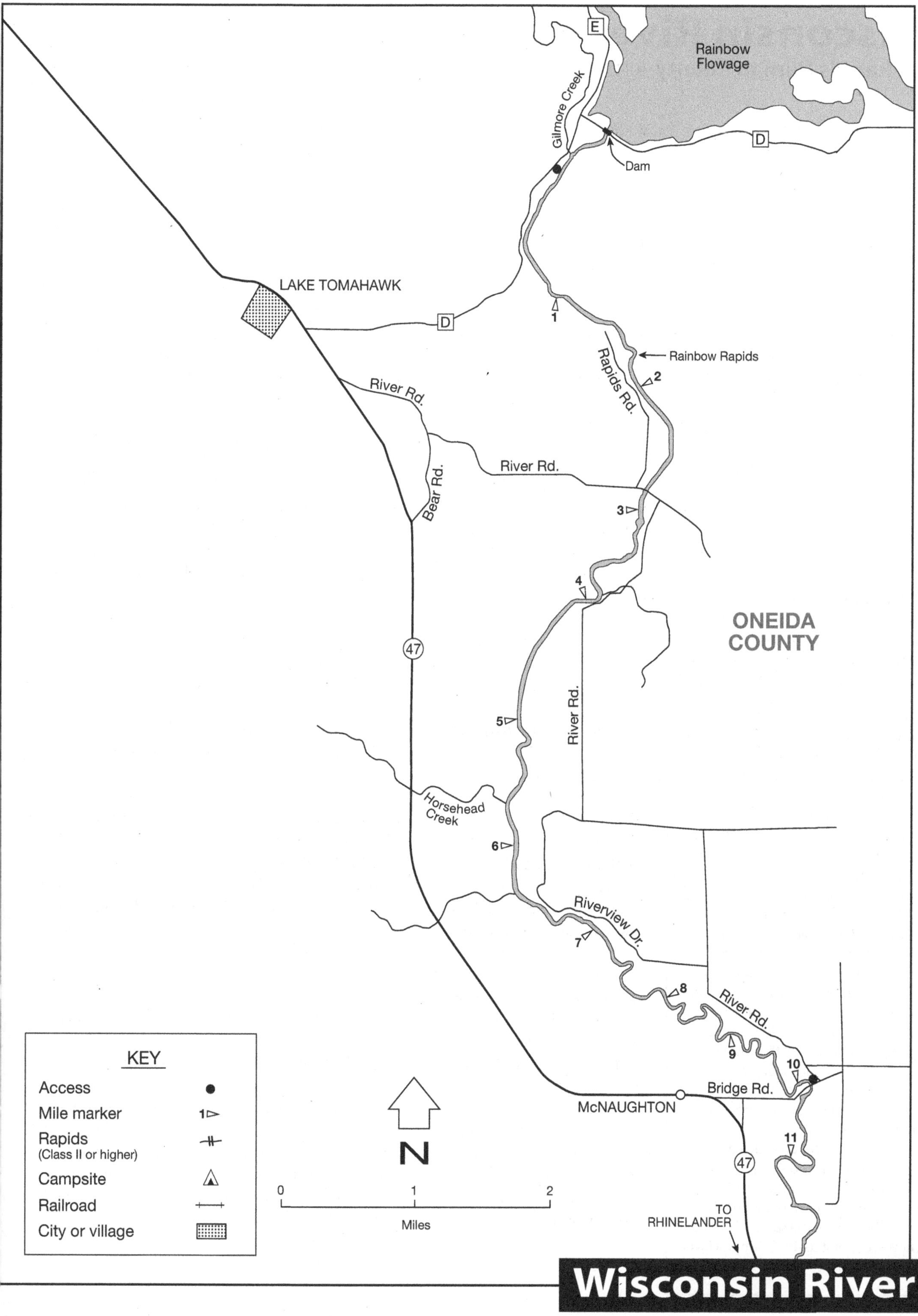

Wisconsin River 4

Wisconsin River 5

Hat Rapids Dam to County A (12.7 Miles)

This section of the Wisconsin—located between the Hat Rapids Flowage and Lake Alice—is like two trips in one: 8 miles of completely natural, quiet river with riffles and rapids, followed by 5 wide, slow miles often frequented by powerboaters. Some of the best rapids on the Wisconsin River (there aren't many!) are found on this section.

Unfortunately, there are no intermediate accesses except at the 3-mile point. Thus, paddlers who wish to enjoy the isolation and excitement of the first part must reconcile themselves to the less tranquil environment of the second part. If possible, paddle this last stretch at times other than weekends and holidays, in order to minimize the chances of encountering motorboat traffic.

There are several private **campgrounds** in the area.

Water levels are almost always adequate for good canoeing. A gauge maintained by the Wisconsin Valley Improvement Company at Whirlpool Rapids indicates the average daily flow of the river in this section; call 715-842-1284 for the recorded data-line. Also check the Hot Rapids flow data on the Wisconsin Public Service website: www.wisconsinpublicservice.com.news/hydro/hydrodata.asp.

The average **GRADIENT** is 4.7 feet per mile.

The **shuttle route** is via Hat Rapids Road, Highway 17 and County A.

PUT IN upstream from the **Hat Rapids Road bridge,** just below the **dam.** A canoe-portage sign and path lead down to the river below the powerhouse, river-right.

The river begins about 125 feet wide, with heavily wooded shorelines. For many miles there is no development at all. Current is usually brisk all the way to Menard Island.

Noisy Creek enters on the left. Farther downstream, soon after an overhead power line, Squaw Creek also comes in from the left, followed by a sharp right-hand bend.

Still a Mystery

In 1660, just 26 years after Jean Nicolet became the first white man to set foot in Wisconsin, Father Rene Menard was sent to establish missions. The Jesuit priest had come to Canada from France in 1640 and had spent 20 years working with the Algonquins and the Iroquois.

When the call came, Menard's health wasn't good. Not surprisingly, the trip to Wisconsin turned out to be a disaster. There were many accidents, and Menard was abandoned by his guides. He spent a cold and hungry winter in a hut, and had minimal success converting the Indians.

Finally, in the spring of 1661, Menard heard of a group of starving Indians on the Black River, and felt obliged to attempt to baptize them. Accompanied by a Frenchman named L'Esperance, he headed south from Chequamegon Bay. Somewhere along the way, L'Esperance ran their canoe alone through a rapids, while the missionary portaged to the end of the whitewater. Never again was Menard seen. Some of his possessions were later found among the Sioux and Sauk, but no one knows what happened to him.

Precisely where the disappearance occurred is still a matter of debate. A historical marker on Highway 107 north of Merrill proclaims Grandfather Falls on the Wisconsin River to have been the spot. Other historians, however, point to the Chippewa River as a more likely place.

Crescent Creek enters from the right, and the only **landing** on the section—Camp 10 Road—appears on the left (3.3 miles). Above Camp 10 there are no rapids, only occasional boulders to dodge.

Misnamed **Whirlpool Rapids** (3.8 miles) is preceded by a Class II boulder garden, then a short pool. At Whirlpool, two islands split the river (a large island on the left and a small one alongside it). The main drop, on the left, is fairly short, with a clearly defined chute and turbulent water beneath; a solid Class II under normal summer conditions, it requires good boat control and can be much more difficult when the water is medium to high. On the right of the large island is a Class II rock garden that is longer but usually easier to run than the left-side drop. Scout Whirlpool by taking out at the upstream side of the large island and examining both sides; boats can be portaged over the island, which is a pleasant spot to relax and perhaps have lunch.

From Whirlpool all the way to Menard Island, there are numerous riffles and Class I rapids—a very pleasant 3.5 miles. Jennie Creek enters from the right in a left-hand bend.

At Menard Island (7.3 miles), which comes after a big right-hand bend, there are riffles and shallows that prevent motorboats from going farther upriver from Lake Alice. For the next 5 miles, however, you can expect to encounter speedboats, jet-skis and pontoon craft. Below Menard Island, the river becomes wide and slow, with marshland vegetation. (Father Rene Menard was a 17th-century French missionary and explorer who is said to have passed this way.)

Dwellings and boat docks come into view after the mouth of Spring Creek on the right (10 miles).

TAKE OUT upstream-right at the County A bridge (the only bridge on the stretch). This **landing** is maintained by the nearby tavern and grill, so it's a good idea to ask permission and voice your thanks.

■ ■ ■

For 24 miles below the County A take-out, the river passes through one impoundment after another: first Lake Alice, then Lake Mohawksin, Grandmother Flowage and Grandfather Flowage. The Grandmother Flowage (7.4 miles from Tomahawk Dam to Grandmother Dam) and Grandfather Flowage (5.5 miles from Grandmother Dam to Grandfather Dam) are canoed, but are wide and slow and require difficult dam-accesses. The next free-flowing section begins below the Grandfather Falls power plant.

Wisconsin River 5

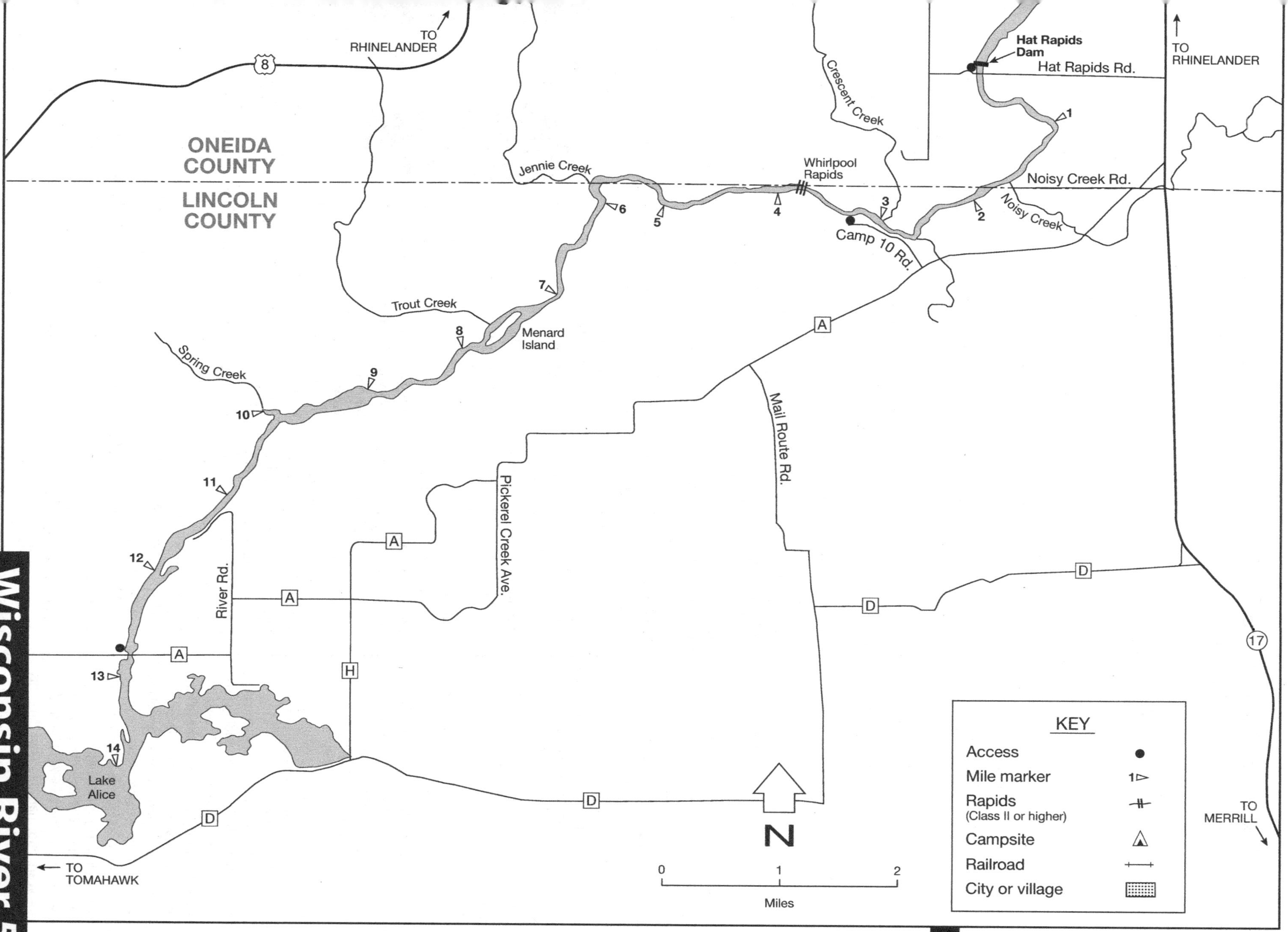

Wisconsin River 6

Camp New Wood County Park to Lokemoen Road (5.3 Miles)

A short trip that can easily be lengthened by using a different take-out, this section flows through a very scenic area and includes some mild rapids. Highway 107 hugs the left shore all the way, but paddlers usually aren't aware of its presence. This is a good beginner's stretch, with a little excitement at the two rapids. The first few miles are undeveloped, but downstream the surroundings become urban. You are likely to see fishermen and a variety of wildlife.

Public **camping** is available on the river at Camp New Wood County Park (the put-in) and downstream at Council Grounds State Park (2 miles north of Merrill off Highway 107).

Water levels are almost always adequate for pleasant paddling. Extra caution is required when the water is medium to high. Because the put-in is located only a mile below the Grandfather Dam hydro station, the water level is affected by dam releases. For flow information from the Grandfather hydroplant, check the Wisconsin Public Service website: www.wisconsinpublicservice.com/news/hydro/hydrodata.asp.

The average **GRADIENT** is 1.8 feet per mile.

The **shuttle route** is via Highway 107 and Lokemoen Road. **Canoe rentals** are available at Backwater Sports, 1 mile north of Merrill (715-536-9056).

While shuttling, take a minute to stop at the stone monument on Highway 107 that honors Father Rene Menard.

PUT IN at **Camp New Wood County Park** north of Merrill, alongside Highway 107. A Civilian Conservation Corps camp in the 1930s, this is an attractive little park with a boat ramp, shelter, picnic tables, toilets and good parking. Directly across Highway 107 are the Nels P. Evjue Memorial School Forest and a Wisconsin Conservation Corps nature trail.

The river begins (and continues) wide, with good current and heavily wooded shores. Be watchful for boulders, especially in low water, unless you like dimples in your boat.

Posey Rapids (Class I) comes up quickly, half a mile downstream. It is easy to find your way through this widely scattered boulder bed. The rapids, which can be viewed from a Highway 107 overlook, are named after Jules Posey, the proprieter of well-known stopping places in Wausau and Merrill in the 1850s.

Two miles of flatwater precede Class I–II **Bill Cross Rapids** (2.7 miles), which begins where the river constricts and boulders litter the river bed. Bill Cross is faster and more obstructed than Posey and requires more maneuvering. The rapids are fairly short and can be run in several places. They bear the name of a colorful trapper, guide, interpreter and trading-post operator who lived in northern Wisconsin in the mid-1800s.

Powerboats can come all the way upstream to Bill Cross Rapids from Lake Alexander, the flowage created by Alexander Dam near Merrill. Turn your boat into the wakes to avoid being swamped.

The New Wood River enters from the right (3.7 miles); there is a house here, and a private landing on the right. There are no houses between the put-in and the New Wood River, but many thereafter.

The current diminishes gradually after Bill Cross Rapids, eventually disappearing almost altogether as you approach the head of the Lake Alexander flowage.

TAKE OUT at the public boat **landing** (5.3 miles) on the left at the end of Lokemoen Road, off Highway 170. There is adequate parking alongside the paved road at the landing.

Monument to Father Menard near the river, north of Merrill.

Paddlers who don't mind adding 3.2 miles of lake paddling can continue downstream, past Arrowhead Island, to an excellent **landing** on the left at **Council Grounds State Park**, not far upstream from the **dam.** The park is a beautiful, densely forested area with camping, nature trails, picnic facilities, beach and plenty of parking. The Ojibwe once gathered here annually for celebrations and council meetings.

■ ■ ■

Downstream, there are 5 miles between the Alexander Dam and the Merrill Dam. Riverside Park, just below the Merrill Dam, is the put-in for the next recommended section.

Who Was Bill Cross?

Many of the rapids in this book bear the names of colorful historical figures whose identities have long since been forgotten by the public. Gilmore's Mistake on the Wolf, Dave's Falls on the Pike and Belille Falls on the Chippewa, for example, are all named after people associated with the logging years of the 19th century.

One of the few rapids left on the Wisconsin River was named after an especially fascinating character, William H. Cross.

Born and raised in the Milwaukee area, Bill Cross headed for the North Woods as a young man. For several years he lived with the Ojibwe, taking an Indian wife and working as a trapper. He became quite proficient in the Ojibwe language, often serving as an interpreter and co-authoring an Ojibwe/English dictionary.

In the 1840s, he and another trapper, Martin Lynch, established a fur-trading post on the west bank of the Wisconsin near the mouth of the New Wood River. In the following decade, Cross worked as a guide for government surveyors, and served as one of the hardy U.S. Mail carriers who regularly traversed the arduous Ontonagon Trail from Wausau to Ontonagon, Michigan.

Later, he left his Ojibwe wife behind and headed south to Wausau, where he lived for several years and married again. After his second wife died, Cross headed north again, spending his last years among the Ojibwe.

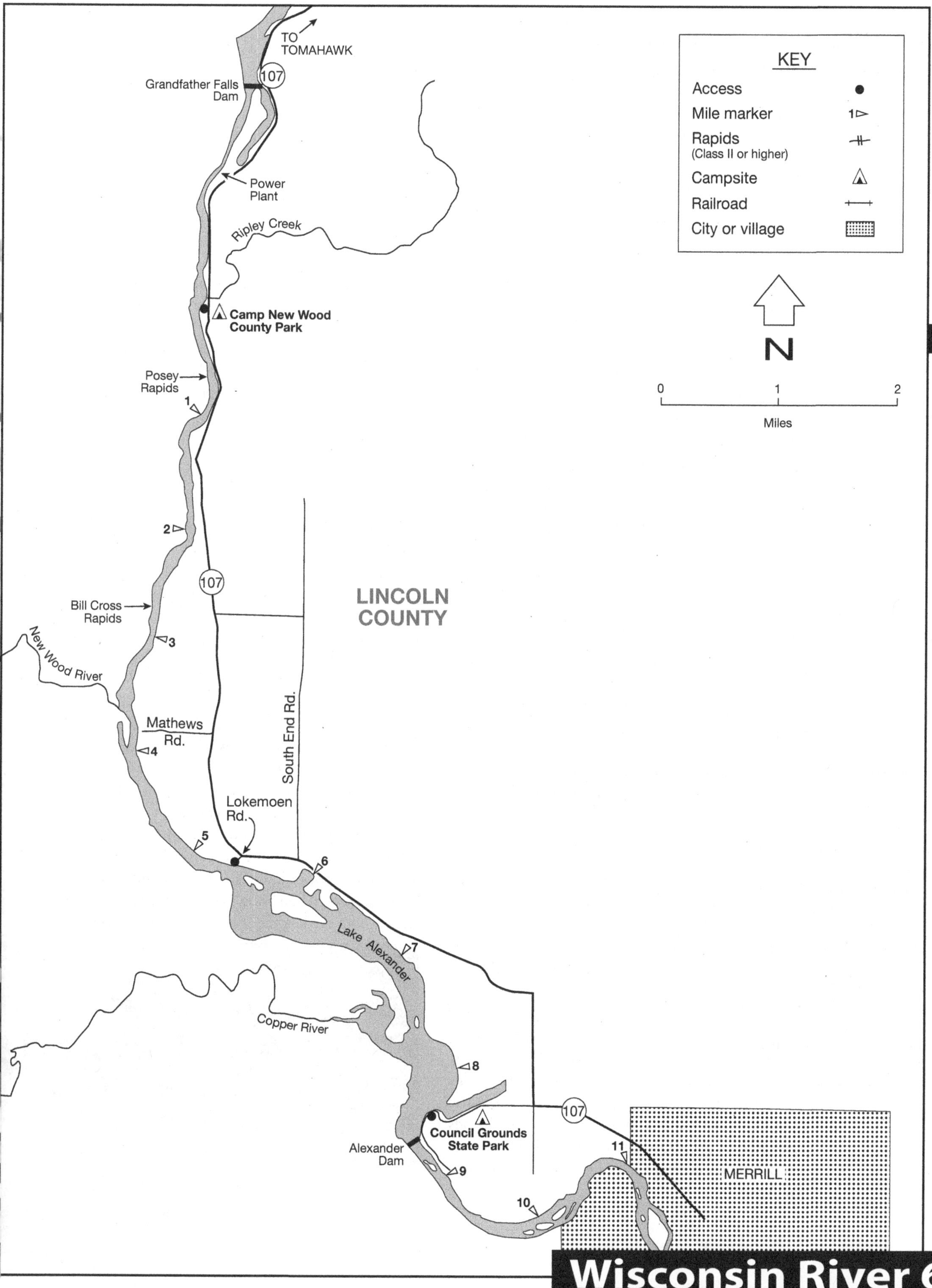
TO TOMAHAWK
107
Grandfather Falls Dam
Power Plant
Ripley Creek
Camp New Wood County Park
Posey Rapids
1
2
107
Bill Cross Rapids
3
New Wood River
Mathews Rd.
4
South End Rd.
Lokemoen Rd.
5
6
LINCOLN COUNTY
Lake Alexander
7
Copper River
8
107
Council Grounds State Park
Alexander Dam
9
10
11
MERRILL
KEY
Access
Mile marker
Rapids (Class II or higher)
Campsite
Railroad
City or village
N
0
1
2
Miles

Wisconsin River 7

Merrill Riverside Park to Granite Heights Road (11 Miles)

Houses and farms are occasionally seen on this stretch, and traffic sometimes heard from nearby roads, but the river still has a relatively undeveloped quality. Banks are high and heavily wooded, the river wide, and current steady. In low water there are shallow riffles here and there, but there is plenty of water to paddle and the shallows are never hard to avoid. Large wooded islands appear periodically, and occasional large boulders in the stream bed are no problem. You will likely see eagles, herons, ducks, kingfishers and turtles.

Public **camping** is available 2 miles north of Merrill at the beautiful Council Grounds State Park, off Highway 107.

Water levels are always sufficient for good paddling, but paddlers should stay off the river when it's high. For water flow data, check the gauge located downstream from the Merrill dam (#05395000) on the USGS website; see "Water Levels" in the introduction. Daily flow data from the Merrill dam is also available in a recorded message at the Wisconsin Valley Improvement Company data line: 715-842-1284.

The average **GRADIENT** is 3.6 feet per mile.

The best **shuttle route** is Highway 64, County W and Granite Heights Road. Canoe rentals are available at Backwater Sports, 1 mile north of Merrill (715-536-9056); and at E-Z Rental in Wausau (715-848-2891).

PUT IN at the Riverside Park **boat ramp** in Merrill, off O'Day Road, downstream-right from the Merrill Dam and the Business 51 bridge. This is an excellent access, with toilets, picnic facilities, water and plenty of parking.

The river makes a big right-hand bend not long after the put-in, then a south straightaway, followed by a big left-hand bend. The Highway 51 bridges soon come into view (3.7 miles). Just upstream from the first bridge is a cluster of islands where a planned hydroelectric dam never materialized; in 1996, two of the islands were donated to the DNR by Wisconsin Public Service Corporation and named after DNR wildlife manager Bill Meier.

Not long after the Highway 51 bridges, the Pine River enters on the left, at the end of a big right-hand bend. (Experienced whitewater kayakers and canoeists often paddle a couple of miles on the Pine when the water is up—from Center Road to County W. This stretch flows through a beautiful dells area, and has numerous Class I and II rapids.)

A short distance downstream from the mouth of County Line Creek (on the right), there is a river-left **landing** in the middle of a big left-hand bend (7.7 miles). A big clump of boulders is visible on the right shore just downstream from the landing. A short path goes up the bank to a pine-covered bluff, where a circle turnaround has room for several cars. Access is from Pine Bluff Road, off County W.

Highway 51 is quite close to the right shoreline. Downstream from the landing, opposite an island cluster, high sand banks appear on the right.

Shortly thereafter, as the river swings right, Class I **Trappe Rapids** occurs where a rocky shoal on the right forces the water into a wavy constriction. Run the brief easy-to-spot chute. Railroad tracks can be seen on the left as the rapids near; the tracks will be close by from here to the take-out. After the rapids, the Trappe River enters from the left, with a railroad bridge over the mouth.

Downstream from the mouth of the Trappe is a river-left landing reached from Wisconsin River Road. From County W, turn onto Wisconsin River Road, go a short distance past the Jesse Ball Field, and turn onto a dirt access road on the right; the access is a short walk from there, with room for several cars.

TAKE-OUT: The **Granite Heights landing** is 1.8 miles downstream from the Trappe, on the left, soon after an overhead power line. The river is quite wide here. There are several houses on the left immediately downstream from the landing. Park alongside the road.

A Great Place for Hikers

How many times have you been told by someone giving you directions that "you can't miss it"—only to do just that? Well, there is definitely one landmark in the Wausau area that you can't miss: Rib Mountain.

Conspicuously visible for miles around, this huge and ancient hill was spared by the glaciers because of its tough quartzite composition. Three miles long and one mile wide, Rib Mountain is known to geologists as a monadnock and stands almost 700 feet above the surrounding land. The view from the top is marvelous.

Four color-coded hiking trails wind through the 1,050 acres of Rib Mountain State Park, which also offers an excellent campground in the warm months, and skiing and snowshoeing in the winter.

The park is located just south of Wausau off County N.

Good whitewater in the dells of the Pine River, a tributary of the Wisconsin.

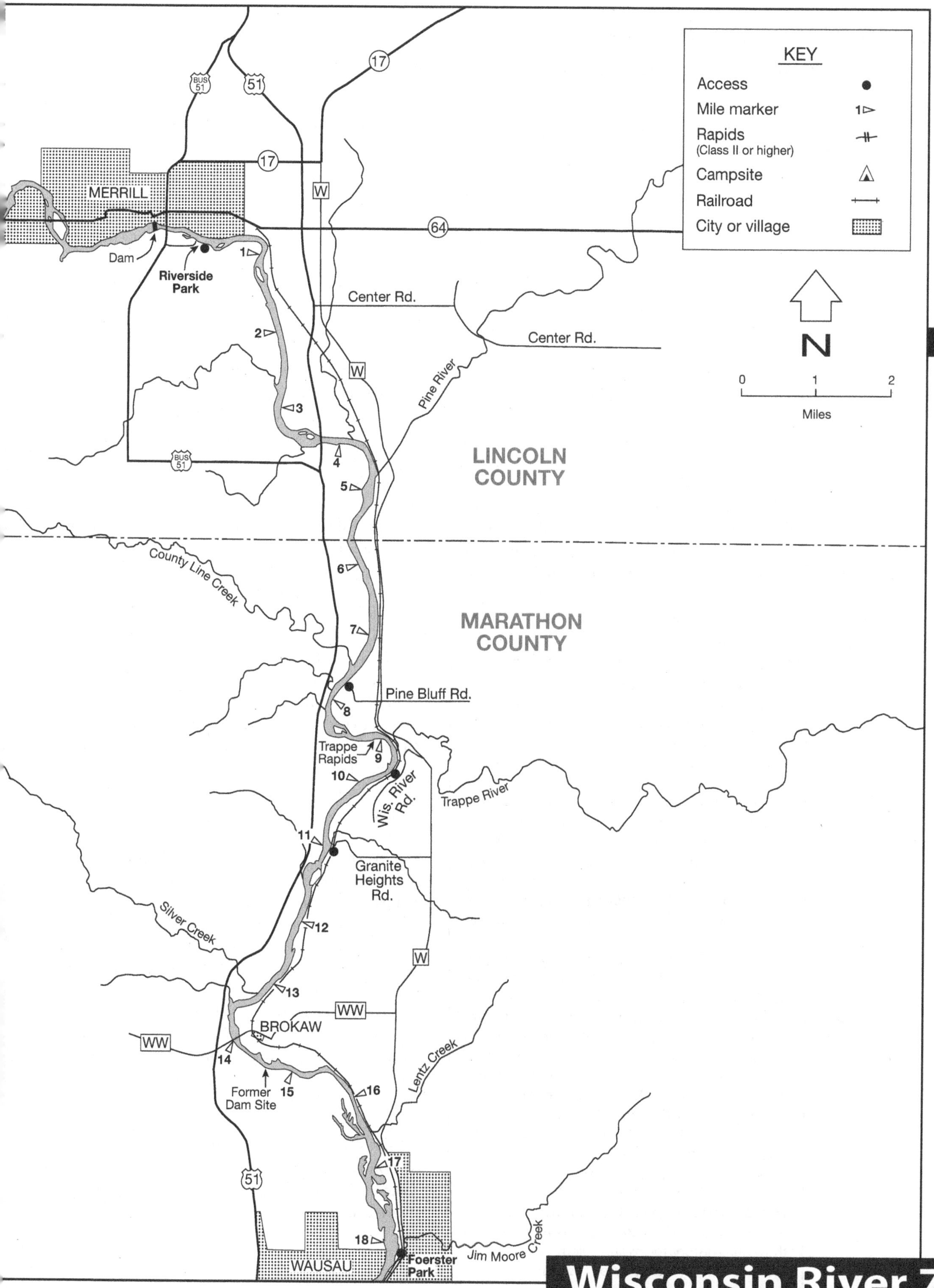
KEY
Access
Mile marker
Rapids
(Class II or higher)
Campsite
Railroad
City or village
N
0
1
2
Miles
MERRILL
Dam
Riverside Park
Center Rd.
Center Rd.
Pine River
LINCOLN COUNTY
MARATHON COUNTY
County Line Creek
Pine Bluff Rd.
Trappe Rapids
Wis. River Rd.
Trappe River
Granite Heights Rd.
Silver Creek
BROKAW
Former Dam Site
Lentz Creek
WAUSAU
Foerster Park
Jim Moore Creek
W
WW
17
51
64
BUS 51

Wisconsin River 8

Granite Heights Road to Foerster Park in Wausau (7.2 Miles)

Not until you approach Wausau near the end of this section does the environment become semi-urban. Until then, the only significant signs of development are near the midpoint, where the river passes a paper mill at Brokaw. The first few miles of the stretch are very wide, and wind can be discouraging. The trip includes not only wide expanses but also grassy banks, wooded bluffs, a gradually lessening current and a short rapids.

Public **camping** is available in Wausau at Marathon Park, and at Rib Mountain State Park southwest of Wausau.

Water levels are always adequate for good paddling, but the river is dangerous when high. For water flow data, see Wisconsin 7.

The average **GRADIENT** is only 1.2 feet per mile.

The **shuttle route** is via Granite Heights Road and County W.

PUT IN at the **landing** on Granite Heights Road (river-left). There is room for a few cars along the road.

Not far downstream, you'll spot traffic on the right on Highway 51 for a short time. In the distance, you can often see smoke rising from the Wausau Paper Company in Brokaw. The river widens, with slow current, all the way to Brokaw.

More About the Wisconsin

If you want to delve more deeply into the lore of the Wisconsin River, the following sources are very enjoyable and informative:

August Derleth, *The Wisconsin: River of a Thousand Isles* (New York: Farrar & Rinehart, 1942). A little dated, but still a very entertaining history of the river, its commerce and its people, by a well-known Wisconsin writer.

Nels Akerlund and Joe Glickman, *Our Wisconsin River: Border to Border* (Rockford, Ill.: Pamacheyon Publishing, 1997). A gorgeous 112-page commentary with photographs of the river, from its source to Prairie du Chien.

Michael J. Goc, *Stewards of the Wisconsin* (Friendship, Wis.: New Past Press, 1993). Commissioned by the Wisconsin Valley Improvement Company (a state-chartered company that manages the flow of the river through a system of 21 reservoirs), this is obviously a "company book," but it is nevertheless a fascinating account, with excellent photos, of how the Wisconsin came to have so many dams.

William F. Stark, *Wisconsin: River of History* (1988). This widely available self-published book on the history and culture of the Wisconsin is imbued with the author's lifelong love of the river.

Richard D. Durbin, *The Wisconsin River: An Odyssey Through Time and Space* (Cross Plains, Wis.: Spring Freshet Press, 1997). A comprehensive account of the natural history, towns and colorful characters of the river, with excellent photos and maps.

Upstream from Brokaw, before the river bends left, there is a private landing on the left; this is on the property of the paper company.

The high County WW bridge comes into view as you pass the mouth of a creek coming in on the right. The river begins to narrow, and the current picks up a little.

The remains of old wooden pilings are found upstream from the bridge, extending out to the middle from the right shore. Getting around them is not a problem.

Downstream from the bridge, where the papermill buildings come out to the river on the left, there is a narrow spot where the old **dam** used to be, with concrete abutments on both sides. Some debris remains in the river, and there is a gradual drop of about 2 feet. It is easy to get out on the right, where a pile of rocks juts out into the water, to scout (and portage, if desired). The middle or right is usually the best place to run this manmade Class I rapids. Some paddlers report seeing pieces of metal reinforcement bar here: Be careful. A deep pool follows.

The surroundings are hillier as you approach Wausau. There are numerous wooded bluffs and few dwellings, so the setting is still fairly wild, except for the electrical transmission lines and railroad tracks that follow the left shore.

The current slows to a creep after Brokaw, and the river acts more like a flowage, although there is some current all the way to the take-out.

A few private boat docks and some houses, especially on the left, announce the northern city limits of Wausau.

TAKE-OUT: The access, **Foerster Park** (also known as Gilbert Park), is on the left immediately after a small railroad bridge over the mouth of Jim Moore Creek. This is a public park located on County W (Sixth Street) on the north side of Wausau, considerably upstream from the dam. In addition to the boat **landing,** there are picnic tables and 12 parking spaces.

Other trips: Below Wausau, the river crosses Highway 29 and thus is outside the scope of this book. Dams and flowages continue all the way to Prairie du Sac, where the Lower Wisconsin State Riverway begins. From Prairie du Sac to the Mississippi, there are no more dams, and the river flows freely for its final 92 miles. For maps and descriptions of 10 additional sections of the Wisconsin River—from Castle Rock Lake to the Mississippi River—see *Paddling Southern Wisconsin.*

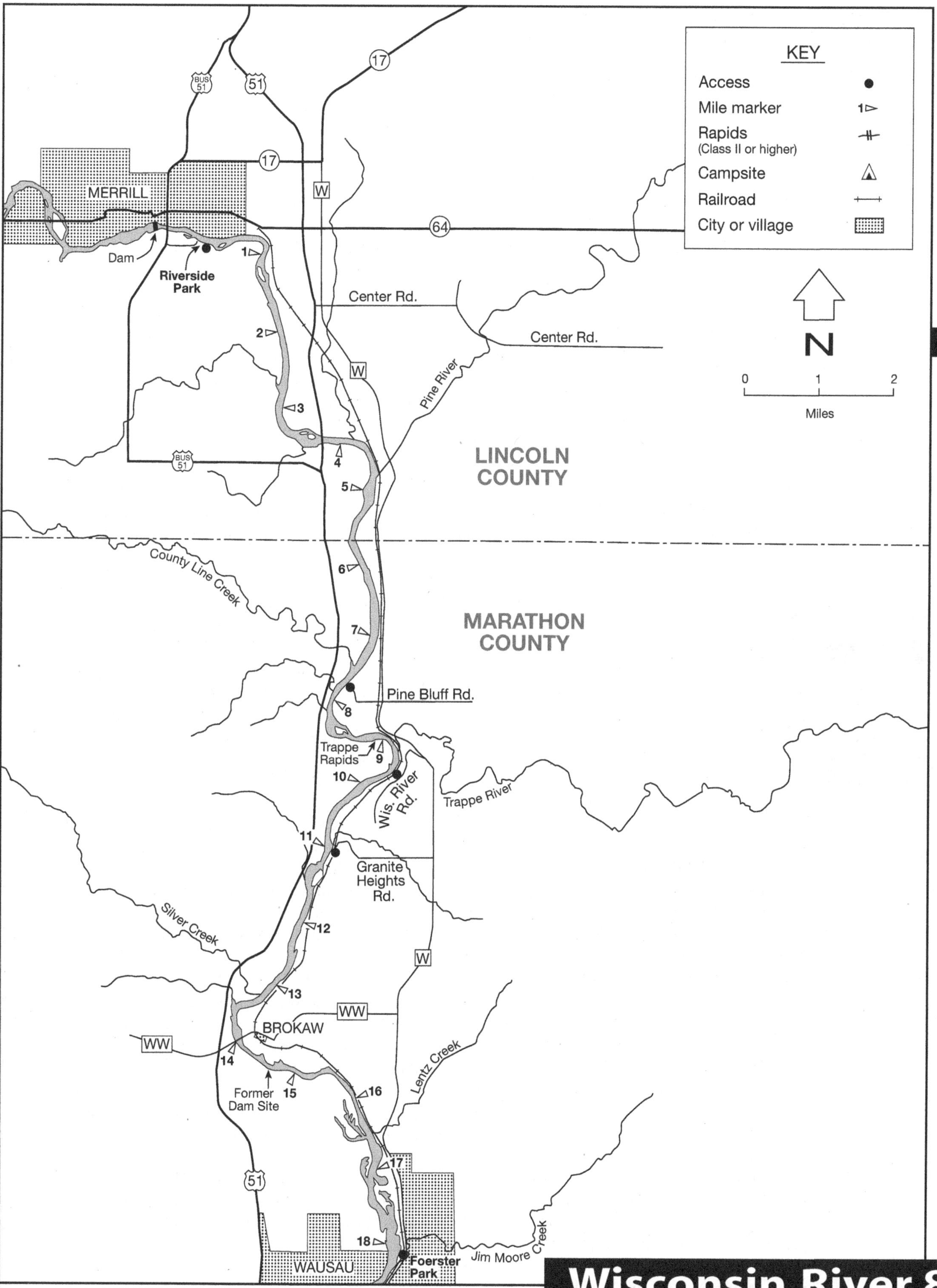

Wisconsin River 8

Wolf River 1

Post Lake Dam to Pearson (10 Miles)

This popular and famous river begins at the outlet of Pine Lake in Forest County and quietly wends its way to Langlade County, where it becomes a top whitewater and trout stream. From Shawano it flows deeply and slowly to Lake Poygan and the Fox River.

After it emerges from Post Lake, the upper Wolf flows freely all the way to Shawano before it is confined by another dam. Beginning quietly, then gathering momentum and plunging through rapid after rapid, the 48-mile segment from Post Lake to the Menominee Indian Reservation is one of the most popular paddling destinations in Wisconsin.

The first 10 miles below Post Lake provide a peaceful outing for flatwater enthusiasts, including beginners. A mixed forest environment predominates during most of the trip, with some attractive sand banks, marshland and wild-rice beds. Eagles and waterfowl are common here, and you're likely to see a beaver lodge or two. Fishermen take northern pike, smallmouth and panfish.

Flatwater on the Wolf.

Public **campgrounds** (both in the Nicolet National Forest) are located to the south at Boulder Lake near Langlade, and to the east at Richardson Lake near Wabeno. Camping is also available near Crandon on Lake Metonga (Forest County Memorial Park). There are numerous private campgrounds in the area.

Water levels can get a little scrapy after prolonged dry periods, but there is almost always enough water for good paddling.

The **GRADIENT** averages only 1.0 feet per mile on this section.

The **shuttle route** is via Clear Lake Road, County U and County T. The trip can be shortened by using the Lost Lake Road landing (3.8 miles) as the take-out or put-in; Lost Lake Road is reached from County K and Highway 55.

PUT IN downstream-left from the **Post Lake dam.** The park here has toilets and plenty of parking, and is a popular fishing spot. During the logging era, a wooden sluice dam occupied the site of the modern structure.

After the pool below the dam, the river flows quietly between oak, pine, birch and popple.

After nearly a mile of straightaway paddling, the river curves sharply to the left, with a marshy area on the right. A right-hand bend comes next, followed by two high sand banks on the left. The Langlade County park located here is a pleasant place to stop. A path through the woods connects the two sand banks, which are separated by a big bend in the river.

Wild rice then grows thick in the river, but there's a clear channel to paddle through it. Several docks and cabins come into view at Turtle Lake, a wide place in the river.

A short distance downstream from Turtle Lake, the river makes a big left-hand bend. Here, after several islands, there is a private access on the right for a Boy Scout camp (the Robert S. Lyle Troop of Racine). After the river swings back to the right, Swamp Creek enters from the left (2.7 miles).

This is a very peaceful area of the river. Occasionally, fallen trees are encountered, but getting around them is usually no problem. There is a lot of marsh vegetation, but woods are never far away. Look for signs of animal activity on the grassy banks: otter and muskrat slides, deer sets, beaver lodges, etc. You'll see wood-duck boxes in the trees along the shore.

A large boulder in the middle of the river at a sharp right-hand turn signals the river-left **access** from Lost Lake Road (3.8 miles). This can be used as an alternate take-out or put-in.

After Lost Lake Road the river becomes very curvy, with many oxbows, and a marshy environment dominates. At 7.5 miles, there are cabins on both sides and a power line overhead. An attractive pine-covered bank follows.

In a right-hand bend, another pine-covered sand bank lies on the left. This area, known locally as the Turtle High Banks, can be reached from Pickerel Creek Road off County T. Located on county forest land, it's a good place to relax for a while.

Not far downstream, the wide mouth of Pickerel Creek appears on the left, in a right-hand bend (8.7 miles). This is a well-known rice-gathering area. (A DNR permit is required to harvest wild rice). Immediately afterward on the left is a red-pine knoll with a private access (Goose Island). Houses and docks begin to appear as you approach the village of Pearson.

TAKE OUT at the river-left **landing** just downstream from the County T bridge, accessed by a spur off County T. There is room for only a few cars.

Other trips: The first leg of the Wolf—from its source at the Pine Lake Outlet dam to the Little Rice Lake dam (7 miles)—is quite narrow and winding, with numerous beaver dams to carry over. The trip is strictly flatwater, except for a brief rocky spot before Little Rice Lake. Marshland vegetation prevails, and the forest is usually at least a hundred yards from the banks. Water levels can be a problem in dry periods. As a rule of thumb, don't start the trip if there isn't plenty of water to float through the culverts at the put-in. A highlight of the trip is the dense area of wild-rice beds at the northern end of Little Rice Lake, which can be avoided by taking out at a gravel dead-end road, running west from County S to the Little Rice Wildlife Area.

Except for a few rock beds, the 15-mile stretch from Little Rice Lake to County B offers more of the same: a meandering stream, marshy vegetation, wild rice, beaver dams and wild seclusion.

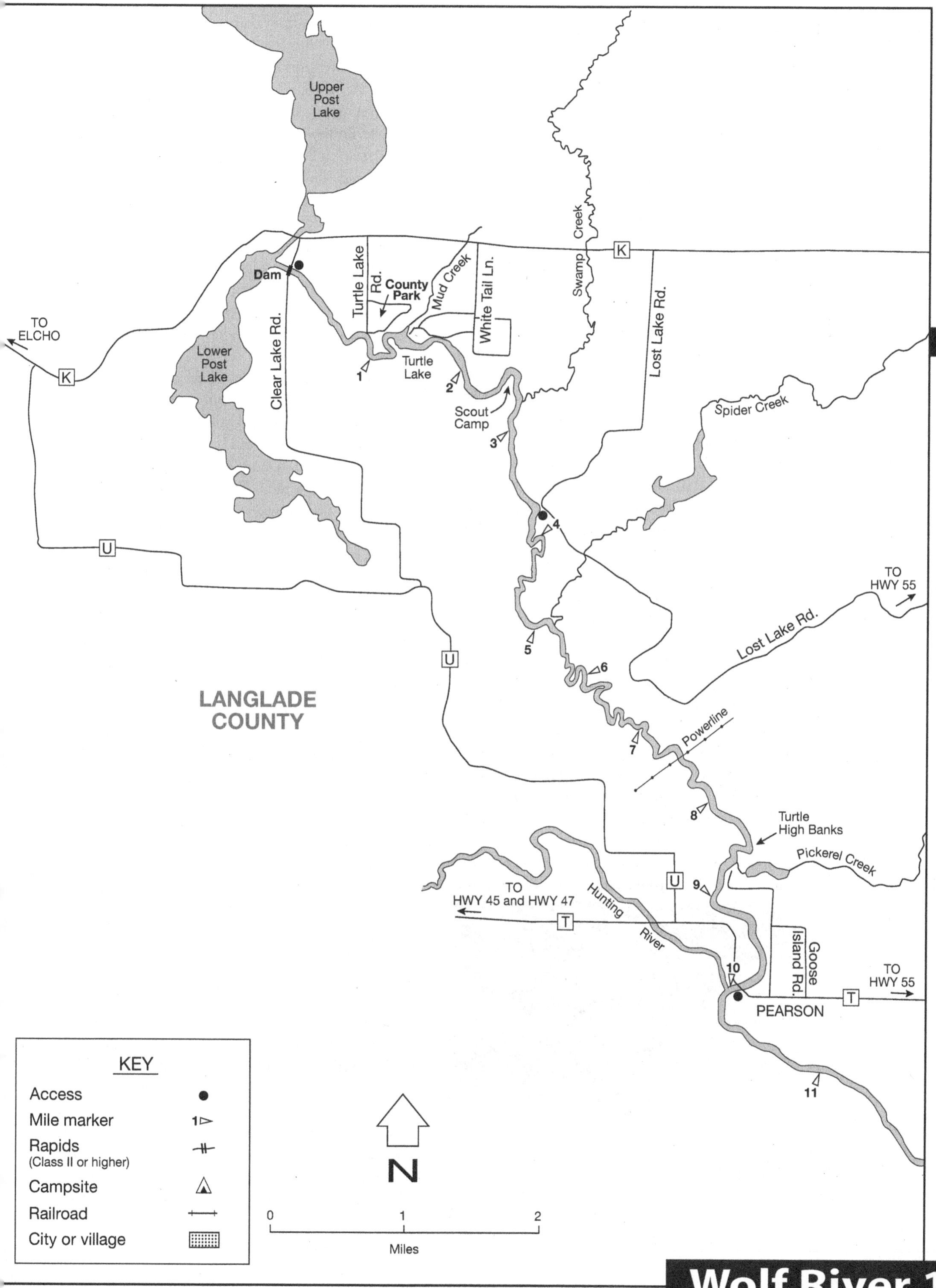
Upper Post Lake
Lower Post Lake
Dam
TO ELCHO
K
Clear Lake Rd.
Turtle Lake Rd.
County Park
Mud Creek
White Tail Ln.
Swamp Creek
Lost Lake Rd.
Turtle Lake
Scout Camp
Spider Creek
U
TO HWY 55
Lost Lake Rd.
LANGLADE COUNTY
Powerline
Turtle High Banks
Pickerel Creek
TO HWY 45 and HWY 47
T
Hunting River
Goose Island Rd.
PEARSON
1
2
3
4
5
6
7
8
9
10
11
KEY
Access
Mile marker
Rapids (Class II or higher)
Campsite
Railroad
City or village
N
0
1
2
Miles

Wolf River 2

Pearson to Lily (12.5 Miles)

The whitewater for which the Wolf River is famous begins in this section, but most of the 12-plus miles is quietwater. Paddlers experience both narrow, wooded stretches and marshy lowlands, together with three sets of rapids and riffles. Alternate accesses make it possible for novice paddlers to avoid most of the whitewater. Much of the land along the river has been purchased by the Wisconsin DNR, so there's a minimum of development.

Camping is not allowed along the river, but is plentiful in private campgrounds throughout the area, especially to the south along Highway 55. Public camping is available to the west at Ada Lake, Boot Lake and Fanny Lake, to the north at Richardson Lake, and to the south at Boulder Lake.

Except during dry spells, **water levels** are usually adequate for good paddling, especially when the USGS gauge at Langlade (#04074950) reads 200 cfs or more; see "Water Levels" in the introduction. There is also a commonly used local gauge at Langlade, measured in inches: 200cfs equates to 4 inches on this gauge. You can contact the Bear Paw Outdoor Adventure resort near Langlade for water-level information (715-882-3502 or www.bearpawoutdoors.com).

The **GRADIENT** averages 6.4 feet per mile.

The **shuttle route** is via County T, County TT, County A, Highway 55 and Highway 52. Alternate accesses (described below) are reached from County A and Highway 55.

PUT IN at the **County T bridge,** downstream-left. There is room to park a few cars.

Downstream, the Hunting River enters on the right. A major tributary, the Hunting is a good trout stream. Old wooden pilings are found below its mouth. About 1.3 miles from the put-in, a creek enters on the right.

Play-boating at Gilmore's Mistake on the Wolf River.

The 2.2 miles from Pearson to County A are rather wide, with lots of marsh grass and no houses.

A couple hundred yards upstream from the County A bridge, the river gets faster and rockier. There is a rock garden beneath the bridge and beyond.

The **County A bridge** can be used as a **put-in,** downstream-right. The rocky stream bed makes this a tricky access, however, so it should be used only by experienced boaters. Marshland gives way to wooded banks below County A.

Wendigo Rapids (Class II) begins in the first left-hand curve past the bridge. There are many rocks to dodge even before the rapids begins. Several hundred yards long, Wendigo requires considerable maneuvering, and can be a miserable exercise in boat-scraping when the water is low.

About half a mile below Wendigo, in a right-hand bend, there is a hard-to-spot public **access** on the left, just upstream from a huge boulder in midriver. A long path through the woods leads to a dirt road that comes out on County A 0.4 mile east of the County A/ County TT intersection. This is by no means an easy access, but it does provide a means of putting in below the most difficult rapids of the trip.

Cabins begin to appear upstream from the River Road **landing** on the left (4.2 miles), where the road parallels the river. This access is a good spot to begin or end a shorter trip, but there is room for only a few cars.

Marshy vegetation reappears after River Road, with a few cabins here and there, and the river curves a great deal.

About half a mile before Military Park, the river narrows, quickens and returns to wooded upland surroundings. The swift water and canopied trees make this one of the prettiest places on the Wolf River.

Strauss Rapids (8.5 miles), usually a low-level Class I–II, comes in two pitches above **Military Park.** Named after the old Military Road (now Highway 55) built during the 1860s, this lovely river-left park has toilets, picnic facilities, good parking and a landing at the bottom of the last pitch. It is a very convenient access point.

A private wooden bridge lies downstream from Military Park in brisk current; be careful of the pilings. Highway 55 now parallels the river for a while, and traffic can be heard occasionally.

Overton Rapids (9.5 miles) is approximately half a mile of riffles, enjoyably wavy when the water is high.

In the middle of a big left-hand bend, the outlet from Turtle Lake comes in on the right (11 miles). It is possible to put in on the lake (**accessed** by Turtle Lake Road from Highway 52) and paddle out to the Wolf under the small bridge at the outlet's mouth. Be sure to look for eagles in the trees near the outlet. They often nest there.

TAKE OUT at the **Highway 52 bridge,** downstream-right; some parking is available.

Wolf River 2

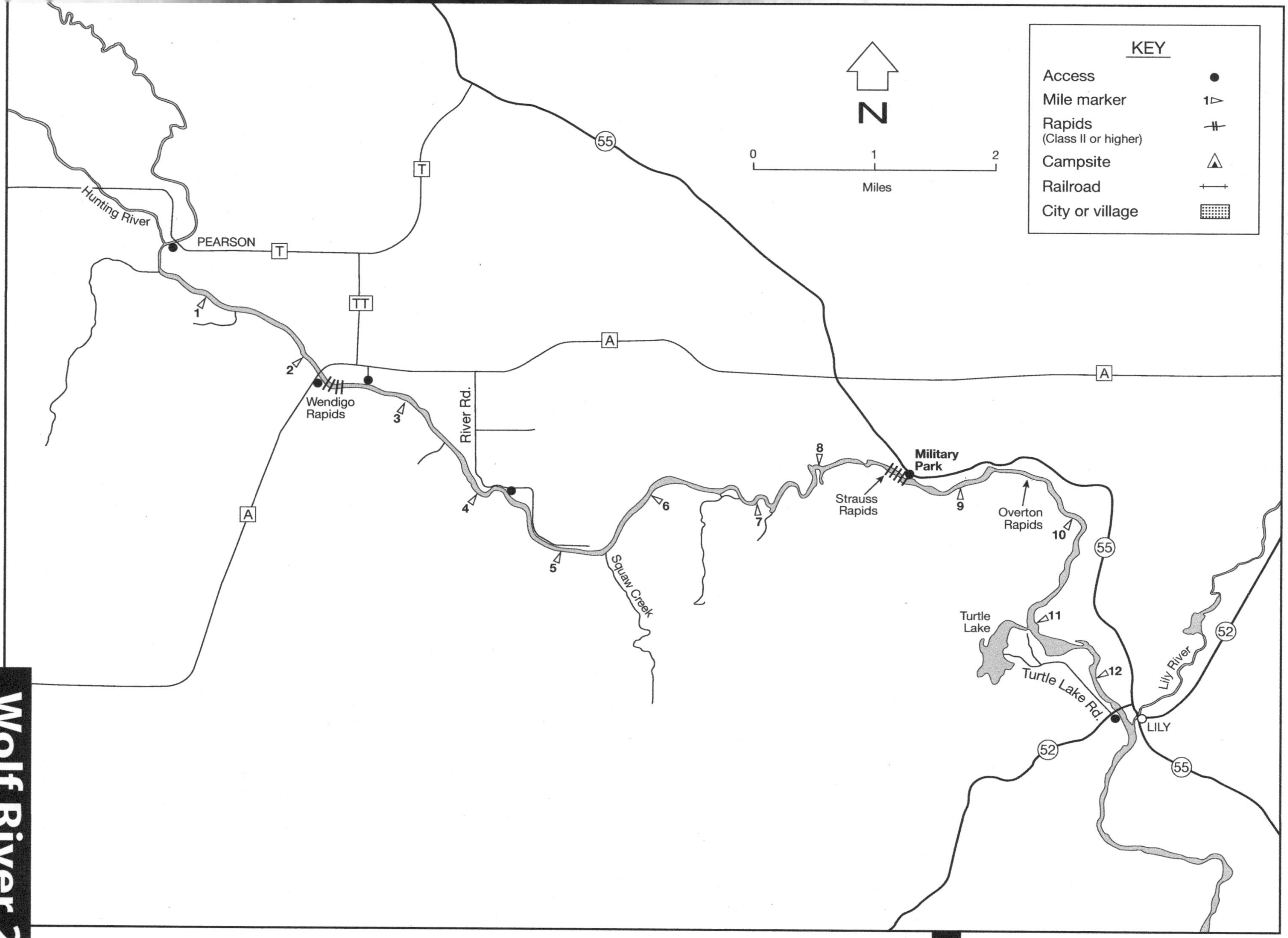

KEY
Access
Mile marker
Rapids
(Class II or higher)
Campsite
Railroad
City or village
N
0
1
2
Miles
PEARSON
Hunting River
T
TT
A
55
52
Wendigo Rapids
River Rd.
Squaw Creek
Military Park
Strauss Rapids
Overton Rapids
Turtle Lake
Turtle Lake Rd.
Lily River
LILY
1
2
3
4
5
6
7
8
9
10
11
12

Wolf River 3

Lily to Langlade (15 Miles)

This is the section in which the Wolf begins to earn its reputation as a whitewater river. Many Class I and II rapids enliven the trip, which also features long and scenic flatwater stretches. Several rapids require considerable boat-handling skill, so this is not an appropriate trip for beginners. Whitewater paddlers often break the section into smaller trips: Lily to Wolf Road (3.5 miles), Hollister to Langlade (8.5 miles) or Irrigation Hole to Langlade (2.7 miles).

Because most of the section is owned by the DNR, the heavily wooded shoreline is broken by few dwellings. Fishing for brown, brook and rainbow trout is good, especially in the "restricted area" below the railroad bridge near Hollister. Eagles, waterfowl, and deer are frequently spotted, among other animals. Please note that Wolf River Township does not allow glass containers or cans on the river.

Camping is not allowed on the river, but there are numerous private campgrounds in the area, especially near Langlade. The Wolf River Lodge Campground is located on river-left immediately after the Taylor Road access. A National Forest campground is available to the south, on Boulder Lake.

For information on **water levels,** see Wolf 2.

The **GRADIENT** averages 12.0 feet per mile.

The **shuttle route** is via Highway 55. Intermediate accesses at Wolf Road, Hollister Road and the Irrigation Hole are all reached from Highway 55. **Rafts and inflatable kayaks may be rented** from several companies in the area, including Herb's Rafts (715-882-8612), Bob's Rafts (715-882-8304) and River Forest Rafts (715-882-3351).

PUT IN at the **Highway 52 bridge** at Lily, downstream-right. There is room for several cars.

After a couple of wide, lazy bends of slow water, the river constricts at the site of an old logging dam. The fast chute is a good play spot to practice ferries and eddy turns. Snags are often found on one or both sides.

Hereafter, the current quickens and marsh vegetation largely disappears. Big boulders are scattered in the stream bed.

St. Claire Rapids (1.3 miles)—or Eagle Run—is a long, winding series of riffles in a gentle boulder-strewn gradient. The lovely forested setting and riffly stream bed make this an especially attractive area. Be on the lookout for eagles, which often nest here. A mile of flatwater follows.

Big Slough Gundy is next (2.5 miles), a wide Class II boulder garden with a fairly steep gradient. About 150 yards long, the rapids requires maneuvering but gives you a number of paths from which to choose.

Just downstream from Big Slough Gundy you will see the horizon line of **Little Slough Gundy,** a solid Class II drop and boulder garden that should be scouted on the right. Portage if in doubt. After the initial drop, the channel is swift and narrow, with big boulders in tricky locations—an easy place to broach a boat. Big waves form here in high water.

The Wolf Road **access** (3.5 miles) is a short paddle downstream, on the left, across from two small islands and in the midst of a riffle **(Big Sheen Rapids).** After a short stretch of flatwater, **Little Sheen Rapids** appears—another riffle—followed by quietwater all the way to Hollister Road.

Downstream from Wolf Road, there is a long DNR streambed improvement project running down the middle of the river (a gravel and rock **wing-dam** and channeling berm, built in 1995). Another project, completed in 1994, is just upstream from the Hollister Road access.

Burnt Point Rapids, an easy Class II, is located at the end of Hollister Road (6.5 miles). If you wish to **put in** or **take out** here, do so on river-left before the rapids. Below Hollister, cabins appear occasionally.

After two small Class I rapids, the mouth of Ninemile Creek appears on the left. Just downstream, around a bend, is a railroad bridge (7.5 miles) that marks the beginning of the catch-and-release fishing area; only artificial lures may be used here. The rapids beneath the bridge is not difficult.

Another long flatwater stretch follows the bridge, eventually ending at **Oxbow Rapids,** a series of boulder gardens in a big left-hand turn. The first two pitches are easy Class I–IIs, but the third, a solid Class II, has a high gradient, is several hundred yards long, and requires considerable maneuvering. Soon afterward, a rapids called **Cedar** by fishermen begins in a right-hand turn: There is a huge boulder on the left at the beginning of the rapids, with a big pour-over rock in the middle of the channel. Stay toward the center; canoeists often get hung up on the rocks to the left. The next boulder garden (just downstream) is steep but short—fishermen refer to it as **Hemlock.**

After two miles of quietwater, the DNR **landing** at the Irrigation Hole is tucked away on the left behind several islands (12.2 miles). Two large boulders at the end of a quiet straightaway are a sign that Irrigation is approaching. A good parking lot is provided.

Three challenging boulder-garden **rapids** remain in the 2.7 miles to Langlade: All are solid Class IIs.

The first rapids (13 miles) goes by various names—**Upper Sherry** by fishermen and the U.S. Geological Survey, Cedar by paddlers, and H.H. Taylor by an earlier guidebook. In any case, it makes a big sweeping S-curve, with many opportunities for practicing your whitewater maneuvers.

A short flatwater-and-riffle stretch precedes **Lower Sherry Rapids** (13.5 miles), a fast quarter-mile with a steep gradient and many boulders to avoid. This is the most difficult of the set of three rapids. (Sherry, incidentally, was a prominent lumberman of the 1800s.)

Larzelere Rapids (14 miles)—named after one of the first settlers in Langlade County—is a much shorter rapids, with numerous opportunities to execute eddy turns. Be careful of the group of boulders near the bottom.

From Larzelere to Highway 64, there is only one easy Class I rapids at the end of Taylor Road, where the gauge for the Wolf River Lodge is located on a huge river-left boulder.

TAKE OUT at the DNR **landing** at the Highway 64 bridge, downstream-right. Toilets, water and excellent parking are available.

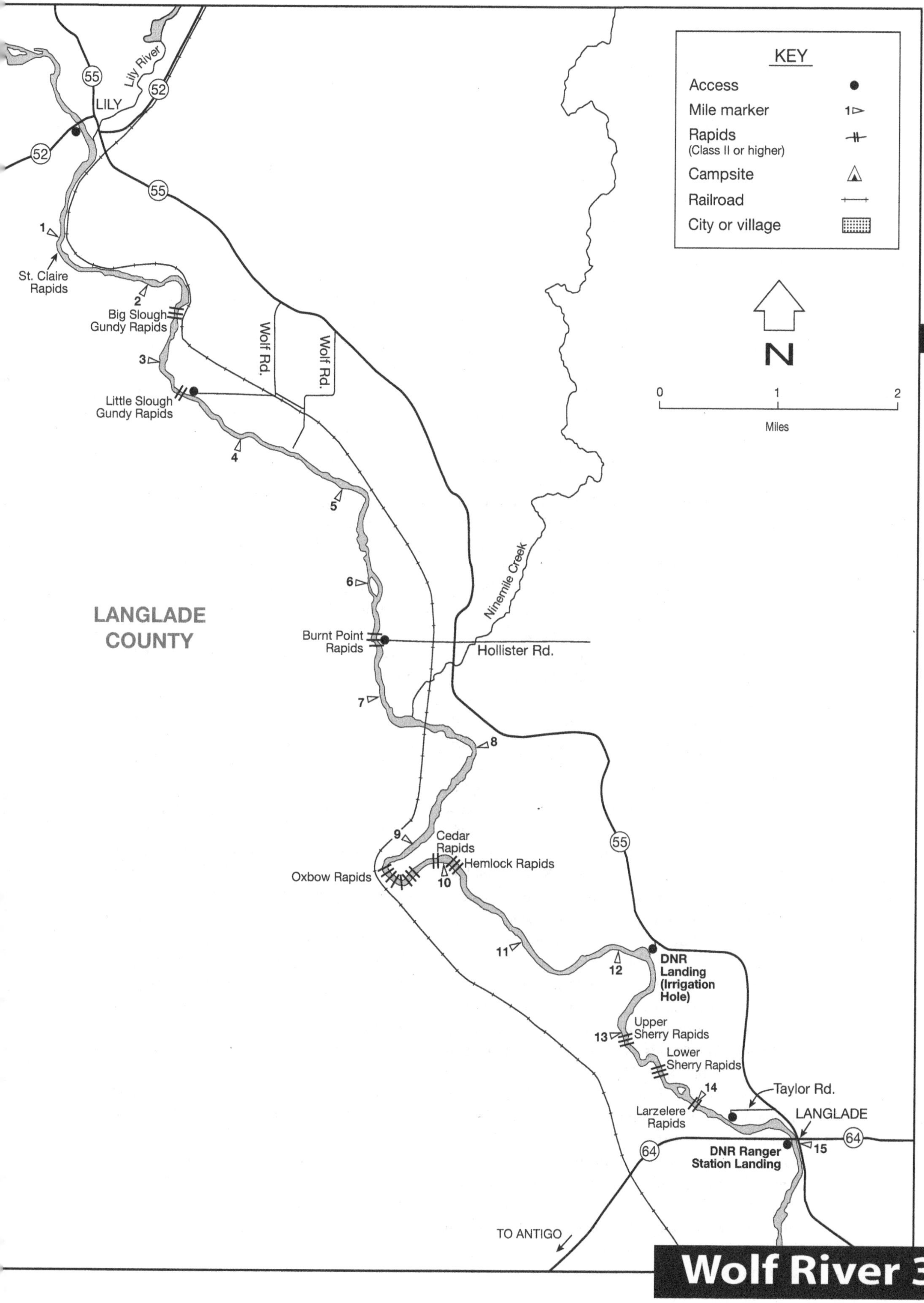
KEY
Access
Mile marker
Rapids
(Class II or higher)
Campsite
Railroad
City or village
N
0
1
2
Miles
LILY
Lily River
55
52
St. Claire Rapids
Big Slough Gundy Rapids
Little Slough Gundy Rapids
Wolf Rd.
Wolf Rd.
LANGLADE COUNTY
Burnt Point Rapids
Hollister Rd.
Ninemile Creek
Cedar Rapids
Hemlock Rapids
Oxbow Rapids
DNR Landing (Irrigation Hole)
Upper Sherry Rapids
Lower Sherry Rapids
Larzelere Rapids
Taylor Rd.
LANGLADE
64
DNR Ranger Station Landing
TO ANTIGO

Wolf River 3

Wolf River 4

Langlade to Gilmore's Mistake (10.5 Miles)

For paddlers who enjoy both whitewater and scenic quietwater, this is an ideal stretch. Six long, complex rapids make it suitable only for intermediate and advanced canoeists and kayakers; in high water, some of its normally Class II whitewater becomes Class III. Over the years, there have been a number of drownings on this section, especially at Boy Scout Rapids.

The rapids have made this a popular rafting venue, and several local enterprises rent equipment to large numbers of rafters on weekends and holidays. Boaters and rafters alike can shorten the trip by starting at a landing 3 miles upstream from the take-out, thus eliminating the flatwater. Please note that Wolf River Township prohibits cans and glass containers on the river.

Camping is not allowed on the river, but there are many private campgrounds in the area, especially along Highway 55. A Nicolet National Forest campground is located nearby at Boulder Lake.

For information on **water levels,** see Wolf 1.

The average **GRADIENT** is 17.1 feet per mile.

The **shuttle route** is via highways 64 and 55. The intermediate access at Herb's Landing is reached from County M (see below). For **raft rentals,** see Wolf 3.

PUT IN at the DNR **landing** at the Highway 64 bridge, downstream-right. Toilets, water and excellent parking are available.

The river begins wide and slow, passing the pilings of an old railroad bridge. At a boulder pile downstream, the river narrows; this was once the site of a logging dam. **Rocky Rips,** an easy Class I–II rapids, begins here, with several cabins along the left shore.

After a stretch of quietwater, Class II **Crowle Rapids** (1.4 miles) begins with a constriction on the left and a fast chute, followed by an S-curve boulder garden. Like the next two rapids, Crowle has a steep gradient; thus, it's very scratchy in low water.

Horserace Rapids (1.8 miles) begins on a right-hand curve; there is a cabin on the right two-thirds of the way through this Class II boulder garden. The following 2-mile flatwater stretch has one small rapids in it.

A long, flat boulder bed announces the beginning of **Twenty-Day Rapids** (4 miles). The first pitch is steep and fast but short. After a short pool, the second pitch begins with a right turn over a small ledge, then a long boulder bed, and finally a steep rapids bending to the left. For the last part of the rapids, stay to the left to avoid getting hung up. At the bottom, on river-left, a rocky ledge is a popular spot for lunching and relaxing.

Three miles of quietwater follow Twenty-Day. About halfway through this stretch, another river-left ledge provides a second good lunch stop. Eagles are often seen in this area.

Two miles below Twenty-Day, **Herb's Landing** (once called Schneck's Landing) appears on the right. This access is on DNR land, but the gated lane to the landing is on private property off County M. (The lane is located on County M 2.5 miles west of Highway 55.) Ask permission to use this access at the Wild Wolf Inn on Highway 55.

A boulder bed and suspension footbridge signal the approach of **Boy Scout** (or Garfield) **Rapids** (8 miles), a solid Class II under normal summertime conditions. For half a mile, this complex boulder garden gains in intensity. There are two brief pools between the two footbridges, and a convenient river-left eddy just upstream from the second bridge. A path runs alongside on the right. The Gardner Dam Boy Scout Camp (named after an Indian who had an inn near here in the mid-1800s) lies on both sides of the rapids.

After Boy Scout Rapids, there are three Class I–II **boulder gardens** that require rock dodging. The last of these is sometimes called **False Hanson's** because (like the bigger rapids to follow) it starts on a right turn, then swings left.

Hanson's Rapids (9.2 miles) is a favorite play spot because of its fast chutes, strong eddies, and surfing waves and holes. Take out on the right and scout from the path, which runs along the river all the way from the County M bridge to the Boy Scout camp. A rocky ledge along the right shoreline is a popular vantage point for onlookers. Like Boy Scout, Hanson's is a challenging Class II+ rapids, often the site of slalom competitions.

A mile of flatwater follows Hanson's. There is an alternate take-out downstream-right from the County M bridge at the DNR **landing** (good parking).

The trip ends dramatically with another solid Class II rapids, **Gilmore's Mistake** (named after an unfortunate timber estimator who told his boss that the Upper Wolf wasn't worth logging). Beginning immediately after an attractive log home on the left, Gilmore's begins with a narrow chute, speeds up in big wave-trains, drops over a ledge into turbulent water, and concludes with a brief rock garden. The rapids is a favorite play spot for whitewater boaters who wish to hone their skills.

TAKE OUT immediately after the rock garden, on river-left, at the Wild Wolf Inn raft **landing.** Carry your boat and equipment to one of the designated parking areas, taking care not to block the landing. The owner of the inn generously allows boaters to use the landing, so please show your gratitude and don't abuse the privilege.

Wolf River 4

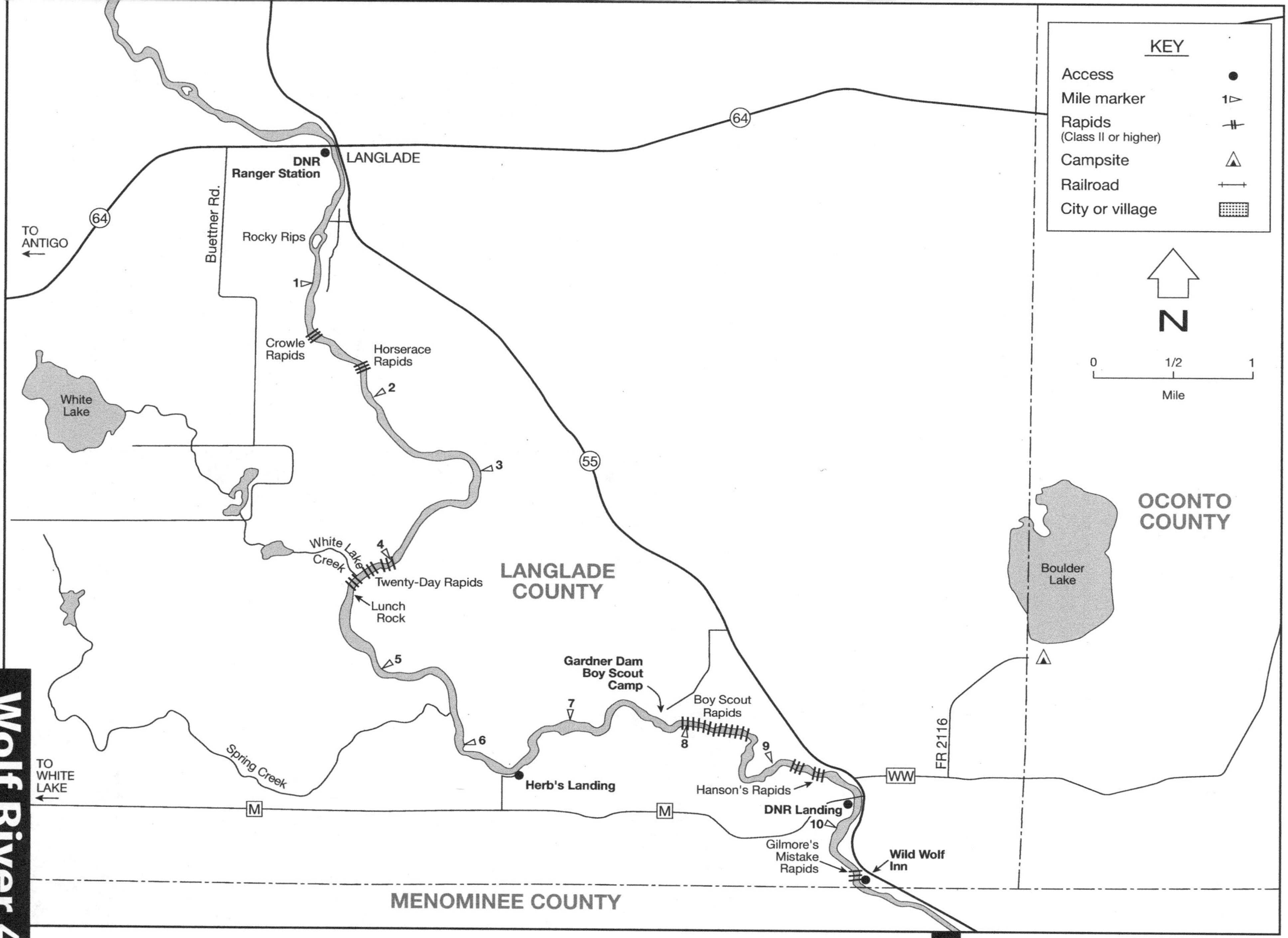
KEY
Access
Mile marker
Rapids
(Class II or higher)
Campsite
Railroad
City or village
N
0
1/2
1
Mile
64
LANGLADE
DNR
Ranger Station
TO
ANTIGO
Buettner Rd.
Rocky Rips
1
Crowle
Rapids
Horserace
Rapids
2
White
Lake
3
55
4
White Lake
Creek
Twenty-Day Rapids
Lunch
Rock
LANGLADE
COUNTY
5
Gardner Dam
Boy Scout
Camp
7
Boy Scout
Rapids
8
9
6
Herb's Landing
Spring Creek
TO
WHITE
LAKE
M
Hanson's Rapids
DNR Landing
10
Gilmore's
Mistake
Rapids
Wild Wolf
Inn
WW
FR 2116
MENOMINEE COUNTY
Boulder
Lake
OCONTO
COUNTY

Wolf River 5

County M to Big Smoky Falls (12.3 Miles)

Much to the delight of advanced paddlers, the Menominee Nation allows kayakers and canoeists to paddle this splendid whitewater stretch. In order to do so, however, boaters must purchase a permit for each paddling day, and must restrict themselves to authorized accesses (Shotgun Eddy Campground and Rafting, Otter Slide, and Big Smoky Falls Rafting). The most popular day trip on the reservation section begins at the Otter Slide, thus eliminating some flatwater, and ends at Big Smoky Falls. This trip includes the biggest drops on the Wolf River, and is arranged through Big Smoky Falls Rafting, which sells permits and provides boat shuttles upstream to the Otter Slide put-in. Only highly skilled, experienced whitewater paddlers should venture onto this section.

A trip on this section not only allows paddlers to experience some of the Midwest's best whitewater, but also gives them a glimpse of great scenery. Not a single house is seen on the whole stretch, and beautiful old-growth forest is obvious all along the shoreline. The Menominee are renowned for their prudent forest management, which is apparent everywhere you look.

Surfing at Teakettle Rapids.

Public **camping** is available at the Boulder Lake Campground off County WW, and there are numerous private campgrounds in the Langlade area.

Water levels are almost always adequate for enjoyable paddling from Otter Slide downstream; if the water is low, the section can become scrapy in rapids. When the USGS gauge at Langlade (#04074950) reads 500 cfs or higher (i.e., 10 inches or higher on the commonly used local gauge at Langlade), the whole section is quite pushy, with big holes and waves; even at lower water levels, however, the river demands a great deal of respect. You can contact the Bear Paw Outdoor Adventure resort near Langlade for water-level information (715-882-3502 or www.bearpawoutdoors.com).

The average **GRADIENT** is 14.6 feet per mile.

The **shuttle route** for the whole 12.3-mile trip is via County M, Highway 55 and Big Smoky Road. Shorter trips are more common: County M to Shotgun Eddy Campground and Rafting, with advance permission from Shotgun Eddy and a reservation permit; or Otter Slide to Big Smoky, with a shuttle provided by Big Smoky Falls Rafting, and a permit. Raft trips are available at Big Smoky Falls Rafting (715-799-3359) or Shotgun Eddy Campground and Rafting (715-882-4461).

PUT IN at the DNR **landing** near the County M bridge, downstream-right. There is plenty of parking.

Half a mile of flatwater takes you past several homes to **Gilmore's Mistake,** a solid Class II rapids alongside the Wild Wolf Inn, a restaurant/motel. The river constricts, then flows swiftly in a big wave-train over a 3-foot ledge, followed by a short boulder garden. Because of its excellent surfing waves and its proximity to Highway 55, Gilmore's is a very popular play spot for whitewater paddlers.

The river-left landing just below Gilmore's is the private take-out for Herb's Rafts, but is also used as a take-out by whitewater boaters. Such boaters must take care not to block the landing area, however, and must use designated parking.

Immediately after the landing, Langlade County ends and the Menominee Reservation begins. In order to continue, boaters must have a valid permit to paddle in the reservation and to use authorized accesses.

The river gets fairly wide below Gilmore's, with some traffic noise from Highway 55 on the left. When the road becomes visible, **Burnt Shanty Rapids** begins—a Class II boulder garden with a ledge at the bottom that can be run left or right. A series of islands follows.

continued page 178

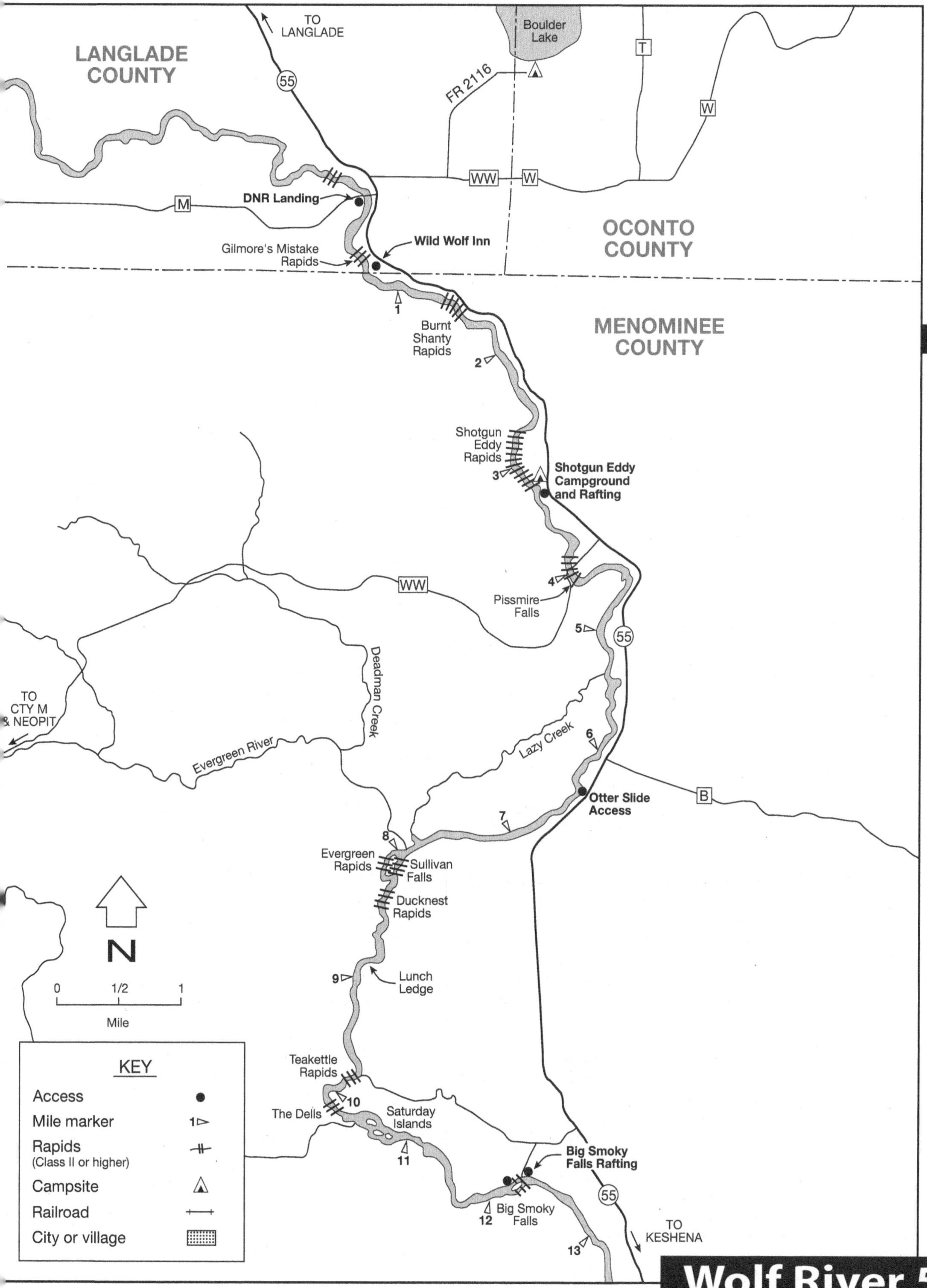
TO LANGLADE
LANGLADE COUNTY
Boulder Lake
55
FR 2116
T
W
WW
W
M
DNR Landing
Wild Wolf Inn
Gilmore's Mistake Rapids
OCONTO COUNTY
1
Burnt Shanty Rapids
MENOMINEE COUNTY
2
Shotgun Eddy Rapids
3
Shotgun Eddy Campground and Rafting
WW
4
Pissmire Falls
5
55
Deadman Creek
TO CTY M & NEOPIT
Evergreen River
Lazy Creek
6
Otter Slide Access
B
7
8
Evergreen Rapids
Sullivan Falls
Ducknest Rapids
N
9
Lunch Ledge
0
1/2
1
Mile
KEY
Access
Mile marker
Rapids (Class II or higher)
Campsite
Railroad
City or village
Teakettle Rapids
10
The Dells
Saturday Islands
11
Big Smoky Falls Rafting
55
12
Big Smoky Falls
TO KESHENA
13

Wolf River 5

Wolf River 5 *continued from page 176*

Over the edge of Sullivan Falls.

Then, as the river swings southwest away from Highway 55, it narrows and winds back and forth, with almost continuous Class II **rapids** in the bends. Deadfall is not usually a problem in this stretch, but be watchful.

The long series of rapids ends with a steeper, faster, more difficult boulder garden alongside **Shotgun Eddy Campground and Rafting** (left). Big boulders halfway through the rapids require care. You can take out at the Shotgun Eddy landing if you have secured advance permission to do so.

A short distance downstream, a solid Class II **rapids** begins upstream from the County WW bridge, ending in a river-wide ledge 100 yards downstream from the bridge (**Pissmire Falls**—Class II–III). At some water levels, a keeper wave develops below the ledge, so caution is obligatory.

A long, quiet stretch follows Pissmire, much of it paralleling Highway 55. About halfway through this flatwater section, the clearing for **Otter Slide Landing** appears on the left. (This was once the location of a stopping place on the 19th-century Military Road.) The landing is now used as a put-in for rafting, and for boaters who secure permits to paddle the reservation. Under no circumstances should the landing area be blocked with vehicles. In the quietwater that follows Otter Slide, there are some small islands.

Where are the Dams of Yesteryear?

The next time you approach the first footbridge at Boy Scout Rapids on the Wolf, look beneath the bridge at the right bank. There you'll see the remnants of an old logging dam.

One of the first on the river, Gardner Dam was named after an Indian, George Gardner, who in the 1800s had a well-known "stopping place" nearby. The earth and log dam enabled lumbermen to build up a "head" of water. They would then open one or more of the four big sluice gates, and send logs careening downriver with enough water to float them over the rapids.

No trace remains of the other big "driving dam" on the Wolf, downstream at the dells. But you can still see some of the shoreline structure of the old dams below Lily and Langlade.

Altogether, there were a dozen dams on the Wolf, from the source at Pine Lake to Keshena. Other rivers in the pinery—including the Chippewa, Peshtigo, Eau Claire, Jump and Oconto—used a similar series of driving dams to send logs downstream to the mills.

About a quarter mile before the next big drop, a rock outcropping appears on the right, and the Evergreen River enters from the right just upstream from a large island. Scratchy, often unrunnable rapids are found on the right of the island, and **Sullivan Falls** on the left. A short Class II **rapids** precedes Sullivan, which is a 7-foot riverwide waterfall (Class III). If you get out on the left to scout, don't linger. On weekends, there's usually a concession stand and toilets here: It doesn't hurt to buy a little something, especially if you want to scout or portage. The drop is typically run left of center, on a diagonal line, skipping off a short ledge below the lip in order to avoid diving straight down.

A short stretch of flatwater follows Sullivan before **Ducknest Rapids** (Class II+). There are rocky walls and ledges on both sides for several hundred yards through the two pitches of Ducknest. The first pitch can be run down a left channel—usually easier—or down the right, where there's a hole to avoid. The two routes come together in a big wave train, followed by a short boulder garden. The river then narrows to about 30 feet, gets fast and wavy, and ends in a series of big waves (including Dave's Wave, a popular surfing spot). Avoid the shallow maze of boulders on the left.

A large rock outcropping—the first of many—appears on the left a half mile after Ducknest. Shortly thereafter, the river narrows to about 20 feet, with a large rocky **ledge** on the left and a Class I+ wavy drop. This is a popular lunch spot.

After another flatwater stretch, **Teakettle Rapids** (also called the Upper Dells) comes after a right turn. Class II+ Teakettle, found in a small 100-yard-long canyon with a concession and toilets on the left, can be scouted on the left side. At the beginning, the river drops over a river-wide ledge with a diagonal tongue left of center; this drop is a favorite spot for surfing and enders. Fast water leads to a tricky, diagonal drop at the end, with a quiet pool below. Not far downstream is a small island with a short rapids on both sides (often scratchy).

The **Dells** (Class III) follows a left turn. Near the end of a Class II rapids, where you can see steep walls looming up ahead, get out on the left to scout. The entrance rapids can be run on the left (through two holes), diagonally down the center (the most common route), or (in higher water) on the far right. Sheer rock walls rise 30 feet on both sides after the entrance drop, and the view is quite beautiful (if you're not swimming). There is a scratchy pile of boulders near the end of the canyon, and a wide pool after the Dells. Look back upstream and enjoy the view.

The Saturday Islands and 1.5 miles of flatwater follow the Dells. Finally, a large island announces that **Big Smoky Falls** is near. There are big drops on both sides of the island. The one on the left, a Class IV–V doozie, choked with debris, is to be avoided under any circumstances. There is a **take-out** on river-left in a small eddy just before the falls, upstream from a footbridge. You can hug the left shore and take out here if you do not want to run Big Smoky, but you must exercise utmost care not to get swept into the current beneath the bridge!

To scout Class III Big Smoky Falls (on the right side of the island), get out at a rocky outcropping on the right shore of the river near the head of the island. A small ledge begins the long, fast run alongside the rocky island walls, ending in a heart-stopping launch off a 7-foot sheer drop at the bottom. A swim here is quite nasty.

TAKE OUT below the falls on the left, at the **landing** used by Big Smoky Falls Rafting.

■ ■ ■

Below Big Smoky, the Wolf is off limits to paddlers. The river continues to flow through the reservation, with at least half a dozen rapids and falls. A few miles downstream from Keshena Falls, dams slow the river in Shawano County. Wide, slow and meandering, the lower Wolf eventually flows into Lake Poygan, then meets the Fox River at Lake Butte des Morts, west of Lake Winnebago.

Running the entrance to the Dells.

Shuttle Along an Indian Trail

When you run a shuttle along Highway 55, you're driving on one of the most historic roads in Wisconsin history.

For centuries, the route was used as a footpath by Native Americans, perhaps by people of the Copper Culture who secured their metal in the Upper Peninsula. Because it led from Green Bay to Shawano, north along the Wolf and eventually all the way to Lake Superior, it became known as the Lake Superior Trail.

In the 1800s, whites used the well-established trail as they settled the North. Places where travelers could spend the night sprang up along the way: at Otter Slide, Langlade and Military Park, for instance—locations familiar to today's paddlers.

During the Civil War, President Lincoln, fearing a British/Canadian invasion from the North in support of the Confederates, ordered a Military Road to be built from Green Bay to Lake Superior, covering much of the same ground as the trail. Although the road was never used to move troops, it later was used extensively by loggers. In modern times, the route became Highway 55.

Yellow River

Miller Dam to County H (16 Miles)

Emerging from the Chequamegon Waters Flowage, the Yellow River runs southwestward until joining the Chippewa River at Lake Wissota near Chippewa Falls. Along much of its course, it flows placidly through an agricultural setting. However, most of the 16-mile stretch below Miller Dam is heavily wooded, scenic, intimate and filled with enjoyable riffles and rapids. At times, trees almost canopy the river. Maples and pines predominate along the shore, and eagles, heron, ducks and deer are frequently seen. Fish include northern, smallmouth, walleye and panfish.

The water is a little dark from organic material, sometimes making submerged rocks difficult to see. You'll see few buildings, particularly upstream from Gilman, and the section has a pleasantly remote quality.

The 16 miles described here are easily broken into two trips by taking out or putting in at Gilman. The river is dangerous when high, especially the portion below Gilman: rapids in the oxbow are difficult and have ruined the day of many a canoeist.

Camping is available on the river at the Gilman Village Park, and in the nearby Chequamegon National Forest (at Chippewa Campground on the flowage, and at nearby Kathryn Lake). There is also a private campground at Miller Dam, downstream right.

Water levels are best in the spring, and after sustained rainfall in the summer and fall. Releases from Miller Dam are a significant factor, of course: If no water is flowing from the dam, you can be in for a lot of scraping. A checkpoint for canoeability is the rocky ledge in Gilman at the village park. There should be enough water to float comfortably over the ledge.

The average **GRADIENT** is 8.7 feet per mile.

The **shuttle route** is via Miller Dam access road, County G, Highway 73, County S and County H. **Canoe and kayak rentals** are available at Silent Glide Canoe & Kayak Shop in Medford (715-748-0148 or www.silentglidecanoeandkayakshop.com).

PUT IN below the **dam** on the right behind the Miller Dam Resort, which offers camping and rents canoes in the spring. The Miller Dam Recreation Area, administered by the USFS, provides picnic facilities, toilets, water and parking. Another good access is the public **landing** just across the river (that is, downstream-left from the dam) at the end of Memorial Drive, accessed from Beaver Creek Drive off County G.

The river begins delightfully narrow and winding, with one riffle, Class I rapids and rocky ledge after another. After the Beaver Creek Drive bridge (a small wooden structure), the river widens somewhat and the riffles and rapids become less frequent. Then the channel narrows and speeds up when the river bends to the northwest.

Except for the bridge, there is no sign of human habitation until the national forest boundary is passed and River Road comes close on the right. At the end of a short south straightaway, pleasant S-curve riffles lead to a big lawn and house on the left; the river then swings right (west) past a deep fishing hole. The setting is very quiet, with grassy, wooded banks and occasional riffles.

A few houses appear at the Highway 64/73 bridge, where the stream bed is deep and narrow. Two sharp left-hand bends lie downstream from the bridge: At the peak of the second bend there is a Class I ledge followed by rocky riffles.

After a long, flat straightaway approaching Gilman from the east, houses appear on the right, followed by a series of nice riffles. The County B bridge passes overhead, followed by an old iron bridge. There is a good **access** on the right at the **village park** and **campground**, just below an old stone building (7.5 miles).

After a small rocky ledge at the park, the river loops left through Gilman under a couple of pedestrian bridges and a railroad bridge. A river-wide ledge is found in a right-hand curve at the edge of town, followed by a narrow, deep and peaceful stretch.

At the oxbow, a long, almost continuous series of Class I–II **boulder gardens** begins, extending for a mile. The current is quick and the stream bed strewn with boulders. The oxbow section is an exciting run in high water, particularly near the end where the water piles up on the west side in a left turn. The last rapids in the oxbow ends at a stone formation on the left.

Quiet, deep water follows, then a series of winding Class I rapids announced by several small islands (be careful of deadfall in the channels). Occasional riffles, rapids and stone formations are found all the way to the Polley Lane bridge (no good access) and beyond, and a few farm buildings are seen on the right as the river parallels Polley Lane.

More farm buildings follow on the right, together with a half mile of riffles and rapids, then the River Road bridge. There is another delightful series of Class I rapids after River Road and many shoreline stone outcroppings. After a good-sized island and overhead power lines, the river follows a long, wide, scenic straightaway to the west. Another large island precedes County H, with riffles almost all the way to the bridge.

TAKE OUT downstream-left at the **County H bridge.**

Other trips: Upstream from the Chequamegon Waters Flowage, the upper Yellow is canoeable when the water is fairly high. A long trip begins on the North Fork of the river at Forest Road 108 (Lake 19 Road) and ends at County M, just upstream from the flowage. Intermediate accesses at Yellow River Drive and Forest Road 575 (Sheep Ranch Road) can be used for a shorter trip. This part of the river flows through the national forest and is quite secluded, with occasional marshes, extensive woodland, beaver dams and a few easy riffle/rapids.

Yellow River

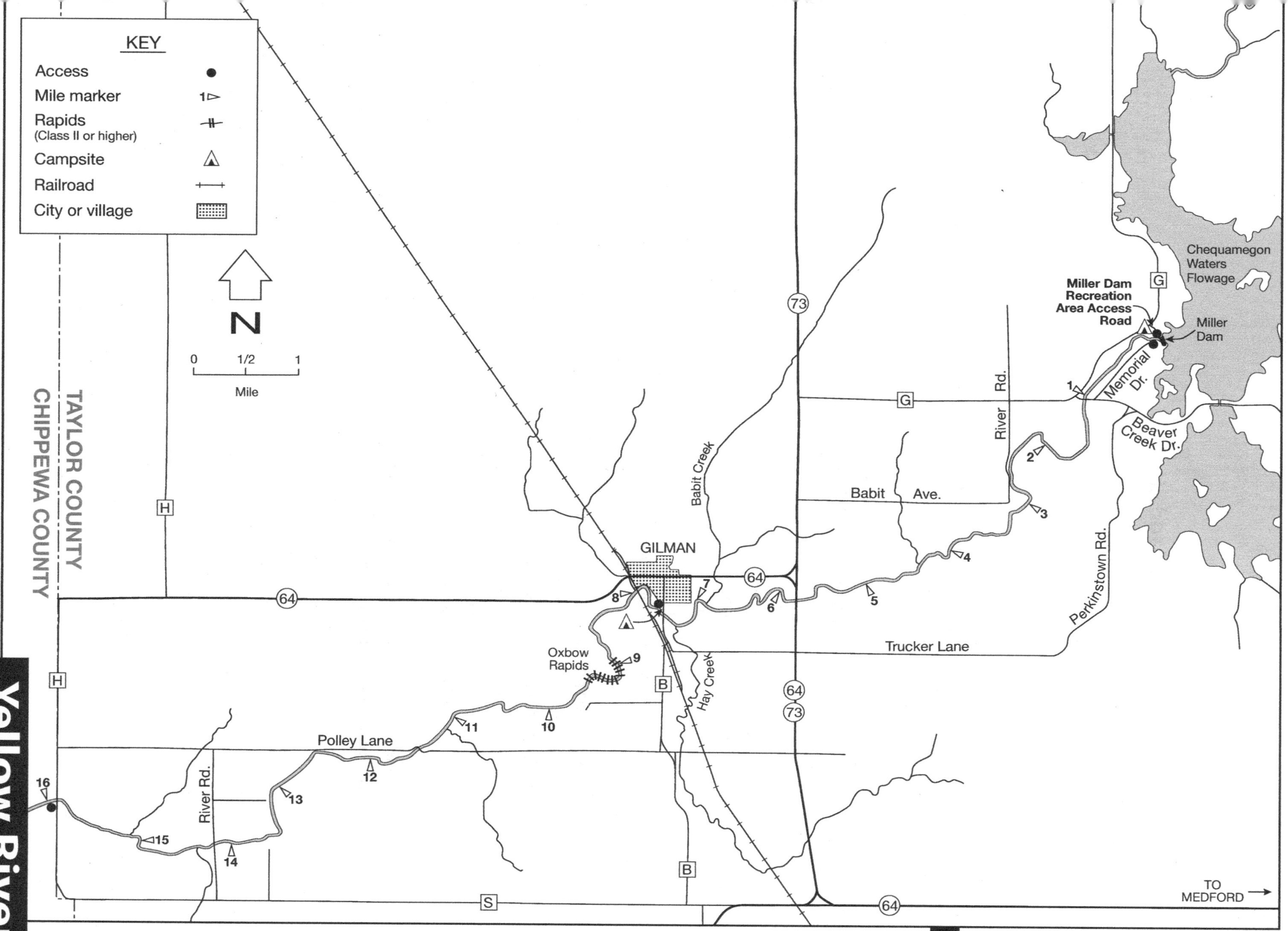

Appendix 1

Selected Resources For Paddlers

BOOKS

American Canoe Association, *Introduction to Paddling: Canoeing Basics for Lakes and Rivers*. Menasha Ridge Press, 1996.

Gordon, I. Herbert. *The Complete Book of Canoeing*. Globe Pequot, 2001.

Gullion, Laurie. *Canoeing: A Woman's Guide*. International Marine Publishing, 1999.

Mattos, Bill. *The Practical Guide to Kayaking and Canoeing*. Lorenz Books, 2002.

Ray, Slim. *The Canoe Handbook: Techniques for Mastering the Sport of Canoeing*. Stackpole Books, 1992.

Whiting, Ken, and Kevin Varette. *The Ultimate Guide to Whitewater Kayaking*. Heliconia Press, 2004.

VIDEOS

Complete Guide to Canoe Trips and Camping (45 mins.)

Essential Boat Control (58 mins.)

From Here to There: Canoe Basics (80 mins.)

Grace Under Pressure: Learning the Kayak Roll (47 mins.)

Kayaking 101: Mastering the Basics (45 mins.)

River Rescue: the Video (55 mins.)

The Kayaker's Edge (55 mins.)

Whitewater Kayaking Basics for Women, with Anna Levesque

INTERNET SITES

American Canoe Association: www.acanet.org

American Whitewater: www.americanwhitewater.org.

Midwest River Inventory: www.geocities.com/midwestrivers/index.html

Paddleguides: www.paddleguides.com

River Alliance of Wisconsin: www.wisconsinrivers.org

Topographic maps: http://topozone.com

Water levels: http://waterdata.usgs.gov/wi/nwis/current/?type=flow

Wisconsin DNR: www.dnr.state.wi.us

Appendix 2

Highly Recommended Reading

The following is a selective listing of a few outstanding publications that are particularly recommended to serious canoeists and kayakers. Other works are mentioned elsewhere in the book.

Akerlund, Nels, and Ted Landphair. *Our Rock River.* Washington, D.C.: Chelsea Publishing, 1995. This stunningly illustrated book traces the Rock from its origin in the Horicon Marsh to its union with the Mississippi, with a wealth of interesting historical detail.

Akerlund, Nels, and Joe Glickman. *Our Wisconsin River: Border to Border.* Rockford, Ill.: Pamacheyon Publishing, 1997. A gorgeous commentary and photo collection on the river, from the source to Prairie du Chien.

Durbin, Richard D. *The Wisconsin River: An Odyssey Through Time and Space.* Cross Plains, Wis.: Spring Freshet Press, 1997. An exhaustively researched history of the river, with splendid photos and maps. Follows the river downstream from the source, pointing out fascinating features and anecdotes along the way.

Gard, Robert E., and L. G. Sorden. *The Romance of Wisconsin Place Names.* New York: October House, 1968. In a very engaging manner, the authors trace the origins of place names back to original sources. The classic book on the subject is Virgil Vogel's *Indian Names on Wisconsin's Map* (Madison, Wis.: University of Wisconsin Press, 1991)—much older, but still quite useful.

Gard, Robert E., and Elaine Reetz. *Trail of the Serpent: The Fox River Valley Lore and Legend.* Madison, Wis.: Wisconsin House, 1973. This entertaining and informative volume is filled with wonderful anecdotes, photos, and historical details, including the story of steamboating on the river.

Hattes, Anne. *Country Towns of Wisconsin: Charming Small Towns and Villages to Explore.* Chicago, Ill.: Country Roads Press, 1999. Has excellent chapters on many towns included in *Paddling Southern Wisconsin*: Spring Green, Kohler, Pepin, Alma, etc.

Martin, Lawrence. *The Physical Geography of Wisconsin.* Madison, Wis.: University of Wisconsin Press, 1965. First published in 1916, this classic work is dated in terms of some of its statistics, but it is still an extraordinarily informative and authoritative account of the processes that determined the topography of the state. There's a wealth of fascinating information on the rivers covered in *Paddling Southern Wisconsin.*

Metcoff, Jill. *Along the Wisconsin Riverway.* Madison, Wis.: University of Wisconsin Press, 1997. A beautiful collection of 104 photos of the Lower Wisconsin River, with text.

Piraino, Frank F. *Small River Canoe Adventures of Wisconsin,* 1999. This 33-page self-published booklet provides brief descriptions of 79 sperate sections of 41 different rivers and creeks throughout the state. The focus is on isolated, seldom-paddled streams. Author's address: 200 Campus View Drive, Baraboo WI 53913

Svob, Mike. *Paddling Northern Wisconsin.* Madison, Wis.: Trails Books, 1998, revised 2003. A complement to *Paddling Southern Wisconsin,* this book describes 85 day trips on 27 different rivers—all north of Highway 29. Several rivers in northern Wisconsin continue past Highway 29, including the Black, Red Cedar, Chippewa, and Wisconsin, and are included in both books.

Svob, Mike. *Paddling Illinois.* Madison, Wis.: Trails Books, 2000. Describing 64 day trips on 33 rivers and streams, this book includes a number of rivers that begin in southern Wisconsin (the Apple, Galena, Pecatonica, Sugar, and Des Plaines), and many others that are just across the border.

Wisconsin Department of Natural Resources. *County Surface Water Resources.* Madison, 1961–1985. Each booklet describes in detail the geology, topography, and other characteristics of a Wisconsin county, including the physical dimensions, wildlife, recreational uses, water quality, and other aspects of the lakes and streams in that county.

Appendix 3

Internet Sites Related to Paddling in Southern Wisconsin

The Internet is an increasingly rich source of information that is directly and indirectly valuable to paddlers. In addition to the information available at a given Web site, "links" often point to a multitude of other sites. For Web sites of paddling clubs and organizations, see Appendix 6. Appendix 4 also lists numerous Web sites.

AMERICAN CANOE ASSOCIATION
www.acanet.org

AMERICAN RIVERS (ORGANIZATION)
www.amrivers.org

AMERICAN WHITEWATER
www.americanwhitewater.org

BEAR PAW OUTDOOR ADVENTURE RESORT
www.bearpawoutdoors.com

CANOE & KAYAK magazine
www.canoekayak.com

CANOEING AND KAYAKING INFORMATION
(a) www.paddling.net
(b) www.canoeing.com

CAPITAL WATER TRAILS
www.capitolwatertrails.org

CHAPPARAL CAMPGROUND & RESORT
www.chapparal.com

CHICAGO AREA PADDLING & FISHING PAGES
www.chicagopaddling.com

CHICAGO AREA SEA KAYAKING ASSOCIATION
www.caska.org

CHICAGOLAND CANOE BASE
www.chicagolandcanoebase.com

DRIVING DIRECTIONS www.mapquest.com

EXPEDITION OUTDOOR SUPPLY (SHEBOYGAN)
www.eosoutdoor.com

FRED FLASHER'S CANOE CAMPING TRIPS
www.canoegrue.com

GREAT OUTDOOR RECREATION PAGES
www.gorp.com

HORICON MARSH
(a) www.horiconmarsh.com
(b) www.horiconchamber.com

INFOHUB
www.infohub.com/TRAVEL/ADVENTURE/RECREATION/kayaking.html

KICKAPOO VALLEY RESERVE
http://kvr.state.wi.us

LAACKE & JOYS (MILWAUKEE & MEQUON)
www.laackeandjoys.com

MECAN RIVER OUTFITTERS & LODGE
www.mecanriveroutfitters.com

MIDWESTERN PADDLESPORTS
www.rivers-end.org

MIDWEST MOUNTAINEERING (MINNEAPOLIS)
www.midwestmtn.com

NATIONAL WEATHER SERVICE
www.nws.noaa.gov

NATIONAL WILD AND SCENIC RIVERS
www.rivers.org

PADDLER MAGAZINE
www.paddlermagazine.com

PADDLES AND PATHWAYS THROUGH THE UPPER MIDWEST
www.webchord.com/padlpath

PADDLEWISE (SEA KAYAKING)
www.paddlewise.net

PECATONICA CANOE FESTIVAL
www.darlingtoncanoefest.com

PRAIRE STATE CANOEISTS (CHICAGO AREA)
www.prairiestatecanoeists.org

RIVER ALLIANCE OF WISCONSIN
www.wisconsinrivers.org

RIVERSIDE JUNCTION (EAU CLAIRE RIVER)
www.riversidejunction.com

ROCK RIVER COALITION
http://rockrivercoalition.org

RUTABAGA PADDLESPORT SHOP (MADISON)
www.rutabaga.com

SIERRA CLUB RIVER TOURING SECTION
http://wisconsin.sierraclub.org/rts

SILENT SPORTS magazine
www.silentsports.net

TIPACANOE CANOE RENTALS (BURLINGTON WI)
www.tipacanoellc.com

UPPER SUGAR RIVER WATERSHED ASSOCIATION
www.usrwa.org

WATER LEVELS
(a) http://waterdata.usgs.gov/wi/nwis/current/?type=flow
(b) http://iwin.nws.noaa.gov/iwin/wi/hydro.html

WEATHER CHANNEL www.weather.com

WISCONSIN DEPARTMENT OF NATURAL RESOURCES
www.dnr.state.wi.us

WISCONSIN DEPARTMENT OF TOURISM
www.travelwisconsin.com

WISCONSIN DEPARTMENT OF TRANSPORTATION
www.dot.state.wi.us

WISCONSIN EVENTS www.wisconline.com

WISCONSIN NATURAL RESOURCES magazine
www.wnrmag.com

THE WISCONSIN PAGE
www.uwsp.edu/geo/wisconsin